The
Samizdat Register

edited by

ROY A. MEDVEDEV

W · W · NORTON & COMPANY INC ·

New York

Library of Congress Cataloging in Publication Data
Main entry under title:

The Samizdat register 1.

   Translations of eight essays which originally appeared
in the first three issues of ''XX Century,'' a journal
published in Moscow.
   1.   Underground literature—Russia—Addresses, essays,
lectures.   2.   Dissenters—Russia—Addresses, essays,
lectures.   3.   Russia—Politics and government—1917-
—Addresses, essays, lectures.   4.   Political prisoners—
Russia—Biography—Addresses, essays, lectures.
I. Medvedev, Roi Aleksandrovich.
DK274.S288 1977   320.9'47'085   77–24984

ISBN 0-393-05652-X

1 2 3 4 5 6 7 8 9 0

Publisher's Note

The eight essays published in this volume are taken from the first
issues of "XX Century", a journal edited by Roy Medvedev and
published in Moscow. This journal is part of the *samizdat*, and
circulates clandestinely in Russia in typescript. The contents have a
twofold in' est for us, both for the matter of the articles
themselves, and not less for the light they shed on the Russian scene
— what are the ideas and preoccupations of that section of the
intelligentzia that reads *samizdat*? Most striking of these attitudes,
as revealed by the choice of subject and approach, is that of the
contemporary opposition to Solzhenitsyn. There is clearly awareness of the extent to which the ideas of this writer have drowned
other voices of dissent, and many of the contributors to "XX
Century" have been at pains to dissociate themselves from the well-
publicised views on political and religious issues expressed by him
after he had been deported to the West.

This brings us to the second characteristic, which many Western
readers may find surprising; the concern of the socialist opposition
with Christianity. A *samizdat* journal, more than a normally
published one, argues a close relationship between contributor and
reader, though this by no means implies an identity of outlook.
Who is going to take the trouble to copy out long typescripts, and
who is going to take the risks involved, if they do not share a basic
concern with the issues under discussion? It is clear that
Solzhenitsyn is not alone in taking up a Christian stance of
opposition to the Soviet regime, but this collection makes equally
clear that his is far from being the only interpretation of
Christianity now to be heard in Russia.

Thirdly the reader is bound to be impressed by the wide range of these articles. The two Memoirs, by Mironov who was shot in 1921 and by Yakubovich who survived more than 20 years in the labour camps to write of the events of 1917, show an interest in Russian history of this period which is also dealt with in a detailed analysis by the editor. This interest is far from 'academic'; the period is the key to a critique of a regime which rests ideologically on claims to Leninist legitimacy. Similarly, the discussion of the Asiatic Mode of Production, while it has been a popular subject with historians at various times, is immediately related to a more contemporary phenomenon. Krasikov's article on the production of vodka is an informed investigation of a situation the Soviet government has been at some trouble to ignore.

The essays published here are not a selection: we have taken all the articles from the first three issues of ''XX Century'' with some exceptions that are not dictated by editorial choice. One or two articles have been dropped on the grounds of duplication, and some of the literary essays have been omitted because they have been translated and have appeared, or will appear, elsewhere. Again, some articles in the original were translations from foreign sources, including *Socialist Register*. These omissions do not distort the emphasis or balance of the original. We have also exercised restraint in leaving all the articles exactly as they were written. One of the problems of *samizdat* writers is the difficulty in checking facts about the recent history of their own country — let alone facts about the outside world. What is remarkable is how well informed these writers are, not the small number of errors which bear witness to their working conditions. (In some cases where we have felt this to be necessary we have set the record straight in a footnote).

Finally there is one exception to this editorial non-interference, which concerns dates. In Russia the Old Style calendar was in use until February 1918. This was, in the nineteenth century, twelve days, and in the twentieth century thirteen days behind the New Style calendar. Dates before 1918 have generally been given in Old Style with, when relevant, the New Style date in brackets.

Contents

The October Revolution and the Problem of History as a Law-Governed Process

ROY A. MEDVEDEV

Translated by Brian Pearce

Foreword

Historians and politicians of various tendencies have differed in their attitudes to the events of 1917 in Russia. But amid all the diversity of estimations and conceptions even the most outspoken anti-Communists usually acknowledge that the Russian revolution of 1917 was the most important historical event of the 20th century. It is not surprising that the attention accorded to everything that happened in Russia in that year, which might now seem far in the past, does not slacken, and that the body of writing devoted to the most diverse aspects of the revolutionary events in Russia continues to be enormous. Historical science concerns itself both with "historical facts" and with the conceptions based upon these which seek to explain them. And it is probably no exaggeration to say that no other great event of the past has given rise to so many conceptions not merely different, but contradictory, as has the revolution in Russia — meaning, first and foremost, of course, not the February but the October revolution.

A process of gradual accumulation of factual knowledge and revision of many estimations and conceptions that were formed in the past is under way in the Soviet Union as well as in the West, and in the world of official historical studies as elsewhere. For all its frequent hesitations and changes of direction, there has obviously been a development in historical science in the U.S.S.R. in the last twenty years, and many of its achievements have also been put to use by Sovietology outside the U.S.S.R. To be sure, this development follows extremely complicated and contradictory

1

paths in our country, where, alongside the most shameless and gross falsification of historical events, with the hushing-up of many highly important facts, a courageous search for the truth is also in progress. Even the most honest of Soviet historians, slowly advancing the cause of truth, must even today manoeuvre cautiously amid the artificial obstacles constituted by all sorts of prohibitions, the number of which, though reduced since the 20th Congress of the C.P.S.U., continues to be very great. To this day, for example, historiography in the U.S.S.R. is not allowed to evaluate objectively the activity of many outstanding participants in the October and February revolutions, which naturally results in numerous distortions in describing and considering the significance of some highly important events of those days and months. Nor are Soviet historians at liberty to discuss certain conceptions. And even those historians who have long since refused to follow the "official" line continue to be subject to the influence — of which they are often unaware — of the stereotypes of pseudo-history they have grown up with since childhood.

In my book *Let History Judge* I expressed myself very sceptically regarding the ability of Western Sovietology to clarify many difficult problems of our Soviet history. I now see that I was wrong, and that besides the rather large number of unobjective or simply dishonest historians there are in the West quite a few who are sincerely striving to know the truth and to give a true picture of the actual causes of the events that have taken place in our country. Nevertheless I am still convinced that only Marxist historians, and above all Soviet ones, are capable of carrying out the main work needed in order to formulate events which occurred in 1917 and also in all the subsequent years. I think so not only because I still believe in the power of Marxism but also because I believe in the power of history in our country. I do not believe that the Soviet Union is doomed, as Amalrik prophesies, to suffer the fate of Byzantium or of Ancient Rome. But I also see clearly the difficulties that lie in the path of historical science in our country.

In his day, Marx wrote: "Bourgeois revolutions, like those of the eighteenth century, storm swiftly from success to success; their dramatic effects outdo each other; men and things seem set in sparkling brilliants; ecstasy is the everyday spirit; but they are short-lived; soon they have attained their zenith, and a long crapulent depression lays hold of society before it learns soberly to assimilate the results of its storm-and-stress period. On the other hand, proletarian revolutions ... criticise themselves constantly, interrupt themselves continually in their own course, come back to the apparently accomplished in order to begin it afresh, deride with unmerciful thoroughness the inadequacies, weaknesses and paltrinesses of their first attempts, seem to throw down their adversary only in order that he may draw new strength from the earth and rise again, more gigantic, before them, recoil ever and anon from the indefinite prodigiousness of their own aims, until a situation has been created which makes all turning back impossible, and the conditions themselves cry out: *Hic Rhodus, hic salta!* (Here is Rhodes, leap here!)"[1]

To those who know how un-self-critical the proletarian revolutions of the 20th century have proved to be, Marx's words may seem naive and utopian. I am sure, however, that there is a significant element of truth in what he said. For it is only by stopping and critically surveying the road that has been traversed, without being afraid resolutely to criticise their own derelictions, mistakes and even crimes, that Marxist revolutionaries can succeed in realising their aims, both practical and scientific. Guided by these very words of Marx's I have decided to undertake a number of studies of the history of the October Revolution and the Civil War, the present essay being the first of them.

I *Was the October Revolution an inevitable event?*

a. Various points of view

One of the propositions most frequently repeated by many Western historians is that the October revolution in Russia was not a natural consequence of the social, economic and political processes which had occurred in the country, and even less can it be regarded as a natural consequence of the events of that period in Europe or throughout the world. This revolution, it is said, resulted from an unforeseen confluence of accidental circumstances which was cleverly exploited by Lenin and the Bolsheviks. The British Sovietologist David Lane wrote, for instance, in one of his books, that, "with the abdication of the Tsar, a political vacuum existed," which the Bolsheviks filled, but "the Bolshevik Revolution was not an inevitable event in history."[2] The American historian R.V. Daniels also declared in one of his articles: "From any rational contemporary standpoint the Bolshevik Revolution was a desperate gamble, unlikely to succeed and still less likely to hold out ...

Chance put Lenin in power, and chance kept him there during the dizzying days that followed ... It was a series of such unpredictable events that diverted Russia from the customary course of modern revolutions and paved the way for the unique phenomenon of twentieth-century Communism.''[3]

These views are often countered by directly opposite views to the effect that the launching and the triumph of the October Revolution were in fact inevitable.

"Even if Lenin and the men around him can be said to have 'made the October Revolution,' it is still more true to say that they were made by it,'' writes the former Comintern official Joseph Berger. "I honestly believe that there was a movement which nothing could have broken or stopped ... and it was this movement which brought Lenin and his disciples to the fore. I do not wish to minimise the work of preparation carried out for decades by the Russian revolutionary movement, but the reason why, at a given moment, the Bolsheviks came to power is, I believe, because at that moment they had the people behind them ... Peace, the distribution of the land, government by workers' and peasants' soviets — all this, I think, was in accordance with the people's will, and in fact the Bolshevik slogans were formulated in response to it ... This was why the Bolsheviks were able to seize the leadership of the country.''[4]

The idea of the fatal inevitability of the October Revolution and the victory of the Communists was also often expressed, in his own way, by the Russian philosopher Berdyaev.

"It is very important to remember,'' he wrote in his book *The Origin of Russian Communism,* "that the Russian communist revolution came to birth in misery and from misery, the misery of a disintegrating war; it was not born of a creative abundance of strength. Revolution, as a matter of fact, always presupposes misery, always presupposes an intensifying of the darkness of the past ... The new liberal democratic government which came on the scene after the February revolution proclaimed abstract human principles; abstract principles of law and order in which there was no organising force of any sort, no energy with which to inspire the masses ... The position of the Provisional Government was so difficult and hopeless that it is hardly possible to judge it severely and condemn it. Kerensky was a man of revolution in its first stage. Moderate people of liberal and humanist principles can never flourish in the elemental sweep of revolution and especially of a revolution brought about by war. The principles of democracy are suitable to times of peace, and not always then, but never to a revolutionary epoch. In the time of revolution men of extreme principles, men who are disposed to dictatorship and capable of exercising it, are those who will triumph. Only dictatorship could put an end to the process of final dissolution and the triumph of chaos and anarchy ... Only Bolshevism could control the situation. It only corresponded to the instincts of the masses and their real attitude to things ...

"Russia was threatened by complete anarchy and this was checked by the communist dictatorship, which found the slogans to which the people agreed to submit ... In this respect communism rendered Russia an indisputable service."[5]

Many Soviet writers too, of course, often uphold the thesis of the inevitability of the October revolution, though expressing it differently. Thus, for example, V.S. Vasyukov and V.I. Salov affirm in their article that the constellation of class forces in Russia in 1917 "predetermined the inevitability of a proletarian revolution."[6]

What can be said about these and similar opinions and assertions? I think that it is not possible to agree completely with any of them, although each of the writers I have quoted could bring forward to support his view a considerable number of striking facts and persuasive arguments.

b. Social revolution in the broad and the narrow sense of the term.

Before considering the question of the inevitable or accidental character of this or that revolution, it is necessary to agree on how to interpret the concept "revolution," or "social revolution," itself. Like many other concepts in the social sciences it is not monosemantic, and has a different content in different contexts — a circumstance which sometimes gives rise to extremely scholastic disputes. I think that this concept can most often be employed in two senses.

By "social revolution" is understood, first, a radical change in the socio-economic structure of society, a transition from one socio-economic order to another, regardless of the concrete political form this transition may take. In this *general* sense Marx wrote about "social revolution" in his *Contribution to the Critique of Political Economy:* "At a certain stage of development, the material productive forces of society come into conflict with the existing relations of production, or — this merely expresses the same thing in legal terms — with the property relations within the framework of which they have operated hitherto. From forms of development of the productive forces these relations turn into their fetters. Then begins an era of social revolution. The changes in the economic foundation lead sooner or later to the transformation of the whole immense superstructure."[7]

In this broad sense of the term, social revolutions are indeed inevitable. The political movements in Germany and Austria-Hungary in 1848-1849 ended in defeat: nevertheless, in the second half of the 19th century a radical turn took place in Central Europe from feudalism to capitalism, that is, a social revolution, which was merely completed by the series of political movements that occurred after World War I. A genuinely social revolution has taken place in the last 20 or 25 years in Iran, Afghanistan and Egypt, and in many other countries in Asia, Africa and Latin America. In essence, the set of reforms "from above" which was put into effect in Japan in the last third of the 19th century was also a social revolution, although it was not accompanied by collapse of the traditional forms of state structure or radical changes in the make-up of the ruling classes. And have there been so few examples in Europe of a former feudalist becoming gradually transformed into a model capitalist?

As seen by Marxists, capitalism is not a universal optimum form of socio-economic structure, either, and therefore that transition to a new social order, more just and more in accordance with the higher level of development of the productive forces, which is already taking place in many countries in the 20th century is seen by them as inevitable. If the question posed at the beginning of this section be approached in this way, the October revolution in Russia can be appreciated as merely the outward realisation of this profound historical necessity, which in other countries and in another period may take on quite different forms.

The concept "social revolution" can be used, however, in a narrower sense (and this is what is usually done in Soviet writing), to signify the spasmodic and rapid passing of political power out of the hands of one class into those of another, brought about through direct action by the "lower orders," that is, by popular demonstrations or uprisings. "Social revolution," writes, for example, the Soviet historian Ya. S. Drabkin, "is a radical overturn in the life of society, altering its structure and signifying a qualitative leap in its progressive development ... [Social] revolution always means an active political deed of the popular masses, in which are combined the spontaneity of an upsurge with conscious purposefulness in bringing about, above all, a transfer of the leadership of society, state power, into the hands of a new class or class grouping ... It must also be mentioned that by its manysidedness, embracing all the fundamental aspects of the activity of society, a social revolution is distinguished from narrower, partial overturns which affect only one sphere or another; for example, from political (governmental) revolutions, which merely change the personnel making up the governing body while preserving the previous structure of society and the fundamentals of the political course being followed; and also from an industrial revolution, a scientific-technical revolution, and so on. At the same time, a social revolution is distinguished from those progressive transformations in society which take place comparatively slowly, without direct participation by the popular masses, by the fact that it is concentrated into a short period of time and by the role played by direct action on the part of the 'lower orders.' It is in this way that revolutionary and evolutionary processes, revolution and reform, are usually distinguished from each other.''[8]

In this narrower sense, any social revolution is determined not only by the operation of the internal laws of social development and the inevitably-formed alignment of social factors, but also by the activity of particular political groups and parties, and by that of the particular leaders who happen to be in the given period of the revolutionary process, at the head of the revolutionary camp, or of the reactionary one. The behaviour and decisions of these historical personages are not and cannot be wholly determined, but depend upon many subjective and accidental factors, and this gives a nuance of indeterminacy and accidentality to the entire concrete course of historical events.

c. The course of history and the role of the individual in history

The ideas of primitive "absolute determinism," according to which all events in history were determined and could not have happened otherwise, are not at all characteristic of Marxism. On the contrary, any *concrete* historical event, even one which has very important consequences, is determined by a complex interweaving of necessary and accidental processes, which compels us in each

7

particular case to speak of the greater or lesser probability of a given event, but not of its absolute inevitability. In historical and social reality, every situation necessarily contains several real alternatives, the fulfilment of which depends on a multitude of circumstances and actions, far from all of which are foreseeable. The facts of history bear witness that by no means always is the most probable historical alternative the one realised: often what might have seemed very improbable events take place. "We do not believe either in the vocation of peoples or in their predestination," wrote A.I. Herzen: "We think that the destinies of peoples and of states can change in the course of time, like the destiny of every individual, but we have the right, basing ourselves on real factors and in accordance with the theory of probability, to draw conclusions about the future."[9] Every genuine Marxist can agree with these words of Herzen's.

It can be clearly seen from history that the concrete course of even the largest-scale historical events depends to a large extent not only on various socio-economic conditions but also on the activity of particular "historic" individuals. The deeds, the decisions and the entire activity of any individual, including the greatest, are not so highly determined and predetermined as are socio-economic processes. The historical events in Europe at the beginning of the 19th century were, as everyone knows, very fundamentally bound up with the personality and deeds of Napoleon. But if we recall the extremely risky undertakings and the many defeats which preceded the proclamation of Napoleon as Emperor of the French, we can say with confidence that Napoleon's dictatorship was one of the least probable alternatives, which nevertheless was realised.[10] Certainly, France needed at that time a "good sword", as Plekhanov correctly put it. A military dictatorship was then *almost* inevitable. But Plekhanov acknowledges that a different general who might have secured the place of dictator might have been more peaceful than Napoleon, and would not have roused the whole of Europe against himself, so that all subsequent events would have assumed a different character.[11] True, it can be said that everything that men do depends on the conditions, external and internal, governing their lives and activity, on the influence of the environment and of the physiological make-up of a man, that the original cause of human actions lies outside the individual personality, and therefore, as I.M. Sechenov expressed it in his day, the "apparent possibility" of free will "is merely a delusion of self-consciousness."[12] "Man is 'free'," says a contemporary

American philosopher, "in so far as he is able to do what he wants to do, and is 'bound' in so far as he has to do what he does not want to do. But all his actions, whether performed from free choice or under compulsion, have their causes and their effects."[13] Of course every human action has a cause. However, because he combines in himself both material and spiritual principles, man is integrated in the system of connexions of cause and effect in a quite different way from inanimate nature. "It would be absurd," wrote Herzen, "to regard man as an exception to the general laws of nature and attribute to him a subjective spontaneity *outside law*. However, this in no way prevents man from cultivating in himself a faculty, composed of reason, feeling and memory, which 'weighs' the possibilities and decides on the choice of action to be performed. This happens not through divine grace, nor through an imaginary spontaneity, but is developed by man's organs, his innate and acquired faculties, which are shaped and combined in a thousand ways by social life. From this standpoint the *deeds* of men certainly result from the organism and its development; nonetheless, this result is not so obligatory and involuntary as breathing and digestion. Physiology analyses the consciousness of freedom into its component elements: simplifies it in seeking to find the explanation for it in the individual organism — and completely loses sight of it."[14] Herzen is, of course, closer to the truth here than Sechenov, who declared that "the question of whether the most voluntary of all voluntary actions of man depend on external and internal conditions has been answered in the affirmative. From this it inevitably follows that *given the same internal and external conditions the activity of man will be similar.*"[15]

But I would go further than Herzen in acknowledging the possibility of freedom of choice. The combination in each human being of the material principle and a spiritual principle that cannot be reduced to matter renders his conduct in many cases unpredictable, even though its influence on the course of external events may also be not very important. People are not omnipotent; but the behaviour and thoughts of every person are not at all predestined, and each of us is capable of a (very limited) freedom of choice, and so can take independent decisions and be answerable for what he does.

Human consciousness is not a mere reflexion of events taking place inside and outside a man: as a spiritual being, man is capable of a definite activity which can change, within certain bounds, the course of external material events and processes, especially in the sphere of man's own history. Without going deeply, however, into discussion of these complex philosophical problems, let me just say that my view coincides with that of the Soviet historian D. Rendel, who wrote in one of his interesting but, alas, unpublished works: "It is expedient to look at the historical process in a dual way. First, as a process in which men's conduct is determined by laws and external conditions which are independent of it. This enables us to grasp the true position of the personages on the historical scene. Secondly, as a process which is *freely* directed by those who participate in it. This enables us to evaluate better the negative and positive consequences of the willed decisions of these personages."[16]

Passing to the question about the October revolution which I put at the beginning of this section, it must be plainly stated that this event was not only the result of what was apparently an irrepressible mass movement, nor was it merely due to the purposeful activity of the Bolshevik Party. The victory of the October revolution was inseparably linked with the activity of certain individuals in the Party, such as, for example, Trotsky, Sverdlov and Raskolnikov and, above all, with that of V.I. Lenin, whose decisions and actions left upon his epoch an imprint no less remarkable than those of Napoleon in his epoch. Nobody could replace Lenin in our Party. His closest associates understood this, and so, in the sharpest of inner-Party disputes, Lenin's threat to leave his post acted upon them more effectively than any other argument. Nearly all Lenin's adversaries understood this, too. "To be left without Lenin," wrote N. Sukhanov, "would that not mean tearing the heart out of the organism, or cutting off the head? ... There was nobody in the Party but Lenin ... A few big generals, without Lenin, would be nothing, like a few immense planets without the sun."[17] But Lenin was not a prophet, representing on earth some higher powers. Berdyaev was profoundly mistaken when he saw Lenin as "a man of destiny, a man sent by fate," and thought that in this lay his strength. No, Lenin was only a man, not guaranteed against mistakes, and not too well protected from the many dangers that lay in wait for him. And if Lenin's fate had taken a different turn in 1917, or during the world war, the fate of the socialist revolution he proclaimed might also have taken a different turn. Nor was the activity either of the opponents or of the temporary allies of the Bolshevik Party predestined. And, looked at in this way, it is quite obvious that the victory of the October Revolution in Russia was not inevitable. In any of the periods before the revolution actually occurred, the situation admitted of several quite different alternative lines of development, and the same was true after the October victory in Petrograd.

What actually happened, of course, cannot be changed. And yet study of the various alternatives and the opportunities that were missed must also form part of the historian's task. This knowledge is useful not only for futurologists and for scientific workers in other disciplines. It is useful and necessary also for practical politicians — provided, of course, that the latter are willing to learn something from history. Unfortunately, this desire has hitherto been found to exist among only a tiny minority of politicians. And Hegel's well-known saying that "what history teaches is that nobody has ever learnt from history" is true even for those politicians who never stop telling us that they are guided in their activity exclusively by the only truly scientific ideology of our time.

d. The bourgeois-democratic revolution of February 1917

If the propositions argued above are accepted, it naturally follows that we must conclude that the February Revolution, too, was not an absolutely inevitable event. The unsuccessful prosecution of the war, which had become more and more unpopular with the masses of workers and peasants, the ever-heavier burdens borne by the soldiers in the trenches — all this gave rise to a ferment of discontent among the masses and made a revolutionary overthrow of the autocracy increasingly likely. And this likelihood of a revolutionary development of events grew steadily with every month of 1916 that passed and with every week of January-February 1917. But this was still only a probability, that is, one of the alternatives created by the historical situation.

Actually, Russia had entered the world war already pregnant with revolution. The retention in Russia of the foundations of the autocracy and of the power of the landlords of a semi-feudal type, bureaucratism and corruption, inequality of rights for the national minorities, growing dependence of Russia upon foreign capital, progressive impoverishment of a substantial section of the urban and rural population, and at the same time the on-going process of a comparatively rapid development of capitalism — all this was eroding and breaking up the basis of the old regime of Imperial Russia. Nor could the Orthodox Church withstand these processes.

"No," even A.I. Solzhenitsyn declared not long ago, "truth compels me to say that the condition of the Russian Church at the beginning of the 20th century, the age-long debased situation of its clergy, bowed down before the state and merged with it, the loss of spiritual independence and thereby the loss of authority among the bulk of the educated class and the mass of the urban workers, and, what was most dreadful, the shaking of this authority even among the peasantry at large — this condition of the Russian Church *was one of the principal reasons why the revolutionary events were inevitable* [Solzhenitsyn's own emphasis] ... Alas, the state of the Russian Orthodox Church at the time of the revolution completely failed to measure up to the gravity of the spiritual dangers menacing our age, and menacing our people in the first place. The live forces in the Church, who believed in reforms that would save it and in the Synod, oppressed by a tyrannical state machine and bogged down by the drowsy placidity of their colleagues, *failed* — so patently failed that the guns of the Red Guards opened fire on the roofs and domes of the Synod as it was in session".[18]

The possibility of revolution was so obvious that even not very far-sighted monarchists were able to perceive it. After the dispersal of the First State Duma, which seemed to the Tsar to be too radical, Prince Yevgeny Trubetskoy (who described himself as "landowner and monarchist") wrote to Nicholas II: "Sire, the striving of the peasants for the land is an irrepressible force ... Everyone who opposes compulsory alienation will be wiped off the face of the earth. The approaching revolution threatens us with confiscation, puts our very lives in danger. Civil war is only a question of time ... It may be that the Government is at the moment succeeding, by repressive measures, in putting down the revolutionary movement. All the more fearful will be the consequent and final explosion which will overthrow the existing order and raze Russian culture to the ground ... And you yourself will be buried beneath the ruins."[19]

Although the revolution of 1905 suffered defeat, the latent forces which had engendered it continued to grow. The reforms undertaken by Stolypin and A.V. Krivoshein in 1906-1912 were an attempt to avert a new revolution. But these reforms were too inconsistent and insufficiently far-reaching to achieve the aim set. While accelerating economic development in town and country alike, Stolypin's reforms failed to eliminate the chief hindrances standing in the way of Russia's capitalist development.

Eventually it was in war (which the Tsarist court expected would be short and victorious) that the monarchy sought salvation. But, by beginning badly and, what mattered most, by assuming a protracted character, World War I only intensified all the basic contradictions of Russian society.

In 1915-1916, however, the monarchy still had some opportunities left for political manoeuvring, for retreat, for compromise with the Duma. And such a compromise was also being sought by those groups and parties in the Duma which were united in the so-called "Progressive Bloc." It is wrong to suppose that the "Progressive Bloc" embraced only "all the bourgeois parties and groups" in the State Duma, as is alleged by Academician I. Mints in his three-volume *History of the Great October*, which is full of the crudest inaccuracies and distortions.[20] In the Octobrist Party, which entered the "Bloc", the landlord element was predominant, and the Centre and Nationalist groups participating in the "Bloc" also contained many representatives of extreme landlord reaction. The formation of the "Progressive Bloc" showed that Nicholas II and his entourage were losing support even among those who had not long before been devoted to them. And although the speeches made by the members of the "Progressive Bloc" were sometimes very harsh and evoked a lively echo in the country, nevertheless, in raising their voices against the Government the leaders of the opposition parties called only for reforms that were very modest in relation to the needs of that period — counting on being able by means of such reforms to avert revolution, that is, direct action by the workers, soldiers and peasants. Yes, indeed, the parties of the "Progressive Bloc" demanded that a "Government of Confidence" be formed, which should be responsible not only to the Tsar but also to the Duma. They did not want to take *all* power, but only to share it with the monarchy. One of the leaders of the "Bloc", V. Shulgin, wrote some years after the revolution: "We were born and brought up to praise or blame the Government while remaining under its wing ... We were capable, in the last resort, of moving painlessly from our deputies' seats into ministerial armchairs, provided that the Imperial Guard assured us its protection ... But faced with the possibility that the Government might fall, thinking of the bottomless pit that such an event would open up, our minds reeled and our hearts went numb. Impotence looked out at me from behind the white columns of the Tauride Palace. And this gaze was scornful to the point of horror."[21]

But neither Nicholas II nor the Empress, nor the Court camarilla that surrounded them were able to judge the situation that was taking shape: they were unwilling to offer any concessions even to those who had recently been their adherents. Continually reshuffling his Council of Ministers, Nicholas appointed to key posts representatives of that same talentless monarchist bureaucracy which was incapable of ruling the country — more so than ever under war conditions. The Court lacked even men. of the calibre of P.A. Stolypin. This blindness of the ruling Tsarist team resulted, of course, from class prejudice — from the Tsar's unwillingness to surrender even a share of his power, and that of the landlord-bureaucratic upper crust to give up the smallest fragment of their privileges. And yet the decisive role in the given situation was played by such factors, which were far from being "determined", from the historical standpoint, as the intellectual nullity and lack of willpower of the last Tsar and the equally obvious nullity of his fanatical wife, with her disposition towards a sort of hysterical mysticism.

"Be Peter the Great, John [*sic*] the Terrible, Emperor Paul — crush them all under you,"[22] the Tsar's wife urged him in her letter of 14 December 1916, having in mind, in the first place, the opposition in the Duma. But she also wrote: "You are too kind and gentle — sometimes a good loud voice can do wonders, and a severe look ..." "They must learn to tremble before you ..." "Remember you are the Emperor, and that others dare not take so much upon themselves ..."[23]

Of course, Nicholas II was neither kind nor gentle. He was merely sluggish, inert, foolish, confused, and sometimes simply overwhelmed by events and therefore incapable of taking any resolute initiative.

The Rasputin business was only one manifestation of this moral disintegration, mental degradation and impotence of the "leading circles." All that the Tsarist Court could think of when it sought a way out of the blind alley was to prepare for secret negotiations with Kaiser Wilhelm for a separate peace with Germany, with a view to which B.V. Stürmer, an open Germanophil and supporter of Rasputin, was appointed Chairman of the Council of Ministers. Historians still to this day argue about how far Nicholas II went in his attempts to arrange contacts with "the enemy". But even the most timid moves in this direction reinforced the rumours of treason and hastened the preparations for a palace revolution and the assassination of Rasputin — a killing which caused rejoicing not only in Duma circles but also among many people at Court.

A palace revolution was undoubtedly one of the possible

alternative lines of development for Russia in 1916, and was the one promoted by the leaders of the "Progressive Bloc" and many Entente statesmen. A number of prominent politicians and some military men took part in preparations for this revolution. "We considered," A.F. Kerensky testified, "that a spontaneous revolutionary movement was inadmissible in wartime, and so we made it our task to support the moderate and even conservative groups, parties and organisations which were to prevent the catastrophe of a spontaneous outbreak by carrying out a palace revolution."[24]

"While visiting military units in 1916 as chief representative of the Red Cross," wrote N.I. Bilibin, a Colonel in the Tsar's Army, "Guchkov expressed to me, in private conversation, his grave fears regarding the outcome of the war. We both concluded that the unskilful operational leadership of the armies, the appointment of talentless courtiers to the highest posts of command, and, finally, the ambiguous conduct of the Empress Alexandra, directed towards obtaining a separate peace with Germany, might end in a military catastrophe and another revolution, which in our view would threaten the collapse of the state. We considered that a palace revolution might serve as the way out of this situation: Nicholas must be forced to abdicate."[25]

However, both in Court circles and among the men of the "Progressive Bloc" preparations for a palace revolution proceeded too slackly, with inadequate vigour: there was no-one among them who was capable of resolutely heading this movement — and that circumstance also was not "determined".

At one time Soviet historiography practically ignored the role played by the Duma opposition in the *de facto* preparation of the masses for revolution, for overthrowing the autocracy. Books have now begun to appear in which detailed accounts are given of the struggle of the Duma opposition against Tsardom, and the authors of these books acknowledge that the moves made by bourgeois and liberal monarchist leaders against the Government, whatever their motives may have been, did arouse the masses of the workers and soldiers against Tsardom. But, strange to relate, some of these writers, who claim to be Marxists, essentially blame the "Progressive Bloc" not for its irresoluteness in the fight against Tsardom but, on the contrary, for its insufficient patriotism and failure to rally round even a bad monarch while the World War was being fought. The political parties of the "Progressive Bloc" are condemned for trying to force the Tsarist bureaucracy out of power and thereby hindering the consolidation of Russia's forces in the struggle against the external foe. This is the position taken up, for example, by N.N. Yakovlev, author of the book *1 August 1914*.[26] For all his criticism of Tsardom, the Tsarist administration and the Rasputin episode, Yakovlev aims his sharpest criticism precisely at those bourgeois circles which, in his opinion, not only sought to seize power in Russia but also deliberately created difficulties at the front and in the rear, exaggerating the shortcomings and defects of the Tsarist war machine, which in 1916, he claims, were not so very great or insuperable. "But then," says Yakovlev, "what about the bourgeoisie's famous slogan of 'war to a victorious conclusion'? This was meant by those who raised it to apply only to a Russia in which power was held exclusively by the bourgeoisie. A victory by Imperial Russia would, from the point of view of the bourgeoisie and its ideologists, have put incredible obstacles in the way of ousting Tsardom from power. Hence the extremely complicated tactics of the bourgeoisie and its parties, aimed at creating difficulties for Tsardom in the conduct of the war. The well-known doctrine of 'the worse the better' became the operational principle of the Russian bourgeoisie."[27] Juggling with facts, Yakovlev tries, for example, to prove that it was the bourgeoisie and its agents that contributed at the beginning of 1917 to the creation of a serious food crisis in the army and in the rear, a shortage of munitions, and so on.[28]

These notions of Yakovlev's fail to stand up to criticism. Essentially, they do not differ from Solzhenitsyn's blaming of the Cadets for the "furious and unthinking storm" they "raised against Goremykin and Stürmer in 1915-1916"[29], which he considers to have been a big political mistake on their part, playing into the hands of the Bolsheviks. The political parties of the bourgeoisie did, of course, seek to obtain a larger share of power and influence. But every political party does this, always and everywhere. Of course the bourgeoisie tried to make money out of the war, out of supplies to the army. But every bourgeoisie did this, in every belligerent country at that time. For an accusation that the Russian bourgeoisie deliberately sabotaged the efforts of the Russian Army there are, though, no serious grounds whatsoever.

Unsubstantiated and unconvincing also are Yakovlev's "revelations" regarding the decisive role played by the Masonic lodges, the Freemasons, in preparing the overthrow of Nicholas II. Naturally, like any other conspiracy, preparation for a palace revolution called for some kind of secret organisation. Connexions through the Masonic lodges may have come in useful here. But the activity of these lodges, as is clear even from Yakovlev's own book, had only very slight influence on the shaping of the political situation in the country, or even directly on the doings of the conspirators, which in essence went no further than preliminary conversations and "soundings" of the ground. Yakovlev himself does not show why, after describing attempts to form a secret organisation "of the type of the Masonic lodges" (on page 8 of his book he calls the Freemasons merely the "ideological precursors" of the conspirators), he has to go on to describe the Masonic organisations and their imagined power. All this is as unconvincing as the attempts made by some writers both in our country and abroad to explain by the secret influence of the Masons the external and internal politics of the U.S.A. and of some other Western governments.[30]

One way or another, by the beginning of 1917 Nicholas II and his Government were utterly isolated. In the country, in the army, in the capital, a situation had been brought about in which a relatively slight cause could produce a general rising by the people. "This tense state of public opinion could be compared to a keg of gunpowder in which a single spark is enough to cause an explosion," the secretary of the Narva district committee of the Party, S.I. Afanasyev, was later to recall.[31] Speaking on 14 February 1917 in the State Duma, the Menshevik leader N. Chkheidze declared: "Gentlemen, the street is beginning to speak! Whether this is a good thing or a bad thing, you cannot deny that it is a fact ... And I think that you cannot avoid taking account of what the street is telling you."[32] In those days, however, it was not only Nicholas II but also many representatives of the bourgeoisie who failed to appreciate the terrible nature of coming events. In reply to the request of the leader of the Octobrists, Rodzyanko, to prolong the life of the Duma, Nicholas II, as is well-known, issued a decree dissolving it. And at that same time the strikes in 22 Petrograd enterprises due to the food-supply difficulties were answered with a lockout, that is, with mass dismissal of all the workers. It is not surprising that the demonstrations and strikes in the capital began, already in the second half of February, to develop into an armed revolt, in which the military garrison of the city were also involved. Therefore the Tsar's order to General Khabalov: "I command you to stop the disorders in the capital as from tomorrow", could only accelerate the revolution, which it then proved impossible to halt either by the hurried abdication of Nicholas II or by the proclamation of a fresh

17

Tsar, Michael. The revolution began and triumphed almost at once and everywhere. The ending of the autocracy in Russia was certainly "law-governed": but in the particular form it took it was certainly not the only possible outcome of the political, social and economic processes which were under way in Russia in those years.

e. The October socialist revolution

If it is impossible to say that the February revolution was an absolutely inevitable phenomenon, even less can this be said of the October socialist revolution. True, so early as the spring of 1917 a definite possibility of a new, proletarian revolution arose in Russia. This enabled Lenin not merely to proclaim the slogan "All power to the Soviets" but also to conclude his brief speech at the Finland Station with a call for a socialist revolution. The possibility of another revolution in Russia, determined by a capricious combination of many objective and subjective factors, increased until July 1917, and then began to decline. In any case, an alliance between Kerensky and Kornilov against the Bolsheviks was considerably more probable than what actually happened, namely, the unexpected alliance between Kerensky and the Bolsheviks against Kornilov, which led to the legalisation of Lenin's party and strengthened its prospects of victory in a fresh revolution. We know that already in September 1917 Lenin considered a Bolshevik victory fully possible, and therefore continually pressed and prodded the hesitating majority in the Central Committee. When in October they took their final decision to launch an armed uprising, Lenin and his closest colleagues showed themselves brilliantly able to exploit a favourable situation, well knowing that this might change to their disadvantage within a few days. "Under no circumstances," wrote Lenin on 24 October (6 November) 1917 to members of the Central Committee, "should power to left in the hands of Kerensky and Co. until the 25th — not under any circumstances; the matter must be decided without fail this very evening, or this very night. History will not forgive revolutionaries for procrastinating when they could be victorious today (and they certainly will be victorious today), while they risk losing much tomorrow, in fact, they *risk losing everything*" (my emphasis, R.M.)[33]

Lenin's letter shows once more the very great personal role he played in the revolutionary events that took place in Russia in 1917.

It was Lenin who managed to over-persuade and reorientate the majority of the Party's leading cadres, who at first did not understand either the "April Theses" or the new opportunities opening up before the Party. Without Lenin the Party would, it is clear, have been unable to overcome successfully the several political crises which followed each other in the summer of 1917. It was Lenin who worked out the concrete tactical plan for the rising and drew up the programme for the first measures to be taken by the future Soviet Government. These examples could be added to. It is therefore impossible to agree with those historians who write nowadays about the inevitability of the October victory. Nearer the truth, indeed, was Academician A.M. Rumyantsev, when he wrote: "The road from February to October was not straightforward, the victory of the Bolsheviks was not, so to speak, 'programmed', that is, on the cards from the very start. Before they could win to their side the majority of the people the Bolsheviks had to overcome gigantic difficulties."[34]

Nor was the activity of the Menshevik and Social-Revolutionary parties "programmed" in advance. These headed the majority in the Soviets immediately after February, and for a few months also headed the Provisional Government. They too considered themselves socialist parties, and by the end of the summer of 1917 they were *de facto* in power. Despite their organisational weakness, the S.R.s and Mensheviks were not only swept by the revolutionary flood into the forefront of political life — for several months they held the decisive positions therein. However hard the S.R.s and Mensheviks tried to cling to their coalition with the Cadets, at the beginning of September 1917 the latter were, against their will, excluded from the Government, and they were not represented in the "Directory" (the Council of Five) proclaimed by Kerensky. But neither the S.R.s nor the Mensheviks did anything substantial in those decisive weeks to put into practice their own political programme and thereby to win to their side the majority of the revolutionary people. One might have expected, for instance, that the initiative in solving the agrarian question in Russia would have fallen in 1917 precisely to the S.R.s. It was, after all, in their programme that pride of place was given to the demand for "socialisation" of all privately-owned land, that is, "its removal from private ownership by individual persons or groups, to become the property of the people as a whole". According to the S.R. programme, "all land is to come under the control of the central and local organs of popular self-government ..., use of the land must be put on a basis of equality in labour, that is, must guarantee a standard of living based upon the labour performed by individuals either separately or in association."[35]

It was under the guidance of the local S.R. organisations that during the summer of 1917 242 local peasant mandates were drawn up, which then served as the basis for the general peasant mandate published in the Bulletin of the All-Russia Soviet of Peasants' Deputies for 19 August 1917.[36] But it was left to the Bolsheviks, after October, to make of this mandate a (provisional) *law*. Addressing the Second All-Russia Congress of Soviets, Lenin said: "Voices are being raised here that the decree itself and the Mandate were drawn up by the Socialist-Revolutionaries. What of it? Does it matter who drew them up? As a democratic government, we cannot ignore the decision of the masses of the people, even though we may disagree with it."[37] The Bolsheviks thus put into effect the programmatic demand of the S.R. party, which this party had itself failed to implement, mainly owing to a number of subjective reasons. Settlement of the agrarian question was obstructed by the right-wing leaders of the party (N.D. Avksentiev, V.M. Chernov, A.F. Kerensky), who in some cases even sanctioned the sending of military detachments to prevent unauthorised seizure of landlords' land. Only in October, when the peasant movement in Russia had begun to assume the character of an agrarian revolution, and the influence of the Bolsheviks was growing rapidly, did the attitude of the right-wing S.R.s begin to change. On 16(29) October 1917 the joint commission of the Provisional Government and the Council of the Republic hastily brought forward a bill for *provisionally* handing over the land to the peasants. But this measure came too late to produce the impression on the masses on which Kerensky counted. In the localities few people even knew about the new bill.

Nor was the external policy of the Provisional Government absolutely "determined". It is known that the fall of the autocracy was hastened by the Court's attempts to make a separate peace with Germany. The Russian bourgeoisie did not want peace, its watchword was "war to a victorious conclusion," and so the Provisional Government, in which the Cadets predominated in the spring of 1917, began to prepare at the front for an offensive by the Russian armies. But already after the failure of the June offensive the mood in the country and in the army altered sharply, and this led to a change in the composition of the Provisional Government. By the beginning of autumn the question of peace had become the chief political question in the country. Not only the Bolsheviks but the Left elements among the Mensheviks as well were calling for peace. Speaking in the Council of the Republic, L. Martov attacked those who "insist upon postponing peace until later, until nothing is left of the Russian army, until Russia becomes the subject of bargaining between the different imperialist groups."[38]

Not long before the October rising, the War Minister in the Provisional Government in its final form, A.I. Verkhovsky, also came out in favour of immediate peace negotiations. At a closed session of the Pre-Parliament Verkhovsky drew the conclusion that "we are not able to go on fighting" and proposed, with a view to combating Bolshevism, "to raise at once the question of making peace". He voiced his confidence that news of peace "will bring an access of vigour to the army. Then units will be found which will be ready to crush anarchy and disruption both at the front and in the rear". Verkhovsky also called on the Provisional Government to urge Russia's allies to hurry up with their peace proposals. Verkhovsky's suggestions failed, however, to win the majority of votes, as did many similar resolutions introduced in the Pre-Parliament. Verkhovsky himself was removed from office — one week before October.[39] In those same pre-October days the prominent S.R. leader A.R. Gotz also came out against Kerensky. "The policy of the Bolsheviki," declared Gotz in the Council of the Republic, "is demagogic and criminal in their exploitation of the popular discontent. But there is a whole series of popular demands which have received no satisfaction up to now ... The questions of peace, land and the democratisation of the army ought to be stated in such a fashion that no soldier, peasant or worker would have the least doubt that our Government is attempting, firmly and infallibly, to solve them ... We Mensheviki do not wish to provoke a Cabinet crisis, and we are ready to defend the Provisional Government with all our energy, to the last drop of our blood — if only the Provisional Government, on all these burning questions, will speak the clear and precise words awaited by the people with such impatience."[40]

But the Provisional Government was unable to find in itself either the resolution or the political wisdom, or even the measure of political resourcefulness needed in order to take up the questions of peace and land, adequately and in time. This does not mean at all, however, that there was no possibility that it might have done this. We know that within a month after the October revolution in Petrograd a congress of the right-wing S.R.s was held. The majority of the speakers saw as the chief reason for their defeat the wrong tactics of the S.R. Party, the conduct of its Central Committee, which had proved incapable of resolute action. In the Congress resolution on the current situation it was stated that the stage of coalition with the bourgeoisie, which was necessary for socialist democracy, and which had rendered great service in 1917, was not justified as the policy for the future, and must be abandoned. But the party "did not show sufficient resolution in difficult moments, did not take power into its own hands in time, but left it to the end in the hands of a weak and colourless government which had lost popularity and become easy prey for the first conspiracy."[41]

The Russian bourgeoisie wanted to carry on the war "to a victorious conclusion". But it did not want to carry on the war *at all costs*, at any price, even the price of its own existence and power. Only a few months after the October revolution the counter-revolutionary government of General Krasnov on the Don made a *de facto* alliance with the German army command, and not only began to receive arms from the Germans but also allowed a number of large units of the German forces to enter the territory of the Don Region.

While the Don Army was taking the line of alliance with the Kaiser's Germany, Denikin and the Volunteer Army relied upon the Entente. However, in August 1918, while the World War was still going on, the Cadet leader P. Milyukov wrote to General Denikin, in a confidential communication, that it was necessary to agree to peace with Germany, to independence for Poland and Finland, and even to benevolent neutrality in relation to Germany — if only the Germans would help in setting up a central national government for Russia, to be headed by the Grand Duke Michael Alexandrovich (who, as Milyukov put it, "must be sought for"). Now, even the leaders of the Cadets were for peace.[42]

Nor was the policy of the Provisional Government regarding the Constituent Assembly predestined. The slogan of a Constituent Assembly, which first appeared in February, was supported by all parties, and it was dear to the masses not for its own sake but because with it was linked the settlement of the country's principal problems, and above all the land question. But the Provisional Government delayed convening the Constituent Assembly, several times postponed the date of the elections, dragged out the drafting of the electoral regulations, and still did not arrange for the elections to be held even when the party lists were ready. The date for the elections was announced only in October, they were to take place at the end of November and the Assembly itself was to meet in December. But by that time the situation in the country had become so incandescent that the decision adopted by the Provisional Government could make little impression, and could not prevent the revolution.

From what has been said it is clear that the October revolution was not at all an absolutely inevitable event. Even more than the February revolution, it was the realisation of one of the possible alternatives for the development of the situation in Russia. This event was neither accidental nor absolutely necessary, but, like every other concrete historical event, was a combination of necessity and accident.

f. Spontaneity and organisation in the mass actions of 1917

The question of the relation between spontaneity and organisation in the actions of the popular masses preoccupied all of Russia's revolutionary parties from early times. Referring to the experience of revolutionary actions in Europe, the Mensheviks asserted that mass popular revolutions begin spontaneously. Therefore it was not possible for any party to "set a date" for a revolution in Russia, the revolution would "come by itself" and it could not be "organised." The party must be ready for the revolution, carry on agitation and propaganda so as to clarify the aims of the revolution and help popular leaders to emerge. But a people's movement could not be led in the way that a military commander leads his troops in action during a battle. After the great movements of January 1905 the Mensheviks wrote in *Iskra* (then still a Menshevik organ) that this upsurge of spontaneous, mass proletarian struggle decisively refuted both the liberal doubters who had not believed that "the people would speak", and the Bolsheviks, those "utopians of conspiratorial organisation" who thought it possible in the name of "formally-organised discipline", to "set in motion at their discretion, by means of a mechanical lever consisting of agents, the million-fold army of the working class."[43]

The task of the Social-Democrats, Martov wrote in those days, was "not so much to organise the people's revolution as to unleash it."[44] The same view was maintained at that time by leading Social-Democrats in Western Europe. "Revolutions allow no-one to play schoolmaster to them," wrote Rosa Luxemburg. "The masses will be the active chorus, and the leaders only the 'speaking parts', the interpreters of the will of the masses.'' She regarded as utopian even the Bolsheviks' demand for military-technical preparation of the rising.[45]

The Bolsheviks' attitude was different. They did not deny the possibility or the importance of spontaneity in revolutionary outbreaks, such as the January demonstration of the Petrograd proletariat, or the mutiny on the battleship *Potemkin*. But it was precisely the spontaneity, the lack of organisation, and, connected with this, the unco-ordinated character of these revolutionary outbreaks that, in the opinion of the Bolsheviks, was the chief reason for their failure. ''A people's revolution, true, cannot be timed,'' wrote Lenin. ''But if we have really prepared an uprising, and if a popular uprising is realisable by virtue of the revolutions in social relations *that have already taken place*, then it is quite possible to time the uprising.''[46] To one of his articles in *Vperyod* Lenin gave the title: ''Should we organise the revolution?'' His answer was fundamentally affirmative.

The revolution of 1905-1907 did not settle this argument. In those years the spontaneous mass actions of the workers, peasants and sailors met with defeat, but those actions arranged and planned in advance by the Bolsheviks (with participation by the S.R.s), such as the December armed rising in Moscow, did not prove victorious either.

The February revolution of 1917 was to a significant extent the result of a spontaneous explosion of mass discontent among the workers and the garrison soldiers who backed them. There also joined in the revolution, quite unexpectedly for the Government, those Cossack regiments which the Tsarist authorities had since the end of 1916 been gradually assembling in Petrograd, Moscow and the chief strategic centres. The resistance put up by certain police sub-units was quickly suppressed, and the revolution swept like a conflagration over the whole country, meeting with support on all the fronts of the World War. Berdyaev came close to the truth of the matter when he wrote: ''It cannot even be said that the February revolution overthrew the Russian monarchy. The monarchy in Russia fell of itself. No one defended it. It had no adherents.''[47] In other words, the February revolution took place approximately in the way that the Mensheviks conceived a political revolution: nobody ''set a date'' for this revolution, nobody drew up beforehand a plan for its unfolding, either in Petrograd or over the country as a whole. ''Not a single

24

organisation," wrote V. Bazarov, "can claim for itself the honour of having led the revolution in its first days."[48] A prominent participant in the February events in Petrograd, N. Sukhanov, also testified that "no party was prepared for the great revolution. They were all dreaming, having presentiments, 'sensing'."[49] The S.R.,V. Zenzinov wrote, soon after the fall of the monarchy: "The revolution struck us like thunder out of the sky and took by surprise not only the Government, the Duma and the established public bodies ..., it was not expected by us revolutionaries, either."[50] Ten years after the revolution the Menshevik O.A. Yermansky recalled: "The street was finally captured by the worker masses, who advanced like an avalanche. This was an elemental movement without any formulated, immediate purpose. Whether there were any attempts at leadership within it I don't know. Apparently there were none."[51]

The predominantly spontaneous nature of the February events was more than once remarked upon by Lenin, too. "In February 1917," he wrote, "the masses had created the Soviets even before any party had managed to proclaim this slogan. It was the great creative spirit of the people, which had passed through the bitter experience of 1905 and had been made wise by it, that gave rise to this form of proletarian power."[52]

The unexpected and rapid revolutionary explosion of 23 February, which no one had actually foreseen *in this form*, and nobody had prepared,[53] was, of course, connected with the very great deal of preparatory work done by all the revolutionary parties in the preceding years. The revolution of 1905-1907 had already served, in fact, as an important "dress rehearsal" for the revolutionary events of 1917. Tsardom itself, by calling up into the army and training in the use of arms millions of peasants and workers, unintentionally promoted the military-technical preparation of the revolution and gave it a material-technical basis. Of enormous importance for future events was the mass reinforcement of the junior commissioned ranks of the army, which before the war had possessed a thoroughly "caste" character, by representatives of the intelligentsia and the students, and also by Cossacks and soldiers who had distinguished themselves in the war. The probable allies of the working-class — the peasants — stood armed and organised in every large town, including Moscow and Petrograd, in the shape of military garrisons. It must be mentioned that the bourgeois and liberal-monarchist parties also facilitated the preparation of the revolution by their public criticism of the Tsarist government. Many of the speeches delivered by well-known Duma orators were disseminated, in manuscript or through newspaper reports, all over the country, and were subjected to lively discussion not only in bourgeois-liberal circles but also among the students, the intelligentsia and part of the working class. P. Milyukov considered that by criticising the Government the Duma was holding back the mob and so protecting the regime. But this was an illusion. V. Shulgin was nearer the mark when he persistently asked himself whether the Progressive Bloc was not criticising the Government too strongly, when it asserted that the latter was good for nothing. Did this not amount to helping the revolution? "Are we bridling [the revolution] or are we kindling it?" And when the mob of revolted workers and soldiers flooded the Tauride Palace, when with unconcealed hatred Shulgin observed the beginning of the revolution and dreamt of machine-guns ("machine-guns, that was what I wanted, but we had none and could not have had any") he clearly understood that the activity of the Progressive Bloc, given the uncompromising attitude of the Tsarist Court, had objectively served to prepare this February revolution.[54]

The activity of the petty-bourgeois parties — Mensheviks, S.R.s and similar groups — in the Duma and in the country generally also contributed to preparing the February revolution. Though they followed a defencist line, they nevertheless subjected the Government and the monarchy to sharp criticism. In one of their appeals the Menshevik-Defencists, in autumn 1916, spoke plainly of the "removal, overthrow or annihilation of the regime which has brought the country to the brink of ruin," and said that "democratisation of the country cannot be separated from its defence."[55]

Even more work, however, was done to prepare the revolution by the Bolsheviks, especially during 1916 and in January-February 1917, although their activity was not so apparent to the outside observer as that, for example, of the "Progressive Bloc". In fact it was only the Bolsheviks who were able to maintain in the army and in the chief proletarian centres, a ramified underground organisation. During the war the Central Committee sent A.G. Shlyapnikov into Russia, where he headed the Russian Bureau of the C.C. and was at the beginning of 1916 co-opted to membership of the Central Committee itself.[56] Reporting to the C.C. on the eve of February, Shlyapnikov wrote: "Our position is excellent in comparison with that of the others. It can be said that only we possess an all-Russia organisation at the present time ...

Mensheviks, Unity-ites and others who broke away from us are returning to our Party's ranks ... The political struggle is intensifying day by day. Discontent rages throughout the country. The revolutionary hurricane can start to blow any day now. There is a threatening mood about."[57]

Nearly all the strikes and demonstrations that took place in Petrograd in January and February 1917 were led and co-ordinated by the district committees of the Party and the Petrograd Committee itself. In February 1917 the Bolshevik organisations in Russia as a whole had 24,000 members, of whom about 2,000 were in Petrograd and about 600 in Moscow.[58] "In those days," wrote Sukhanov, referring to the Bolsheviks, "those people were absorbed in a quite different kind of work, looking after the technical needs of the movement, pressing for a showdown with Tsardom, organising agitation and illegal publications."[59]

From all these facts it is impossible, however, to deduce that the revolution that happened in February was not mainly a spontaneous affair, that it was largely organised by the Bolsheviks, or that the revolutionary events developed according to some secret but well-defined plan worked out by the Russian Bureau of the C.C. and the Petrograd Committee of the Bolsheviks. At the same time it is wrong to suppose that the revolution actually happened without any preparation by anyone, and caught everyone by surprise, as N. Sukhanov and V. Zenzinov allege.[60] The truth lies somewhere between these two extreme views.

The Bolsheviks, of course, both prepared for the revolution and were ready for it. They assumed that revolution was already near. But they did not think that events would develop at such impetuous speed. It is revealing that on 23 February the Bolshevik organisations in Petrograd were not planning either political demonstrations or political strikes. A member of the Petrograd Committee, I.D. Chugurin, testifies that "we [i.e., the C.C.] intended to organise a decisive demonstration, in the form of a general strike, on 1 May 1917."[61] Events developed otherwise, however, and on 23 February the revolutionary initiative of Petrograd's working men and women broke through with elemental force: the soldiers of the garrison, and then the Cossacks, joined in the movement, and this began the February revolution. While it can be said that the very rapid development of the revolutionary events proved unexpected to the Bolsheviks as to everyone else, it is not the case that these events took them by surprise and that all control over what was happening was lost. All the Party committees immediately joined in the movement, striving to advance their representatives and to give form to the spontaneous movement of hundreds of thousands of workers and soldiers. A considerable role was also played in the events of the first days and weeks of the revolution by certain groups and individual members of the Menshevik and S.R. parties — all the more so because only a minority of the workers, not to mention the soldiers, were at that time under Bolshevik influence. Thus, for example, in the first days of the revolution the actual leadership of the Petrograd Soviet was in the hands of three men: Yu. Steklov, who at that time considered himself neither a Bolshevik nor a Menshevik; N. Sukhanov, who belonged to the group of Mensnevik-Internationalists; and N.D. Sokolov, who in February 1917 was a member of the left wing of the Menshevik party.[62] It was with the participation of these men that the famous "Order No.1" of the Petrograd Soviet was drawn up, which contributed to the rapid revolutionising of the army. With the return to Petrograd of other, better-known Social-Democratic and S.R. leaders, these initial activists of the Petrograd Soviet fell into the background.

It is interesting to trace the attitudes of V.I. Lenin in January-February 1917. Cut off from Russia, far from the front line, Lenin followed closely, through the press and through the confidential information that reached him, the development of events in Russia and throughout the world. Of course he expected revolution in Russia and in the other countries of Europe, and did all he could to bring this revolutionary outbreak nearer. He was sure that the world war would end in revolution in the majority of the belligerent countries of Europe, but he naturally could not foresee exactly the concrete course events would follow.

Lenin could not foresee how long the battles of the world war would continue. He appreciated very well that Russia was the weakest link among the belligerent countries, he knew about the possibility of a separate peace between Nicholas II and Wilhelm, and he weighed attentively the various possible ways in which events might devleop. In his article "A Turn in World Politics," published on 31 January 1917, Lenin wrote: "It is possible that a separate peace between Germany and Russia *has been concluded* after all ... The Tsar may have told Wilhelm: 'If I openly sign a separate peace, then tomorrow you, my august partner, may have to deal with a government of Milyukov and Guchkov, if not of Milyukov and Kerensky. For the revolution is growing, and I cannot answer for the army, whose generals are in correspondence with Guchkov and whose officers are mainly yesterday's high-school boys. Is there any point in my risking my throne and your losing a good partner?'''[63]

Frequently quoted is Lenin's lecture to young Swiss workers in January 1917 about the revolution of 1905 in Russia. In particular, these words: "We must not be deceived by the present grave-like stillness in Europe. Europe is pregnant with revolution. The monstrous horrors of the imperialist war, the suffering caused by the high cost of living everywhere, engender a revolutionary mood; and the ruling classes ... are more and more moving into a blind alley from which they can never extricate themselves without tremendous upheavals ... In Europe the coming years, precisely because of this predatory war, will lead to popular uprisings under the leadership of the proletariat against the power of finance capital, against the big banks, against the capitalists; and these upheavals cannot end otherwise than with the expropriation of the bourgeoisie, with the victory of socialism. We of the older generation may not live to see the decisive battles of the coming revolution. But I can, I believe, express the confident hope that the youth which is working so splendidly in the socialist movement of Switzerland, and of the whole world, will be fortunate enough not only to fight, but also to win, in the coming proletarian revolution."[64]

It is quite obvious that the phrase about "we of the older generation" perhaps not living to see the revolution (which broke out in Russia only six weeks later) was nothing more than a rhetorical device. Lenin was sure that the revolution was not far off. N.K. Krupskaya recalled: "Never before had Vladimir Ilyich been in such an uncompromising mood as he was during the last months of 1916 and the early months of 1917. He was positively certain that the revolution was impending."[65] and Lenin realised clearly enough that, under the conditions of world war, spontaneity would predominate in the movement of the popular masses in the first stages of the coming revolutions. He regarded this spontaneity as a sign of the depth of the popular movement. "It is beyond all doubt," he wrote, "that the spontaneity of the movement is proof that it is deeply rooted in the masses, that its roots are firm and that it is inevitable."[66] "Spontaneous outbreaks," he observed later, "become inevitable as the revolution matures. There has never been a revolution in which this has not been the case."[67]

★　　★　　★　　★

While spontaneous movements and outbursts predominated in the development of events during the maturation of the February revolution, the October revolution matured and developed in an entirely different way. The combination in the actions of the masses of spontaneity and organisation, blind indignation and conscious awareness, was in October 1917 already different from what it had been in February. This is understandable, for the February revolution had taken place in a country deprived of fundamental democratic freedoms. It was practically impossible to prepare and organise the revolutionary forces beforehand: one had to expect a spontaneous, elemental (and therefore badly-led) outbreak of mass discontent, which could then grow into a revolt. An altogether different situation existed in Russia in the period leading up to October. Between March and October the popular masses enjoyed almost complete political freedom. All the left-wing parties were legalised, their numbers (especially those of the S.R.s and Bolsheviks) increased very rapidly, and the Bolshevik Party was the best organised and disciplined force on the left: its influence grew, first and foremost, in the principal industrial centres of the country. Although the bourgeoisie came to power for a few months after the overthrow of the monarchy, they were unable in so short a period and in such an unstable situation to create any effective machinery of government, that is, really to take power into their own hands and put an end to the situation of "dual power". While the old apparatus of Tsarist rule was visibly disintegrating (prisons and police-stations were destroyed, officers lost most of their former authority over the soldiers, the courts practically ceased to function, and. so on), the feverish efforts of the bourgeois parties (supported by the Mensheviks and S.R.s) to create a new state machine produced no very noticeable result.

Under these conditions the Bolsheviks were able to engage in something more than agitation and propaganda and to create not just a *political* army for the next revolution. They could and did also carry on a great deal of organisational work to establish a real *military* support for that revolution. Arming of the workers went forward at a rapid pace, and units of the Red Guard were formed in all the enterprises and districts, with a unified command. The Bolsheviks became the preponderant force in the revolutionary organisations of the Baltic Fleet. Their influence grew in the army units, including the garrisons of Petrograd and many other cities, and also on the North-Western front. Of special importance was the passing of the Petrograd and Moscow Soviets under Bolshevik influence and control, since the Provisional Government had maintained itself up to that time not so much through the support of the army or the state apparatus as through the active, or at least passive, support given it by the Soviets.

The Bolsheviks did, of course, rely in the period of the preparation for October upon the spontaneous upsurge of the mass movement. Seen from outside, however, this spontaneous movement seemed to have become weaker, as Lenin's opponents in the C.C. pointed out. They said that the masses showed no disposition to rush out into the streets, and that, on the contrary, the pogromist, Black-Hundred, anti-Bolshevik press was everywhere increasing its circulation. But Lenin confidently rejected these conclusions: "Absenteeism and indifference on the part of the masses," he declared at the Central Committee meeting of 10(23) October, 1917, "is due to their being tired of words and resolutions."[68]

Clarifying his view of the matter, Lenin wrote a few days later that it was true that the masses were "not in a mood that would drive them into the streets". But, "if we approach this characterisation of the mass mood from the point of view of the entire development of the class and political struggle and of the entire course of events during the six months of our revolution, it will become clear to us how people frightened by the bourgeoisie are distorting the question. Things are not as they were before April 20-21, June 9, July 3, for then it was a matter of *spontaneous excitement* which we, as a party, either failed to comprehend (April 20) or held back and shaped into a peaceful demonstration (June 9 and July 3), for we knew very well at that time that the Soviets were *not yet* ours, that the peasants *still* trusted the Lieberdan-Chernov and not the Bolshevik course (uprising), that consequently we could not have the majority of the people behind us, and that consequently the uprising would be premature. At that time the majority of the class-conscious workers did *not* raise the question of the last decisive struggle at all; not one of all our Party units would have raised it at that time. As for the unenlightened and very broad masses, there was neither a concerted effort nor a resolve born out of despair; there was only a spontaneous *excitement* with the naive hope of 'influencing' Kerensky and the bourgeoisie by 'action', by a demonstration pure and simple. What is needed for an uprising is not this, but, on the one hand, a conscious, firm and unswerving resolve on the part of the class-conscious elements to fight to the end; and on the other, a mood of despair among the broad masses who *feel* that nothing can now be saved by half-measures ... The development of the revolution has in practice brought *both* the workers *and* the peasantry to precisely this combination of a tense mood resulting from experience among the class-conscious and a mood of hatred towards ... the capitalists that is close to despair among the broadest masses."[69] And subsequent events showed that Lenin was right. Basing itself on his counsels regarding the art of insurrection, the Military Revolutionary Committee of the Petrograd Soviet were able to draw up a precise plan of action, making detailed arrangements for the coming battle, and this plan was carried out exactly according to schedule, and crowned with complete success. With somewhat greater difficulty and heavier losses, but also successfully, an armed uprising was launched in Moscow. In many other cities it proved possible to dispense with an armed uprising, and power there passed into the hands of the Soviets peacefully, without shooting or casualties.

The October revolution was in essence the first great people's revolution in which the factor of spontaneity had no decisive importance, but which was carried out in an organised and precise way, almost completely in accordance with a prearranged plan. Thus was confirmed Lenin's idea that it was possible and desirable not merely to prepare the revolution politically but also to "plan" and "organise" it. It turned out that, contrary to Rosa Luxemburg's opinion, revolutions can be "schooled."

g. The degree of risk in the actions of the Bolsheviks

In so far as the October revolution was not the result of a spontaneous outburst, the question naturally arises: to what extent did the actions taken by the Bolsheviks involve an element of risk, and how great was the danger of defeat?

It is not hard to believe that in October 1917 victory for the Bolsheviks was practically certain and beyond question in Petrograd and Moscow, as Lenin had sought to convince his Party comrades during nearly two months. The decisions of the Sixth Congress of the R.S.D.L.P. (B.) on the course to be taken towards an armed uprising was no secret to the Provisional Government. As October approached, the Provisional Government, though it did not know all the details and timetables of the uprising, was well enough aware that the Bolsheviks were preparing to revolt, and it strove in every way to prevent this from happening. But neither in September nor in October was Kerensky in a position to repeat what he had partly succeeded in doing in July, namely, to force the Bolsheviks to retreat or to go underground. Not only in Petrograd but in nearly all the other industrial centres of Russia the Bolsheviks were in September 1917 already stronger than their adversaries, both politically and in the military sense. The Western Sovietologist B. Wolfe, talking with the aged ex-Premier A.F. Kerensky, who lived in the U.S.A. until his death at the end of the 1960s, put this question to him: "Why did you not suppress the Bolsheviks after they openly declared their intention to wage war on [your] Government?" Kerensky answered: "What force did I have to suppress them with?"[70]

Soviet historians' calculations have shown that in Petrograd alone, on the eve of the October insurrection, the Bolsheviks had on their side not less than 300,000 armed workers, soldiers and sailors, whereas the Provisional Government had only a little over 30,000 men. In the evening of 25 October, when the storming of the Winter Palace was being prepared, about 20,000 Red Guards, soldiers and sailors were concentrated against this last refuge of the Provisional Government, while in the Palace itself and in the square in front of it the defenders totalled no more than 3,000. The seizure by the Bolsheviks of all the other strategic centres of Petrograd proceeded almost without bloodshed. Owing to the overwhelming superiority possessed by the Bolsheviks there was no serious fighting in Petrograd on 24-26 October (6-8 November) 1917, and the total number of killed on both sides came to no more than 15, with 60 wounded, at most.[71] The ordinary non-political citizens of Petrograd learnt of the change of government only when they read their morning papers or heard announcements.

In the country at large, however, the situation was rather more complicated, and the relation of forces was not at all so clear and definite as in Petrograd. Russia was still at war on all fronts, and there were more than ten million men under arms. Not only the generals and officers but also most of the elected army committees were hostile to the new government in the capital. Many military units which had kept their fighting capacity might support the Provisional Government. For this reason the latter endeavoured (though without much success) to transfer from Petrograd the soldiers of the garrison who had been worked upon by Bolshevik propaganda, and replace them with "fresh" units. When he fled from the Winter Palace, Kerensky was still able to persuade a few commanders, and especially General P. Krasnov, to move their forces against Petrograd. True, after their first clashes with the Red Guards and sailors, Krasnov's Cossacks refused to fight. Krasnov himself was arrested, and Kerensky had to flee once more, and soon left the country. Nevertheless, at the end of October the Bolsheviks were forced to make a much bigger effort to defend Petrograd than had been needed a few days earlier to capture the Winter Palace. Another extremely risky step was Lenin's decision to dismiss the commander-in-chief of Russia's field army, General Dukhonin, and replace him by the Bolshevik Ensign N. Krylenko. Let us turn to Stalin's recollections of this event. "I recall," he wrote, "that Lenin, Krylenko ... and I went to General Staff Headquarters in Petrograd to negotiate with Dukhonin over the direct wire. It was a ghastly moment. Dukhonin and Field Headquarters categorically refused to obey the order of the Council of People's Commissars. The army officers were completely under the sway of Field Headquarters. As for the soldiers, no one could tell what this army of fourteen million would say, subordinated as it was to the so-called army organisations, which were hostile to the Soviet power."[72]

But still more complicated and difficult to forecast was the general international situation. The Russian army, weary, enfeebled and demoralised, was faced at the front by the still sufficiently powerful and disciplined armies of the Austro-German coalition. The countries allied to Russia — Britain, France, the U.S.A., Japan — had millions of men under arms, some of whom the Entente might use to put down the Russian revolution and re-establish the Eastern Front.

When he called on the Russian proletariat to begin the socialist revolution in a Russia at war, Lenin counted on their being backed up very soon by the proletarians of the principal European countries. In 1917 neither Lenin nor the other Bolshevik leaders even hoped that a revolutionary Russia could last very long amid a hostile capitalist encirclement. It was a question merely of *beginning* what was not so much a Russian as a world revolution, and holding on as long as possible — until the revolutions in the other countries "ripened". This was Lenin's main strategic calculation at that time, and in this lay the principal risk, for it was impossible to guess in advance at all the innumerable important factors that might determine the international situation and the course of the war. And Lenin did not deceive himself: he knew quite well that to raise a rebellion in the rear of a fighting army under conditions of world war was not merely taking a risk, it was staking everything on one card. The other Bolshevik leaders realised this too.[73]

But it would be wrong to blame the Bolsheviks for playing too risky a game. Engels wrote: "In revolution as in war, it is of the highest necessity to stake everything on the decisive moment, whatever the odds may be ... It is a matter of course that, in every struggle, he who takes up the gauntlet risks being beaten; but is that a reason why he should confess himself beaten, and submit to the yoke without drawing the sword?"[74] Every revolution contains an element of risk, and all the more so must the first socialist revolution in world history be a leap into the unknown. One can understand those who are against all revolutions and all forms of revolutionary violence, on principle. But, in spite of them, revolutions keep on happening in our imperfect world. Agreeing with Engels, Marx wrote, in one of his letters: "World history would indeed be very easy to make if the struggle were taken up only on condition of infallibly favourable chances."[75] Referring to these words of Marx's, Lenin also wrote: "To attempt in advance to calculate the chances *with complete accuracy* would be quackery or hopeless pedantry."[76] The Bolsheviks had been guided by these ideas in December 1905 and had suffered defeat. Guided by the same ideas in October 1917, they were victorious.

II *Was the October Socialist Revolution premature?*

a. Various points of view

If the October revolution of 1917 was not the result of an uncontrolled and spontaneous outburst of popular indignation, but was organised and planned by the Bolsheviks, the question naturally arises: were not the actions and decisions of the Bolsheviks too hasty and misconceived, and was not the October Revolution itself, therefore, "premature"?

As we know, all the political adversaries of the Bolsheviks have answered this question in the affirmative. Even if they considered, or consider, themselves to be socialists, they have no doubt that the Russia of 1917 was not ripe for a "socialist" revolution and "the dictatorship of the proletariat".

But it is also known that among the Bolsheviks themselves, too, there was no uniformity of view on this question in 1917. Before Lenin's return to Russia none of the leaders of the Bolshevik Party had seriously raised the question of a transition to direct preparation for the socialist revolution. Even the slogan "All power to the Soviets" was not heard in those days among the Bolsheviks, and even more premature than that would have seemed the slogan of the dictatorship of the proletariat. Many Bolsheviks referred in justification of their then standpoint to Lenin's writings of the 1905-1907 period. It appeared to them that the question of a socialist revolution could be raised only when all the fundamental tasks of the bourgeois-democratic revolution had been solved: first and foremost, the agrarian question. It was not surprising that Lenin's famous "April Theses", in which he decalred sharply and clearly that with the passing of State power in Russia into the hands of the bourgeoisie the bourgeois-democratic revolution in Russia had been *completed*, and that the main task of the moment was now to pass "from the first stage of the revolution — which ... placed power in the hands of the bourgeoisie — to its second stage, which must place power in the hands of the proletariat and the poorest sections of the peasants,"[77] and that it was *"impossible* to slip out of the imperialist war and achieve a democratic, non-coercive peace without overthrowing the power of capital and transferring power to *another* class, the proletariat"[78] — it was not surprising that these theses evoked, at first, bewilderment and objections among the Bolsheviks themselves. Lenin had to spend not only time but also tremendous efforts, in order to convince the majority of delegates to the Petrograd City Conference and to the Sixth (April) All-Russia Conference of the Bolshevik Party of the correctness of his political line.

However, doubts regarding Lenin's correctness did not vanish in those circles even after the April conference. And when, at the First All-Russia Congress of Soviets of Workers' and Soldiers' Deputies, replying to the assertion by the Menshevik leader I.G. Tsereteli: "At the present time there is no political party in Russia which would say: put power into our hands, go away, we will take your place,"[79] Lenin exclaimed: "Yes, there is. No party can refuse this and our Party certainly doesn't. It is ready to take over full power at any moment,"[80] some of the leaders of the Bolshevik Party thought that this was too rash a declaration to have made.

Even after the Sixth Congress of the Bolshevik Party had decided on steering towards the organisation of an armed uprising, there were still members of the Central Committee who doubted the rightness of this course. Even at the last enlarged meeting of the C.C. before the insurrection, on 16(29) October the resolution put forward by Lenin was adopted only by 19 votes to 2 (Kamenev and Zinoviev), with 4 abstentions. The resolution moved by Zinoviev was rejected by 15 to 6, with 3 abstentions.[81] Some of the most prominent Bolsheviks considered, down to the last moment, that the Party must stick to its line of working towards the convening of a Constituent Assembly in which, without holding power, the Bolsheviks must function as a strong opposition.[82]

It might have seemed that these disputes would have been settled by the October Revolution itself, with its almost bloodless victory in Petrograd and rapid success throughout the country, which Lenin called, not without justification, the triumphal march of Soviet power. Disputes about the prematurity or otherwise of the October revolution did indeed cease inside the Bolshevik Party. Many of the events, however, which followed that revolution — the three years of cruel civil war, and then, later, the forced collectivisation of 1929-1930, the terror against the peasantry, and even the terror of 1937-1938, caused historians and sociologists of various tendencies to bring up again the question whether the October revolution had been premature, and whether all the excesses committed after the revolution were not to be explained by Lenin and the Bolsheviks having been in too much of a hurry at that time — in October 1917. Many historians, sociologists and Sovietologists continue to affirm, to this very day, that the October revolution was patently premature and that all our country's subsequent sufferings, including the Stalin terror, were due to this fatal "original sin" of Lenin's in taking advantage of the weakness of the state power after the February revolution to proclaim a socialist revolution in a country that was as yet quite unready for socialism.

b. Is a "premature" revolution possible?

One may reasonably ask, though, whether a premature revolution can ever occur. Did not Marx say in one of his fundamental works, that "no social order is ever destroyed before all the productive forces for which it is sufficient have been developed, and new superior relations of production never replace older ones before the material conditions for their existence have matured within the framework of the old society"? Did he not declare that "Mankind ... sets itself only such tasks as it is able to solve, since closer examination will always show that the problem itself arises only when the material conditions for its solution are already present or at least in the course of formation"?[83]

It is not hard to perceive, however, that Marx was here speaking of a social revolution in the broadest sense of the term. So far as

37

particular concrete revolutionary actions and political movements were concerned, Marx and Engels always allowed for the possible occurrence of obviously premature events, that is, for instances of running ahead and mistakenly "jumping over" stages of development not yet completed, on the part of particular revolutionary parties.

In the history of revolutionary movements in any country it has seldom happened that a revolution has taken place "right on time". Nearly every successful revolution has been preceded, as a rule, by several unsuccessful attempts, which ended in defeat and were clearly *premature*. Only some of these premature actions deserve to be condemned. A commander who begins fighting a battle without having either a plan of possible operations or precise intelligence information, and without taking trouble to select the best possible position, and so forth, does, of course, deserve condemnation. But many a commander has been obliged to fight a battle which was *forced* upon him, in unfavourable circumstances and with small chance of success. And no-one can reproach such a commander for being defeated, if he has fought bravely against clearly superior enemy forces. By this one lost battle, he may have contributed to the success of the campaign as a whole. It is the same in the case of revolutions. Spartacus's revolt was doomed to failure, and also the revolts of Razin and Pugachev, and the Paris Commune, and dozens of other revolutionary actions, in their time. Yet they often enriched revolutionary thought, produced traditions and experience, brought revolutionary leaders to the forefront, and thereby helped to bring down a social order which had outlived itself.

Almost always, "premature" or insufficiently prepared revolutionary actions ended in defeat, as happened with the revolt of the Paris Communards in the spring of 1871, or with the Russian Revolution of 1905-1907. But Marx and Engels also gave serious consideration to the possibility of *victory* for "premature" revolutions and, in particular, to the possible coming to power of the proletariat and its party in a situation in which neither the objective nor the subjective conditions for the fulfilment of their radical socialist programmes had matured.

Engels forecast two possible variants for the development of events after such a premature political overturn.

In the first case the extremist party, having come to power, will put into effect not those changes which it *would have liked* to put into effect, and which are contained in its basic party programme, but only those which *can* be put into effect in the given social and economic conditions. Engels's forecast for this case was very pessimistic.

"The worst thing that can befall a leader of an extreme party," he wrote in 1850, "is to be compelled to take over a government in an epoch when the movement is not yet ripe for the domination of the class which he represents, and for the realisation of the measure which that domination implies. What he *can* do depends not on his will but upon the degree of contradiction between the various classes, and upon the level of development of the material means of existence, of the conditions of production and commerce upon which class contradictions always repose. What he *ought* to do, what his party demands of him, again depends not upon him or the stage of development of the class struggle and its conditions. He is bound to the doctrines and demands hitherto propounded ... Thus he necessarily finds himself in an unsolvable dilemma. What he *can* do contradicts all his previous actions, and the principles and immediate interests of his party, and what he *ought* to do cannot be done. In a word, he is compelled to represent not his party or his class, but the class for whose domination the movement is then ripe. In the interests of the movement he is compelled to advance the interests of an alien class, and to feed his own class with phrases and promises, and with the asseveration that the interests of that alien class are their own interests. Whoever is put into this awkward position is irrevocably lost."[84]

In the second case, the extremist party which has come to power may nevertheless try, Engels supposed, to put into effect some of its own party demands, regardless of the objective, material conditions prevailing. Engels's forecasts about what would happen in this case were even more pessimistic.

"I have a presentiment," he wrote to Weydemeyer in 1853, "that, thanks to the perplexity and flabbiness of all the others, our Party will one fine morning be forced to assume power and finally to carry out the measures that are of no direct interest to us, but are in the general interests of the revolution and the specific interests of the petty-bourgeoisie; on which occasion, driven by the proletarian populace, bound by our own printed declarations and plans — more or less falsely interpreted, more or less passionately thrust to the fore in the Party struggle — we shall be constrained to undertake communist experiments and perform leaps the untimeliness of which we know better than anyone else. In so doing we lose our heads —

only physically speaking, let us hope — a reaction sets in, and until the world is able to pass *historical* judgment on such events, we are considered not only beasts, which wouldn't matter, but also *bêtes*, which is much worse. I do not quite see how it can turn out otherwise. In a backward country like Germany, which possesses an advanced party and is involved in an advanced revolution with an advanced country like France, the advanced party must get into power at the first serious conflict and as soon as *actual danger* is present, and that is, in any event, ahead of its normal time. All that does not matter, however, and the best thing we can do is for our Party to have established its historical rehabilitation in its literature ahead of time, should events take such a turn.''[85]

Nearly forty years later, in 1891, Engels again returned to the question of the possibility of a premature socialist revolution. The situation both in Germany and in Europe as a whole was then substantially different. In Germany there was the strongest Social-Democratic Party in the world. Engels rendered very great support to this party and set especially great hopes upon it. From his letters of 1890-1891 it is clear that he considered that Germany, thanks to the development in that country, side by side, of industry, the working class and the Social-Democratic Party, would by the end of the century, or in any case in not more than a decade, be ready for a socialist revolution, which would set socialist revolutions going in the other Western European countries. Engels was afraid, however, that long before that moment came, Russia and France would start a war against Germany; that, faced with such powerful adversaries on two fronts, Germany would suffer defeat; and that this would mean the destruction of the socialist movement in Germany and in other countries, and a prolonged rein thereafter in Europe of the spirit of nationalism and *revanchisme*. In those circumstances Engels did not advocate the line of ''defeat of one's own government''. On 13 October 1891 he wrote to August Bebel: ''If the danger of war increases, we can tell the Government that we should be ready, provided it makes this possible through proper treatment of us, to support it against the external enemy, on condition that it wages the war unwaveringly and making use of all means, including revolutionary ones. If Germany is attacked from both East and West, then any and every means of defence is justified. National existence is at stake, and for us also the maintenance of the position and the prospects for the future which we have won. The more revolutionary the way that the war is waged, the more will it be waged in our spirit. And it may happen that, owing to the cowardice of the bourgeois and Junkers, seeking to safeguard their property, we shall prove to be the only truly energetic war-party. Naturally, it may also happen that we shall be obliged to take the helm ourselves and act as in 1793, in order to throw out the Russians and their allies.''[86]

Ten days later, Engels expressed the same idea in a letter to Friedrich Sorge: "If the Russians start war against us, German Socialists must go for the Russians and their allies, whoever they may be, *à outrance*. If Germany is crushed, then we shall be too, while in the most favourable case the struggle will be such a violent one that Germany will only be able to maintain herself by revolutionary means, so that very possibly we shall be forced to come into power and play the part of 1793."[87]

Although Engels still thought that it would be premature for the Social-Democrats to come to power at the beginning of the 1890s, he did not on this occasion repeat his former gloomy prophecies. He thought that the German Social-Democratic Party was already strong enough to retain power and begin to build the new socialist society. Considering, however, that subjectively, the country was not yet ready for revolution, Engels thought it possible that the newly established Social-Democratic government would have to make greater use of compulsion, and even terror, than if it had come to power under conditions that were "riper" for this development. In late October 1891 Engels wrote to Bebel again: "In order to take possession of and set in motion the means of production, we need people with technical training, and masses of them. These we have not got, and up till now we have even been rather glad that we have been largely spared the 'educated' people. Now things are different. Now we are strong enough to put up with any quantity of educated rubbish and to digest it, and I foresee that in the next eight or ten years we shall recruit enough young technicians, doctors, lawyers and schoolmasters to enable us to have factories and big estates administered on behalf of the nation by Party comrades. Then, therefore, our entry into power will be quite natural and will be settled relatively quickly. If, on the other hand, a war brings us to power prematurely, the technicians will be our chief enemies; they will deceive and betray us wherever they can and we shall have to use terror against them, but shall get cheated all the same. It is what always happened, on a small scale, to the French revolutionaries: even in the ordinary administration they had to leave the subordinate posts, where the real work is done, in the possession of old reactionaries who obstructed and paralysed everything. Therefore I hope and desire that our splendid and secure development, which is advancing with the calm and inevitability of a process of nature, may remain on its natural lines.''[88] The dark forebodings of Engels in 1850-1853 about a premature accession to power by the socialists were well known to Russian Marxists. His letters of 1890-1891 were not at all so well-known, as they were published in full only after October. (Not very accurate translations of them could be found in various collections of the 1920s: more accurate ones were published only in 1940, in the first edition of the collected works of Marx and Engels.) But despite this, the question whether Russia was ripe for socialist reconstruction was being discussed in Russian revolutionary and Narodnik circles as early as the middle of the 19th century, and also became a subject of lively dispute in the Russian Social-Democratic Party at the turn of the century. Without recounting the entire history of this discussion, let me say merely that by 1917 the views of the Bolsheviks and the Mensheviks, respectively, on this question had become substantially different.

c. The socialist revolution in Russia and the position of the
   Mensheviks and the Socialist-Revolutionaries

Both the Mensheviks and the S.R.s mostly always considered themselves socialists, and there is no reason to doubt the sincerity of their belief. In 1917, however, both of these parties looked on a socialist revolution in Russia as something obviously premature. All factions in the Menshevik Party and all the Menshevik leaders dissociated themselves sharply from Lenin's "April Theses", a document which in their view was erroneous and adventuristic, written "in utter abstraction from circumstances of time and place".[89] G.V. Plekhanov had declared, already at the time of the first Russian revolution in 1905-1907, that there could be no talk of a socialist revolution until the democratic revolution had been completed. "These two moments," Plekhanov considered, "will necessarily be separated by a substantial interval."[90] In 1917, Plekhanov, who was then on the right wing of the Menshevik Party, wrote: "If, in a given country, capitalism has not yet reached the level at which it becomes a hindrance to the development of the productive forces, it is absurd to call on the workers of town and countryside, and the poorest section of the peasantry, to overthrow it ... The dictatorship of the proletariat will become possible and desirable only when the wage-earners have become the majority of the population ... It is clear that no-one who has even the slightest grasp of the teaching of Marx can talk about a socialist revolution here.''[91] But Martov, too, the leader of the left-wing faction of Menshevik-Internationalists, shared this view in 1917.[92] The Mensheviks considered that after February Russia would undergo a further long period of bourgeois development, and therefore the Soviets must act only as the "tribune" and "supervisor" of the revolution. This line of the Mensheviks was reiterated in the decisions of their May conference, at which it was said that, since a bourgeois-democratic revolution was going on in Russia, "the working class cannot take up as its immediate task the socialist reconstruction of society.''[93] Similar statements were made in the speeches at the unity congress of the Menshevik Party in August 1917. It would be utopian, said Martov on that occasion, to think of transforming the bourgeois-democratic revolution into the socialist revolution at that moment.[94] "We do not know what the future of the revolution will be, we do not know in what forms the socialist revolution will come,'' said Avilov, echoing him.[95]

The S.R. Party considered itself socialist, although it proceeded in its programme and propaganda from ideas that were far from Marxist. The S.R.s thought, for instance, that even under capitalism one could create socialist enterprises in the form of co-operative societies. They regarded the socialisation of the land as a socialist measure and practically the main thing in the socialist revolution, although in the opinion of the Marxists the measure belonged completely within the framework of the bourgeois-democratic revolution. The S.R. programme contained propositions about a revolution in the collective character of labour, with abolition of private property and of the division of society into classes. It also stated that the realisation of the Party programme as a whole and the expropriation of all capitalist property, presupposed complete victory by the working class, reorganisation of the whole of society on socialist principles and, *if need be*, the establishment of a revolutionary dictatorship of the working class. However, the S.R.s used the concept "working class" quite differently from the Marxists. They wrote in their programme that "it is necessary to get all strata of the exploited population, from the industrial proletariat to the labouring peasantry, *to appreciate that they form a single working class*, to see in their class unity the guarantee of their emancipation, and to subordinate their partial, local and temporary interests to the one great task of social-revolutionary change.''[96]

With such a conception of socialism as this the S.R.s considered that the victory over Tsardom opened the way for starting the socialist revolution as they understood it. In 1917, however, there was a big gap between the S.R.s' programme and their practical political activity. In the decisive months after February the S.R. Party, which was considerably larger than the Mensheviks, and wielded more political influence than they did, nevertheless followed their lead on many theoretical questions, adopting their view of the nature, current tasks and prospects of the bourgeois-democratic revolution in Russia. For this reason the majority of the S.R. leaders, after the victory of the February revolution, not only did not try to impose their demand for "socialisation" of the land, but hindered in every way the introduction of agrarian reform. Echoing the Mensheviks, the S.R. paper *Dyelo Naroda* wrote, for instance, in one of its leading articles: "Until the socialist revolution has been accomplished in Western Europe there can be no question of overthrowing the capitalist order in Russia."[97] "Until the triumph of socialism in Western Europe,'' said the same paper, "capitalism will be the basis of the economic situation in our country as well.''(98]

It must be mentioned, though, that such a sharp difference between the programmatic demands of the party and the actual policy being followed by the S.R. leaders gave rise in the summer of 1917 to a split in the S.R. party, with the formation first of a Left faction and then of a separate Left S.R. party, which stood for the implementation of the party programme, with immediate introduction of agrarian reform and many other revolutionary changes. And while the main body of the S.R.s allied themselves first and foremost with the Mensheviks, the Left S.R.s gradually drew nearer to the idea of supporting the Bolsheviks.

If we take into account only their theoretical systems, it would be wrong to say about all those tendencies and groupings in the R.S.D.L.P. which did not agree with the "April Theses", and considered it their duty to prepare the proletariat for the prospect of a more protracted struggle for socialism under conditions of bourgeois democracy, that they had no right to call themselves socialist. And both among the Mensheviks and also among the S.R.s there were many sincere socialists who considered themselves, not without justification, as forming one of the detachments of world socialism. In the circumstances of the Russia of that time various views had the right to exist so far as the paths and timing of the socialist revolution were concerned, and so not only the bulk of the rank-and-file but also a considerable section of the leadership of the Mensheviks and S.R.s were, subjectively at any rate, far from being "agents" of the bourgeoisie among the workers and peasants.

But the Mensheviks and S.R.s did not confine themselves to putting forward various theoretical propositions. In the impetuously changing political situation of 1917 these parties could not evade taking important political decisions and measures. In this way it frequently happened that a dogmatic striving to act only in accordance with their previously-established doctrines placed the Mensheviks and S.R.s in the position of being objective allies of the bourgeoisie and the bourgeois parties.

Although after February the Soviets at once became a real force, and the actual masters of the situation in Russia, the Mensheviks and S.R.s who were at the head of the Soviets never put forward the slogan "All power to the Soviets" and did not even organise the "dual power" which came about *de facto*. Remembering Engels's gloomy prophecies, the Mensheviks *feared* to take power, and the S.R.s were in full solidarity with them on this point. According to the testimony of M.P. Yakubovich, the then leaders of the Mensheviks — F.I. Dan, I.G. Tsereteli, A.R. Gotz — and the leaders of the S.R.s — V.M. Chernov and N.D. Avksentiev — were by virtue of their personal qualities little fitted to take part in political activity under conditions of a rapidly developing revolution, when the masses were in a state of "storm and stress". They did not understand the logic of revolution, and were afraid of any "revolutionary excesses."[99] Consequently, the S.R.s and Mensheviks actively co-operated in forming the first Provisional Government, which was made up of Octobrists and Cadets. Because of their idea about the bourgeois character of the revolution that was under way, the Mensheviks and S.R.s *wanted* the country to be ruled, for the time being, by the bourgeois parties, and promised that the latter would receive the support both of their parties and of the Soviets.

In this behaviour by the leaders of the Mensheviks and the S.R.s there was, of course, no conscious betrayal of the interests of the people, such as the Bolsheviks accused them of and Soviet historians continue to lay at their door. The Mensheviks in 1917 not only *considered* themselves a party of the working class, they did in fact reflect the views of a considerable section of the workers, just as the S.R.s reflected those of a considerable section of the peasants and soldiers. But many of the leaders of these parties were unable to overcome their doctrinairism: they did not want to assume responsibility for fulfilling the tasks of the bourgeois revolution, fearing to find themselves in that false position of which Engels had written that it would mean ruin for a workers' party.

It was, however, the bad luck of the Mensheviks and S.R.s that the bourgeois Provisional Government proved to be quite incapable of solving even the most essential tasks of the bourgeois-democratic revolution. Not only did it oppose the realisation of many long-since-mature tasks of the bourgeois revolution, it tried at first to restore the Romanov monarchy in some form. The prestige of this government among the people and in the army declined so fast that its fall was a matter of a very short time indeed. Already following the April crisis, the Prime Minister of the Provisional Government, G.E. Lvov, asked in a letter to the Chairman of the Petrograd Soviet, N.S. Chkheidze, that they discuss the entry of representatives of the Soviet into the Government. This proposal gave rise to stormy argument in all the factions in the Soviet, and the Menshevik leaders at first rejected Lvov's request. However, the Provisional Government continued to press them. The first to come out in favour of entry into the Government were the Trudoviki and the Popular Socialists (N.S.s), then the leaders of the S.R.s and Mensheviks, Chernov and Tsereteli. The first coalition government, formed with their participation, proved, however, lifeless and short-lived. No less ineffective was the second coalition government, headed by the S.R. Alexander Kerensky. Although the representatives of the socialist parties predominated numerically in this government, it was the Cadets who continued to exert the main influence on the government's activities. This was the government which, under pressure from the Allies, attempted to prepare and carry through an offensive at the front. According to Yakubovich, who belonged to the left wing of the Mensheviks and was then one of the leaders of the military department of the All-Russia Central Executive Committee of the Soviets, the decision to launch the offensive was "nonsensical". The Russian army "was psychologically quite incapable of an offensive." The Russian soldiers both in the trenches and in the rear dreamt ardently of peace, of soon returning home, where there would at last be a dividing-up of the landlords' estates ... How could these soldiers go into the attack? "At best, the army was capable of defensive action if the Germans were to attack." But there could be no question, after the revolution, of any offensive on Russia's part. The defeat suffered was without precedent in the history of the Russian army. When news of this offensive and of its defeat reached Petrograd, it made a tremendous impression on the workers there, and also, and especially, on the soldiers of the city's garrison. The result achieved was, of course, the direct opposite of what Kerensky and Tereshchenko had expected, and of which the coalition government and the leaders of the Menshevik and S.R. parties had also been confident.[100]

It is well known what the end was to the political and governmental crisis which broke out in the first days of July. The huge demonstration of workers, soldiers and sailors on 3 July was a spontaneous affair: the Bolsheviks, having failed to prevent it, did all they could to make it peaceful in character. Chernov and Tsereteli tried to address the demonstrators, but no-one listened, though no violence was used against them. And then the leaders of the Mensheviks and S.R.s, the heads of the Central Executive Committee of the Soviets and of the Provisional Government, fell into that sin against which Engels had warned in 1850 and 1853. They called in Cossacks to break up the July demonstrations, followed by military units withdrawn from the front. Many Bolsheviks were arrested, and Lenin and Zinoviev were obliged to go underground and hide themselves away at Razliv. The new coalition government which was formed only at the end of the month included once more seven socialists of various shades and the same number of Cadets and politicians associated with them, though the S.R.s and Mensheviks were at that time perfectly capable of forming a government without the bourgeois parties and starting to introduce the reforms which the whole people had long been waiting for. The political influence of the Cadets (not to mention the Octobrists) had greatly declined by August 1917, whereas that of the S.R.s and Mensheviks had, on the whole, continued to increase. Even in numerical strength the S.R. party was in the summer of 1917 the biggest in the country. The Menshevik party numbered nearly 200,000 members. Power in Russia had been put into the hands of these parties against their will, so to speak, but the leaders of the S.R.s and Mensheviks, in a state of confusion, did not know how to grasp this power and use it. Trying to maintain at any price their coalition with the bourgeois parties, fearing to alienate the "propertied elements", or, to put it more plainly, the bourgeoisie, from the revolution, the S.R.s and

Mensheviks continued to hold back from implementing those democratic and social changes which had nothing socialist about them and which were not in the least premature even from the standpoint of these "moderate" socialist parties. This attitude of theirs frequently earned them praise from the leaders of the bourgeoisie. In one of his speeches the Cadet leader Milyukov said: "The socialist parties now see the immediate tasks of the Russian revolution in a much more reasonable light, they seem to have learnt much from what has happened, and regard it as axiomatic that the Russian revolution cannot, any more than other revolutions in our time and in the past, be a victory for socialism and the socialist order; that this revolution is predominantly political, a revolution which is, in their terminology, bourgeois in character, and not at all directed toward an immediate victory of socialism."[101]

Thus the Mensheviks and S.R.s, these two parties which were socialist in their slogans and programmes (and in the subjective intentions of many of their leaders and most of their members), found themselves in an even more ambiguous and false position than that which Engels had forecast and which, as he saw it, could ruin for good the reputation of any revolutionary socialist party.

This was exactly what happened in 1917 to the Mensheviks and Right S.R.s. Although they continued to regard themselves as revolutionaries and socialists, the Russian masses began to turn their backs on them and increasingly to support the Bolsheviks, whose views on the prospects and possibilities of the revolution that was going on were quite different.

Actually, the break-up of the Menshevik party began even before October, as was shown at the meetings of the Menshevik fraction in the so-called Democratic Conference. N. Zhordania, who was elected chairman of this fraction, wrote later: "Utter confusion. Nobody knew what to do or how to act ... The Mensheviks and Socialist-Revolutionaries were alike isolated both from the people and from the soldiers."[102] The breakdown and decay of the Menshevik Party was noted in its press at the time. In the newspaper *Novaya Zhizn* at the end of September, R. Grigoryev wrote that "the Menshevik wing of the Social-Democrats has collapsed and is ceasing to exist."[103] In Plekhanov's paper *Yedinstvo* L. Deutsch wrote: "The Menshevik faction has suffered setback after setback, and it is not necessary to be a prophet to forecast that it will soon perish. Its days are certainly numbered."[104] The S.R. paper *Dyelo Naroda*, commenting on the

48

make-up of the Moscow Region Congress of Soviets, wrote: "The Congress has once again revealed that ... the party of the Menshevik Social-Democrats has vanished from the political arena."[105] At the end of September and in October the S.R.s still maintained their positions, as was shown, especially, by the elections to the Constituent Assembly. But their influence was important mainly in the provinces and the rural areas, and also on those fronts which were farthest from the centre and where political life moved at a slower pace. In the principal and decisive centres of the country the influence of the S.R. party had already fallen to the lowest level by the middle of October. This was what eventually determined the rapid success of the October revolution.

Even after October the S.R.s and Mensheviks continued to insist that the revolution which had been accomplished was "premature." When he learnt that the Provisional Government had been overthrown, Plekhanov addressed an "Open Letter" to the Petrograd workers in which he wrote: "I am disappointed by the events of the last few days not because I do not desire the triumph of the working class in Russia but precisely because I pray for it with all the strength of my soul ... [We must] remember Engels's remark that there could be no greater historical tragedy for the working-class than to seize political power when it is not ready for it."[106] Plekhanov prophesied that the October revolution would oblige the workers to retreat a long way from the positions won in February and March of that year. In other words, Plekhanov again tried to persuade the Russian workers that "Russia's history has not yet ground the flour from which, in due course, the wheaten loaf of socialism will be baked."[107] About a month after the October insurrection, another congress of the Menshevik party took place. In the decisions of this congress the participants expressed their firm conviction that the new revolution would not prove capable of realising socialist changes, because "these changes have not yet begun in the more developed countries of Europe, and because of the low level of development of the productive forces in Russia."[108]

d. Concerning the timeliness of the first revolutionary measures taken by the Soviet power

As mentioned above, Lenin convinced the majority of his party that the "second revolution" was timely and necessary: he constantly affirmed that only the passing of power in the country into the hands of the proletariat would enable Russia to quit the hated war and propose a democratic and just peace to the peoples and governments of all the belligerent countries. It is not surprising that the Decree on Peace was adopted by the Second Congress of Soviets immediately after the resolution on transferring power to the Soviets. This decree did not, of course, mean an immediate end to the war between Russia and the Triple Alliance — that still required prolonged and painful negotiations. Nevertheless, the armistice which was soon concluded gave the country the breathing space it needed so badly.

Lenin also declared that only the dictatorship of the proletariat would enable all the survivals of feudalism in the Russian countryside to be abolished and a rapid and just solution of the land question to be effected. And, indeed, immediately after the Decree on Peace, the Second Congress of Soviets adopted the Decree on Land, by which landlords' ownership of land was abolished forthwith and without compensation, and all estates, with all appanage, monastery and church lands, were placed at the disposal of the county land committees and the district Soviets of Peasants' Deputies, for distribution among the peasants. The latter were relieved of all their previous obligations, and more than 150 million hectares of land were handed over to them.

It is difficult not to accept that these great decisions of the Second Congress of Soviets were quite timely. No less timely were the decrees of the Council of People's Commissars and the All-Russia C.E.C. recognising the independence of Finland and Poland, and also the "Declaration of the Rights of the Peoples of Russia", which acknowledged the right of these peoples to self-determination, abolished all forms of national oppression, and cancelled all the enslaving treaties between Russia and the colonial and dependent countries. It is hardly possible to regard as premature, either, such decisions of the Soviet Government as the decree abolishing social "estates", ranks and titles, or the decree "on civil marriage, on children and on the maintenance of registers of civil status", which established equality of rights between women and men. Also a long-since-mature democratic reform was the decree separating the church from the state and the school from the church, and providing for complete freedom of conscience and creed. Quite timely too was the Soviet Government's decision to annul all state debts, which cancelled Russia's colossal indebtedness, releasing her from semi-colonial dependence.

The list of such long-overdue and absolutely timely revolutionary reforms which were introduced only thanks to the October revolution could be extended. There was, of course, nothing socialist in any of these reforms. They c⌐nstituted merely a very radical carrying through of the tasks of the bourgeois-democratic revolution, tasks which neither the bourgeois parties nor the Mensheviks and S.R.s had shown themselves able to fulfil. In effecting these reforms, however, the Bolsheviks were not in the least afraid of putting themselves in the false position of which Engels had written in 1850 and 1853. For, unlike Plekhanov, they did not consider that Russia was not ripe for socialism, that the dictatorship of the proletariat was for her an unneccessary and harmful utopia. While recognising the economic and cultural backwardness of Russia, Lenin and his co-thinkers believed that Russia had already attained a level of capitalist development at which it was desirable, possible, and, under the conditions of the imperialist world war, even necessary to introduce not only bourgeois-democratic changes but also *some* changes of a socialist character. As the Bolsheviks saw it, Russia in 1917 was substantially different from the Germany of 1850-1853. With all its backwardness, Russia had already entered the phase of monopoly capitalism and imperialism, and so a socialist revolution in such a country could not, *generally speaking*, be premature. And if now, in 1917, the proletariat was offered the possibility of taking power, it would be a crime for the proletarian party to refuse this opportunity. For in a few years' time, when the Russian bourgeoisie had acquired experience of political rule, when they had created their own state in place of the disintegrated Tsarist administration, and when they had succeeded in consolidating themselves economically and organising their forces in every way, it would be much more difficult for the proletariat to vanquish this bourgeoisie. Consequently, the weakness of the Russian bourgeoisie and the comparative economic backwardness of the country even gave some additional advantages, in Lenin's view, to the Russian proletariat, which, though small in numbers, was politically very mature. Lenin considered that by taking power and introducing not only the long-overdue bourgeois-democratic changes but also some socialist reforms for which Russia was ripe, the Russian proletariat could advance the country's socio-economic development much more effectively and rapidly than the bourgeoisie could. Moreover, Lenin was firmly convinced that Russia would not have to remain for long on her own, that the socialist revolution in Russia would hasten and facilitate the triumph of the revolution in the other belligerent countries of Western Europe as well. In their turn, these economically developed countries would help Russia to overcome more rapidly her economic and cultural backwardness.

What *specifically socialist* changes did Lenin regard as possible in Russia under the conditions of her war economy of 1917? These were comparatively few. Already in the April Theses Lenin had written: "It is not our *immediate* task to 'introduce' socialism, but only to bring social production and the distribution of products at once under the *control* of the Soviets of Workers' Deputies".[109] The most important pre-condition for this control was, according to Lenin, the merging of all the country's banks into one national bank and the establishment of control over *this* bank by the Soviets of Workers' Deputies. Clarifying these theses of his later on, Lenin wrote that the Soviet power "does not intend to 'introduce', and must not introduce, *any* reforms which have not absolutely matured both in economic reality and in the minds of the over-whelming majority of the people."[110] Besides nationalisation and unification of all the banks, Lenin included among such "absolutely matured" measures the nationalisation of the capitalist syndicates, "or, at least, the *immediate* establishment of the *control* of the Soviets of Workers' Deputies, etc., over them."[111]

A somewhat more detailed programme for the very first socialist changes to be introduced was set out by Lenin in his pamphlet *The Impending Catastrophe and How to Combat It*, which he wrote in mid-September 1917. In Lenin's view, in order to prevent an economic and military catastrophe the new revolutionary government should introduce the following principal measures:

"(1) Amalgamation of all banks into a single bank, and state control over its operations, or nationalisation of the banks.

"(2) Nationalisation of the syndicates, i.e., the largest, mono-polistic capitalist associations (sugar, oil, coal, iron and steel, and other syndicates.)

"(3) Abolition of commercial secrecy.

"(4) Compulsory syndication (i.e., compulsory amalgamation into associations) of industrialists, merchants and employers generally.

"(5) Compulsory organisation of the population into con-sumers' societies, or encouragement of such organisation, and the exercise of control over it."[112]

52

Explaining his proposals, Lenin observed that some of them — for example, the compulsory organisation of the population into consumers' societies, with really equal distribution of all articles of consumption among the people and control by the poorer classes over consumption by the rich — were called for by the concrete conditions of wartime, when the people were starving, despite the rationing system which had been introduced in all the belligerent countries.[113]

Of course, wrote Lenin, the introduction of all the measures listed above is *"a step towards socialism.* For socialism is merely the next step forward from state-capitalist monopoly. Or, in other words, socialism is merely state-capitalist monopoly *which is made to serve the interests of the whole people* and has to that extent *ceased* to be capitalist monopoly." "Imperialist war," wrote Lenin, "is the eve of socialist revolution. And this not only because the horrors of the war give rise to proletarian revolt — no revolt can bring about socialism unless the economic conditions for socialism are ripe — but because state-monopoly capitalism is a complete *material* preparation for socialism, the *threshold* of socialism, a rung on the ladder of history between which and the rung called socialism *there are no intermediate rungs."*[114]

We see, then, that Lenin formulated very cautiously the question of the specifically socialist measures of the "second" revolution. And these measures were indeed introduced very cautiously during the first months after the October revolution.

"Workers' control" over production, as one of the most important tasks of the workers' and peasants' government, was proclaimed already in the famous appeal of the Petrograd Military Revolutionary Committee "To the citizens of Russia!" On 14 November 1917 the All-Russia Central Executive Committee adopted a proposal for workers' control as a legislative act of the Soviet Government. Henceforth, factory committees, shop-stewards' committees, economic control commissions and some other elected organisations of the workers in the enterprises were given the right to interfere in the direction of production and in administrative arrangements. At the end of November a Supreme Economic Council (V.S.N.Kh.) was formed to deal with general problems of the organisation of the economy and government finance. The first days following October saw the nationalisation of the State Bank, and then that of all the private banks. After the formation of the V.S.N.Kh. the Party and the Council of People's Commissars began to prepare a measure for nationalising key branches of industry — first and foremost, the oil, iron and steel and coal industries. At the same time, particular enterprises in other branches of industry were nationalised, primarily those factories which belonged to members of the Imperial family and also those which, for one reason or another, had been left without owners. In January 1918 the most important railways and the merchant navy became state property. Altogether, between November 1917 and March 1918 according to the industrial census of 1918, the Soviet state, controlling 31 of Russia's provinces, took over 836 enterprises.[115]

Of course, the activity of the Council of People's Commissars, the All-Russia C.E.C., the central Party authorities and the V.S.N.Kh. in the first months after October was not free from mistakes. On the whole, however, this work followed the right lines, and so in these first months after the revolution the overwhelming majority of the people supported the Bolsheviks. In the period between November and January the Bolsheviks' influence among the masses grew steadily and generally, while that not only of the Mensheviks but also of the S.R.s fell to a considerable extent. This was shown in the "triumphal march" of the Soviets all across the country, the rapid and almost bloodless victory of the Soviet power over the entire basic territory of Russia — and it provided the best proof possible of the timeliness of the October revolution. The Bolsheviks were therefore not far from the truth when they said that the Constituent Assembly, which met in January 1918, having been elected in November 1917 on the basis of lists drawn up in September, reflected the "yesterday" of the revolution. And although the dispersal of the demonstration in defence of the Constitutent Assembly which was organised by the parties opposed to the Bolsheviks, and which was accompanied, according to a number of reliable witnesses, by firing on the demonstrators, was a seriously blameworthy action, the dissolution of the Assembly by a decree of the All-Russia C.E.C. was a perfectly natural step for the then newly-established Soviet power to take.

e. Concerning the premature character of the "Red Guard attack" on capitalism and commodity production in the spring of 1918

The Soviet Government's task in altering the economic life of the country and creating various organs for state regulation and control was made easier, of course, by the armistice concluded with the Triple Alliance countries — an armistice which, however, was not to last indefinitely. It does not come within my province here to discuss all aspects of the making of the peace treaty of Brest-Litovsk: merely to point out that Russia's exit from the war proved to be a far more difficult affair than could have been foreseen. In one way or another, though, peace was at last achieved, and Soviet Russia obtained the breathing space she had desired for so long. Despite the attempts of the counter-revolutionary forces to develop their activity, both in the industrial centres and in the borderlands, and the decisions already being taken for intervention by the general staffs in several Western countries, the position of the Bolsheviks and of the Soviet Government they headed was secure enough, and conditions in the country were sufficiently favourable for them to consolidate their position still further, improving the economic and political situation in the new Soviet state and avoiding civil war, or, at least, localising and quickly suppressing the particular attempts that might be made to start such a war.

In Soviet historical writing the period from the beginning of March to the end of May 1918 has been entitled "the approach to the building of socialism" or "Lenin's plan for socialist construction," names which emphasise the predominantly peaceful character of the Party's work in this period. I am not going to undertake here any detailed analysis of this extremely complex, contradictory and instructive period. That would require a more specialised study. It is, however, impossible not to observe that in these few peaceful months the Bolsheviks did not manage to remain in the positions they had won in January-February 1918, so as to reorganise themselves and give deep and thorough consideration to a plan for further advance, which would be realistic in the stages and methods laid down for socialist construction, taking account of the actual possibilities before them in a huge country, petty-bourgeois and peasant in character, which had not only been awakened but had also been fundamentally ruined by the four years of war.

Carried along by the tide of events, but also to a certain degree intoxicated by the success of the first revolutionary changes and the support given them by the majority of the working people, the Bolsheviks began in the spring of 1918 — that is, *before* the civil war had begun — to go a great deal further in the changes they made and the decrees they issued than the prevailing political, economic and social realities permitted. In full conformity with Engels's prophecy, the Bolsheviks, who had hitherto shown

55

themselves great realists, began suddenly to "undertake communist experiments and perform leaps" the "untimeliness" of which they had themselves acknowledged not long before.[116] Moreover, many mistaken reforms were introduced without there being any pressure for them on the part of the proletarian masses, and which were not even in accordance with "our own printed declarations and plans — more or less falsely interpreted, more or less passionately thrust to the fore in the party struggle."[117] The Bolsheviks did in fact attempt, in the spring of 1918, to pursue that policy of "immediately introducing socialism" against which Lenin had so cogently spoken in the "April Theses" and in many other speeches and articles during 1917, but which, strangely, he himself supported in the spring of 1918. To be sure, the policy of spring 1918 was influenced by some hasty thoughts about socialism which had been uttered before the revolution not only by Marx and Engels but also by Lenin himself. The main cause of the mistakes made, however, was rather that psychological atmosphere of "storm and stress" when it seemed that everything was possible, that all that mattered was what the revolutionary party which had come to power wished to do. "Everything was swept along by a tumultuous flood, filled with revolutionary enthusiasm," said A.V. Lunacharsky, only three years later, about this period. "What was necessary, above all, was to proclaim our ideals in their entirety, and ruthlessly to crush whatever did not suit us. It was difficult in those days to talk of half-measures, of stages, of moving step by step towards the realisation of our ideals. That was regarded as opportunism, even, perhaps, by the most 'cautious' among us."[118]

"Borne along on the crest of the wave of enthusiasm," wrote Lenin, also in 1921, "rousing first the political enthusiasm and then the military enthusiasm of the people, we expected to accomplish economic tasks just as great as the political and military tasks we had accomplished by relying directly on this enthusiasm. We expected ... to be able to organise the state production and the state distribution of products on communist lines in a small peasant country directly as ordered by the proletarian state."[119] Of great importance also was the simple fact that the Bolsheviks simply did not know, in most cases, how to go about building a socialist society, for they were the first to take this as yet untrodden path. They therefore often operated experimentally, advanced by trial and error, and they answered painfully for the mistakes they made in this way. In his address to the Tenth Party Congress (1921), speaking of the previous economic policy of the Bolsheviks, which had begun in March 1918, Lenin frankly acknowledged that in that phase they had "made patent mistakes, and it would be a great crime not to see it, and not to realise that we have failed to keep within bounds, and have not known where to stop ... It is an unquestionable fact that we went further than was theoretically and politically necessary."[120]

The most serious mistakes were committed by the Party in their policy regarding exchange with the rural areas. The food situation in the country in the spring of 1918 was, though complicated, not catastrophic. By March of that year the army had been almost completely demobilised, a considerable section of the soldiers having returned home without permission even much earlier. The Government thus no longer had to face the very difficult task of feeding an army of ten million men. The system of victualling the army had been established in the first months of the war, with grain being purchased from the landlords and peasants. The Provisional Government had extended the grain monopoly. According to a decision of the Provisional Government dated 25 March 1917, all purchases of grain except for the needs of the army and navy had to be carried out through special food offices. It was provided that all the marketable grain of the landlords and peasants was to be bought at fixed prices by the state organisations and then sold, again at fixed prices, to the urban population, according to a rationing system, or else used to feed the army. Alongside this system there went on, of course, both before and after October, parallel, comparatively unrestricted selling of grain through various illegal channels.

This grain monopoly was retained after the October revolution. Certainly, the need to smash the old state machine and create a new, proletarian state led, in the winter of 1917-1918, to a temporary slackening of state control over the working of the grain monopoly. Also, the continued depreciation of paper money made it less advantageous to the peasants to sell grain at fixed prices, and resulted in an increase in speculative trade. For this reason, despite demobilisation, the food situation in the towns deteriorated in the spring of 1918, although the 1917 harvest had not been a bad one and there was a good deal of grain in the country. According to the Agriculture Commissariat's calculations, the deficit in the districts which consumed grain amounted to 180 million poods, while the grain-producing provinces had a surplus of 635 million poods.[121] In order to remove the threat of famine in the towns the Soviet

Government increased *threefold* the price paid for grain. At the same time, a procedure was introduced whereby the peasants could buy manufactured goods from the state only if they supplied grain. However, these measures did not produce the desired result. State procurement of grain accounted for only one-tenth of the amount required. There were several reasons for this failure. The break-up of the landlords' estates, which previously had supplied the bulk of the marketable grain, had its effect. The transfer of the landlords' land and other property into the hands of the peasantry increased the consumption of grain in the countryside itself, where a considerable proportion of the people had previously been underfed. But this was not the main factor. In the spring of 1918 the rate of inflation exceeded the increase in the price paid for grain, while industry, going over with difficulty from war to peace production, was still unable to supply the countryside, which was starved of manufactured goods, with even a minimal quantity of these goods.

What might have served as a more rational way out of the situation? Complete abolition of the grain monopoly and introduction of free trade, as proposed by the S.R. party? Such a decision would have suited the interests of a considerable section not only of the rich peasants but also of the middle peasants, but it could not be acceptable to a proletarian state, since it would undoubtedly have led to a worsening of the material situation of the working class. What could have been done?

Looking at this question with the benefit of hindsight it is not hard to find the answer, since this was provided by the New Economic Policy (N.E.P.), which was introduced in a very much more complex and difficult situation, and the successful implementation of which alone saved the dictatorship of the proletariat in that situation. Clearly, if the N.E.P. succeeded in the spring of 1921, it would have brought even more tangible results in the spring of 1918. In other words, already in the spring of 1918 the Soviet Government should have introduced a tax in kind, exacted in order to cover the bulk of the deficit of the grain-consuming districts, while at the same time free buying and selling of surpluses of grain and other produce should have been permitted.

Such a measure would soon have removed the growing tension between town and country and strengthened the alliance of the proletariat not only with the poorest peasants but also with the middle peasantry. It would not only have cut the ground from under the anti-Soviet propaganda of the S.R.s, but might have opened the way to some kind of compromise between the Bolsheviks, on the one hand, and the Mensheviks and S.R.s, on the other. The game was worth the candle, for such a compromise would have made it quite impossible for the counter-revolution to start civil war — which cannot be waged without mass support. It must be said that Lenin did not look upon all compromise with the Mensheviks and S.R.s as ruled out on principle. Here we should recall what Lenin wrote after the suppression of Kornilov's mutiny, which was also one of the first outbursts of civil war in Russia.

"An alliance of the Bolsheviks with the Socialist-Revolutionaries and Mensheviks against the Cadets, against the bourgeoisie, *has not yet been tried*," he wrote in his article "The Russian Revolution and Civil War". "Or, to be more precise, such an alliance has been tried *on one front only*, for *five days* only, from August 26 to August 31, the period of the Kornilov revolt, and this alliance at that time scored a victory over the counter-revolution with an ease never yet achieved in any revolution; it was such a crushing suppression of the bourgeois, landowners', capitalist, Allied imperialist and Cadet counter-revolution, that the civil war *from that side* ceased to exist ... If there is an absolutely undisputed lesson of the revolution, one fully proved by facts, it is that only an alliance of the Bolsheviks with the Socialist-Revolutionaries and Mensheviks, only an immediate transfer of all power to the Soviets would make civil war in Russia impossible, for a civil war begun by the bourgeoisie against such an alliance, against the Soviets of Workers' Soldiers' and Peasants' Deputies, is inconceivable; such a 'war' would not last even until the first battle; the bourgeoisie, *for the second time* since the Kornilov revolt, would not be able to move even the Savage Division, or the former number of Cossack units against the Soviet Government ... For [the bourgeoisie's] resistance to reach the stage of civil war, *masses* of some kind are necessary, masses capable of fighting and vanquishing the Soviets. The bourgeoisie does *not* have these masses, and has nowhere to get them. The sooner and the more resolutely the Soviets take all power, the sooner both Savage Divisions and Cossacks will split into an insignificant minority of politically-conscious Kornilov supporters and a huge majority of those in favour of a democratic and *socialist* (for it is with socialism that we shall then be dealing) alliance of workers and peasants."[122]

Unfortunately, this "absolutely undisputed lesson of the revolution, one fully proved by facts," mentioned by Lenin, was not learnt, and no alliance between Russia's left-wing parties was ever concluded. The chief responsibility for this regrettable course taken by events lay, in the period before the October revolution, with the Mensheviks and S.R.s *After* the revolution, however, the possibility of a definite compromise and alliance between the three parties mentioned was left unrealised largely through the fault of the Bolsheviks, who were unable to find in the spring of 1918 a method of solving the country's food problems which would be more acceptable to the majority of the peasantry.

Among Marxists as a whole, and in particular among the Bolsheviks, there had long prevailed a dogma that had never been proved, namely, that socialism is incompatible with commodity production, buying and selling, money and so on. Marx and Engels thought that even in the first phase of Communist society, that is, under socialism, the production and circulation of commodities would wither away, and commodity-exchange would be replaced by direct distribution of goods. Engels, for example, wrote: "With the seizing of the means of production by society, production of commodities is done away with, and simultaneously, the mastery of the product over the producer."[123] Uncritically repeating what Marx and Engels had said, Lenin too wrote, in 1908: "Socialism, as we know, means the abolition of commodity economy ... So long as exchange remains, it is ridiculous to talk of socialism."[124] It is likely that these profoundly erroneous dogmas had some influence on the economic policy devised by the Bolsheviks in the spring of 1918.

As the Soviet researcher L.M. Spirin has written: "The workers' and peasants' state, applying itself in the spring of 1918 to the task of laying the foundations of a socialist economy, counted on establishing between town and country, between socialist industry and basically petty-commodity-producing agriculture, a mode of economic linkage based upon products-exchange. The town would send manufactured goods to the rural areas, and the peasants would provide the workers with agricultural produce. Commodity and money relations, the market, would be excluded. In April 1918 the People's Commissariat for Food Supplies had at its disposal, to serve as an exchange fund, 400 million arshins of textiles, two million pairs of galoshes, 200,000 pairs of footwear, 17 million poods of sugar, kerosene, matches, ironmongery, hardware, agricultural implements. It was proposed to barter these goods with the peasants for 120 million poods of grain. But very little grain was procured. Its value was immeasurably less than that of the manufactured goods given in exchange. For 600 wagonloads of these goods the Commissariat received no more than 400 wagonloads of grain, that is, about 400,000 poods. Procurement of grain by way of products-exchange broke down.''[125]

To get only 400,000 poods of grain in return for 600 wagonloads of manufactures was, of course, extremely disappointing for the Commissariat concerned. (During the first six months of 1918 42,000 wagonloads of manufactures were sent into the rural areas, and 36,000 wagonloads of agricultural produce, mostly grain, received in exchange.) But to expect, in the spring of 1918, when grain was the most important commodity in Russia, to obtain through products-exchange 120 million poods, or 120,000 wagonloads of grain, was patently utopian. Under the prevailing conditions, direct products-exchange was unrealistic, and the breakdown of grain-procurement was not to be explained by the resistance of the rich peasants and kulaks, though there was indeed such resistance. With the coming of peace, freedom of trade was demanded by the majority of the peasants, including the middle peasants, and the Bolsheviks could not but take account of this in their calculations. The Bolsheviks must have realised that the broad masses of the people will accept, in the first place, only those slogans which correspond to their own interests. The October revolution was therefore timely in so far as it put in the forefront the slogans of peace, land and bread. These slogans corresponded to the interests of the broadest masses of the people, who were suffering from the protracted war. Hatred of the war was the chief catalyst of all the political processes which occurred in 1917. It would be strange to suppose that the broad masses, having read Lenin's articles, marched out to die for socialism, or, having read the no less fervent articles of Martov, went back home. Only certain individuals can behave in that way. A slogan arouses the masses only when it corresponds to a mood which has already developed among them, owing to the conditions in which they are living. It was this that the Bolsheviks began to forget in spring 1918, and so their influence among the broad masses of the peasantry began to decline, while that of the S.R.s, who stood for freedom of trade, began to grow. The peasants' discontent was what gave the S.R. party its second wind.

The attempt to establish direct products-exchange between town and country also required of the Soviet Government that it intervene more resolutely in the activity of not only the largest industrial enterprises but also the middle-sized and small ones, ading to the grain monopoly the establishment of a state monopoly of other food products as well, and then of all the basic manufactured goods destined for individual consumption. Curtailment of commodity-money relations was accompanied by attempts to establish an extremely cumbersome and badly administered apparatus for regulating the production and distribution of goods, although neither the competent personnel nor the economic conditions existed for such an apparatus to function normally.

Thus, for example, in the middle of March (early April, new style), the Council of People's Commissars adopted a decree "on the organisation of the supply to the population of all kinds of products and objects of individual consumption and domestic use." The very first point of this decree announced: "In order to replace the private-trade apparatus and to establish planned supply to the population of all kinds of products from state and co-operative distribution-centres, the People's Commissariat for Food Supply is assigned the task of procuring all goods which enter into individual consumption or domestic use."

Distribution of these goods in accordance with the decree was to be effected through state and co-operative wholesale depots and retail shops, under the control of the Commissariat mentioned. A real dictatorship of "Komprod", as this Commissariat was called, came into being. No other institutions, central or local, were allowed to take any measures to regulate trade. Private trade was, in principle, completely forbidden and excluded. Point six of the decree declared: "All supply to the population of goods, whether subject to monopoly or not, produced by industry or craft workshops, is to be ensured by the Chief Administration of Products-Distribution in the People's Commissariat of Food Supply (Glavprodukt). The board of Glavprodukt is to include two representatives of the Supreme Economic Council and one of the People's Commissariat of Trade and Industry." It was further laid down that all enterprises must hand over what they produced to Glavprodukt and its local organs.[126] This sort of interference in the activity of every enterprise, and the abolition of private trade could, in the circumstances of 1918, result only in the decline of medium and small-scale production and the self-liquidation of a multitude of enterprises which were capable of playing a useful role in the country's life. All this affected also the work of large-scale enterprises, which could not get enough raw material and whose workers were unable to buy with their wages the food that they needed. Frequently this food was not even available on ration. Naturally, the mood of the working class deteriorated, and

Menshevik agitation found fertile soil. It was in this period that the special conference of representatives of factories in the city of Petrograd was held, the proceedings of which were published by Solzhenitsyn in No. 2 of the journal *Kontinent*.[127] One may not agree with many of the extremely sharp accusations levelled at the Bolsheviks in the "Declaration" adopted by this conference. Nevertheless, many of the charges and critical pronouncements in the speeches made by participants were undoubtedly justified. The Petrograd workers had at this time accumulated a great many causes for discontent.

Having failed, for quite comprehensible reasons, to establish direct products-exchange between town and country, and being unwilling to permit, or even to facilitate through certain channels, free trade between country and town, the Soviet Government decided to intensify measures of coercion and even terror in order to ensure a supply of food to the hungry cities. As Spirin writes: "In these circumstances nothing was left for the Soviet power but to consolidate the grain monopoly on a new basis, forbid free trade in grain, and proceed to adopt new methods for procuring the latter."[128] But these new methods of procurement essentially amounted to confiscation, since, owing to the headlong progress of inflation, the so-called "fixed prices" were purely fictitious, the paper money used to pay them being worthless and backed by no security. This meant, fundamentally, the introduction of the regime which came to be known as "war communism". In our historical writings the principal measures characteristic of "war communism" are usually associated with the difficulties of the civil war. More often than not there is a failure to mention that the foundations of the policy of "war communism" were laid between March and May 1918, that is, in the period of the peaceful breathing-space, the time of the "approach to socialist construction". It was as early as May 1918 that the Council of People's Commissars and the All-Russia C.E.C. approved the decree on the "food dictatorship". In his corrections to the draft of this decree Lenin wrote: "Emphasise more strongly the basic idea of the necessity, for salvation from famine, of conducting and carrying through a ruthless and terrorist struggle and war against peasant or other bourgeois elements who retain surplus grain for themselves: lay down precisely that owners of grain who possess surplus grain and do not *send it* to the depots and places of grain collection will be declared *enemies of the people* and will be subject to imprisonment for a term of not less than ten years, confiscation of

all their property and expulsion for ever from the community."
[129] This punishment Lenin also wanted imposed on all
unauthorised distillers of vodka.

Already in May 1918 the first decisions were taken for peasants
who were propertyless and did not possess surpluses, to unite for
"ruthless struggle against the kulaks". These associations soon
became the Poor Peasants' Committees. This month of May also
saw the decision to mobilise "the most advanced, organised and
conscious workers" in order to help the rural poor in their struggle
against the kulaks — from which decision soon emerged the
famous Food-procuring Detachments.[130]

Such draconian measures did, of course, result in a certain
increase in the supply of food to the towns. But they also had big
negative consequences.

f. The beginning of the civil war

The introduction of these severe measures stirred up against the
Bolshevik Party and the Soviet Government not only the kulaks
but also the majority of the middle peasants as well. Even Stalin, in
one of his letters to Lenin, describing the very unfavourable
situation in the southern (grain-producing) areas of the country,
and trying to discover the reasons for this failure, put in the first
place "the fact that the front-line soldier, the 'competent muzhik,'
who in October fought for the Soviet power, has now turned
against it (he heartily detests the grain monopoly, the fixed prices,
the requisitions and the measures against bag-trading)".[131]

To the discontent of the majority of the peasants must be added
the discontent of the urban petty-bourgeoisie, the petty and
medium entrepreneurs and traders, and even part of the working
class. A really dangerous situation for the Soviet Government was
created in Russia. The tension rose everywhere to such a pitch that
only one small spark was needed to kindle the conflagration of a
great civil war. This spark was provided by the revolt of the
Czechoslovak Corps, which was to a large extent provoked
by Trotsky's irresponsible telegram* ordering that they be

* *"Trotsky's irresponsible telegram."*
When Soviet Russia made peace with Germany, at Brest-Litovsk in March 1918, the
Czechoslovak Corps — formed mainly from Czechs and Slovaks who had deserted
for patriotic reasons from the Austro-Hungarian Army — which had been fighting
alongside the Russian Army, expressed the desire to leave Russia in order to go to
France, there to continue the struggle which they hoped would result in the

disarmed, together with the actions of a number of local Soviet authorities. From the military standpoint this corps was a unit of no very great importance, embracing less than 50,000 men, who, moreover, were spread out along the railway from Ufa to Vladivostok. But this was the spark which, together with the Cossack revolts on the Don and the Ural, served to set ablaze the three-year civil war. Within a few weeks the Soviet power, which only six months earlier had been established all over the country, was overthrown in Siberia, in the Volga region and almost everywhere in the South — in other words, over most of Russia. Thus, historical responsibility for the civil war lies not only with the Russian counter-revolution or the interventionists but also with the Bolsheviks themselves, who raised a substantial section of the population against their rule through their premature "introduction of socialism". More detailed and documented examination of this question calls, however, for a special study which lies outside the limits of the present essay.

From what has been said here, though, it is clear enough, I think, that all those concessions to the middle peasant and to the petty-bourgeoisie of town and country which the Party was forced to grant in the spring of 1921 could and should have been granted in the spring of 1918. Thereby it would have been possible to avoid, if not completely then at least in the majority of cases, those excesses of the civil war and the "Red Terror" on account of which, even today, not only many bourgeois historians but also many sincere supporters of socialism still look upon the Bolsheviks of the civil war period not as heroes but as "beasts". And although the holding of such an opinion about Communists worried Engels very little, and Lenin not very much, it is impossible not to admit that this sort of "terrorist" fame has done grave harm to the cause of socialism throughout the world.

establishment of an independent Czechoslovakia. The Soviet Government arranged for these troops to travel by rail across the entire width of Russia, to Vladivostok, where they were to take ship for America and thence proceed to Western Europe. An agreement was drawn up, at Penza, regulating the quantity of arms the Czechoslovaks were to be allowed to take with them.

This troop-movement did not go smoothly, however. "Local soviets, which at that time sometimes paid little regard to instructions from Moscow, often delayed the movement of the Czechs, and demanded the surrender of more arms than the Penza agreement had prescribed," and irritation was also caused by harassment at the railway stations on the part of Communist agitators "endeavouring to persuade the soldiers to join the Red Army" (W.H. Chamberlin, *The Russian Revolution, 1917-1921* [1935], Vol.II, pp.4-5). The trains carrying the Czechoslovaks eastward were sometimes halted on various pretexts at stations where trains with westward destinations were standing which were full of German, Austrian and Hungarian ex-prisoners on their way to repatriation. On such occasions, tension inevitably developed. Some of the Czechoslovak volunteers said: "Here are we, struggling to reach France to help the Allies, and yet not only are we unable to move forward, but we actually have to permit fresh and thoroughly rested enemy soldiers to slip through our hands back to the Fatherland so that they may be ready to fight us when eventually we reach the Western Front" (Gustav Bečvar, *The Lost Legion* [1939], p.84). For their part, the returning ex-prisoners often jeered at the Czechoslovaks.

On 14 May an exceptionally grave "incident" occurred. At Chelyabinsk a Hungarian soldier threw from his carriage a piece of iron at a Czech who was on the platform, and it killed him. The Czech's comrades then set upon the Hungarian, who died under their blows. "During the investigation of the affair by Bolshevik authorities, a number of Czechs called as witnesses were imprisoned by the Soviet. A delegation sent by the Czechs to demand their release was also placed under arrest. This occurrence enraged the Czechoslovaks. On the 17th they released the prisoners by force, disarmed the Red Guards, and took possession of the arsenal. The Chelyabinsk affair was soon peacefully settled by the local disputants, but Moscow decided on a more drastic policy towards the Czechoslovaks" (James Bunyan, *Intervention, Civil War and Communism in Russia* [1936], pp. 86-87).

The Soviet Government had been getting more and more worried about what to do with these men since April, when some Japanese Marines had landed at Vladivostok, "to protect Japanese lives and property. If the Czechoslovaks were allowed to reach that city, might not the interventionists" try to use them for a campaign against the Bolsheviks in Siberia? On 20 and 23 May, Aralov, Trotsky's assistant in the War Commissariat, sent telegrams to the local Soviets along the railway line, ordering them to get the Czechoslovaks off the trains, disband them, and either organise them into labour units or enrol them in the Red Army. The President and Vice-President of the Czechoslovak National Council in Moscow were arrested and forced to sign an order to the Czechoslovak soldiers to give up *all* their arms. And on 25 May Trotsky despatched a telegram to the Soviets of every town along the railway line, couched in very strong terms: any Czechoslovak found armed was to be shot on the spot, and every unit in which even a single armed man was found was to be sent to one of the prisoner-of-war camps lately vacated by the Germans, Austrians and Hungarians. (Some of the latter, who had joined the Red Army, were actually used by the Soviet authorities in their attempts to enforce Trotsky's order.)

The Czechoslovaks resisted, and soon there was a situation, at numerous points along the railway, of which anti-Soviet elements were not slow to take advantage. The series of centres of armed resistance by the Czechoslovaks became the poles around which counter-revolutionary forces gathered, in order to launch full-scale civil war. And when a quarter of the Corps reached Vladivostok, the fears of the Soviet Government about what would happen then came true. These Czechoslovaks decided "that they would have to turn their forces west again to rescue their compatriots" who were still fighting their way along the Trans-Siberian Railway, and "urgently requested" that the Allies help them to do this, before there could be any question of their embarking for the U.S.A. (Richard H. Ullman, *Anglo-Soviet Relations, 1917-1921: Vol.I, Intervention and the War* [1961], pp.212-213). Large-scale intervention was well and truly launched, with a pretext that appealed to sentiments of loyalty and humanity in the Allied countries.

As Chamberlin points out (op.cit., Vol.II, p.7), "it was not in the power of the local Soviets" to carry out decisively and effectively what he calls "Trotsky's drastic order", which thus provoked the Czechoslovaks in a context where the consequences of this provocation could not be contained. Roy Medvedev has commented elsewhere (*Politichesky Dnevnik, 1964-1970*, Vol.I, pp. 565-566) that there was no probability at all that the Czechoslovaks would willingly surrender their arms to the as yet very weak Red Army units, and no forces were available to enforce the order in the event of a serious resistance — while the political effect of this order was to wipe out the important difference in attitude to the Soviets which had till then distinguished most of the rank-and-file Czechoslovaks from some of their officers.

The text of Trotsky's telegram is given in Bunyan, op.cit., p.91.   —Trans.

NOTES

1 Marx, *The Eighteenth Brumaire of Louis Bonaparte*; in Marx and Engels, *Selected Works in Three Volumes*, Moscow, Progress, Vol.I, 1969, p.401.
2 David Lane, *Politics and Society in the U.S.S.R.*, London, Weidenfeld and Nicolson, 1970, pp.48, 50.
3 R.V. Daniels, "The Bolshevik Gamble", in *The Russian Review*, Oct. 1967, pp.337-340 (included in *The Russian Revolution: An Anthology*, ed. M.K. DZiewanowski, New York, Crowell, 1970, pp.180-182).
4 Joseph Berger, *Shipwreck of a Generation*, London, Harvill, 1971, p.16.
5 N. Berdyaev, *The Origin of Russian Communism*, London, Geoffrey Bles, 1937, pp.166-168, 159 (*sic*).
6 In the symposium, *Kritika burzhuaznoy istoriografii sovetskogo obshchestva* (A critique of bourgeois historical writing about Soviet society), Moscow, 1972, p.34.
7 Karl Marx, *A Contribution to the Critique of Political Economy*, London, Lawrence and Wishart, 1971, p.21.
8 *Istoricheskaya nauka i nekotorye problemy sovremennosti* (Historical science and some problems of contemporary life), Moscow, 1969, pp.211-212.
9 A.I. Herzen, "Russia and Poland: Fourth Letter" (1859), in *Sobranie sochinenii* (Collected Works), Moscow, Vol.14 (1958), p.46.
10 The Soviet historian A. Manfred, writing of Napoleon's return to France from Egypt in 1799, compares this to a game of chance which is won by a player against whom the odds are a hundred to one. But was this a unique case among Napoleon's adventures in that period?
11 G.V. Plekhanov, "The Role of the Individual in History," in *Fundamental Problems of Marxism, etc.*, London, Lawrence and Wishart, 1969, p.167.
12 I.M. Sechenov, *Selected Physiological and Psychological Works*, Moscow, F.L.P.H., 1962, p.135.
13 *Amerika*, 1962, No.68, p.31. The philosopher quoted is Curt J. Ducasse — *Trans.*
14 A.I. Herzen, "Letter on Free Will" (1868), in *Sobranie sochinenii* (Collected Works), Moscow, Vol.20, book I (1960), p.435. [Translated from the French original. The version given in Herzen, *Selected Philosophical Works*, Moscow, F.L.P.H., 1956, p.572, is inadequate — Trans.)
15 I.M. Sechenov, op.cit., p.135.
16 D. Rendel, *Ob osobennostyakh istoricheskogo razvitiya Rossii* (On the peculiarities of Russia's historical development), manuscript, p.159.
17 N. Sukhanov, *Zapiski o revolyutsii* (Notes on the revolution), Vol.III, Berlin-

Petrograd-Moscow, 1922, pp.54-55.
18 *Vestnik russkogo khristianskogo dvizheniya* (Bulletin of the Russian Christian Movement), Paris, 1974), no.112-113, pp.106-107.
19 *Sotsialisticheskii Vestnik* (Socialist Courier), 1960, no.2-3; from the article by M. Vishnyak, "19 fevralya 1861 g." ("19 February 1861").
20 I.I. Mints, *Istoriya Velikogo Oktyabrya* (History of the Great October), 3 Vols. Moscow, 1966, 1967, 1973.
21 V. Shulgin, *Dni* (Days), Belgrade, 1925 p.148.
22 Empress Alexandra Fedorovna, *Letters to the Tsar, 1914-1916*, London, Duckworth, 1923, p.455. [These letters were written in English — Trans.]
23 Ibid., letters of 4 April, 10 June and 4 May, 1915, pp.62, 86, 79.
24 In the Paris Russian newspaper *Dni*, 22 May 1932.
25 Quoted in N. Yakovlev, *1 avgusta 1914* (1 August 1914) Moscow, 1974, p.156.
26 This book, which caused a great sensation among Soviet historians, was published in a large edition by the *Molodaya Gvardiya* press.
27 Yakovlev, op.cit., pp.121, 205, etc.
28 Yakovlev, op.cit., pp.121, 205, etc.
29 Solzhenitsyn, "Peace and Violence" (1973), in *Solzhenitsyn: A Documentary Record*, ed. Leopold Labedz, London, Penguin, 2nd edition, 1974, p.353.
30 And utterly beyond the bounds of scientific history lie the efforts of certain historians to attribute the sabotage of Russia's war effort in 1914-1917 to certain "Zionist" circles which had got control of the Russian press and numerous industrialists' organisations, and also subjected Rasputin to their influence — and through him the Tsaritsa.
31 *Partiya bolshevikov v fevralskyuyu revolyutsiyu v Rossii* (The Bolshevik Party in Russia's February Revolution), Moscow, 1971, p.138.
32 State Duma, Fifth Session, Stenographic Report, 1917, p.1297.
33 Lenin, *Collected Works*, 4th edition, English version, Vol.26, p.235.
34 A. Rumyantsev. *Problemy sovremennoi nauki ob obshchestve* (Problems of contemporary social science), Moscow, 1969, p.23.
35 *Programmy russkikh politicheskikh partii* (The programmes of Russia's political parties), Moscow, 1917, pp.18-19.
36 *Izvestiya Vserossiikogo Soveta Krestyanskikh Deputatov*, Petrograd, No.88, 19 August 1917. This newspaper reflected at that time the attitude of the *right wing* of the S.R. Party.
37 Lenin, op. cit., Vol.26, p.260.
38 John Reed, *Ten Days That Shook The World*, ed. Bertram D. Wolfe, New York, Modern Library, 1960, p.26.
39 Editorial note in Lenin, *Polnoye sobranie sochinenii* (Complete collected works, i.e., the 5th edition of the Collected Works), Vol.34, p.533. See also *Revolyutsionnoye dvizhenie v Rossii nakanune oktyabrskogo vooruzhennogo vosstaniya* (The revolutionary movement in Russia on the eve of the October armed uprising), pp.224-229.
40 Reed, op.cit., p.94.
41 L.M. Spirin, *Klassy i partii v grazhdanskoi voine v Rossii* (Classes and parties in the Russian Civil War), Moscow, 1968, pp.82-83.
42 S. Piontkovsky, *Grazhdanskaya voina v Rossii* (The Civil War in Russia: a reader), Moscow, 1927, pp.206-207. [Michael Alexandrovich had been shot by the Bolsheviks in the previous month, shortly before his brother Nicholas II — Trans].
43 *Iskra*, 1905, no.84.
44 *Iskra*, 1905, no.85.

45 Rosa Luxemburg, "Mass Strike, Party and Trade Unions," in *Selected Political Writings*, New York, Monthly Review Press, 1971, pp.245-246, 270.
46 Lenin, *Collected Works*, 4th edn., English version, Vol.8, p.153.
47 Berdyaev, op.cit., p.159.
48 V. Bazarov, "Pervye shagi russkoi revolyutsii" (The first steps of the Russian revolution), in *Letopis*, 1917, no.2-4, p.379. (V. Bazarov was a Social-Democrat "belonging to no faction.")
49 N. Sukhanov, op.cit., Vol.I, 1922, p.19.
50 In *Dyelo Naroda*, 15 March 1917.
51 O. Yermansky, *Iz perezhitogo* (From my past), Moscow and Leningrad, 1927, pp. 141, 148.
52 Lenin, *Collected Works*, 4th edn., English version, Vol.27, p.90.
53 *Sverzhenie samoderzhavija* (The overthrow of the autocracy), Moscow, 1970, p.33, P. Volobuyev's article. See also the objection to this raised by the reviewers in *Voprosy istorii K.P.S.S.* (Problems of the history of the C.P.S.U.), 1972, no.9.
54 V. Shulgin, op.cit., pp.163, 166.
55 *Kanun revolyutsii* (The eve of the revolution), Petrograd, 1918, p.104.
56 *Voprosy istorii K.P.S.S.*, 1965, no.9, p.81.
57 Ibid.
58 *Istoria K.P.S.S.* (History of the C.P.S.U.), Vol.2, Moscow, 1967, p.653.
59 Sukhanov, op.cit., Vol.I, p.50.
60 The thesis of the complete unexpectedness of the February revolution is repeated in many Western historical works, too. "The Revolution to which all the revolutionary parties had looked forward," wrote, for example, M. Fainsod, "took them all by surprise" (Merle Fainsod, *How Russia Is Ruled*, Cambridge [Mass.], Harvard U.P., 1963, p.60). The American historian W.B. Walsh likewise wrote: "The February-March Revolution was in no sense a Bolshevik or Marxist movement in causation, organisation or direction. It was a chaotic happening" (W.B. Walsh, *Russia and the Soviet Union*, Ann Arbor, University of Michigan Press, 1958, p.371).
61 *Bolsheviki v fevralskoi revolyutsii 1917 g.* (The Bolsheviks in the February revolution), Moscow, 1971, p.142.
62 *Iz zhizni idei* (From the History of Ideas), the reminiscences of M.P. Yakubovich, Part I.
63 Lenin, *Collected Works*, 4th edition, English version, Vol.23, p.264.
64 Ibid., Vol.23, p.253.
65 Krupskaya, *Reminiscences of Lenin*, Moscow, 1959, pp.334-335.
66 Lenin, "The Russian Revolution and Civil War" (September 1917) in *Collected Works*, 4th edition, English version, Vol.26, p.31.
67 Ibid., Vol.29, p.396.
68 Ibid., Vol.26, p.188.
69 Ibid., Vol.26, pp.209-210.
70 Bertram D. Wolfe, *An Ideology in Power*, London, Allen and Unwin, 1969, p.146.
71 E.F. Krykalov, *Oktyabrskoye vooruzhennoye vosstaniye v Petrograde* (The October insurrection in Petrograd), Leningrad, 1966, pp.303-304, 434-435, 461-462. See also *Kritika burzhuaznoy istoriografii Sovetskogo obshchestva*, op.cit., p.44.
72 Stalin, *Works*, English edition, Vol.6, p.65.
73 Ibid., Vol.6, p.64.
74 "Revolution and Counter-Revolution in Germany," in Marx and Engels,

Selected Works in Three Volumes, Vol.1, pp.361-362.
75 Marx to Kugelmann, 17 April 1871: in *Selected Correspondence*, Moscow, F.L.P.H., 1956, p.320.
76 "Preface to the Russian Translation of Marx's Letters to Kugelmann" (1907) in *Collected Works*, 4th edition, English version, Vol.12, p.111.
77 Ibid., Vol.24, p.22.
78 Ibid., Vol.24, p.67.
79 *Pervui Vserossiiskiy Syezd Sovetov R. i S.D.*, Vol.I, p.65.
80 Lenin, *Collected Works*, 4th edn., English version, Vol.25, p.20.
81 *The Bolsheviks and the October Revolution*, trans. Ann Bone, London, Pluto Press, 1974, p.109. Neither in the minutes of the Central Committee, as published in Moscow in 1958 (p.104) nor in *Istoriya K.P.S.S.*, Vol.3, Book I, are the names given of those who abstained or voted for Zinoviev's resolution.
82 Lenin, *Collected Works*, 4th edn., English version, Vol.26, p.202.
83 Marx, *Contribution to the Critique of Political Economy*, op.cit., p.21.
84 Engels, *The Peasant War in Germany*, Moscow, F.L.P.H., 1956, pp.138-139.
85 Letter of 12 April 1853, in Marx and Engels, *Selected Correspondence*, Moscow, F.L.P.H., 1956, p.94.
86 Marx and Engels, *Werke*, Berlin, Dietz, Vol.38, 1968, p.176.
87 Letter of 24 October 1891, in Marx and Engels, *Selected Correspondence*, London, Martin Lawrence, 1934, p.492.
88 Letter of 24 October 1891, in Marx and Engels, *Selected Correspondence*, London, Martin Lawrence, 1934, p.493. (Translation modified by reference to the German original, in *Werke*, op.cit., Vol.38, p.189.)
89 The newspaper *Yedinstvo*, No.9, 9 April 1917.
90 Plekhanov, *Polnoye sobranie sochinenii* (Complete collected works), ed. D. Ryazanov, Vol.XIII, p.340.
91 Plekhanov, *God na Rodine* (A year in the homeland), Vol.I, Paris, 1921, pp.26, 28, 30.
92 L. Martov, *Sotsialisti-revolyutsionery i proletariat* (The S.R.s and the proletariat), Petrograd, 1917.
93 *Vserossiiskaya konferentsiya menshevistskikh organizatsii R.S.D.R.P.* (All-Russia conference of the Menshevik organisations of the R.S.D.L.P.), Petrograd, 1917, p.46.
94 *Sotsialisti o tekushchem momente* (The socialists on the current situation), Moscow, 1917, p.268.
95 Central Party Archives, Institute of Marxism-Leninism, collection 275, series 1, document 12, sheet 20. (B.V. Avilov, previously a Bolshevik, joined the Mensheviks in 1917.)
96 *Programmy russkikh politicheskikh partii*, op.cit., Moscow, 1917. (My emphasis, R.M.)
97 *Dyelo Naroda*, 1 September 1917.
98 Ibid., 6 October 1917.
99 M.P. Yakubovich, op.cit. (Manuscript).
100 Ibid., pp.59-60.
101 Central State Archives of the October Revolution, collection 579, series 1, document 854 a, sheets 3-4.
102 N. Zhordania, *Moya Zhizn* (My Life), pp.77-78.
103 *Novaya Zhizn*, 29 September 1917.

104 *Yedinstvo*, 4 October 1917.
105 *Dyelo Naroda*, 4 October 1917.
106 *Yedinstvo*, 28 October (10 November) 1917. This letter of Plekhanov's is quoted, in the first volume of *The Gulag Archipelago*, by A.I. Solzhenitsyn (op. cit., Eng.ed., p.194), who, unlike Plekhanov, considers that the socialist revolution was not merely premature but, in general, not needed by Russia and the Russian people.
107 Plekhanov, *God na Rodine*, op.cit., Vol.I, p.218.
108 *Novy Luch*, no.5, 6 December 1917.
109 Lenin, *Collected Works*, 4th edn., English version, Vol.24, p.24.
110 Ibid., Vol.24, p.69.
111 Ibid., Vol.24, p.74.
112 Ibid., Vol.25, p.39.
113 Ibid., Vol.25, p.346.
114 Ibid., Vol.25, pp.358-359.
115 *Istoriya K.P.S.S.* Vol.3, Book I, Moscow, 1967, p.473.
116 See note 85.
117 Ibid.
118 *Otchet Narkomprosa IX syezdu Sovyetov* (Report by the People's Commissar for Education to the 9th Congress of Soviets), Moscow, 1921, p.4.
119 Lenin, *Collected Works*, 4th edn., English version, Vol.33, p.58.
120 Ibid., Vol.32, pp.219-220.
121 E. Ambartsumov, *Vverkh k vershine* (Up to the summit), Moscow, 1974, p.106.
122 Lenin, *Collected Works*, 4th edn., English version, Vol.26, pp.36-37.
123 In *Anti-Dühring*: Marx and Engels, *Selected Works in Three Volumes*, op.cit., Vol.3, p.149.
124 In "The Agrarian Question in Russia towards the close of the 19th century": Lenin, *Collected Works*, 4th edn., English version, Vol.15, p.138.
125 Spirin, op.cit., p.148 (based on N. Orlov, *Prodovolstvennaya rabota sovetskoy vlasti* [The work of the Soviet Government in the field of food-supply], Moscow, 1918, p.351.
126 S. Piontkovsky, op.cit., p.65.
127 *Kontinent*, 1975, no.2, pp.385-419. In his foreword to this document Solzhenitsyn presents the conference as an expression of the feelings and views of the entire working class of Petrograd. However, the formulations used in the speeches and in the resolutions show that it had been organised by the Mensheviks. Nevertheless, the holding of such a conference was a grave and threatening symptom of the decline in the Bolsheviks' influence among the workers.
128 Spirin, op.cit., p.150.
129 Lenin, *Collected Works*, 4th edn., English version, Vol.27, p.356.
130 Ibid., Vol.42, p.93.
131 Stalin, 4 August 1918: in *Works*, English ed., Vol.4, pp.125-126.

Mironov's Last Letter

Translated by Brian Pearce

Introductory note

The document which follows is the letter written at the end of
March 1921 from Butyrki Prison in Moscow to the heads of the
Soviet Communist Party and the Soviet State by F.K. Mironov.
Three days later, on 2 April, Mironov was shot dead while taking
exercise in the prison yard, without any formal trial having been
held or sentence passed upon him. An official statement issued
later by the Cheka announced that he had been executed for having
organised a conspiracy against the Soviet power.

Who was Mironov? The first edition of the *Large Soviet
Encyclopaedia* contains, in the relevant volume, published in 1938,
nothing about him, nor does the second edition, the relevant
volume of which appeared in 1954. In the relevant volume,
published in 1974, of the third edition of this standard Soviet
reference work, there is, however, an article about Mironov. He
appears as a devoted revolutionary and a distinguished cavalry
commander on the Red side in the Civil War; the date of his death
is given, but nothing is said about its circumstances. Mironov had,
in fact, been quietly "rehabilitated" in 1960. Here is a brief outline
of his political and military career, the "Mironov affair", and the
struggle for his rehabilitation, together with some notes on certain
persons mentioned in his letter.

Born in 1872 at Ust-Medveditskaya, a stanitsa (Cossack village)
in the Don Region (now called Serafimovich, after the author of
The Iron Flood), Filipp Kozmich Mironov attended the Cossack

officers' training school at Novocherkassk, from which he entered the Tsar's Army. He fought in the Russo-Japanese War of 1904-1905, and his experiences turned him into an opponent of the Tsarist regime. Having joined the "Trudoviki", a radical peasant group linked with the left wing of the Socialist-Revolutionary Party, he took part in the revolutionary outbreaks among sections of the Don Cossacks in 1906 during the "First Russian Revolution". For this activity he was dismissed from the Army.

When the First World War began, Mironov was recalled to the colours. He was decorated four times for bravery, and promoted to *voiskovoi starshina*, the Cossack rank equivalent to Lieutenant-Colonel. After the February Revolution of 1917 he was elected commander of the 32nd Don Cossack Regiment, and after the October Revolution he led his regiment back from the Romanian front to its home base in the Upper Don country. There he played a prominent part in the fight for recognition by the Cossacks of the Soviet Government and against attempts to draw them into "White" revolts against the new ruling power. Between July 1918 and March 1919 he commanded the 23rd Infantry Division of the Red Army in the successful campaign against "White" Cossack forces led by Krasnov and others, and was presented with a gold watch, in acknowledgement of his outstanding services, as well as with the Order of the Red Banner.

Once the Bolsheviks had become masters of a large part of the Don Cossack territory they applied a highly repressive policy there — what was called "de-Cossackisation." All Cossacks who possessed military experience were treated (unless, like Mironov, they had come over to active support of the Soviet power) as *ipso facto* "enemies of the people". Cossacks were forbidden to wear the traditional coloured stripe down their trouser-legs, their horses were confiscated, and the very word "Cossack" was outlawed. The Don Region was split up and parts of it detached and joined to neighbouring administrative areas. All this, together with a particularly ruthless local enforcement of the general policy of requisitioning all "surplus produce," caused grave discontent to spread among the Don Cossacks at every level.

Mironov criticised these features of Bolshevik policy, and, as a result, local Party leaders asked for his removal from the Don. He was transferred to the Western Front, where he commanded the forces of the "Soviet Republic of Lithuania and Byelorussia" against the Poles. Then, in June 1919, the "White" Army in South Russia, under Denikin, began a powerful offensive. The Red Army's

Southern Command, aware both of Mironov's military ability and of his popularity among the Cossacks, asked for his return to their front. He was put in charge of a "Special Don Corps", to be formed from Cossack supporters of the Soviet power, at Saransk, in the Penza region, well in the rear.

Formation of his Cossack corps proceeded more slowly than Mironov considered really inevitable, and he suspected that delays in the supply of equipment, etc., were due to an ambiguous attitude on the part of the Soviet authorities toward the whole idea of creating such a force, under his command. He frequently quarrelled with the political commissars over their treatment of the Cossack soldiers. Then, in mid-August 1919 came Mamontov's raid — the remarkable break-through achieved by Denikin's cavalry commander, sweeping across the Upper Don country and capturing important centres on the road to Moscow, notably Tambov and Kozlov.

It seemed to Mironov that the military situation was so desperate as to justify him in moving his 5,000 men without authorisation towards the front, in order to check the "White" advance. Other Red Army forces were ordered to head him off, and on encountering them he surrendered without resistance, near Balashov. (A falsified version of this incident, in which Mironov is presented as intending to help Denikin, appears in Konstantin Fedin's "historical" novel *No Ordinary Summer*.) Mironov was court-martialled and sentenced to death for his insubordinate behaviour — but immediately pardoned on instructions from the Political Bureau of the Party. This was in October 1919. It is worth noting that Mironov was not the only Red Commander to act in an "unauthorised" way during this period of acute crisis and confusion on the Southern Front. According to John Erickson, in *The Soviet High Command* (pp. 71-72), in October Budenny's cavalry "had moved into the Voronezh area, in defiance of orders to proceed to the south-east. Going north, Budenny had heard that Mamontov was about to stage another of his raids and sought to forestall him and bring him to battle. In the subsequent engagement Mamontov was defeated and Budenny occupied Voronezh on 24th."

Mironov expressed contrition for his impulsive behaviour, asked for an opportunity to redeem himself in the eyes of the Soviet leadership, and applied to join the Bolshevik Party. He was appointed to serve on the Executive Committee of the Soviets for the Don Region (which now received a measure of temporary autonomy), and became head of its Land Department. In this capacity he again came into conflict with what he considered a harsh, undemocratic Communist officialdom, among whose members he acquired unpopularity balancing his popularity among the Cossack masses.

In January 1920 Mironov was accepted into membership of the Communist Party. When the "White" forces in South Russia, now commanded by General Baron Wrangel, launched a fresh offensive, in which they succeeded in crossing to the right (west) bank of the River Dnieper, Mironov was summoned back to military service to help save the situation. He was appointed in September 1920 to command the Second Cavalry Army, then only recently formed. (Budenny commanded the *First* Cavalry Army, whose actions on the Polish front form the background of Isaac Babel's *Red Cavalry*.)

Mironov successfully threw Wrangel's forces back across the Dnieper and pursued them into the Crimea, where, with Budenny, he completed their rout by occupying Sebastopol, from which Wrangel was forced to flee to Constantinople. In December 1920 Mironov was presented with a gold-hilted sword of honour, together with another Order of the Red Banner, in recognition of his outstanding contribution to the triumph of the Soviet power in the South.

After participating in the liquidation of Makhno's anarchist bands in the Ukraine, Mironov was appointed Inspector of Cavalry. The period which had now opened, with the ending, by the military defeat of the "Whites", of all direct threat of restoration of the landlord's power, saw the discontent of Russia's peasantry with the regime of "War Communism", which had been held in check so long as the Civil War was still going on, ready at last to break out in open revolt — it was the period of the Kronstadt mutiny and of the great peasant rising led by Antonov in Tambov region. Very soon the Bolshevik Party was to acknowledge, at its Tenth Party Congress (March 1921), the need for a radical change in policy towards the peasantry, ending the regime of requisitions and permitting a degree of freedom of trade in farm produce. It was Mironov's misfortune to come forward a few weeks before time as a "premature" advocate of this New Economic Policy, and by his vigorous championing of the grievances of the Don Cossack countryfolk to give his enemies a chance to put him out of the way.

While on leave in his home district of Ust-Medveditskaya, Mironov was arrested. It is perhaps significant that the telegram reporting this to Moscow mentions that the arrest was carried out "without the knowledge of the population or troop units" (*The*

Trotsky Papers, Vol. II, p. 383.) From Butyrki Prison, where he had been taken, Mironov appealed in this letter to the leaders of Party and State, but without success, and he died soon afterward in the manner already mentioned.

Mironov was an "un-person", to be referred to, if at all, only in opprobrious terms, until after the Twentieth Party Congress, in 1956. In the new atmosphere created by Khrushchev's "secret" speech, Mironov's surviving relatives, together with many of his comrades-in-arms and people from his home district, began approaching the authorities to re-examine his "case." Eventually they succeeded. The Military Collegium of the U.S.S.R. Supreme Court undertook an investigation, and concluded that there was no basis for the accusation brought against Mironov by the Don Region Cheka. On 15 November 1960 he was rehabilitated by the Supreme Court, and on 9 December the Political Directorate of the Soviet Army restored him, posthumously, to Party membership.

★   ★   ★   ★

Kalinin, who was nominal head of the Soviet state in 1920-1921, and figured as the particular friend of the peasants in the Soviet leadership, travelled around the fronts during the Civil War in an "agitational" train, making speeches to the troops. In this capacity he was present, as Mironov mentions, when the forces commanded by the latter inflicted their historic defeats upon Wrangel in October 1920 in the Kakhovka area.

Kaledin was the first "White" General to try to raise the Don Cossacks against the Soviet power. Finding himself deserted by his men, partly as a result of Mironov's agitation, he killed himself in February 1918.

The "White" forces commanded by Wrangel, though they had been forced to quit Russian soil, remained in being as an organised force in early 1921 ("not yet finished off", as Mironov puts it) in Turkey in Europe, which was then under Allied occupation.

The "White" Cossack Generals Krasnov and Shkuro emigrated after the Civil War, and kept up their struggle against the Soviet power. They fought alongside Hitler's forces in the Second World War, fell into the hands of the British Army, and were handed over to the Soviet authorities and hanged in Moscow in 1947.

Budenny, Mironov's comrade (and rival) as a cavalry commander, lived until 1973. When the history of the civil war was rewritten so as to exclude the contributions of such as Mironov, the latter's victories were ascribed to Budenny (or to Voroshilov), and he is said to have opposed and delayed, to the best of his ability, the rehabilitation of the leader of the Second Cavalry Army.

Brian Pearce

Addressed, as a Party communication, to the Chairman of the Central Executive Committee of the All-Russia Congress of Soviets, Citizen Mikhail Ivanovich Kalinin.

Copies to: the Chairman of the Council of People's Commissars, V.I. Ulyanov; the Chairman of the Revolutionary Military Council of the Republic, L.D. Trotsky; the Chairman of the Central Committee of the Russian Communist Party L. Kamenev; and the Central Control Commission of the Russian Communist Party.

Dear Citizen and Comrade Mikhail Ivanovich,

In the letter from the Central Control Commission published in No. 61 of *Pravda* it is said that "the Party sees itself as one united army, the vanguard of the working people, leading and guiding the struggle. So that those who have lagged behind may catch up, and so that those who have run too far ahead may not lose contact with the broad masses who must carry out our constructive tasks ... "

In another letter, from the Party Central Committee to all members, in No. 64 of *Pravda*, we read, among other things: "Events have shown that we were all in too much of a hurry when we spoke about the approach of a peaceful period in the life of the Soviet Republic, and that the task of all Party organisations is to penetrate more deeply into the rural areas, to intensify work among the peasantry, and so on. The Party has resolved to put an end, at any cost, to bureaucratism and isolation from the masses ... " This letter concludes with the call: "To the masses ... this is the main slogan of the Tenth Congress."

During four years of revolutionary struggle I have not isolated myself from the masses, and I don't know whether I lagged behind or ran too far ahead, but, lying in Butyrki Prison with pain in my heart and broken in spirit, I feel that I am suffering here on account of that very slogan.

From Comrade Lenin's speech to the Tenth Congress, on the tax in kind (in *Pravda* No. 57), I will quote, for the moment, just one passage; "But at the same time it is an unquestionable fact that we went further than was theoretically and politically necessary, and this should not be concealed in our agitation and propaganda."

I have taken this excerpt in order to ask, of myself and others: who, in the end, has turned out to have become isolated from the broad masses, and who has turned out to have run too far ahead?

But however I may answer this question, so far as I myself am concerned, I am not in a position either to catch up with the

Communist Party or to wait for it to catch up with me, in order to take my place in its ranks on the new front proclaimed by the Party Congress, in the struggle for a better future for mankind, for I have been deprived of my freedom. You, Mikhail Ivanovich, in your greetings to the congress of railwaymen and water-transport workers on 23 March (in *Pravda* No. 63), declared, among other things: "The Soviet Government says that we must, everywhere, come to the aid of weary and exhausted people."

Well, it is one of the weariest and most exhausted of men who is appealing to you from Butyrki Prison for such aid, as you can see from this medical certificate given me on 29 March (No. 912): "Certified to Filipp Kozmich Mironov, detained in Butyrki Prison, that he is suffering from chronic degeneration of the heart muscle and a severe form of neurasthenia."

The one who is appealing to you is he who, at the cost of his life and what was left of his nerves, on 13-14 October 1920 wrested victory at the village of Sholokhovo from the hands of Baron Wrangel, but whose lot it has been to be cast into Butyrki Prison: the one who struck down in mortal combat General Babiyev, on whom Wrangel relied: the man whose skilful operations on 27 October caused Count Tretyakov, the general commanding the Markov Division, to shoot himself.

He is appealing to you who, in your presence on 25 October 1920, on the right bank of the Dnieper, at the village of Verkhne-Tarasovka, called on the Red warriors of the 16th Cavalry Division to capture that same night the monastery which was gleaming white across the broad river, and by Christmas to hoist the red banner of labour over Sebastopol.

You experienced these moments of lofty enthusiasm together with the 2nd Cavalry Army, and how that army and its commander, Mironov, performed their revolutionary duty is eloquently witnessed in the Order of the Revolutionary Military Council of the Republic No. 7078, dated 4 December 1920.

The man who is appealing to you is he who snatched the initiative of victory from Wrangel on 13-14 October, and who on that occasion captured General Shkuro's black flag bearing the wolf's head emblem, the emblem of the capitalist beast of prey, with the inscription "For Russia One and Indivisible," and presented it to you, as a pledge of loyalty to the social revolution, as between the political leaders and the Red Army, with its leaders ... It is, indeed, a weary and exhausted man who is appealing to you for social justice ...

And if, Mikhail Ivanovich, you are still deaf to my appeal by 15 April 1921, I shall end my life in prison by dying of hunger.

If I felt that I were even a little guilty I should think it shameful to go on living and to appeal to you with this letter. I am too proud to bargain with my conscience.

The whole of my hard life and 18 years of revolutionary struggle testify to my insatiable thirst for justice and deep love for the working peple, to my disinterestedness and to the honesty of the means of struggle that I have used in order to see equality and fraternity established among men.

A monstrous charge has been brought against me: "organising a revolt on the Don against the Soviet Government."

What has served as the basis for this nonsense is the fact that the bandit Vakulin, who raised a revolt in Ust-Medveditskaya district, referred to me in his proclamations, because I enjoyed popularity in the Don area, and said that I was supporting him with the 2nd Cavalry Army.

He also said that Comrade Budenny was supporting him.

Vakulin's revolt broke out on 18 December 1920, at a time when I was in the Ukraine, smashing Makhno's bands, and I learnt of this revolt from the operational summaries.

Besides the revolt in the district mentioned, almost at the same time there were outbreaks in other districts, under the influence, it may be supposed, of Antonov's revolt in Voronezh province.

For Vakulin to claim Antonov's support was natural, but his allusion to me and to Comrade Budenny was a lying provocation.

I shall not stop to describe here how I spent the year of life that was given me and how this year taught and convinced me not only to shun revolts but also what to think of them.

I am, first and foremost, neither bloodthirsty nor vindictive, as four years of direct and persistent struggle should have taught anyone.

I have always seen the success of the social revolution in the slogan: "to the masses", about which I had the honour to write on 30 July 1919 to our respected leader, V.I. Lenin, in a letter which was quoted during my trial on 7 October 1919. I wrote at the time, too, about what Comrade Kurayev writes, very, very belatedly, in his article "Our Course", in *Pravda* No. 65: "We need, accordingly, to change the procedures and methods of our work among the peasantry and our approach to them ... The old ways of working can prove more harmful than enemy agitation ... "

Life has shown us, brutally, how true this is. I did not depart from this slogan, "to the masses", in the interests of the social revolution, throughout the whole period of struggle, as is confirmed by the great trust which the masses showed towards me right down to the last moments before my arrest. And if now it is written (*Pravda* No. 65): "We must regard as the best organiser in our ranks the one who wins the greatest trust and arouses the greatest degree of initiative among the peasant masses, and who by means of persuasion makes coercion unnecessary ... ", then I dare affirm that the strength of my authority among the broad working masses of the Cossacks and peasants of the Don area is based precisely on persuasion, and not on violence, to which I was frankly opposed. Consequently I am incapable of causing the masses of the people to endure further sacrifices, and I know the cost of rebellion from what I have seen in the Ukraine.

This is my last confession before I die.

People generally do not lie when faced with death, and this is all the more so in my case because I have still not lost faith in my God, who is embodied in my conscience, at the command of which I have, all my life, acted in the same way towards friend and foe alike.

The darker the night, the brighter the stars, the deeper in sorrow, the closer to God.

That is why I listen so keenly to the voice of my conscience.

Truth, impartial truth, is often hard and unpleasant, for truth is, in general, disagreeable to what is evil — but it is truth ...

Under the protection of truth, as behind a trusty shield, I bore the blows of the Tsarist Generals, and in truth I still place my hope ...

I repeat, this is my God, and to Him I have never ceased to pray, nor shall I cease, while the spirit remains in my mortal body.

Once again I venture to say that I am not going to dwell on those facts, which I learned while I was a member of the Don Executive Committee, that made me a foe to all revolts and their disastrous consequences. I steadfastly expressed this attitude at all my meetings. I do not wish to maintain that the great meeting which I held on 6 June 1920 at Mikhailovka settlement, one of the centres of Vakulin's rebellion, when I addressed more than two thousand White Cossack prisoners, brought together from all the stanitsas, called upon them only to fear any and every revolt against the Soviet power, like fire (for, by order of the Front Command, stanitsas and hamlets were to be destroyed by fire for this offence) — that this meeting was the reason why the Cossacks of Ust-Medveditskaya district did not support Vakulin's rebellion, but, on the contrary, threw him out of the Don region. I repeat, I do not wish to maintain that this was the case, but I do make so bold as to say that the power of the appeal I made was very great, and was felt by all who were there.

During the civil war on the Don the White Guard command recognised this power, and openly declared that wherever Mironov was present it was useless to try and raise a revolt against the Soviet Government. In their newspapers they wrote of this power: "If the bacilli of Mironov infect anyone, they infect the whole family." And now, suddenly, Mironov has gone mad and organised a rebellion in the place where for four years he summoned the people to fight for the Soviet Government.

Already in those days, in June 1920, there was inflammable material in that district, material heaped up through the evil deeds of the former chairman of the District Executive Committee, Yerovchenko (a White Guard whom I had banished at the beginning of February 1919 from Ust-Medveditskaya stanitsa to Bolshaya hamlet), and of the former head of the District Militia, Polezhayev (another White Guard), whom Yerovechenko and others bailed out of custody, thereby enabling him to escape revolutionary justice. That much was clear to honest Communists and citizens.

And there was, too, the activity carried on by the head of the Area Militia, Grigoryev, whom I frightened away from Ust-Medvidits kaya by announcing an inspection — Grigoryev, whose persecution brought the people's judge Kovalev to his death. The densely-charged atmosphere of popular anger and discontent can be appreciated from the following incident.

On 4 June 1920 I went from Ust-Medveditskaya to Mikhailovka settlement, accompanied by the Inspector of Infantry of the Don Army — this can be checked, if need be. Peasants were working in the fields.

"Comrade Mironov, is it you?" called out a strapping peasant woman, in a loud voice, when our car passed near her.

"Yes, citizeness, it's me ... "

The peasant woman fell on her knees and, lifting her arms to heaven, cried despairingly: "Comrade Mironov, save the people!" This scene made a painful impression on all of us. That was what life was like in Yerovchenko's "manor."

I think that there was nothing surprising in the fact that, at my subsequent meetings, on 6 June and after, in connexion with the activity of the local representatives of the Soviet power, as illustrated by the episode just described, I called upon the masses to endure even this evil, which was perhaps of provocational origin (I have grounds for thinking so) and to believe that the central Soviet authority had no desire to behave as an enemy of the working people. Just as you will find nothing surprising in my mentioning this event.

At the Conference of Party members at the Regional Congress in the second half of June 1920 I spoke about the banditry that had developed in Ust-Medveditskaya district, with the benevolent assistance of the militia, and of the possibility of a revolt breaking out. However, not only was I not listened to, but I was made to shut up, for there were still people who had not had their fill of blood. (There are none left now, except one.)

Please do not think that I want to point a finger at any member of the former Presidium of the Don Executive Committee.

Now I come to the fact that they have put me in Butyrki Prison. Looking back from within these walls, it has become plain to me that I have been hunted for a long time. I shall not say much about the moment, a painful one for me, when, having encountered at Archadinskaya Stanitsa a former White Guard, whom I had taken prisoner in 1918 and who had fled to join General Krasnov a second time on 17-18 June 1918, near Skurishenskyaha stanitsa, one Baryshnikov, now in the role of chairman of the stanitsa Executive Committee, I let myself be affected by his provocative rudeness and mockery towards me, lost my temper, and struck him, as a White Guard, an enemy of the working people.

I regretted having done this, of course, a few hours later.

I will briefly describe what happened on 8 February at Ust-Medveditskaya stanitsa, where I spent only two days, and for that "indulgence" was thrown into prison.

The Chairman of the Three-Man Commission for re-establishing the Soviet power in the district, Comrade Stukachev, had proposed to me, in an official conversation over the direct wire, that I hold a series of meetings in the district at which I should refute Vakulin's provocational reference to me.

During the evening of 8 February, after my meeting, five men came to call on me. Three of them I knew well, one I knew slightly, and the other I was seeing for the first time.

Being still under the impression left by the incident at Archadinskaya, as well as by Vakulin's provocational appeal, and also by the famine that had begun in the stanitsas and villages, and by the hundreds of complaints I received, oral and in writing (I was going to give these to you when I arrived in Moscow), which were accompanied by tears and painful scenes; affected especially by the statements of the delegates from the local guard company (their report was taken from me when I was arrested), complaining about hunger and cold (they were dressed like beggars), and seeing all this as so much inflammable material for a rebellion — I decided that not only the population but the Red Army men as well had lost faith in the local organis of power and their Red leadership, and, when they heard of my arrival, these people who did not know me had come to ask for help. I promised them help, in the name of the Chairman of the Revolutionary Military Council of the Republic, as soon as I should reach Moscow.

However, my journey to Moscow was delayed ...

Taking into consideration the four outbreaks of revolt which had occured on the Don, Antonov's rebellion, which had strongly aroused the masses, the universal confused murmuring among the rural population generally, the rumble of which came to my ears very easily, since these people and their representatives always approached me with trust, if only for the moral support they received in the form of sound advice — I, having nothing criminal in mind and not even allowing myself thoughts that, concealed in the depths of my heart, might lead to crime, openly expressed the hidden, tormenting idea of a coming counter-revolution from within, which would be much more dangerous than Denikin, Wrangel and the whole bourgeois world. A better proof of my political reliability, of my loyalty to the proletarian revolution (the tasks of which I understand very well), could hardly be imagined.

But no, alas ... Judas the betrayer was sitting there. It is loathsome to speak of the provocational tricks with which he set to

I began by talking about what was worrying and distressing me, and ended by saying that if the policy of the ruling party did not come to terms with the demands of life, which could not be met without making concessions, then the spring might see a rebellion that would reduce the country to anarchy. In my address I spoke especially about some passages in the speeches on the role of the trade unions delivered by Comrades Lenin, Zinoviev, Trotsky and others — not in order to criticise them, but to point out that the enemies of the working people were using all this for provocational purposes, so as to stir up a popular movement against the Soviet power. I dwelt on the letter from the Party's Central Committee about the requisitioning of farm produce, in order to compare a point in this letter with one of the points in the measures of coercion devised by the department in Yeisk responsible for carrying out this requisitioning, a point such as not even the most malicious enemy of the social revolution could have thought up. I spoke of all these matters, I repeat, as facts that were playing into the hands of the counter-revolution. *Byednota* (no. 885) saw the situation similarly, though a little latter than I, on 26 March: "Our enemies have tried [on 8 February, I said "are trying"] to represent disagreements on particular questions as the beginning of a split and the break-up of the Party."

I repeat that I did what I did in order to bring out the seriousness of the moment we were living through, and what needed to be done to prevent any attempt at a rebellion,

After an exchange of views, having stressed the danger to the Soviet power, I proposed (since I was going away from there, in obedience to the orders of the Commander-in-Chief) that they carry out the following plan. The five of them should constitute themselves a basic cell and then, in accordance with certain conditions (from the pamphlet *The Republic of Soviets*), should subsequently organise collateral cells, so as:

(1) to fight in an organised way, through Communist Party cells, Party and non-Party assemblies and conferences, against White-Guard and other harmful elements that had attached themselves to the Party and the Soviet power;

(2) in the event of a rebellion and the onset of anarchy, leading to a breakdown of communications with the leading organs, to enable these cells to function as the shield and stronghold of the Soviet power in the localities;

(3) to ensure that, if foreign bayonets (the Poles and Romanians) or Wrangel, not yet finished off, should, with the Entente's encouragement, begin to threaten Moscow, then all the cells, with all available volunteers would, at my call, go to the defence of the central Soviet Government — though I emphasised that this last task might not arise.

This was not denied by the informer when questioned at our confrontation.

I was only unable to provide a precise definition of these cells, though their essential nature was beyond any doubt.

Pravda No. 57 has suggested to me, while in prison, a name for them, by its article "On Soviet Cells." Hitherto there have only been Communist cells ...

In order that the cells might understand better the work they were to perform I handed to them the pamphlet *The Republic of Soviets*, promising to send them a sufficient number of copies.

Since a struggle against evil at the local level in the shape of some

requisitioning agent or other would do no good, it was decided that
the cell should send me privately from time to time information
about abuses, so that I could take action through prominent
members of the All-Russia Central Executive Committee.

That was the fundamental reason for the code which we arranged
to use between us.

All this brought me to my tribulations in prison.

But where is there in all this even the slightest suggestion of the
organising of a revolt on the Don against the Soviet power?

If I am guilty, then my guilt lies only in the fact that, as a
Communist, I ought not to have organised this cell outside the
framework of the Party; but, I repeat, given the terrible realities of
the situation, I saw nothing criminal in this. If I am guilty, what I
am guilty of is a breach of Party discipline. (Like the "Workers'
Opposition.")

Delation is a nasty word. In some it arouses fear, in others a
feeling of contempt, like a shot fired from behind a corner, or a
stab in the back. This attitude towards delation is not accidental —
it comes down to us from the dark past, when an accusation
suddenly fell upon a man like a bolt from the blue, when the
informer did not have to prove the guilt of the man he denounced
and the latter had no chance to establish his innocence. This is
in fact the situation I am now in, and I appeal to you to restore
the truth.

I wore myself out doing my duty to the workers' and peasants'
revolution in the struggle against Wrangel. After wiping out the
disgrace of the offensive I had felt obliged to launch in 1919, I went
on leave. And then, suddenly — I was in prison again.

While the Whites did not manage to catch me and hang me "on
a dry aspen", as they wrote in their papers, despite the prize set on
my head by General Krasnov (22 June 1918 — 200,000 roubles;
then, in August — 400,000 roubles), I have been betrayed for this
purpose to my own Government, by some shady functionary, some
self-seeker.

Mikhail Ivanovich! Have a look at the White publications which
were taken from me when I was arrested and which are in the
archives of the revolution and you will see what my betrayers' aim
is. They are sorry for Baron Wrangel, sorry for the bourgeoisie of
Europe.

I do not want to admit the possibility that the Soviet Government
may, as the result of a base, groundless delation, send to the
guillotine one of the best of its warriors — "the valiant commander

87

of the Second Cavalry Army'' (Order of the Revolutionary Military Council of the Republic, 4 December 1920, no. 7078.)

I do not want to believe that a base slander has proved stronger than the evidence of my political and military services to the social revolution and the Soviet power, my honesty and sincerity in relation to them.

I do not want to believe that a base slander has eclipsed the bright image of the Order of the Red Banner, that symbol of the world proletarian revolution which I wear with unconcealed pride: I do not want to believe that the poisonous breath of slander has tarnished the blade of my gold sword of honour, and that the minute-hand of my gold watch stopped when the betrayer gripped my throat with a devilish guffaw.

I do not want to believe that an old revolutionary, who stood with the Soviet power from the first moment of its birth (25 October 1917), that an old revolutionary from among those Tsarist officers who were persecuted for their ''redness'', who helped General Kaledin to depart this life and leave the workers in peace, and who beat Krasnov and Wrangel, has been doomed to languish in prison, to the joy of the enemy.

I want to believe that I shall lead Red regiments victoriously to Bucharest, to Budapest and beyond, as I said on that unlucky 8 February, to that ''group of five,'' so unlucky for me, among whom there were provocateurs.

From what source do I draw my hope?

First and foremost, from my guiltlessness towards the Soviet power: secondly, from what we have been forced to appreciate, what has been importunately hammered into our heads, and has now been admitted by the Tenth Party Congress and by you.

''Without a firm alliance between the peasants and the workers, victory is impossible. These basic forces upon which the revolution depends are breaking apart. Our task is once more to rally them, to unite them, so that everyone may realise that weariness is a threat not only to the Communist Party but to all the working people of the Republic'' (*Pravda*, no. 63).

I stood up for the initiative of the working masses, as can be seen from my testimony to the investigator on 26 February. On 22 March an article appeared in *Pravda* No. 61 which said; ''we need the farmer's initiative'' ... Whether I lagged behind in this case, or ran too far ahead, I don't know ...

All the foregoing, in connexion with ''the new turn in the economic policy of the Soviet Government'' (*Pravda* no. 62), with "the course taken towards resolutely drawing closer to the masses" (*Pravda* No. 58), gives me confidence that the A.-R. C.E.C. will, when you have reported to them, hasten my release from prison, for I am conscious of no guilt.

The prison regime is having a ruinous effect on my weak health, shattered as it is by the hard struggle I have waged over many years. I am slowly losing strength.

What helped me to make the Second Cavalry Army within a month (between 5 September and 5 October) not merely capable of fighting, but invincible, despite the fact that it had twice been defeated, and despite the motley character of the replacements hastily brought together from all corners of the Republic?

Only the sincere voice with which I called upon this army to smash Wrangel. Only such a voice can carry the masses with it. You will find an echo of this voice in my memoirs, *How the Rout of Wrangel Began*, which were taken from me when I was arrested.

"To the masses!" is the main slogan of the Tenth Congress.

And if this appeal is being implemented in the decree, published in *Izvestiya* No. 67, giving permission for the free exchange, buying and selling of grain and fodder-grain produce, it might have seemed that the very moment had come for the Soviet Government, acting through me as a Party member and on behalf of the Party, to put into practice in full force the slogan that has been proclaimed, and resolutely draw closer to the masses. Instead, however, I have been thrown into prison.

This new decree has made me remember past events and it leads me to tell you about a very characteristic phenomenon of our stormy times.

Among the papers and documents that were taken from me when I was arrested there were a number of statements about the way the inhabitants of Ust-Medveditskaya district were driven by hunger to move into the neighbouring Upper-Don District, where there were still, in remote stanitsas and steppe hamlets, some stocks of bread, so as to barter their last shirts for a crust of bread for their swollen-bellied children, and about the shameless way they were robbed there. The procedure followed by the Government agents in the localities was a simple one. If what they wanted was the people's belongings, they took these off them without letting them get so far as to exchange them: if what they wanted was bread, they left the people free to carry out the exchange and then, after allowing their intended victims to go on their way, overtook them and seized the bread.

The suffering and tears of the hungry, plundered people compelled me to bring this question up at the district Party conference, on 12 February 1921, and to go into it thoroughly in order that some measures might be taken both against the threatening famine and against the tyrannical treatment inflicted on the hungry people, and also in order that supplies be obtained for the spring sowing, so that there should not be a repetition of what happened last autumn, when the fields remained unsown because no seed was available.

My proposal gave rise to heated arguments on the part of short-sighted politicians, who lost no time in charging me with a tendency in favour of freedom of trade, almost counter-revolution, which obliged me to protest against such a distortion of my idea. I think this was written into the minutes of the meeting so as to be used for the denunciation of my seditious notions which was to follow.

Whether I was lagging behind or running too far ahead in this matter was shown us by life, in the fact that the central government, by its decree of 23 March 1921 on freedom of exchange, buying and selling, has adopted the same standpoint as mine. And now they are going to put me on trial for this perspicacity. The Soviet Government has abandoned the front of coercion for the front of persuasion, on which I was so strong (the rout of Kaledin, of Krasnov and of Wrangel), but I am not considered fit for a place in the ranks of the fighters on this vital front.

If Comrade Steklov's angry protest against the French bourgeoisie for having flung four Communists into prison, kept them there for ten months, until they contracted tuberculosis, and then acquitted them, was published in *Pravda* No. 62 not merely to fill up the required number of lines in his article "A Doomed Regime," but as the deeply-felt protest of an indignant spirit, then you, Mikhail Ivanovich, will understand my confidence, my profound hope, that the Soviet Government is not going to follow the example of the French bourgeoisie, is not going to keep me in prison even one day more, let alone for ten or twelve months (there are cases like that in Butyrki), and is not going to reduce me to slow death from hunger. After all, I, too, am a Communist ...

Once more I repeat your own words back to you: "The Soviet Government says that we must, everywhere, come to the aid of weary and exhausted people." I flatter myself with profound faith in the sanctity of these words, and want to believe that I myself am one of these people who have grown weary and exhausted in struggle for the Soviet power, and that these words of yours must, above all, mean justification for me.

The Republic of Soviets and its brain, the Russian Communist Party, are still far from having completed their great task: "New paths, new tasks and new dangers open up before the Republic of Soviets," says Comrade Krassin in *Pravda* No. 62.

I want once again to believe that, when I have cleared myself of this slander and the grave, undeserved suspicion that hangs over me, and restored confidence in myself, as before the defeat of Wrangel, the A.-R. C.E.C. will find in me, as in the past, one of the staunchest fighters in the struggle for Soviet power.

This testing-time for Communists is surely not far off.

Commodity Number One

PART I

A. Krasikov

Translated by Brian Pearce

Let us raise our glasses, let's move them together!
A toast to the Muses, a toast to reason!
> (Pushkin, *Bacchic Song* (1825))

From ancient times wine has added pleasure and animation to talk between friends. In those countries where vines are cultivated, in the homeland of wine, people did not gulp it down. Draining one's glass did not mean "knocking it back." One sought the bouquet in wine just as in talk one seeks the truth. Drinkers savoured their wine, and their tongues did not falter, even if an old, mature wine should affect their legs and gradually spread a sweet languor all through their bodies.

The art of drinking sprang from the art of winemaking. The winegrower's aim was not to produce as much wine as possible but to produce the best wine, in terms of aroma and taste. Wine brought joy to the heart and boldness to the mind.

In countries where the vine was not grown, the people brewed beer and ale, hymned by Burns in *John Barleycorn*:

"John Barleycorn was a hero bold,
Of noble enterprise,
For if you do but taste his blood,
'Twill make your courage rise."

Style in drinking depends very much, of course, on what is being drunk. Unlike wine and ale, vodka intoxicates immediately, and people drink it down at one gulp, so as not to notice its taste and smell. (Only in comparatively recent times has it become possible

93

to purify it of fusel oil.) And instantaneous intoxication is a very different matter from the protracted enjoyment of a drink which sharpens consciousness and stimulates thought.

Speedy intoxication raises from the depths of a man's heart not courage but violence, not joy of living but maudlin tears, not a feeling of benevolence but causeless and senseless rage. Russian popular sayings about vodka and drinking are characteristic in this respect. Unlike those related to the partaking of wine among a group of friends, they speak only of the evil arising from drink — with the sole exception of the basic proposition that "Russia's gaiety lies in drinking." What sort of gaiety is meant by this? Popular sayings provide the answer. "Drink, and beat people up — that's the life." "Drink, and smash your glass — and if anybody doesn't like it, smash his face in." "Drink beer and hit your father-in-law in the face, eat pies and beat your mother-in-law." "They drank with Phil, and Phil got beaten." "He went out to celebrate and came back home to mourn." "They spend a day celebrating and have sore heads for a week from the hangover." "He sticks it out through a bad day, and when a good day comes he gets drunk." And, as a direct reply to Prince Vladmimir's saying about Russia's gaiety, we have this: "That sort of gaiety will bring on a hangover."

In Tsarist times people drank heavily, as anyone must realise who has read our classics. But statistics show that the quantity of alcohol consumed per head of population was not so large, and in any case was a great deal less than, say, in France, where everyone drinks, but what they drink is mainly a rather weak wine (5 or 6 degrees.) They drink this wine not in order to get drunk and find oblivion, but as an accompaniment to meals, just as in other countries people drink water while they eat. When considering wine and vodka it is necessary to keep in mind the way in which they are taken. The sort of drinking-bout which calls, the morning after, for "a hair of the dog that bit you", is fraught with a principle of rapid development.

From the statistical yearbook *Narodnoye Khozyaistvo SSSR* [*The Soviet Economy*] we learn that in 1913 about 120 million decalitres of vodka were produced, and 800 million decalitres of beer. (A decalitre — ten litres — is approximately the capacity of an ordinary large domestic bucket.) Translating these figures into terms of pure alcohol, we get the figure of 3.35 litres per head of population.

In 1955 the country reached, and a year later surpassed, the level of Tsarist times, and by 1970 was producing nearly twice as much: 6.35 litres of pure alcohol per head of population. These figures are not presented straightforwardly in the statistical publication mentioned, but have to be deduced by comparing various data which are given in it. These data throw little light, unfortunately, on this question. They do not provide much information, especially so far as the amount spent by the Soviet citizen on the purchase of alcoholic drinks is concerned. But even a few years ago this item of expenditure was not such a hush-hush subject, and in earlier issues of the yearbook (which began to be published in 1956) it was possible to find something about it.

Thus, in the section "Trade" there appeared, year after year, a table headed "Commodity structure of the retail turnover in state and co-operative trade," with a column showing the consumption of drink, even though this was somewhat less than fully explicit, being entitled: "Alcoholic and non-alcoholic beverages." This column continued to appear for several years, but then in 1964 vanished. A mysterious obscurity began to gather around the subject of alcohol. Could it be that "drinking" had ceased to constitute our national "gaiety"? Or had we gone over to kvass? But, if so, what would be the point of concealing such remarkable progress?

It is necessary to look into this matter of the missing column. If we compare successive issues of the yearbook over a number of years we observe that the figures for consumption of all the goods shown in the table increase more or less steadily from one year to the next. Only one of the columns — "Other foodstuffs" — suddenly makes an incredible jump in the year 1963. Until then it had shown a comparatively small expenditure, much smaller than for butter. But now, all of a sudden, it has increased tenfold, and by 1970, has reached the figure of nearly 27 milliard roubles, nine times as much as the expenditure on butter (p. 582 of the 1970 handbook.)

Let us try to discover what is meant by "other foodstuffs." Down to 1963 the yearbook itself provided the details. It listed, between brackets: "Coffee, spices, vitamins, mushrooms, soya-bean products, etc." Mushrooms, soya-bean products and so on accounted, of course, for only a very small proportion of the total amount spent by the working people in state shops — according to my calculation, 3.2 per cent of all expenditure on foodstuffs. But since it is obvious, even to the naked eye, how disproportionately "other foodstuffs" increased after 1963, this fact, together with the

95

disappearance of the "beverages" column, reveals to the attentive reader the whole essence of the manipulation of figures which the compilers of the yearbook have effected. They have merged two columns which before had been presented separately: the one for "beverages" and the one for "other foodstuffs". In order to establish this clearly, let us just take a look at the yearbook for 1960, turn to the table that interests us, and compare this with the corresponding table in the yearbook for 1970. In the first case two columns appear, in the second they have been merged. In the first case we see that 110,230 million roubles was spent on "beverages", and 13,730 million on "other foodstuffs." These figures are given in old roubles: translating them into the new values we get 11,023 million and 1,373 million — altogether, then, 12,396 million. In the 1970 issue of the yearbook, in the column "other foodstuffs", against the year 1960 (page 582) we find precisely that total figure, obtained by combining the figures from the two previously-published columns — a combination the editors have forgotten to draw the reader's attention to. Similarly, they have forgotten to enumerate, as they did before, between brackets, what these "other foodstuffs" consist of (coffee, mushrooms, etc.) For, if they were to list them honestly, then they would have to add beverages to the mushrooms, while if they were to omit beverages from the list, then something utterly absurd would appear to have happened — mushrooms, laurel leaves and coffee being sold on a scale that is hard to conceive.

And so, without going carefully through all the figures, and merely by reading those for one category of goods, we are taken aback, and find that there is something odd here. The table lists 25 different groups of commodities. Separate mention is made of butcher's meat and poultry, tinned meat, tinned vegetables and tinned fish, cheese and eggs. Even salt and tea are accorded separate columns. In a special column we find mention of various fruits, berries, water-melons and melons. Everything is named, everything, it would seem, has been accounted for — but even after this there remain certain articles of consumption left unnamed, on which, nevertheless, the colossal sum of 27 millard roubles has been spent, or nearly a third of the total expenditure on all foodstuffs. And now we notice that in this remarkable table everything that people *eat* has been named, but of what people *drink* only tea is mentioned by name. Before us we have a highly-moral, absolutely sober table, without any trace of wine or vodka. Oh, well done!

Let us re-establish the true situation, if only in the form in which it was shown to us in the first issues of the yearbook. In those years, as I calculated above, the relative weight of "other foodstuffs" was, on the average, 3.2 per cent of total purchases of foodstuffs. By calculating what this meant in roubles and deducting it from the new, post-1963 combined total for "other foodstuffs", we recover the figure formerly given for "alcoholic and non-alcoholic beverages," which has been so clumsily hidden up the editor's sleeve.

True, we do not obtain the previous accuracy to a million roubles, for the figures we have deduced are not direct figures but have been established through collation, by effecting a sort of "confrontation" between indices scattered in a number of different places. But our error, inevitable in such calculations, cannot be of any great significance: even if the sale of mushrooms in the state shops had increased tenfold, would this seriously effect the trade turnover as a whole?

It is better to know the truth with a few inexactitudes than to remain content with the half-truth of unscrupulous manipulations.

Still keeping to the previously-published column, with non-manipulated values, which showed "other foodstuffs", let us calculate its magnitude for 1970 in terms of roubles. Total purchases of foodstuffs by the population in that year came to 86 milliard roubles, which means that the item we are looking for came to 2.8 milliard roubles (3.2 percent of 86.) Deducting this sum from the current, half-honest total for "other foodstuffs", amounting to 27 milliard roubles, we obtain the figure for what, in the early issues of the yearbook, was entitled, almost artlessly: "Alcoholic and non-alcoholic beverages." It is 24.2 milliard roubles. This, then, is the expenditure on alcohol, diluted with the expenditure on kvass and Narzan water. What we now have to do is to separate the components of this mixture. This is not an easy task, but it is worth making the effort needed. It is reasonable to begin with the non-alcoholic beverages, since they are much cheaper than the alcoholic ones, and the inaccuracies unavoidable in calculating what they represent in the total will have less bearing on the ultimate result.

What quantity of soft drinks was produced (and drunk) in 1970? However strange it may seem at first glance, the output of soft drinks has paralleled the output of vodka for many years now. In the handbook *Promyshlennost SSSR (Soviet Industry)* for 1964, the production of vodka and of soft drinks, respectively, was given for the years between 1950 and 1964. Let us take these figures year by year. As numerator we will put the figure for soft drinks, in millions of decalitres, and as denominator the figure for vodka, in the same terms. In this way we get:

1950 –	72	soft drinks	/	62	vodka
1953 –	87.8	... ...	/	95.4	...
1955 –	97.8	... ...	/	116.9	...
1956 –	97.2	... ...	/	122.9	...
1957 –	115.2	... ...	/	140.2	...
1958 –	120.1	... ...	/	145.3	...
1959 –	134.6	... ...	/	137.3	...
1960 –	141.5	... ...	/	138.1	...
1961 –	142.8	... ...	/	145.7	...
1962 –	149	... ...	/	162	...
1963 –	155	... ...	/	152	...

As was to be expected with a planned, socialist system of production, output rose in a planned way, and the production of vodka decreased only in years when the harvest was poor (1959 and 1963). The general picture is that the annual output of soft drinks lagged slightly behind that of vodka, but in those particular years vodka had to yield first place. It may be that, besides the failure of the harvest, socialist emulation between workers in different branches of the food industry played a certain role here, too.

The annual increase in the output of soft drinks was sometimes 5, sometimes 6, sometimes 7 millions of decalitres — sometimes even only one million. In only two cases out of eleven did it exceed 7 millions (once it was 18 millions and once 14 millions). Let us assume, so as not to make any mistake, that after 1963 the rate of increase was 9-10 million decalitres each year. We thus get the figure of 220-230 million decalitres of soft drinks produced in 1970. Taking into account the installation in recent years of automatic vending machines for aerated water, let us increase this figure to 250-300 million decalitres. If all the soft drinks sold were sold in bottles, that would mean 5-6 milliard bottles, or 20-25 bottles per person — quite a lot, it would seem, since soft drinks are purchased mainly in the towns and mostly in the summer.

Let us work out the average price of a bottle of one of these drinks. Fruit juices do not come into our calculation, as they figure in the "fruit" column, and in any case they are not a large item of consumption. Mineral water costs 10 kopecks a bottle. Aerated water and kvass are sold more cheaply. Only fruit-flavoured drinks are dearer. If we take 18 kopecks as the average we are certainly overestimating: however, let us stay with this hypothetical price. On that basis, we obtain a figure between 900 million roubles and something a little over one milliard. Let us assume the figure is one milliard.

Accordingly, the cost of non-alcoholic beverages comes to no more than one-twenty-fourth of total expenditure on drink, taking the latter to amount to the already-calculated sum of 24.2 milliard roubles. Deducting from that figure, therefore, one milliard roubles for soft drinks, we see that 23.2 milliard roubles was spent on alcohol. And so, at last, we have found where the dog lies buried, in the table called "Commodity structure of retail turnover."

According to this table, total purchases by the population in state and co-operative shops in 1970 amounted to 155.2 milliard roubles. This means that alcohol accounted for almost 15 percent of total purchases: and if we make the comparison with foodstuffs alone, it accounted for 27 percent of *that* total. Every rouble received by a food shop was due, for 27 kopecks out of the 100, to sales of alcohol. But, as the Roman Emperor Vespasian said when he put a tax on the public urinals: "Money doesn't smell."

However successfully the drink business may have developed, we still need to compare it with the overall dynamic of popular consumption over a series of years: when we have done this, our picture will be complete. In the table "Dynamic of sales of most important commodities" (on p. 558 of the yearbook for 1970), the readings are taken with the year 1940 as 100. On this basis the sale of alcoholic products in the last thirty years emerges as follows: in 1950 — 75 (a decline fully explicable in the period just after the war), in 1960 — 200, in 1965 — 283, in 1970 — 439. An increase to a figure almost four-and-a-half times that of 1940! In this table everything is shown not in roubles, as in the "commodity-structure" table previously analysed, but in percentages calculated in comparable prices. The increase by four-and-a-half times is therefore an increase in the actual physical quantity of alcohol drunk. The purchase of many other commodities has increased since 1940 to a greater extent than that of alcohol: e.g., radio sets 38-fold, milk 13-fold, furniture 18-fold, and so on.

This, then, is the picture as compared with the year 1940. But let us try to examine a period closer to the present — say, the decade between 1960 and 1970. What purchases increased, and by how much, during those ten years? To find this, let us take the same table, but use 1960 as our base-year for calculations. A simple division of the figures in the column for 1970 by the corresponding figures in the column for 1960 reveals the dynamic of purchases over the decade: 1.8 times as much meat was bought in 1970 as in 1960, nearly 1.5 times as much butter, 1.6 times as much sugar. Sales of textile fabrics did not increase, they fell: but if we lump textile fabrics together with clothing and knitwear (which is much more reasonable than lumping vodka with kvass, since knitwear and textile fabrics do indeed go together, whereas kvass and vodka do not) we get an increase of 1.7-fold. To do this we have had to bring in data from the "commodity structure" table. That table also shows that purchases of footwear of all kinds increased to more than twice the earlier figure. The increase in purchases of furniture was 2.6-fold.

Sales of alcoholic products increased 2.2-fold, and this ratio of 1:2.2, clearly shown in the "Dynamic" table (the actual figures being 200:439), confirms to a remarkable degree that our previous calculations, in which some of the figures used had to be hypothetical, were broadly correct, since they resulted in this same figure of 2.2-fold for the increase in the sale of alcohol over the ten-year period in question.

For example's sake let us recall the amount spent on alcohol in 1970, namely, 23.2 milliard roubles. The amount of alcoholic and non-alcoholic beverages sold a decade previously is known to us from the yearbook: 11,023 million new roubles. Deducting from this figure the proportion we have calculated for soft drinks, that is, one-twenty-fourth, or 459 million, we obtain 10.5 milliard, which is 2.2 times less than the 1970 figure of 23.2 milliard. Let us recall that during these ten years the price of alcoholic drinks did not change, so that the increase in the quantity sold corresponded to the increase in the amount spent. Having obtained yet another proof that we were correct in our calculation of the figure for purchases in 1970, we can now confidently compare the sale of alcohol with the sales of other commodities, for which the yearbook gives direct figures.

The sale of alcohol gave, in money terms, in 1970, as much as the sale of clothing and underwear together with the sale of butter and other dairy produce (cf. the "Commodity structure" table, not forgetting that not a word about alcohol is to be found in it). Perhaps, though, the expression "the sale of alcohol *gave*" is not quite correct, for, after all, what it gave it also took — from the population of the U.S.S.R.

We have compared quantities. But what about rates of increase? In rate of increase, purchases of alcohol in the decade 1960 -1970 were second only to furniture, the purchase of which grew 2.6-fold. We must not forget, however, how many milliards were spent on alcohol (23.2) and how many on furniture (3.6, that is, six-and-a-half times less). In comparison with alcohol, furniture appears as a quite secondary commodity — which, moreover, has a saturation point, just as with sewing-machines and radio sets. Vodka and wine have no such saturation point: he who drank yesterday will want to drink again today, and, furthermore, he who did *not* drink yesterday may want to drink today. As, indeed, we observe.

There is, though, another item of expenditure which in rate of increase falls not far behind vodka. This is "printed publications", i.e., newspaper, magazines and books, including textbooks. In the decade in question the retail turnover of this item increased 2.16-fold. In absolute amount, however, what was spent on "the wise, the good, the eternal", was only 1.7 milliard roubles, or half as much as was spent on furniture, and one-thirteenth as much as was spent on alcohol. Besides, "printed publications" are bought not only by the working people but also by institutions — libraries, schools, and even barber-shops — whereas vodka and beer are bought by nobody apart from the workers, office-workers, collective-farmers and intelligentsia of our country. They alone contribute to the consumption of alcohol, which has increased at such a rate.

Alcohol is, indeed, the leading commodity among all those purchased by our people. It has become Commodity Number One, with Number Two ("clothing and underwear") and Number Three ("meat and sausages") lagging behind not by half a length, not by half a milliard, but by 9 and 12 milliards respectively.

Alcoholic drinks hold the leading position not only in amount purchased and rate of increase, but also in profitability, which exceeds every other branch of trade. Let us now examine this aspect of the matter, and see what we can find out, despite the deep secrecy surrounding it.

We open at page 601 our yearbook of the Soviet economy in 1970, to find "Indices of state retail prices." As compared with 1940, the base year, prices of all foodstuffs, excluding alcohol, had risen to the level of 133 percent. Prices of alcoholic beverages, however, stood at 262 percent of the 1940 level. In other words, the increase in the prices of all other foodstuffs was 33 percent, whereas the price of alcohol had risen 162 percent, or five times as much. Can it for even a moment be supposed that some special increase had occurred in the cost of production of alcoholic drinks, necessitating an increase in their price? Of course not. On the contrary, technical progress and the growth of productivity should have reduced, not increased, the cost of producing them. Later on we shall perhaps be able to determine their cost of production fairly accurately, but to start with we need to establish what relation there is between the cost of production of alcoholic drinks and the price at which they are sold. The mere fact that this price can be raised so simply and easily to any height required tells us that there is no relation at all. During the entire period of 77 years since the state vodka monopoly was introduced, the price has been determined by a variety of considerations, but never by the cost of production.

The *Large Soviet Encyclopaedia* tells us, in the article on "The Wine Monopoly" (2nd edition, Vol. 8, 1951), that "before the First World War the cost of producing all the vodka consumed in one year was 200 million roubles, but the consumers paid 900 million roubles for it." That was written about the Tsarist period. Later the encyclopaedia article says that "vodka prices are fixed by the Soviet state at a level which facilitates the struggle against alcoholism ... In the U.S.S.R. the production of vodka is not governed by fiscal purposes and the income obtained from selling it accounts for an insignificant proportion of the state's revenue." (What is a *significant* and what an *insignificant* proportion? Would it be 10 percent? or 12? or 15?)

What the *Large Soviet Encyclopaedia* says coincides on many points with the statement of Count S. Yu. Witte, who was Minister of Finance under Tsar Alexander III and his son, Nicholas the Last. The wine monopoly, which he introduced, was, according to him, "essentially a measure intended to reduce drunkenness." When he left the Ministry of Finance, however, the line that he had followed was, he wrote, abruptly changed, and the Ministry now saw the function of the monopoly not as struggle against alcoholism but as "increasing revenue from the sale of drink ... The price of wine was seriously increased ... A price was fixed — and has been maintained ever since — which, though accessible to almost everyone, was ruinous for them ... This measure considerably increased the revenue from drink." (Be it noted that "wine", or "grain-wine", was the official name for vodka in those days.) All this can be read in Witte's *Memoirs* (*Vospominanii*, published by "Slovo", 1922, p. 73).

Commodity Number One

From the information given in the *Large Soviet Encyclopaedia* about the cost of producing vodka before World War I we see that the Tsarist Government stung the people for seven-ninths — or 78 percent — of the selling price of vodka. We know how much of it was sold in 1913: 118.9 million decalitres. And the Government received 900 million roubles, which means that a litre of vodka was sold for 75 kopecks. That was already the increased price which Witte condemned, blaming the Ministry of Finance, from which he had departed long since, for setting itself a fiscal task — increasing state revenue from drink and, without combating drunkenness, ruining the people: a price that was "accessible but ruinous."

Our Soviet state's price cannot, of course, be as exorbitant as the Tsarist price (22 percent of which went to the manufacturer, who made a good profit even with that, and 78 percent to the Treasury), for, as the *Large Soviet Encyclopaedia* says, "in the U.S.S.R. the production of vodka is not governed by fiscal purposes." At the same time, though, the price of vodka must be kept, as the encyclopaedia puts it, "at a level which facilitates the struggle against alcoholism", that is, at a fairly high level. What is this level which while not pursuing base fiscal aims of profit, nevertheless helps to carry on a high-minded struggle?

Let us see what goes to make up the cost of production of vodka and its price nowadays. In the book *Ekonomika, organizatsiya i planirovaniye spirtovogo proizvodstva* (The economics, organisation and planning of alcohol production), by V.G. Pykhov, published by "Pishchevaya Promyshlennost" (the Food Industry Press), Moscow, 1966, no data are given regarding the cost of production of vodka, any more than they are to be found in any other generally-accessible work. But in two of the book's tables (on pp. 178 and 201) we find, among other things, the wholesale price of the pure alcohol from which it is made. This is a firm price, fixed by the Government in 1954. A factory must strive to reduce its cost of production, and if this is brought down below the wholesale price, the difference constitutes the factory's profit. The state's wholesale price of pure alcohol is, for first-quality rectified spirit, 5 roubles 90 kopecks a decalitre, and for rectified spirit of the highest purity, 6 roubles 10 kopecks a decalitre. Highest-purity rectified spirit, from which vodka is made, needs no further processing, all that has to be done is to dilute it with water. In the remote northern regions of the U.S.S.R., to which pure alcohol is still sent, its transformation into vodka at the consumer's table is effected quite simply: each person dilutes it according to his taste, or, more correctly, to his capacity. In the factories where liqueur vodkas are produced this procedure is more complicated: in industrial production there is the labour-force to be paid, and the technical personnel too, and there are costs of depreciation to be covered.

There is not much published about the vodka industry, and we have to deduce the cost of production of vodka by analogy with pure alcohol production. In this case the raw material accounts, on the average, for 84 percent of the cost, and processing is responsible for the remaining 16 percent. The technology of transforming pure alcohol into vodka is very much simpler than the manufacture of the pure alcohol itself: diluting the stuff, pouring it into bottles, and corking them, that's all there is to it. The making of liqueurs like *pertsovka* or *spotykach* is more complicated, but their relative importance is slight and has little bearing on the matter in hand. Therefore, if we assume for vodka a cost of production half that of pure alcohol, this will be an extremely generous estimate. Let us add a profit, such as that made by the pure alcohol factories. Together, this comes to 16 percent of the price of pure alcohol, and with this addition we obtain the factory price.

A decalitre of alcohol, leaving the gates of the vodka factory in new containers, will cost not 6 roubles 10 kopecks but 7 roubles 8 kopecks. But to this alcohol water has been added, so that what we have before us now is not, in fact, a decalitre of pure alcohol but 2.5 decalitres of vodka — practically 2.5, that is, maybe a little less, but since we are taking the next higher figure in all these calculations we can neglect the difference. A litre of vodka, fully paid for and also giving a profit to the two enterprises through which it has passed, is now worth 28 kopecks, although we have allowed the vodka factory a very generous cost of production and a healthy profit.

At which stage a fresh metamorphosis, still more striking than the previous chemical changes, takes place in the formation of the price of vodka is immaterial so far as the consumer is concerned. An increase is effected somewhere along the line, at one of the hardly noticeable halts between the factory and the retail shop. It takes the form of payments to the Treasury, levied by way of an allocation from profits and the turnover tax — which, as textbooks of financial science explain, is certainly not an indirect tax, and, indeed, not even any sort of tax at all, but merely an allocation to the Treasury.

(Analysis of this question would take us too far from our subject. I have not been able to decide which definition of the turnover tax to accept — that given in the *Large Soviet Encyclopaedia*, or that given in the official textbook. The former tells us [2nd edition, Vol. 29]:

"The turnover tax is added as the difference between the retail price (allowing for trade discount) and the wholesale price." But the textbook recommended by the Ministry for use in financial colleges, *Finansy SSSR*, written by a group of authors headed by Professor Allakhverdian, Moscow, 1962, says something quite different: "The turnover tax constitutes the difference between the wholesale price for the industry and the wholesale price for the enterprise." Without trying to find who is closer to the truth in this matter, let us stick to the unscientific and simple-minded definition used by every worker: vodka costs the state so-much, but they make us pay so-much. This definition is certainly a lot clearer than "the difference between the wholesale price fot the industry and the wholesale price for the enterprise."

The retail price of a bottle of vodka is just as firm as its wholesale price was. The only difference is that everybody knows the former, but not the latter. And also, of course, the amounts involved.

The retail price must meet the expenses of trade: maintenance of staff, transport, payment for premises, etc. Trade also must make a profit. On the average, trade costs make up 6.24 percent of retail turnover (cf. the table on page 596 of the yearbook of the Soviet economy for 1970.) Can this percentage apply in the case of vodka?

This percentage, applied to the cost of vodka such as was sold at an average price, down to 1971, of 5 roubles 50 kopecks a litre (I have taken as my average the price of ordinary vodka: liqueurs were cheaper, but there were also some kinds of vodka that were more expensive than this), would come to 34 kopecks per litre, the factory price of the commodity itself being 28 kopecks. This mark-up recalls all too well the well-known saying: "The heifer on the other shore costs a quarter of a kopeck, but to ferry it over costs a rouble": yet the ferrying of the heifer in this case, which is done by ourselves and not by anyone on "the other shore", actually costs very little. The expenses incurred in the alcohol trade are much lower than in any other branch. Alcohol does not go bad, as meat and butter do, does not turn sour, like milk, does not go out of fashion, like clothes and footwear, does not require such elaborate packing as china and porcelain. It has no need of refrigerators. It can be transported easily: in order to transport 10,000 roubles' worth of this commodity, all that is required is one three-ton truck, while 10,000 roubles' worth of the potatoes from which the vodka is made would weigh over a hundred tons, for the transport of which 40 three-tonners would be needed. Alcohol does not demand much shop-space: a single counter served by one shop-assistant will bring a food store a larger trade turnover than ten other counters with ten other shop-assistants. And, finally, stock-taking — that operation which testifies to the degree of trust which our state has learned to place in its trading apparatus — is incomparably easier to carry out where alcohol is concerned, even if it be done every week, than in the case of books or haberdashery. So that application of the average percentage of trade mark-up when selling alcohol is illegitimate. And although we have in every case hitherto allowed a more than sufficient "margin" for every hypothetical magnitude, this time it will be reasonable to assume that trading expenses plus trading profit make up not more than half of the wholesale price of the commodity itself, that is, 14 kopecks a litre.

(The trading organisations themselves probably reckon in a different way. In order to cover their high expenditure on other goods, they need to add the average mark-up to those which sell profitably, even if the actual cost embodied in "profitable" goods is less than the average. This seems normal so far as trade as a whole is concerned, but wrong when we calculate what a lot the state actually makes out of the sale of alcohol products. In order to accomplish our task, it is essential to differentiate between trading expenses on the basis of the characteristics of each commodity. Accordingly, the trade mark-up of 14 kopecks per litre of vodka which I have assumed is not too small, but rather an extremely big mark-up.)

What we arrive at finally is this: a wholesale price for vodka of 28 kopecks a litre, plus 14 kopecks trade mark-up, giving 42 kopecks in all. But the selling price is 5 roubles 50 kopecks. The state's share (not counting the profits taken by the industry and by the trade organisations) is therefore 5 roubles 8 kopecks on every litre, or 92.4 percent of what the consumer pays.

Remembering what the encyclopaedia says about vodka production in our country not serving fiscal aims, let us now estimate how much the Treasury gets from the sale of all the vodka produced. About wine and beer we will speak later.

First of all we need to establish the actual dimensions of vodka production, of which the yearbooks have been silent for the last nine years. The table already mentioned, showing the "Dynamic of the sale of commodities", from which we learnt that the realisation of alcoholic beverages had increased 2.2-fold between 1960 and 1970, gave us a general impression, but failed to supply details for each kind of alcohol taken separately. The calculations I propose to undertake start from the figures for the production of vodka alone, which are given in the statistical yearbook, though only for an earlier period. The last year for which this information is supplied is 1962. If we can determine the rate of increase of vodka production in the period 1950-1962 we shall possess a certain basis for supposition regarding subsequent developments.

In the first three years of this period the increase was very significant — 50 per cent (from 62.8 million decalitres to 95.4 million). In the next two years the increase was 22 per cent. In 1956 it was 5 per cent, in 1957 14 per cent, in 1958 3.6 per cent. In 1959 production fell by 5.5 percent, but thereafter the rate of increase turned upward: in 1960 it was 0.6 percent, in 1961 5.5 percent, in 1962 11.3 percent.

The average annual increase over 12 years was about 9 percent. If, however, we ignore the first half of the 1950s, when the increase was especially vigorous, the average comes to 5 percent. If we take this lower variant as applying in the last ten years, we arrive at the figure of 238 million decalitres of vodka produced in 1970. This means an increase of nearly 50 percent in eight years, since in 1962 the amount produced was 162 million decalitres.

Our hypothetical figure can be checked. To do this we need first to determine the average price of wine — a product which comes in many different varieties with different prices. Starting out from the price of vodka as 5 roubles 50 kopecks a litre and the price of beer as 40 kopecks a litre, it is easy to calculate how much of those drinks was bought in 1960, when the yearbook gave figures for the output of all three kinds of alcohol. For vodka (138.1 million decalitres) and beer (249 million decalitres) the sum expended was 8,590 million roubles. Let us deduct this sum from the total expenditure on alcohol, which we calculated earlier to be 10,564 million roubles. This means that the share of the total represented by wine was 1,974 million roubles. And in that year the amount produced was 77.7 million decalitres. The average price of wine therefore, was 2 roubles 54 kopecks a litre.

Now we will proceed to the year 1970. First, let us deduct from the total receipts from alcohol (23.2 milliard roubles) 4 percent, the proportion by which the price of alcohol was raised in 1970 (cf. the table if indices on p.601). The resulting figure is 22,272 million. Now, let us deduct the receipts from wine (263 million decalitres) and beer (419 million decalitres), amounting together to 8,423 million roubles. What remains is the money received from the sale of vodka. Dividing this by the average price of a decalitre, we find that in 1970 257 million decalitres of vodka were put on the market — 19 millions more than we previously calculated, on the basis of an annual growth-rate of 5 per cent in vodka production. Perhaps rates of increase really were higher than we supposed. There is another possibility, too: as a result of the remarkable extension of wine-making (from 77.7 million decalitres in 1960 to 268 in 1970, an increase of 3.3-fold), new and more expensive varieties of wine may have been put on sale, so raising the average price of wine as compared with 1960. It would have been enough to increase this figure by one-and-a-half roubles per decalitre, as compared with 1960, for this to have a marked influence on our calculation.

At all events, this price-check shows that the figure of 238 million decalitres was no exaggeration. Remaining faithful to the rule that it is better to underestimate than to overestimate, let us keep to this figure.

In this case, receipts from vodka in 1970 came to 13.1 milliard roubles, and the net revenue obtained by the Treasury (92.4 percent of the total) to 11.9 milliard. This was vodka's contribution to the budget. How much was obtained from the sale of wine and beer? Deducting 13.1 milliard from 23.2 milliard, we get 10.1 milliard roubles. To work out the cost of production of wine would be a sum with too many unknowns in it. Instead, let us make the following calculation. Let us suppose that wine and beer were sold in the shops in 1940, thirty years ago, at their wholesale price, without any allocations to the budget and without any turnover tax. This did not happen, but let us assume for the moment that it did. In the table of indices already familiar to us, the price prevailing at that time is taken as 100. In the thirty years after 1940 the index for alcohol products rose to 262, whereas their cost of production certainly did not increase, but undoubtedly fell. The increase of 162 percent (index 262 minus 100) therefore represents net revenue to the Treasury. In terms of money, this means 6.2 milliard roubles out of the 10.1 milliard received for wine and beer. The calculation is very rough, but it is certainly an underestimate, since we can be sure that in 1940 beer and wine were not being sold on a purely philanthropic basis, without any benefit accruing to the budget. Thus, then, vodka contributed to the budget to the tune of 11.9 milliard roubles, and wine and beer a good deal less — 6.2 milliard. Altogether, 18.1 milliard. The encyclopaedia was right: 18 milliard roubles is only a small proportion of a budget of 156 milliard, not quite 12 percent. However, although the price of alcohol is not increased for the sake of gain, but in order to promote the fight against drunkenness, there are no grounds for disdaining the revenue obtained. Say what you like, that amount of money can cover the state's expenditure on public health (9.3 milliard) and on science (6.6 milliard), and still leave quite a bit in hand.

All our calculations relate to the period up to 1970 inclusive, when an increase in alcohol prices began and the campaign against alcoholism was raised to a higher level, in accordance with the formulation of the *Large Soviet Encyclopaedia* — a level that would enable a struggle to be waged. Whatever commodity may be involved, the consumer possesses one means of reacting to an increase in its price, namely, ceasing to buy the commodity which has become more expensive. This was the reaction expected when the price of alcohol was raised to such a level that, it was assumed, drinkers would cease to buy it, so that drunkenness would then disappear automatically. This expectation must have been based on the assumption that drunkenness was a phenomenon prevalent precisely among the less-well-off strata of the population, and they would cease to buy alcohol because it had become too dear for them. Otherwise, what would be the point of increasing the price of alcohol? The only advantage from it would accrue to the Treasury.

Between increasing the price of alcohol and increasing any other price there is no difference of principle. There is only one essential consideration here — the repercussions which the given measure is expected to have. An increase in the price of meat or butter is not expected to have any favourable repercussions. With vodka it is another matter: making it more expensive is intended to promote the fight against drunkenness, it is a measure of a positive character. Not to mention that, given the scale that the alcohol trade has attained, every 5 percent increase in the price of alcohol brings in cash to the amount of a milliard roubles, that is, as much as the whole of the dressmaking industry and all the mending done in dressmaking establishments throughout the country. In order to obtain an additional milliard from the work of the dressmaking workshops it would be necessary to double the prices they charge, which is unthinkable. To obtain a milliard from alcohol is so much simpler. A bottle which yesterday cost 2 roubles today costs 2 roubles 10 kopecks — and at the end of the year, a milliard is lying on the little saucer with the blue border, as Ostap Bender used to say.

However, by its very nature, an increase in the price of alcohol makes a much stronger impact on the worker's household than would be made by an increase in the cost of communal services. Expenditure on alcohol comes out of the household budget and not out of some abstract pocket or other. In saying this I do not wish to imply that it is wrong to increase the price of alcohol. That is an excellent step on the state's part: the only thing is, it is not clear how it is supposed to help those workers' households where they drink.

But what if the working people have no need of such help? What if the increase in the consumption of alcohol is a natural consequence of increasing prosperity? In a certain sense this is so. Increased prosperity cannot but result in an increased demand for alcohol. In Tsarist Russia, in the thirteen years between 1900 and 1913, the demand for vodka per head of population rose by 20 percent (*Large Soviet Encyclopaedia*, 2nd edition, Vol. 2, article on "Alcoholism"). The view has long become established that drunkenness in those days was a consequence of the people's poverty and their hopeless subjection. But for all the scandalous poverty in which the people lived, the Tsarist Government was able to fix a price for vodka that did not prevent the people from drinking, as Count Witte noted — "a price that was accessible but ruinous." The years after 1905 were years of reaction. In such periods people drink more. And yet the increase in consumption of alcohol was only 20 percent in 13 years. How slow their growth-rates were in those days!

The Tsarist Government did not advertise vodka or call upon the people to drink it. There was even a temperance society. But that Government's whole policy in this sphere proceeded from the assumption (though this was usually kept concealed) that drunkenness was an unavoidable evil and that it could be combated only by means of vodka. "Russia's gaiety lies in drinking." And, gradually, this gaiety became transformed into a national calamity.

We, however, are struggling against drunkenness! We are waging this struggle by raising the price of alcohol and restricting the hours between which it can be sold. And yet, despite such effective measures, consumption of alcohol during a ten-year period increased (according to the official evidence of the table, already quoted more than once, "Dynamic of the sales of commodities," page 558) 2.2-fold, that is, by 120 percent, or, when reckoned per head of population, by 100 percent.

While an incease in drinking by 20 percent in 13 years corresponded to persistent poverty among the people, the fact that it doubled in 10 years would be unthinkable unless the people had become better off and so able to allow themselves to spend such a lot on alcohol: let me recall that alcohol accounts for 15 percent of all expenditure in stage and co-operative shops.

Undoubtedly, increased prosperity is a factor in this. But that improvement has taken place not in a vacuum but amid concrete, historically-formed conditions of life. Such an enormous increase in the consumption of a commodity could not have occurred unless the consumers had become addicted to it as something they must have.

Alcohol is a drug. The habit of drug-taking spreads much faster than any other. For this reason, any analogy between the consumption of alcohol in our country and in those countries where they drink wine with their meals, morning, noon and night (France, for example) is not to be taken seriously. When people drink with their meals a weakish wine made from grapes, which heightens the appetite, this helps them to swallow their food. But when people drink in order to stimulate themselves, a snack helps them to swallow a glass of vodka. For this purpose of self-stimulation a weak wine will not suffice, and so our people do not drink it. The very style in which wine and vodka, respectively, are taken shows the different places occupied by these drinks in the use that the people make of them.

It is an obvious fact that alcoholic drinks have become an integral part of popular consumption in a number of countries. No less obvious is it that at a certain level of development the consumption of alcohol becomes a national calamity. It seems to me that the most important symptom that this is happening can be seen in the speed with which vodka has become the leading commodity in popular consumption. Having become Commodity Number One, vodka is on its way to becoming also Calamity Number One.

Reading no longer gives any help in this matter. Not in vain has the subject of alcohol completely vanished from the press and is steadily fading even from statistics. And making alcohol more expensive will hardly help, either. It can only lead to the cutting down of other, necessary purchases by those families which have no money to spare, that is, those where such reductions are least to be desired. The increase in the price of alcohol does, of course, also result in a certain *increase* in expenditure on the part of those families which the Government wishes to react in this way — those families which have money in reserve. And reserves of money do exist among the people, they are increasing very fast, and there is nothing to be done with them except to put them in the savings-bank. A certain transference of investment takes place: some of the money deposited in the savings-bank is taken from there and invested in a bottle of vodka which has increased in price. But is *much* money being transferred in this way? Very little, I fancy: the people who drink are not those who go to the savings-bank, and those who go to the savings-bank are not the ones who send their wives round to the shop to buy a half-litre.

Savings-bank deposits have increased to a remarkable extent in the last five years: from 18.7 milliard roubles in 1965 to 46.6 milliard in 1970. It would be odd if this were to be explained by increased thriftiness on the part of the Soviet people: thriftiness does not increase two-and-a-half-fold in five years. It would likewise be groundless to suppose that people are saving up to buy particularly expensive articles such as furniture or motor-cycles. If 3.6 milliard roubles' worth of furniture is sold and 1.2 milliard worth of motorcycles, that certainly confirms that little is available that is worth buying. But what significance have expenditures of this order when you compare them with the amount of money which remains unspent in the savings-bank deposits?

But can the working people manage to buy motor-cars? In the commodity-structure table which I have used several times already there is not even a column for this item. Another table (on page 587) shows "commodities of productive and economic importance made available for sale to the population", and in it we find, after coal, saw-timber and kerosene, 123,000 light cars sold in 1970. (The table shows that in 1960 62,000 such cars were sold, in 1965 64,000, in 1969 87,000 and in 1970 123,000. If we assume that in the years omitted here the number sold was the same as in the years adjacent to them, we get the figure of 800,000 cars sold during the entire eleven-year period.) Despite the fact that the working people bought motor-cars too, they were unable to spend all their money. This also signifies, no doubt, increased prosperity.

For the sale of cars from the Togliatti works (with a planned annual output of 440,000 cars for the first few years) to even half-fill the "goods-vacuum", these cars would have to be sold at the fantastic price of 50,000 roubles apiece. At the usual prices for cars, which our people have come to accept as normal, the sale of cars brings in a sum slightly larger than the sale of furniture. (I have already compared this with the proceeds from the sale of vodka and shown that it amounts to little in comparison with the milliards spent on the latter.)

When talking about the standard of living or the expenditure of the population, we consider the latter as a sort of "average", homogeneous mass. But does vodka attract to itself the money of the same groups of this allegedly homogeneous population as those who put theirs in the savings-banks? Certainly not — though statistics give us no information on that point. However, let us look at the table on p. 564, headed: "Average size of deposits in savings-banks in the different republics." The lowest average amount is shown for Moldavia — 462 roubles. Then, in ascending order, come: Kirghizia, Uzbekistan, Tadzhikistan, The R.S.F.S.R., the Ukraine, Kazakhstan and Byelorussia. The average size of deposit ranges from 519 roubles in Kirghizia to 588 roubles in Byelorussia. Thereafter we find a sharp increase — 647 in Latvia, 672 in Azerbaidzhan, 688 in Turkmenia — and then another big jump: 806 in Estonia, 964 in Lithuania, 980 in Armenia, 1,016 in Georgia.

It is clearly evident that the largest deposits are found in the republics from which southern fruits are sent to the northern and central parts of the U.S.S.R. and in those where they let rooms and sleeping accommodation to summer holidaymakers. And, let us note, the prices of fruits, and also those of rooms, are governed by prices fixed by the State, and are subject to the turnover tax.

Turkmenia, Azebaidzhan, Armenia and the Baltic republics are far from being the republics where people drink the most. We do not need statistical handbooks to tell us that. In Georgia they have been drinkers since ancient times, theirs is an old wine-growing country, but what they drink, for preference, is wine — and, what is most important, they drink it in their own national manner, which is very different from the manner of drinking customary in Russia since the time of the farming-out of the drink trade and the "wine-monopoly."

Statistics provide no key to understanding the reasons why those groups of the working people who put their money in the savings-banks are far from coinciding with the ones who invest heavily in bottles of vodka. Though statistics fail to quantify this fact, they do indirectly confirm it. Thereby they confirm that further increases in the price of alcohol, in extracting money from the population, would not affect the money lying in the savings-banks, which lies there principally owing to the "goods-vacuum." To fill this vacuum by making alcoholic drinks more expensive would probably prove as difficult as to reduce the level of drunkenness by raising the price-level. The solving of both problems is all the more problematical in that on the alcohol front there is another force engaged, with which, though it is not much talked about, it is necessary to reckon very seriously. This is home-distilled vodka — *samogon*. It stands ready in the second échelon: but it does not form part of the high command's reserves — on the contrary, it is not subordinate to the high command at all, and is subject to no planning. Home-distilling has become easier in our time (and the struggle against it made more difficult) because the technology involved is now as simple as can be: no stills are needed for the brewing, saucepans will do.

I have said little about home-distilling: statistics do not take account of it, but this uncontrolled magnitude must not be forgotten. It is capable of upsetting the most optimistic calculations.

If we ignore home-distilling, the visible side of the alcohol trade is easily reducible to figures: so many million bucketsful bring in so much revenue. The reverse, dark side, however, is hard to express in figures, and any such figures can be contested. Even the number of working hours lost through severe hangovers is a doubtful magnitude. Just you prove that it is because of hangovers, and not because the first day, like the first hour, back at work after a break is less productive than those that follow. And, something even more difficult — just you prove that the quantity of material loss inflicted by drunkenness is greater than the material revenue obtained from the sale of vodka.

As for the balance of *spiritual* gains and losses, who shall draw that up? Nobody is interested in doing it. Social statistics, which are prudent enough anyway, are super-prudent on that aspect of things. There are not even any real criteria where this question is concerned. What constitutes drunkenness and what does not? Nobody can say.

Therefore, without trying to answer questions the very formulation of which leaves open the possibility of answering both yes and no, I have kept to the firm ground of official data, from which I have been able to deduce certain figures where the actual statistics themselves are concealed. The significance of these figures is confirmed most convincingly by the very fact that they are concealed. Unimportant facts are not hidden so carefully. On the other hand, the concealment of factual material concerning the question of drink hinders from the outset any attempt to fight against the increase in the consumption of alcohol, for society cannot combat an evil without knowing its locations and its dimensions. But can we be certain that the growth in the consumption of alcohol is really regarded as an evil?

Fighting against the increasing consumption of alcohol is like Don Quixote's campaign against the windmills. Sensible people don't engage in such tomfoolery. Cervantes did not need to tell us what the miller was doing while the Knight galloped, spurring Rosinante, towards his mill. We know it without being told: the miller was calmly pouring corn on to the millstone. What seemed to

Don Quixote a wicked giant was to the miller a means of livelihood.

The increase in the consumption of alcohol has become transformed before our eyes into an uncontrollable process. And a problem which arises entirely from a process that cannot be controlled cannot be solved, either. Such processes are utilised, so far as this can be managed — and that's all. The miller never thinks of governing the wind and struggling against it. All he can do is to turn his mill so that its sails get as much wind as possible in them.

Turning the sails of a windmill into the wind does not mean going against the wind.

On the Question of the Place in History of the Social Structure of the Soviet Union

(An Historical Parallel and a
Sociological Hypothesis)

by A. Zimin

Translated by Brian Pearce

1. About the subject of these notes

The purpose of the following notes is to make an approach to studying the social nature and the place in history of Soviet society as it exists today, the society which Stalin called "complete socialism" and which the neo-Stalinists call "developed socialism." The reader is invited, before seeking to answer this very topical question for mankind in the middle and the second half of the 20th century, and with a view to finding the answer, to consider some long-past and forgotten vicissitudes of the human race. Such a procedure may seem strained, or a mere game with academic paradoxes, but in fact it is not so. And I hope that the reader will be convinced that this attempt to compare two of the major turning-points in the history of mankind — the epoch of transition from class society to classless (post-class) society, at the summit of civilisation, with the age of transition from classless (pre-class) society to class society, at the dawn of civilisation — is not strained, paradoxical or far-fetched academicism. On the contrary, this comparison is forced upon us by the very essence of the question, and it helps to light up certain problems of the path of development taken by human society which have been left in the shadow by science and by social consciousness, but an appreciation of which is of decisive importance for understanding both of these historical changes — and the answer to which may prove decisive for the fate of mankind today, living as it is in the second of these epochs of change. But I have endeavoured, of course, to keep my introductory excursion into ancient times and survivals from those times as brief as possible, freeing it from details and literary

116

references and concentrating it upon a single problem, one that is highly instructive in relation to my subject, namely the so-called "Asiatic mode of production."

2. What the discussions about the Asiatic mode of production did and did not contribute

What we know about the last two-and-a-half thousand years of the existence and development of the peoples of Europe shows that the class-divided part of man's history consists of three successive social formations — slaveowning, feudal and capitalist. The structure and regularity of each formation, the laws governing the rise, shaping and break-up of each one and of its transition to the next, and also the sequence of these transitions, has been studied to such an extent that it was possible already in the 19th century to deduce a general law of the social progress of mankind — or, more precisely, this study facilitated the construction of a general theory of the three-stage character of the progress of class society. Theoretical and logical necessity does not, of course, signify binding force. Like any rule, this development through three stages allows, in its actual realization, not only of variations but also, depending on concrete historical circumstances and specific conditions, of deviations and exceptions, although the very nature of the latter merely serves to confirm its validity. As the three-stage theory is modelled on the history of Europe, the variations, deviations and exceptions are, naturally, observed in the main when it is applied to the history of the peoples of Asia, Africa and Latin America. In themselves, however, failures to conform to the European pattern of the sequence of three stages of class society are not of interest for our theme, although among them are found such fundamental differences as the slaveowning formation following instead of preceding the feudal one, or an uncanonic, i.e., non-European, interweaving (as, for example, in the Russian form of serfdom) of slaveowning and feudal relations, or absence altogether of one of the pre-capitalist formations (for example, a path of development in certain countries which omits the slaveowning stage), or movement towards post-class society without passing through the stage of capitalism, and so on.

Within the framework of the general process of world history there is, however, one phenomenon — with many variants, and yet basically homogeneous enough — which essentially refuses to fit into the three-stage pattern, however this may be varied. The phenomenon in question, this *social organism of a special kind*, cannot be reduced to an exception that proves the rule, owing to its deeply-penetrating importance for many aspects of life, its immense territorial extent and its continued existence over thousands of years. It cannot be treated as a deviation engendered by some accidental confluence of circumstances, owing to its systematic and regular nature. It certainly cannot be seen, from this standpoint, as something episodic and transient, but only as a major and prolonged *departure or diversion* from the natural course of the historical process. In short, the phenomenon referred to — mentioned earlier as the "Asiatic mode of production" — has its own definite *place in history*, in the many thousands of years that mankind has been in existence. What is this phenomenon, and what is its place?

The expression "Asiatic mode of production" was first used by Marx, in the middle of the 19th century, when the phenomenon was most fully known through its Asiatic variants. At that time Marx proposed that it be seen as an independent social formation which preceded the three class-divided formations (see his Preface to the *Contribution to the Critique of* Political Economy, 1859), assuming that its economic basis was primitive communism. This corresponded to Marx's view, established already long before, that in the communal system lay the origins of all mankind's subsequent development.[1] Survivals of this system were, let me repeat, first discovered only in Asiatic countries; but, as the decades passed, science brought forward ever new factual materials and theoretical arguments drawn no longer from the history of the Asiatic countries alone. On the one hand it has proved that the pre-class communal system existing in the countries of the "Asiatic mode of production" was everywhere associated with economic exploitation and political despotism, and consequently distorted by them, but that the shoots of class relations growing out of this situation were *not* the relations of the slaveowning formation. And, on the other hand, it was confirmed that the slaveowning formation — that is the chronologically first of the fully class-divided formations which had been known, described and sociologically analysed — had developed directly out of the break-up of the classless (pre-class) primitive-communal formation. Consequently, in the sequence of social formations there was no place left for the Asiatic mode of production — neither as a formation which, retaining a classless structure, could be seen as succeeding the primitive-communal one, nor as a formation which, possessing a class structure, could be seen as preceding the slaveowning one. And, gradually, the expression "Asiatic mode of production" vanished from scientific language and the terminology of Marx and Engels: we do not find it used even in a work specially devoted to the sources and the rise of class society, namely, *The Origins of the Family, Private Property and the State*. Nor did Lenin use this expression.*

But if the social organism which, more than a century ago, Marx called by the geographical (i.e., obviously provisional) term "the Asiatic mode of production" offers no grounds for our regarding it as a special independent social formation, what is it, then, in reality, and what place does it occupy in the actual course of mankind's historical process? The question is all the more important for our understanding of this process in that, as is becoming ever clearer, almost the majority of the countries of the world — in Asia, Africa, pre-Columbian America, even in parts of Europe — have passed through the stage of the "Asiatic mode of production" in some form or degree and during periods of varying length. However, the rebirth of interest in the problem of the "Asiatic mode of production" which has occurred in the 20th century, and has involved not only Marxists, has been evoked not by concern about the ancient paths of the human race, for their own sake, but by the traces (sometimes profound and deeply-rooted) which these ancient paths have left in the life of present-day mankind, the survivals from them, across the centuries and millennia, which have become lodged in the social order and structure of peoples contemporary with us, and which have continued to exist in one form or another in many corners, and often over wide areas, of our world. This interest has been not so much scientific as political.

Translator's note. The writer's statement that the expression "Asiatic mode of production" is not to be found in Lenin's writings is not correct. See *Collected Works*, 4th edition, English version, Vol. 10, p.332.

At the Stockholm Congress of the Russian Social-Democratic Labour Party, in 1906, Plekhanov had opposed Lenin on the question of whether a revolutionary government in Russia should nationalise the land. Plekhanov proposed, instead, that the land be "municipalised", since nationalisation would put too much power in the hands of the state and bring the danger of a re-establishment of the old autocracy in a new form. Lenin replied to this argument: "Insofar as (or if) the land was nationalised in Muscovy, the economic basis of this nationalisation was the *Asiatic mode of production* ... He [Plekhanov] confused nationalisation based on the Asiatic mode of production with nationalisation based on the capitalist mode of production.... The logical deduction from his premises is the restoration of the Asiatic mode of production — which is a sheer absurdity in the epoch of capitalism".

And when, in the second half of the 1920s, a discussion about the Asiatic mode of production flared up in the U.S.S.R., what lay behind this and motivated it were the concerns of the world socialist revolution[2] — problems of the utilising (or of the paralysing) of pre-capitalist structures and relations in the socialist struggle against capitalism. In this discussion there participated historians, sociologists, economists, orientalists and professional politicians. The Asiatic mode of production was talked about at the Congress of the C.P.S.U.(B.) (see *XV s'ezd VKP(b). Stenografich. otchet (15th Congress of the C.P.S.U.(B.) Stenographic report)*, Vol. I, Moscow, 1961, pp.733, 805-806, 839-840). The "Asiatic mode of production" appeared in the Programme of the Communist International adopted at its Sixth Congress in 1928 (section IV, sub-section 8). But in 1931 the discussion was suddenly cut short by intervention from above, before it had reached any conclusion. Stalin's ideological regime could not permit any broad and even moderately independent examination of problems which had been placed within the competence of the Party apparatus. Besides, as the discussion developed, bringing to the forefront the barbarously oppressive and despotic aspects of the societies of the Asiatic mode of production, parallels and similarities had increasingly suggested themselves between these societies and the society which our country, led by Stalin, had begun to build under the name and using the phraseology of socialism — parallels and similarities which were not only disturbing but, objectively speaking, also quite natural and explicable, even though they had (as we shall see) nothing to do with the essence of the subject under discussion.

In any case, discussion of the Asiatic mode of production was suspended for a long time, and only the thaw following the 20th Party Congress enabled it to be revived. The tremendous changes brought about in the political map of the world by World War II (the collapse of the colonial empires, the winning of independence by the so-called "underdeveloped countries", China's entry on the path of advance to socialism, the formation of "neo-colonialism" and the struggle against it, and so on) placed in a new and considerably wider and more complex world context the problem of the Asiatic mode of production. It was characteristic of the new situation that those who were the first to revive the discussion were not Soviet Communists but Communists of the Western countries. But after there had appeared in Moscow in 1964 a book by a participant in the earlier discussion, E. Varga, containing a special chapter on the Asiatic mode of production (*Politico-economic Problems of Capitalism*), and after a number of foreign writers had sent their studies of the question direct to Soviet scholars, the latter, too, joined in this discussion which had been interrupted for a third of a century. A discussion in many languages — participating in it were not only Europeans but also scholars from Japan, China, India, Vietnam, Mexico, Venezuela, etc. — took place in the mid-1960s and early 1970s, and assumed not only sharper political accents but also a more cultivated theoretical tone than the earlier one. There was spread out before us a whole spectrum of conceptions of the Asiatic mode of production. Some saw in it an independent social formation, supplementing the sequence of the already known and hitherto unquestioned formations. Some identified it with one or other of these formations. Some regarded it as a *phase* of one or other of these formations. Some saw it as replacing, in certain countries, one or other of them. Some introduced the conception of a "transitional formation", and assigned the Asiatic mode of production to this category. Some declined to grant it independence in any sense, considering it to be an intermingling, or mixture, and so a hybrid of two or more formations. And there were other conceptions which were made up of fragments of the conceptions already listed. All these speculative and to a large extent scholastic "nuances" are of no interest in relation to my present subject[3], but there did emerge from the disputes a real *picture of societies* based upon a mode of production which it has now become the accepted practice to call "Asiatic" — and this is just what is relevant to our theme. Let us look at the features which are *typical* of such a society (although, of course, with a lot of variations and gradations.)

(i) At a certain stage of biological overpopulation, there arose in pastoral and agricultural communities of the primitive classless formation an obstacle to their continued existence, in the form of inadequacy in the amount of land suitable for agriculture and stockraising under the climatic conditions and with the water supply with which nature had endowed their territories. The necessary condition for maintaining primitive-communal life which naturally suggested itself, and which was at the same time realisable, given the abundance of labour-power, was artificial irrigation (a system of reservoirs and canals), a system of storing grain against the possibility of years of harvest-failure or natural calamities, and also the building of roads.

(ii) The establishment and maintenance of artificial irrigation systems and the building of storehouses and roads required the mobilisation of great masses of people for compulsory public works (and, in any case, for work that was rewarded by an allowance in kind), the application of considerable technical and material resources, organisation and supervision of the whole task on the scale not of one or a few neighbouring communities but of an entire state. And this naturally led to the establishment of state ownership of the land and of the irrigation and storage installations, and to the circumstance that private property in land did not arise even in its feudal form. Thus, in these centralised societies and states the system of village communes was retained, as their unchanging basis, in *de facto* and hereditary possession of lands belonging to the state — communes which were closed in and isolated from each other, maintaining a patriarchal structure, little economic worlds-in-themselves, in which a primitive division of labour became more or less petrified, over centuries and millennia, into caste distinctions and domestic slavery.

(iii) The state power was thus by the nature of things invested in these societies with the monopoly of fulfilment of those functions which were necessary for the economic life and for the defence of the communes, and which were common and uniform for all, and its sovereignty was based, in one form or another, on the right to be the supreme and unique owner of land. Being, consequently, united with society in a single principle, the state bore here the character and form of a despotism which carried out its economic functions by methods of extra-economic compulsion, that is, relying on political relations of dependence. And this unlimited power over the people's labour enabled the despotism to exploit it not only for the serving of vital economic needs but also for the construction of buildings which multiplied the despotism's terrifying military and political might, and of other buildings which, by their giant size and stupendous luxury, or by their religious functions and mystical aspect, served to inspire the people with admiration and awe in face of the omnipotence and majesty of the ruling despotism. Reproducing itself, century after century, millennium after millennium, all this made of the contrast between the state and the mass of the people a religious mystery not to be questioned and a natural condition of affairs which it was both blasphemous and senseless to try and alter.

(iv) This Oriental despotism was implemented through a bureaucracy, and the independent position of public offices in relation to society inevitably led to the bureaucracy raising itself up and ruling over the people, from society's servant becoming society's master (as priests, *literati*, etc.). Master meant also exploiter of society: the bureaucracy lived on the surplus product of the people's labour. This surplus product was taken by the bureaucracy in the name of the state, which was simultaneously landowner and sovereign, and from the economic standpoint it was ground-rent; but since it was extracted by means of a fiscal apparatus, this was rent of a special kind — "tax-rent", as Marx called it. If to this be added the exploitation of slaves, recruited from captive aliens, we have before us a primary process of the transformation of the servant of society into the master of society, and then the welding of many individual persons in authority into an internally-linked ruling social stratum. This could be called a rudimentary form of state power and, along with that, a rudimentary form of the division of society into classes. Here the state was directly counterposed to the immediate producers, and the state machine was as yet not differentiated from the ruling class, not separated off from it as a formally-independent formation, as the executive committee of this class, expressing, organising and realising its class interests. The bureaucracy which constituted the state machine here still directly *was* itself the ruling class. But while the "state-class" and the "commune-class" and the relations between them can be regarded as rudimentary forms of class society, this is true only in a conditional sense, or, more precisely, in the sense that they were not genuinely but *unnaturally* rudimentary forms. What we have here, strictly speaking, are functional classes without a strictly defined antagonism between exploiters and exploited, and, moreover, classes which exist outside of relations of private ownership (without which genuine classes are not only impossible in reality but even inconceivable), and without property-differences within each of them. Not for nothing do Marx, Engels and Lenin refrain from using the word "classes" when speaking about societies in which they see present the Asiatic mode of production. Instead, we find Marx using, in relation to the Asiatic mode of production, the expression "universal slavery."

(v) And, finally, the durability, the exclusiveness, the disconnectedness, the "self-sufficient inertia" of the economic basis of society, the village communes inherited by the Asiatic mode of production from the primitive communal-clan system which immediately preceded it, with their inherent low standard of living and the tortoise-paced development of the "hereditary divisions of labour", created "immobility of the social basis while there was ceaseless change in the individuals and tribes who wielded the political superstructure" ... "petrified social life" ... "living petrifaction." And "what we call its history is but the history of the successive intruders who founded their empires on the passive basis of that unresisting and unchanging society." (The words in quotation-marks are taken from Marx's articles "The Future Results of the British Rule in India", 1853, and "Chinese Affairs", 1862 [i.e., *"Chinesisches"*, in *Die Presse*, Vienna, 7 July 1862 — Trans.]) And only after private property has invaded the village commune and begun to distintegrate it, at the same time putting an end to its passivity in relation to the state, only then does the stagnation characteristic of this state system of self-sufficient communes come to an end, only then is the road opened for the real history of society.

This picture is *typical* of the society formed on the basis of the mode of production usually called "Asiatic" by present-day Communists (though, of course, it does not always and everywhere fully correspond to that society). Earlier I listed some of the varying interpretations of the nature of this society put forward in the discussions which developed in Communist circles in connexion with the problem of utilising or paralysing the survivals of the Asiatic mode of production in certain countries during their advance towards socialism. One may add the views of some important bourgeois scholars, considered as classics, such as, for example, Max Weber, Eduard Meyer and M. Rostovtzeff, who interpreted a society of this kind — the first by analogy with slaveowning society, the second by analogy with feudalism, and the third by analogy with capitalism. Not so long ago, the sinologist Karl Wittfogel, who began his scholarly career in the Communist movement but later broke away from it, interpreted Stalin's "socialism" by analogy with the "Oriental despotism" of ancient times.[4] And in our own day I.R. Shafarevich has directly identified each and every form of socialism — the very nature of socialism, so to speak — with despotism of the type found in connexion with the Asiatic mode of production.[5].

But none of these artificial and almost always one-sided and to a considerable extent preconceived notions, which intersect and mingle in academic discussions, are of help in answering the *only* question which interests us for the purpose of the present note, where the Asiatic mode of production is concerned, namely, the question of the *place* of this mode of production *in the history and development of mankind as a whole*. Rather do they obscure the question itself, diluting it with details and sub-problems which are of only local significance (in space and time), and thereby removing it from the *larger context* of the world process of human history. I propose, therefore, to develop my consideration of the place in history of the societies of the so-called Asiatic mode of production, not by comparing the different conceptions discussed, but by starting from the typical picture of a society of this kind which I presented earlier on. What does this picture tell us?

The Asiatic mode of production arose out of the disintegration of the primitive clan commune which knew neither classes nor the state, in times when this disintegration had already been prepared by thousands of years of previous development of human life, and when it had become necessary for the further development of this life. But it arose there, and only there, where this inevitable disintegration could not, owing to the empirically given conditions of human existence, take the *natural* path of break-up of the patriarchal village commune and formation of the first great division of society into classes — into slaveowners and slaves. However extensive the territory that the Asiatic mode of production united into a single society-state, and however long the periods that it lasted on these territories, it does not belong among the naturally and logically necessary and consecutive links in the chain of socio-economic formations which constitute the progressive development of mankind.[6] Nowhere and never was it a special and independent social formation, or a variation or gradation of the slaveowning or feudal formation, and still less of the capitalist formation, or a preparatory or preliminary or undeveloped stage of one or other of these, or of any combination of them. Those empirically-given conditions which in many parts of our planet and over long period of time gave rise to the Asiatic mode of production, and thereby interrupted and distorted the natural course of the historical process, are usually called geographical conditions. Such indeed they were, in the direct sense, and as such they blocked man's path in those early times of civilisation when naturally existing productive forces prevailed over those which were created by human hands and human intelligence. But for each given social organism they were *historical* preconditions and formed the basis of its *historical* development. And the crux of the matter is that in the economic structure and social relations of such societies there were unnaturally mingled and interwoven, distorting each other and in distorted form supporting and stabilising each other, *two lines along which history could have advanced*. These were, on the one hand, the line of patriarchal authoritarianism, exclusiveness and immobility, which constitutes the necessary and unchanging basis and source of nourishment of the Asiatic mode of production, wherever and for however long it has existed, and which it has adapted to the requirements of its despotic state: and, on the other hand, the line which was demanded and engendered by the progress of the productive forces and of civilisation, and which only the slaveowning and, subsequently, the feudal formations were capable of realising in adequate form and in the spontaneous process of economic development. But wherever, in consequence of actual historical circumstances such as have been described above, the Asiatic mode of production undertook to follow this second line, then, utilising its despotic state, with its system of political coercion and extra-economic compulsion and combining this with the patriarchalism of the village commune, which it retained and consolidated in a distorted form, it distorted and adapted to itself also the relations of slavery and serfdom which, having been prepared by history, inevitably made their appearance. And so, entering as assimilated and subordinate elements into the structure of the Asiatic mode of production, these relations lost their content and historical significance as expressions and driving forces of social progress.

Not being a necessary stage through which human society had to pass in its progressive development, but merely a local, even though extremely widespread, distortion of this development, the Asiatic mode of production showed itself very stable and enduring — and this, moreover, over extensive and populous areas of the globe. Having appeared in history *before* the slaveowning formation arose in Europe, it outlasted not only that formation but also the feudal one which succeeded it. But this was the stability and endurance of inertia and stagnation. To be sure, on the political surfaces of these Eastern societies stormy and bloody changes of rulers and of whole dynasties, and even of state-formations, took place, but these were, as Marx called them, only sterile movements. Periods of growth of the productive forces alternated with periods in which they were destroyed and fell into decay. But the mode of production, essentially mule-like in character, remained in principle and in practice unchanged for thousands of years, with as its foundation not only the economic functions performed by the despotism, and not only this despotism's apparatus of political power, but also the numerous regularities and traditions — economic, legal, and in the sphere of everyday life — which had taken shape and become rooted in the course of many generations, and in addition, of course, the ideology of a social order which had existed from all eternity, the religious ideology of submission and obedience.

And here we come to the point which for us, people living at the end of the 20th century, the century which has seen the beginning of man's transition from class to classless society, from capitalism to socialism, constitutes our main interest in giving attention to the ancient times of the Asiatic mode of production. What I have in mind is this. The stagnant character of the society of the Asiatic mode of production means that a society of that sort does not grow into anything, and leads nowhere. It possesses neither laws of development nor social forces that could take it out of the limits which fetter it, enabling it to advance to a higher stage of society. Its history is pseudo-history, or, to employ Hegel's expression, "unhistorical history." In short, its development gets stuck in a blind alley of stagnation. And the Asiatic mode of production does not possess the capacity to lead society out of this blind alley. Consequently, looking at the matter theoretically, the only possible way of opening up a prospect of progressive development for society, is in such a case, to liberate it from the Asiatic mode of production and set it on the path of history, replacing the Asiatic mode of production by the slaveowning or the feudal formation, followed by the capitalist formation. If this is not done, then, sooner or later, the social organism is doomed to decay and ruin. And the actual course of history confirms this theoretical notion: in ancient Egypt the Asiatic mode of production gave way to the slave system, in pre-Columbian America it was replaced by early capitalism, in Persia, India and China by feudalism together with capitalism, while the ancient kingdoms of Assyria and Babylon perished one after the other in blood and destruction, rendered helpless by centuries of ceaseless marking-time under the wasteful Asiatic mode of production.

Thus, in the end, history's great plan is realised, which can be postponed for particular social organisms — even very big ones, and for a very long time — but cannot be abrogated. What forces turned these societies out of the blind-alley zigzag of the Asiatic mode of production (if they did not perish in that zigzag) on to the main road of history, thereby shifting them out of their immobility and giving them a stimulus to go forward in the direction of historical progress? These forces could not be economic laws and tendencies engendered within the societies in question, immanent in the Asiatic mode of production, for such forces simply did not exist. They could not be, either, popular movements conscious of a decisive historical task to be performed, and waging a victorious struggle to perform it: given the elemental course of the historical process in those days, movements of that sort could not arise from within the depths and inside the framework of the Asiatic mode of production. They could only be forces coming *from without*. And history set these forces to work, so as to cut off the road, leading nowhere, of the Asiatic mode of production, and thus straighten out the path of human progress. Rome brought slavery to Egypt; the Turks introduced into the countries of Hither Asia which they conquered "a sort of feudal ownership of land" (Engels's expression); in India and China the latent and mutilated potentialities of feudalism were unleashed by the colonialist eruption of European capitalism, both bloody and peaceful, commercial and ideological ...

Summing up now the results of our excursion into the Asiatic mode of production, we see that both discussions, the one in the 1920s and the one in the 1960s, were focused on the problems of the strategy and tactics of a non-capitalist development towards socialism in the colonial and semi-colonial countries — and, therefore, not so much on ascertaining the place in history of the Asiatic mode of production itself, and the ways of escape from it exemplified by history, as on revealing the survivals of this mode of production that were still present in our time, their condition and tendencies. In following this line the discussions were, it must be supposed, not without their value. But this meant that the discussions avoided the problems in which lie hidden the historical and theoretical explanation of this instructive phenomenon in the social development of mankind — instructive not only for understanding those survivals from grey antiquity which are scattered over the face of the earth in the 20th century, and the problems to which such survivals give rise, but also for understanding the 20th century's own problems, and, above all, the most topical and acute of these problems, namely, that of the present-day society of so-called "complete socialism." The discussions avoided this question because from the very start, and throughout, they took place within the ideological and administrative-political setting of Stalinism and neo-Stalinism, and so could not but avoid it. Operating here was not only that *immediate* cause mentioned above, namely the embarrassing similarities which leapt to the eye between the social structure and usages of the society of

Stalin's "complete socialism" and the societies of the Asiatic mode of production. Many of these similarities are, of course, not accidental, and they call for explanation: explanatidn, let it be emphasised, and not those merely outward comparisons, stressed for effect, but without analysis or proof, beyond which, for example, Wittfogel and Shafarevich are incapable of taking the matter. But, however numerous these similarities may be, it was not for their sake that I invited the reader to make this excursion. *The main point does not lie there*: it is hidden in the depths of the socio-historical process of mankind and has hardly ever entered the minds of the Stalinists. The main point is the light that the place occupied by the Asiatic mode of production in man's historical transition from classless (pre-class) to class formations throws upon the place occupied by Stalin's "complete socialism" (and its continuation, the neo-Stalinists' "developed socialism") in the historical transition from class formations to a classless (post-class) formation. And also the light that the ancient problems of getting out of the blind alley of the Asiatic mode of production throw upon today's problems of escaping from the blind alley of Stalinist "complete" and "developed socialism." It is to this main question that I now wish to direct the reader's attention.

3. A hypothesis concerning the place in history of Stalin's society of "complete socialism" (and the neo-Stalinists' "developed socialism")[7]

What can our excursion among the débris of the history of the Asiatic mode of production teach us in this connexion?

First, that in certain countries some empirical circumstances, which prove decisive in the given cases, can divert the course of history even from such important and theoretically obligatory lines of progressive development as the law-governed sequence of socio-economic formations.

Secondly, that as a result of such a diversion, there may be formed a peculiar mode of production which is neither one thing nor the other, corresponding to none of the stages of the sequence of social formations and not being transitional towards any of them. This mode of production does not permit free and rational social progress, and takes society into a blind alley of stagnation. In its stagnation, however, lying to one side of the main road of history, it is capable of stable and enduring existence, even when acute, destructive and devastating political upheavals and revolutions take place within it.

Thirdly, that, since this mode of production lacks internal forces for regeneration in the direction of progress and self-movement, and, consequently, for rescuing society from the blind alley and returning it to the main road, and since it is incapable of engendering such forces within itself, then either this mode of production leads society to eventual destruction, or else external forces liquidate this unnatural system, by one means or another, and in this way open up the road to law-governed historical progress for the given society.

Fourthly, that actual history has known a situation, during the transition from pre-class to class-divided socio-economic formations, when the Asiatic mode of production took shape and was consolidated on huge territories and for very long periods of time.

And, fifthly, that this happened in those parts of the world which, owing to certain confluences of historical circumstances, were chronologically the first to face the task of transcending the limitations of the clan system and going over to a class structure of society. History had, so to speak, no experience of a transition like this, and at the outset it created a mongrel and freakish social formation, in which the village commune of the clan period was retained while elements of slaveowning and serfdom relations came into being — neither of them corresponding to their essential nature, but in distorted form. When, subsequently (and, with the extremely slow course of the historical process in those days, these intervals of time were measured in millennia), the European countries took the road of forming class-divided societies, *they* moved along this road in accordance with the natural, progressive sequence of socio-economic formations — slaveowning, feudal, capitalist.

And now I will put forward my sociological hypothesis, if I may so describe it.

Just as happened in the great change in man's history from pre-class to class society, so in the great change from class to classless society, in the countries in which the change began it was accomplished with a violation of the natural course of the maturation of a new socio-economic formation, prepared by the historical progress of mankind. This violation was expressed in a radical distortion of this formation and in the establishment, *instead of it*, of a social order which, though stable, led nowhere in its growth and development and was in this sense stagnant, a social order which thrust society into a blind alley and which had to be eliminated if the road was to be opened for the natural succession of socio-economic formations required by historical progress. And to the place which in the age of the first change was occupied by the Asiatic mode of production there corresponds, in the present age of history's second great change, the place occupied by the society of Stalin's "complete socialism", which has spread over one-sixth of the globe and with some variations of minor significance has been extended to several other countries.

This hypothesis has, of course, two aspects.

First, it states that in its economic (and so also in its legal and political) structure the society of Stalin's "complete socialism" is not capitalist, nor is it socialist, nor is it transitional — either from capitalism to socialism or from socialism to capitalism.

It is not a capitalist economic order, either of the free-competition variant of capitalism or of the monopoly (including state, or state-monopoly) variant. There is no ownership of the means of production by a class of capitalists, no division into two main and opposed classes — the capitalists, living on surplus value, and the proletarians, living on wages. In this society private ownership of personal property is prevented from becoming transformed into ownership of means of production, and thus into capital. In this society there is no payment of wage workers according to the value of their labour power. Profit is not the stimulus and driving force of production, and the course, co-ordination and development of production is neither directly nor indirectly governed by market relations and objectively-operating value-mechanisms. Consequently, this society is free from the irrationality, waste and cruelty of economic individualism and the system of competition; but, at the same time, it lacks the efficiency, rationality and flexibility and the constantly advancing and (as Marx puts it) revolutionising technical and organisational innovation which are contributed to the production process by the capitalist striving for profit under conditions of ruthless competition.

Yet the social order established in the Soviet Union is not a socialist order — not socialism as the first phase of the communist formation, and not a form of society moving towards such genuine socialism. In these times when the world is overcrowded with all sorts of false definitions and interpretations of socialism and of the road to socialism, both among persons who consider themselves to be in the socialist camp and among those who reject and oppose socialism, it may, perhaps, be appropriate to ask the reader to consider this point in rather more detail.

So then, the economic structure of the U.S.S.R. today is not socialist. The social order is not based on an absence of classes: on the contrary, official recognition is given to the existence of three classes — the workers, the peasants and the intelligentsia (though the term "class" is not applied to the last-named of these). In this society the workers are not paid according to the socialist principle of payment for quantity of labour but according to the anti-socialist principle of payment for quantity *and* so-called "quality" of labour, and consequently there is not and cannot be socialist economic equality in this society. On the contrary, economic inequality constitutes here the basis and law of human relations — it dictates the prevailing ideals of life, interests and aspirations, principles of conduct and ways of estimating men's worth. And this ladder of economic inequality is set up, shaped and strengthened through encouraging and disseminating private property, the accumulation of which is subject to no limits and which can be passed on by inheritance. The contradiction between the social character of production and the private-property form under which objects and means of consumption are appropriated and accumulated is one of the central contradictions of this society. Public ownership of the means of production, which in this society exists in the form of state ownership, is organised and conducted in such a way that between it and the people, who are treated in the Constitution as the owners, there stands a numerous class-like social stratum of state and quasi-state agents. This stratum is not officially recognised as being a class, or quasi-class, but, possessing as it does the monopoly of power to dispose of the means of production, it appropriates, through the system of payment in accordance with quantity and "quality" of labour, part of the labour of the rest of the population, and in this way raises itself economically above them. For here there does not obtain that essential requirement of socialism, namely, that not a single state official, including those holding the highest posts, should receive an income exceeding the average wage of a good worker. In this society labour-power is a commodity (even though not paid in accordance with its value), and this determines the ways in which it enters into the production process and in which production is managed — ways that are such that socialist labour-incentives, socialist collective labour, and workers' self-management in joint labour find no place in the enterprise and are unable to reveal their productive potentialities. As for the economy as a whole, the socialisation of production is here effected in such a way that those mechanisms of economic planning and management which under socialism take the place of value and market mechanisms, and which are based on economic equality both horizontal and vertical, on full control both from above and from below, and on the participation of the masses in the taking of decisions, do not exist. The masses are here kept out of the work of planning socialised production and its management, and, above all, kept out of the taking of decisions. All *that* goes on in privacy, concentrated within the ponderous bureaucratic pyramid of the state apparatus (the Party apparatus being the hierarchical axis of this pyramid, constructed according to the system whereby Party bodies at different levels nominate the staffs of Government bodies at corresponding levels); and, by methods of administrative manipulation, secrecy and misinformation, this apparatus exercises compulsion both economic and extra-economic upon the working people. Society is deprived of the internal mechanisms which could naturally and freely control, correct, and, when necessary, replace this pyramid of power which is counterposed to it.

But neither is this society in transition from capitalism to socialism. To be so, to be a society developing and "growing-over" into socialism, as the first phase of communism, its development and "growing-over", and the results of these processes, would necessarily have to conform to the following requirements.

(a) Public ownership of the means of production and socialisation of production must be realised on the basis of organisation, planning and management of production such that the disposition of the means of production (and control over this) is effected through a combination of centralised public administration with self-management by the producers' collectives themselves. Production-relations must be formed on the basis of the gradual elimination of classes and class differences inherited from capitalism, with prevention of the formation of new classes (or of a new variant of the previously existing ones). First and foremost, it must not be permitted that the individuals standing at the helm of management of the publicly-owned means of production become a class-like social stratum, in privileged receipt of the products of this production: the work of guiding social production must not be allowed to become transformed into any form or degree of exploitation of the labour of the direct producers.

(b) There must be a continually closer approach to the socialist principle of payment of labour in accordance with its quantity, that is, taking account only of the time and intensity of the expenditure of labour, and ignoring the level of qualification involved. On this basis: (i) ever closer approximation to the economic equality between members of society which is theoretically achievable in the first stage of communism; (ii) continual raising of the productivity of labour by non-capitalist methods, that is, by developing and introducing a socialist conception of labour and attitude to labour, a socialist culture of labour; and (iii) bringing physical and mental labour, the production-worker and the intellectual worker, closer and closer to each other.

(c) Not only exclusion of the possibility of enrichment through exploitation of hired or forced labour, but also (in order to safeguard material equality, to the extent that this can be created by the socialist system of payment of labour in accordance with its quantity), refusal to permit such other ways of acquiring private property (or private control of property) as allowing particular individuals privileged control of real estate, material goods or sums of money, special-access stores and shops, so-called representation expenses, and so on; and also gradual abolition of the right to inherit *anything*, including goods obtained through labour. A policy aimed at ensuring that inequality of status between members of society (differences in their social position and importance) should not bring with it material inequality between these persons — that it should neither be based on material inequality, nor confirmed or demonstrated by such inequality.

(d) A policy aimed at increasingly emancipating the economic process and the whole of social life, and all life lived in society, from the principles, laws and norms of commodity economy. Increasing restriction of the function and role of money and shrinkage of the sphere of money-circulation and money-relations, both in the economic relations of society as a whole and in relations between society and individual citizens and between the citizens themselves.

(e) Movement in the direction of the dying-out of the state, and consequently, of the role of political parties in society (in a one-party state, of the role of this single party). After liquidation of the pre-socialist bureaucratic state machine, refusal to allow the formation of a new hierarchically-differentiated ruling social stratum of permanent (professional) officials, separated and isolated from the people, raised above the people, and concentrating in their hands, as a monopoly, the apparatus and organs of state power over the people. Gradual transference of the work of administration by the state and of control over the administration and the judiciary, at every level and in all departments, to the broad masses of the people, through their increasing participation in the preparing and adoption (and not only fulfilment, on orders from above) of political, economic, administrative and other decisions. As the first condition and principal lever of this transference — complete publicity and freedom of criticism in relation to every form of authority, from the bottom to the top, and the right publicly to demand changes and replacements in these authorities.

(f) Refusal to permit violation by the organs of state power of the constitutional rights and individual lives of citizens, including the right to choose one's place of residence, and also the right to go abroad and to return to one's own country. Removal from the competence of the state power of the task of safeguarding socialist morality and, in general, exclusion from the competence of the organs of state of all judgment and decision on moral questions.

(g) Refusal to allow the idea of communism to be transformed, by means of an army of special "ideological cadres", paid by the state, into a compulsorily-disseminated ideology enjoying a monopoly, and obligatory upon all citizens — and refusal to allow the battle of ideas for communism to degenerate into a system of state "ideological" (and then administrative and judicial) persecution of "dissenters."

(h) Freedom of scientific and artistic creation, including the possibility of publication of their results without censorship, freedom of intellectual life, access to sources of information (including foreign sources, and also records), and freedom of ethical (including religious) beliefs.

(i) Full equality in mutual relations and rights for citizens of all nationalities and ethnic groups in the country, and refusal to allow any discrimination or privilege based on national distinctions.

(j) Taking account of the physical and biological differences between the sexes, solution of the task of establishing *de facto* equality between the female and male halves of the human race in their civil, economic and domestic situations and in their opportunities for participating in the country's social and spiritual life.

(k) Replacement of universal military service by universal military training. Refusal to allow the cadres of organisers, trainers and commanders of the armed forces to be transformed into a military caste.

(l) Orientation of the country's international policy otherwise than in accordance with the interests and pre-socialist prejudices and traditions of one's nationally-conceived state and subordination to nationally-limited ambitions and pretensions — whether in a spirit of self-isolation or in one of great-power aspirations, or in any other spirit of exceptionalism. Elaboration and consistent implementation of a foreign policy that renounces every inheritance of national limitedness, and sees itself as representing and participating in the world-wide movement of mankind towards socialism — in relations with capitalist states and likewise with countries seeking the socialist path.

These are the most important constituent features of a society which is advancing towards socialism, as the first phase of communism. They could, of course, be enumerated and arranged in a different way, and additions could be made to the list, but there is, in any case, no room for doubt: without and apart from these features, the advance towards socialism and the attainment of socialism are unrealisable and unthinkable. In different internal and external conditions, prepared by history, and in different empirically-given (economic and national-psychological) circumstances, the concrete forms and ways of implementing these necessary features of the advance toward socialism, as the first phase of Communism, will vary. But Stalin's road of "complete socialism" has nothing to do with this natural and inevitable plurality in the roads to socialism. I set out earlier a factual description of the economic structure and line of development of Soviet society. It is enough to compare with it just one of the economic indications of advance towards socialism given in my list (the reader will easily extend this comparison to the distinguishing features of the political and spiritual life of Soviet society), to see that Stalin's "complete socialism", as built in our country, is not the first stage of the communist social formation, or any advance towards it. But this comparison also shows that its neo-Stalinist continuation, the so-called "developed socialism" of the last two decades, has failed to eliminate even one of the cardinal differences between our society and genuine socialism. On the contrary, these differences have undergone increasing consolidation and, ossifying, have become to an ever greater degree constituent, organic features and relations of the Soviet social system, within the framework of which and by means of which its expanded reproduction proceeds. And this means that the system *per se*, by virtue of its inherent economic and social laws, is not leading to socialism.

If this is so — and it is — then the question naturally arises: is it leading to capitalism, to a capitalist restoration? No, life and theoretical considerations alike return a negative answer to this question. In order to grow and develop in the quantitative limits and qualitative forms required for it to survive, this society does not need to re-establish those fundamental economic relations the absence of which marks it off from capitalism — capitalist production-relations and capitalist private ownership of the means of production. Left to itself, to the inertia of its own economic laws and social foundations, this society is incapable, moreover, of acting to bring about such a restoration.

And so, let me repeat, the society of Stalin's so-called "complete socialism" is neither capitalist nor socialist, nor is it in transition from capitalism to socialism, or *vice versa*. Yet it is a quite well-defined society, unlike any other known to history or described theoretically. During the half-century it has existed, regularity and perfection of form have been acquired not only by its economic structure and economic practices, its class relations, political and state system, legal norms, military machine, principles and methods in dealings with other states, and not only by the objective laws and tendencies which operate in all of these spheres, but also by the moral outlook of its people and both of the ideologies — everyday popular thinking and the official apologia. This is, then, a settled and stable society. But at the same time, it is, *in the historical sense*, a stagnant society, and its stability is the stability of stagnation. This statement is true in two ways. First, as regards the quantitative, so-to-speak purely economic, aspect, the growth attainable by the society of Stalin's "complete socialism" falls short of the possibilities available to present-day mankind and realisable under other social systems — not only the socialism of the future but the capitalism of the present. To speak in concrete terms: in level and pace, and in rationality and efficiency, and in the material, domestic improvement of everyday life, this growth fails, to a greater or lesser extent, to measure up to what could be provided by the first phase of communism or to what is actually provided by contemporary capitalism. And, *secondly*, from the qualitative standpoint, that is, where the forms of social life are concerned (including social psychology and the forms of intellectual and moral life), growth is not accompanied by development: this social order is leading nowhere and, while maintaining itself in being, is capable only of marking time. The prospect of an historical way forward is offered not by this society itself, its self-preservation which is incapable of self-modification, but only by the liquidation of this society, the abolition of the fetters and forces of stagnation which are inherent in it.

That is *one aspect of my hypothesis*. Proceeding from history's lesson of the forming and thousands-of-years'-long existence of the Asiatic mode of production, at the turning-point from a pre-class to a class structure of society, it points to the *possibility* of a stable and enduring diversion from the historically natural sequence of socio-economic formations also at the turning-point from a class to a classless structure of society — a diversion which by its very basis deforms the socialist order which is historically due to arrive, and shunts society's development into a blind alley. My hypothesis sees in Stalin's "complete socialism" the realisation of that possibility. By being realised, of course, a possibility proves that it was objectively determined, and so was in that sense "necessary" — but not necessarily that it was the only possible "necessity", that it was *inevitable*. Living history includes not only what was accomplished but also what might have been accomplished. And this is where the *second* aspect of my hypothesis appears, proceeding from the differences of principle between the epoch of transition from classless to class society and the epoch of transition from class to classless society. These differences are three in number.

First, the transition from class to classless society is taking place in an age when there has been formed — or, to speak more concretely, when capitalism in its imperialist stage has created — *the unity of mankind*, embracing the entire globe, with a world economy, a world culture, world-wide communications and interdependence, and world-scale social problems. Mankind today pursues a line of world-historical development which is uniform for all its sections, and has a common destiny, but it is still divided politically into separate territorial states at varying levels of economic, social and cultural development. We have seen that, where the transition from pre-class to class society was concerned, its initiation, taking place in one or other of numerous human communities scattered over the surface of the planet, could be and actually was an isolated phenomenon, caused by local conditions and, generally speaking, without significance for the course of development of other, contemporary communities. Where the transition from class to classless society is concerned, however, it is a different matter. Here the beginning of the transition, in the country in which history decided this should take place, could not be other than a phenomenon within a unified world system, *immediately* opening the way for a transition of the *entire* system to a classless structure of society, and by definition orientated towards a world-wide system, and having therein its actual significance. The

October Revolution in Russia was, in fact, a beginning *of this kind.* While the very fact that this beginning, made in our country, was conditioned by its special circumstances (a medium-weak link in the world chain of capitalism), the direction and type of historical development opened up by this beginning was determined not by the local conditions of our country but by "the general line of development of world history", "the general line of world development"; and the local, Russian circumstances determined only "details" and "certain amendments (quite insignificant from the standpoint of the general development of world history)"[8] Lenin understood as a phenomenon of world history (and not merely of Russian history), as the beginning of the world socialist revolution, the October revolution which he conceived and organised, and it was so understood by our Russian working class which carried it through, and by the whole world Communist movement which aligned itself upon this revolution.

Secondly, transition from a class to a classless structure of society is taking place in a period when, owing to the real unity of world history, there is an all-embracing breadth and intensity of contacts and connexions between the different countries, when the influence of the course of development of some countries upon that of others has assumed decisive importance, when this reciprocal influence, together with the high level and impetuous progress of science and technique is steadily revolutionising all conditions and aspects of human life, and when ever fresh hundreds of millions of people in more and more new countries are being drawn into the world current of civilisation. In an epoch such as this, owing to all these factors and the other circumstances bound up with them,[9] the pace of the historical process increases tremendously[10] and the intervals between social changes become shorter and shorter. Nowadays it is impossible for a situation to occur such as was natural in the age of transition from pre-class to class society, when one country could maintain inviolable for centuries and millennia the foundations of its social order, walled off from the changes going on in the rest of the world, even in neighbouring areas, and experiencing no influence from outside. Such self-isolation can now be kept up only for incomparably shorter periods of time.

Thirdly, the mechanism of the historical process in mankind's transition from a class to a classless order is radically different from that which prevailed in the epoch of the transition from pre-class to class society. It was then an entirely spontaneous mechanism; social phenomena were directly intertwined with the

139

elemental processes of nature, through the biological rhythm of the life of the primitive human masses, through the preponderant role of the productive forces provided by nature (and not made by man), and through the dehumanisation of human labour and the social relations of ignorance and cruelty characteristic of the exploiting upper stratum that was beginning to emerge. The forces of social necessity operated then as a factor and mechanism of nature, and not as the conscious creativity of the masses; the latter were only objects of the historical process. Today, in the transition from a class to a classless social structure, the decisive role in the implementation of historical necessity is played not by the elemental effect of an unconscious process but by the reasoning power of the revolutionary consciousness of the masses — more concretely, that of the working class, which strives towards a classless society as its conscious aim, and of the political parties which have expressed and given form to this consciousness. And this consciousness is tested, clarified, armed and organised by the science of the paths and laws of social development, the science of Marxism. In short, the million-fold masses must become the *subject* of social creativity, and science, scientific politics, scientific direction of the historical process must become the weapon of these masses, in order to carry through the transition from a class to a classless social order.

We have seen that the Asiatic mode of production was incapable of engendering within itself the social forces that could have liquidated it, so that only the intervention of external forces, acting in a spontaneous way, succeeded in turning the given society on to the road of historical progress. But the socially stagnant system of Stalin's "complete socialism" has arisen and exists in an epoch when the world-wide transition to classless society has fully matured and is ready to happen, and when it is the conscious task of the masses to make this happen. For this reason the liquidation of Stalin's "complete socialism" can be accomplished as an act of self-liquidation. It would, of course, be imprudent to assume that a *regressive* self-liquidation of Stalin's "complete socialism" is absolutely out of the question in our country, that is, a self-liquidation that would lead to the restoration of capitalism in some form or other. But the age in which we live, when the world process of shaking the foundations of the capitalist mode of production is proceeding ever faster, and when the world socialist revolution which began in October 1917, and which on the broad historical plane is far from having exhausted itself, is gathering new forces in new conditions — this age makes more probable, for our country as well, the prospect of a progressive self-liquidation of Stalin's "complete socialism", that is, a returning of society to the road of building socialism, as the first phase of communism.

These are the three differences of principle between the situation in which mankind's transition from pre-class to class society took place and that in which its transition is taking place from class to classless society, which determine the second aspect of my hypothesis. Taken together, these differences show that, whereas in the epoch of the first transition, in the countries where this began, we have to reckon with phenomena that were not only possible, but also inevitable, phenomena of violation and distortion of the natural sequence of socio-economic formations, and the appearance in many areas of Asiatic-mode-of-production societies which were stable and capable of survival for an indefinite length of time, but which led nowhere and remained stagnant — in the second transition, from a class to a classless structure, matters are otherwise. The stable society, leading nowhere, and in that sense stagnant, of Stalin's "complete socialism," which by its appearance and spread violated and distorted the sequence of socio-economic formations, though it proved to be possible, was not and is not historically *inevitable*, even in the area in which it arose.

Historical science does not yet, so far as I am aware, possess rigorous evidence adequate to form a judgment on what is a generally fundamental question, namely, this. In those societies in which a class system first took shape, did the distorted "proto-class" structure, the Asiatic mode of production, grow *directly* out of the break-up of the clan system — avoiding, that is, from the very outset, movement towards the slaveowning socio-economic formation which the empirical conditions did not allow to take shape and which simply could not arise under these conditions? Or did the break-up of clan society proceed *at first* along the natural path of succession of socio-economic formations, and did development then become diverted into the side-road of the Asiatic mode of production only after unsuccessful attempts by history to bring the slaveowning system into existence and *as a result* of a process of distortion of such rudimentary slaveowning societies?

But this question, which still remains unanswered so far as the epoch of transition of a number of Oriental, African and American countries from pre-class to class society is concerned, does not apply in relation to the epoch of the transition from class to classless society in our country, which was the first to open the road for the world to make this transition, by our revolution of October

1917. The beginning of *this* epoch was within the memory of the older generation of those still living, and their memories can be drawn upon. Those were the years when our country was led by Lenin, and also the first few years after his death. They saw progress from capitalism towards socialism along the road of building socialism as the first phase of communism, in accordance with the law-governed sequence of socio-economic formations, by which the last (monopoly) stage of the capitalist formation is followed by the first (socialist) stage of the Communist formation. Thus, the facts of history show that in the specific Russian conditions of the October Revolution there was nothing inherent which made it inevitable that the transition to classless society should begin with the building of socialism in what was not its true form but a distorted one.[11] And, according to my hypothesis, there was no historical inevitability and so no historical justification in that distortion of Lenin's path, the true path, of socialist construction which, beginning in the second half of the 1920s was effected by Stalin under the name of "complete socialism" (and, after his death by neo-Stalinism under the name of "developed socialism").

My hypothesis therefore differs from the very outset from the views of those Western Communists who reject Stalin's "complete socialism" only for their own countries, but who are prepared to see in it an historically legitimate "model of socialism" for Russia, good enough and indeed almost the only one possible for her, and who consider that the wreck of Lenin's initiatives and Lenin's line soon after his death, and the triumph of Stalinism, were inevitable given the conditions of Russian economic and cultural backwardness and the centuries-old traditions of Russian political despotism.

To an even greater degree is my hypothesis opposed to that way of rejecting the system of "complete socialism", that opposition to the system which, at present still politically amorphous, is increasingly characteristic of very wide sections of the "native" Soviet intelligentsia, those who have grown up since the Revolution,[12] and which, identifying Stalinism with Leninism, extends their disappointment with the "socialism" of the Stalinist formation to the October Revolution itself. If October had never happened, these people argue, then Russia, after developing for half a century along the lines of the February bourgeois revolution, would have attained the same, if not greater, economic and social results as today, but without those monstrous sufferings on the part of the people and those inhuman cruelties, without moral and cultural losses that are so hard to repair, without the innumerable violent deaths inflicted. Lenin's October was a mistake, they say, for, given the conditions of Russia at the beginning of the 20th century it was inevitably bound to give birth to Stalinism. In the light of my hypothesis, however, this argument about whether October was or was not necessary for Russia is seen as narrow, false and *unhistorical*. October was not just a matter of saving the Russian people and the Russian state of the early 20th century from disastrous backwardness and ruin — its significance lay in the fact that this salvation was effected by way of the socialist revolution, that it *linked* this salvation with the socialist revolution, with the *world revolution* the task of which is to carry through the great, historically mature change from class to classless society, in the life of *mankind as a whole*.[13] October 1917 was not merely Russia's October, it was the world's October, opening the era of building a classless society throughout the world. And, under Lenin and Lenin's followers, October showed *how to do this*. After Stalin and his followers have shown, for half a century now, *how not to do this*, it is only by turning our attention to the experience of Lenin's time that we can learn how, in a new historical context and on a new social and political basis (and so, not repeating but re-working and carrying further this experience), we can cleanse and renew the interrupted, perverted and betrayed task of the Russian and world October. For the Soviet Union this means opening the way out of the blind alley of neither-capitalism-nor-socialism on to the high road of the historical sequence of socio-economic formations, the road of the legitimate and logical transition to the communist formation.

4. Some concluding observations

The hypothesis set out above regarding the place in history of the society of Stalin's "complete socialism" (and its successor, the neo-Stalinists' "developed socialism") requires, like every hypothesis, to be confirmed. It can, evidently, be considered as having been confirmed if, proceeding from this hypothesis and making use of it, we succeed in finding answers to the following problems:

(i) How could it happen that, so soon as the end of the first decade opened by the October Revolution, the legitimate sequence of formations was violated, and the shoots and buds, tendencies and paths, concepts and aims of socialism began to degenerate and become deformed, and that, under the name of socialism there gradually, but with increasing intensity, began to take shape, instead of socialism, a non-socialist society which led neither forward to socialism nor back to capitalism? How did it occur that, in the history of our country, between the capitalist and communist socio-economic formations there inserted itself a non-socialist system of social relations which historical science and Marxist-Leninist theory had not foreseen and provided for? This is the problem of the *origin* of the society of Stalin's "complete socialism" and of the *stages* of its development along the road from the immature and incomplete socialist relations of the Leninist period of the revolution to the subsequent non-socialist ones.

(ii) Why is it possible for this society to continue to exist — this society which is a product of the distortion of the bases and of all the defined lines for building socialism in our country, as prepared by history and actually begun? Why does this deviation of social development from the highroad of history still go on? This is the problem of the *sources of the stability and stagnancy* of Stalin's society of "complete socialism."

(iii) How long can this society, occupying a huge area of the globe and involving hundreds of millions of people, continue to exist? And what historical factors — economic and political — are capable of putting an end to the hybrid structure of this society — internal ones (maturing within the society itself) or external ones (arising from the society's relations with the rest of the world)? This is the problem of the *limits of the stability and stagnancy* of the society of Stalin's "complete socialism."

(iv) What social forces are capable of carrying through the liquidation of this system and leading Soviet society out of the blind alley of Stalin's "complete socialism" on to the road along which our country's advance towards socialism, begun under Lenin and subverted by Stalin, can be resumed? And by what methods and over what period of time can this be achieved? This is the problem of the decisive *pre-condition for renewing and bringing to completion the building of socialism* in our country.

I invite our historians, sociologists and economists to test my hypothesis against these four problems, all the more insistently because thereby they will be able to work at finding and grounding the ways by which the transition from today's Soviet order to socialism can be accomplished. This will be a transition radically different from the socialist revolution of October 1917 and from the transitional period between capitalism and socialism opened up by this revolution: a transition that will be a great deal more complex and difficult.

NOTES

1 So early as 1844, in the *Economic and Philosophical Manuscripts*, Marx had presented the development of society as proceeding through three stages: a first stage, in which there was as yet no alienation of labour, no private property; a second stage, history as we have known it, in which labour is alienated and private property prevails; and a third stage, in the future, when labour will be disalienated and private property abolished. And at that time, too (in *The German Ideology*, 1845-46), the first stage was directly defined as the reign of the tribal form of property.

2 Just as Marx's ideas about the "Asiatic mode of production" in the 1850s echoed and were perhaps even directly connected with, his thoughtful articles written about the anti-British struggle for freedom that was developing at that time in India (then a British dependency), about the future of this struggle and its significance in world history.

3 Readers who are interested in the subject of the Asiatic mode of production *per se* will find detailed information enough, together with a plentiful bibliography, in these books: *Obschcheye i osobennoye v istoricheskom razvitii stran Vostoka (Materialy diskussii ob obshchestvennykh formatsiyakh na Vostoke: Aziatskiy sposob proizvodstva)* (The general and the particular in the historical development of the countries of the East. [Materials from the discussion on social formations in the East: the Asiatic mode of production]). Symposium published by the Institute of the Peoples of Asia, U.S.S.R. Academy of Sciences, Moscow, 1965. *Problemy dokapitalistichestikh obshchestv v stranakh Vostoka* (Problems of pre-capitalist societies in the countries of the East), Moscow, 1971. Yu. V. Kachanovsky, *Rabovladenie, feodalizm ili aziatskiy sposob proizvodstva?* (Slaveowning, feudalism or Asiatic mode of production?), Moscow, 1971. M.A. Vitkin, *Vostok v filosofsko-istoricheskoy kontseptsii K. Marksa i F. Engel'sa* (The East in the philosophy-of-history conceptions of K. Marx and F. Engels), Moscow, 1972. (The last four titles are all published by "Nauka".) *Premières sociétés de classes et mode de production asiatique: Recherches Internationales à la lumière du Marxisme*, no. 57-58, Paris, Edition de la Nouvelle Critique, 1967. Centre d'Etudes et de Recherches Marxistes: *Sur le "mode de production asiatique"*, with a preface by Roger Garaudy, Paris, Editions Sociales, 1969. Centre d'Etudes et de Recherches Marxistes: *Sur les sociétés précapitalistes. Textes choisis de Marx, Engels, Lénine,* with a preface by Maurice Godelier, Paris, Editions Sociales, 1973.

4 K.A. Wittfogel, *Oriental Despotism: A comparative study of total power*, New Haven and London, Yale U.P., 1957.

5 See his article "Socialism" in the symposium *From Under the Rubble*, 1974.

6 Let it be recalled once more that the natural three-stage development of class society, through slavery, feudalism and capitalism, was established by science on the basis of the history of Europe. The justification for the European schema has been well explained by the French Marxist sociologist Maurice Godelier. "The Western line of development," he writes, "is typical because in its *peculiar* movement it has brought about a *universal result*. It has provided the practical foundation (industrial economy) and the theoretical conception (socialism) needed to free itself and other societies from all forms of exploitation of man by man, both the most ancient and the most recent. Thereby it has provided man-

145

kind as a whole with the conditions for solving a universal problem which has existed ever since classes first appeared, namely, how to ensure maximum development of the productive forces without exploitation of man by man ... It *offers possibilities* which no other distinctive history has offered ..." (M. Godelier, *La Notion de "mode de production asiatique" et les schémas marxistes d'évolution des sociétés*, Paris, Cahiers du Centre d'Etudes et de Recherches Marxistes, n.d., p. 37.)

7 Subsequently, wherever I speak of Stalin's "complete socialism", I mean the neo-Stalinists' "developed socialism" as well. The latter is a continuation of the former, minus a few particularly odious features, as is actually confirmed by the builders of "developed socialism" when they do not allow criticism of Stalin's "complete socialism", and still denigrate or keep silent about those Communists who opposed it in its time, but instead proclaim their own continuity with it. I consider myself justified, therefore, for the sake of brevity, in omitting the additional words "and developed socialism" and on almost every occasion confining myself to the first expression, "complete socialism."

8 The quotations are from Lenin's article "Our Revolution (Apropos of N. Sukhanov's notes)". See *infra*.

9 Among these, of course, must be seen, first and foremost, the world wars and the innumerable "local" wars engendered and provoked by capitalism, which does not want to leave the scene of history.

10 Lenin called it "this tremendous acceleration of world development", and "this great acceleration of the greatest world revolution". See, e.g., his article, "On the Tenth Anniversary of *Pravda*," 2 May 1922.

11 In the year before he died, the sixth year of our country's march towards socialism, Lenin discussed, in his article already quoted, "Our Revolution (Apropos of N. Sukhanov's Notes)", the historical conditions and the special features created by them in Russia, which "stands on the borderline between the civilised countries and the countries which the war has for the first time definitely brought into the orbit of civilization — all the Oriental, non-European countries." He wrote about these special features as "certain periods of development [which] may display peculiarities in either the form or the sequence of this development" in accomplishing the world socialist revolution, and, as we have seen above, called such peculiarities "certain amendments (quite insignificant from the standpoint of the general development of world history)" — mere "details", from this point of view. At the same time, of course, Lenin never forgot what he had said three years earlier, in *'Left-wing' Communism, an Infantile Disorder*: "It would ... be erroneous to lose sight of the fact that soon after the vistory of the proletarian revolution in at least one of the advanced countries, a sharp change will probably come about: Russia will cease to be the model and will once again become a backward country (in the 'Soviet' and socialist sense)."

12 Including — secretly, of course; but isn't this one of those "open" secrets? — a considerable and ever-growing number of members of the Soviet Communist Party.

13 Two years before October Lenin wrote of "the gulf between the chauvinist revolutionaries (revolution for victory over Germany) and the proletarian internationalist revolutionaries (revolution to awaken the proletariat of other countries, to unite it in a general proletarian revolution)" (Letter to A.G. Shlyapnikov, 19 September 1915: *Collected Works*, 4th edition, English version, Vol. 36, p.354.)

From the History of Ideas

PART I

M.P. Yakubovich

Translated by Tamara Deutscher

I

When in the summer of 1914 the first world war was threatening to engulf mankind, Jean Jaurès tried to step in between the enemies poised for attack and separate them with his own hands. By this heroic gesture he entered history and became the symbol of struggle against war. But if the pistol of a fanatic patriot had not destroyed him at the table of a Parisian café, what position would he have adopted after the outbreak of the war and after the avalanche of German troops had swooped across the frontier, around the defensive line of Verdun-Epinal-Belfort, threatening republican France, threatening the freedom of Paris — that haven of political refugees from all over the world? Can one doubt that in spite of all his humanitarian ideals and sentiments Jaurès would have adopted an unreservedly "defencist" position? Even Jules Guesde, his determined opponent within the socialist movement, who consistently and for many years criticized his opportunism and his lack of a proletarian class approach to political problems, submitted with a heavy heart to the decision to enter a national coalition which, without class distinction, aimed at creating a common front in the face of the deadly enemy — Jules Guesde, the stubborn and uncompromising ideologue, the organizer and leader of the independent working class party, independent of any bourgeois influence and any liberal "possibilism". Such was the impact of the German invasion. Was it only Guesde who reacted in this way?

147

And what about G.V. Plekhanov, the theorist and philosopher of revolutionary Marxism, incomparably more steadfast in his socialist faith than Guesde? Plekhanov was also carried away by the wave of panic at the thought of a possible victory of Prussian militarism and the destruction of the French core of international socialism. What then would Jaurès have done? With the approval of both Plekhanov and Guesde, he would have probably joined the French national government long before Guesde.

Among the ideologues and leaders of the Second International, and popular at that time, only one single man resisted the wave of anti-German feelings which took hold of the Russian emigré socialists together with their French comrades. This man was Lenin. One could not say that he did not value the liberties of republican bourgeois France, or did not realize the full danger which the triumph of militarist-imperialist Germany presented for the cause of the revolutionary working classes of Europe generally and for the Russian revolutionary socialists in particular. The Bolshevik party school, under the direction of Zinoviev, at that time a pupil and close companion of Lenin, where Bolshevik cadres were taught and trained for the job of setting up and running party organizations inside Russia, was situated in a suburb of Paris at Longjumeau. If Paris were to fall, the Germans would not have tolerated such activities on their occupied territories. Obviously, Lenin must have been fully aware of this. What then was the motive for his intransigent attitude to the war? What made him break with the whole International, with the Russians who considered themselves revolutionary socialists, among whom there were many comrades belonging to the Bolshevik organization, who all succumbed to "defencism"? What gave him the ideological strength for such a break?

First of all it should be noted that Lenin in all circumstances knew how to withstand moods of panic. (Incidentally, one of his favourite expressions in situations which were not uncommon in the history of any revolutionary party was: "Do not panic!") Yes, he refused to succumb to the panic which overcame French and Russian socialists, leaders and ideologues, at the sight of the Kaiser's battalions marching through the streets of Brussels, moving towards the French frontier, and preparing for their triumphal entry into Paris. Lenin, of course, could not have known that the French General Staff was counting on the help of the Russian army advancing to strike in East Prussia; nor did he know of General Galliéni's plan of attacking the German army on the

Marne, the army which forgot the famous injunction of the head of its General Staff Graf Schlieffen, uttered on his deathbed: "Remember the right flank." Lenin, with his characteristic shrewdness and political intuition, analysed the military-economic potential of both warring coalitions and came to the conclusion that neither side could achieve a speedy victory; and on this conclusion he based his programme of action for the near future. This evaluation of the political and military situation led him to define the task of every proletarian revolutionary as a struggle for the overthrow of "his own" government, for the defeat of its claims for world domination in one form or another.

A unique strength of mind, an exceptional civil courage, and a political imagination were needed to oppose one's own understanding of historical events and one's own historical prognosis to the general outcry about the necessity of "defence" against the predatory aggressors. What followed confirmed Lenin's analysis of the situation. The fields of military operations were soaked in human blood; the war was engulfing ever new countries and the end was not in sight. Fighting went on; defeats followed triumphs; the armies were dug in, neither advancing nor retreating. None of the belligerents could, or wished to, give up the hope of victory and of the plunder which would follow it. Lenin's view, which he entertained at the beginning of the war, hardened into certainty; in this war there could be no victors and no vanquished because two imperialist bandits of nearly equal economic and political power were locked in mortal combat; they were at each other's throats and such was their predatory nature that they could neither give up their ambitions nor achieve a compromise. This life and death struggle of the robbers could have one outcome only: a world proletarian revolution. Only the revolution could put an end to the unbounded greed of the warring bourgeois coalitions. Only a revolution could put an end to the war and also to the existence of the world capitalist system, replacing it by world socialism. Imperialist world war could only end in a world-wide socialist revolution — there was no other way.

This theory of world-wide socialist revolution which was imminent and for which the time had come, inspired Lenin and gave him the strength to swim against the current, to fight dejection and despondency in the ranks of socialists, and allowed him to gather around himself devoted disciples and followers. The intrinsic greatness of this idea fired the imagination of his comrades; but to be strengthened in their beliefs they also needed some clear signs of the approaching revolution. Where would the revolution begin? How and in what way would it spread? This could not be foretold. To determine where precisely the revolution would start was impossible. But Lenin did not exclude the possibility that the revolution might break out in Russia, which was the weakest link in the imperialist chain, and where the chaos brought about by the war and the weakness of the existing regime were particularly striking. Revolution might first break out in Russia, but it would not stop there — it would become "uninterrupted" and embrace other countries involved in the war. This, said Lenin, will be an "uninterrupted socialist revolution". This is how during the years of the imperialist war was conceived in Lenin's mind the theory of "uninterrupted" socialist revolution, which alone would unfailingly bring to a halt world hostilities and would lead to the introduction of a socialist order, if not on a world scale then at least in the advanced capitalist belligerent countries.

2

Lenin's theory of uninterrupted socialist revolution has some superficial (and perhaps not only superficial) resemblance with the theory of permanent revolution elaborated in 1905 by Alexander Parvus and of which Trotsky was the main exponent. But Lenin's theory was constructed on quite different social and historical premises, and the dissimilarity was greater than the semantic difference between "uninterrupted" and "permanent" might imply. Parvus arrived at his theory under the direct influence of the new proletarian methods of revolutionary struggle put into practice in the course of the revolution of 1905, namely the general strike of the whole Russian working class, which alarmed Tsarist absolutism to such a degree that it had to retreat politically — hence the promulgation of the Manifesto of 17 October.

These new specific methods of revolutionary struggle of the Russian proletariat made a tremendous impression on the consciousness of the world bourgeoisie as well as of the world proletariat. Yet none of the theorists of the Socialist International attempted to revise their views on the immediate future of the world movement and on history. None — except Parvus. In the first instance, Parvus drew attention to the discrepancy between the real forces active in the Russian revolution, their methods of action and the political results achieved. Basically, the revolution of 1905 was a "workers'" revolution. It acquired an irresistible strength only when it was joined by the working class which pushed aside the shrill campaign of the "Zemstvo movement" of the bourgeoisie and the nobility; it became victorious only when it resorted to the proletarian weapon of the strike, when by a political strike it brought to a halt the whole economic and social life of the country and thus threw into confusion the very apex of the bureaucracy of absolutist Russia. The confusion was complete. Then Sergei Witte (Count Witte), one of the more intelligent representatives of the Russian bureaucracy, a former enemy of liberalism,* came forward with a plan for a drastic political change and presented a draft of a Manifesto proclaiming the principle of a "true inviolability of the individual" and foreshadowed the calling of a National Assembly on the Western European model. Witte expressed in this case the bewilderment of the high Tsarist bureaucracy in the face of a workers' revolution in Russia. Even he did not think of any political concessions for the benefit of the working class, only of a compromise with the bourgeois intelligentsia, with the bourgeoisie and nobility of the Zemstvo liberal movement. This movement fed on illusions, celebrated its victory and expected the introduction of a parliamentary regime after the election of the Duma.

But what in all this was there for the working class, for the class which organized the defeat of the bureaucracy by resorting to the weapon of the strike? The promised Duma (Parliament) would at best represent the opinion of the liberal bourgeoisie, alien and hostile to socialist ideas. Then, in the mind of the proletariat intuitively and instinctively groping toward future political action, was conceived the plan of Councils of Workers' Deputies, organs of workers' power, which at their very first appearance had no defined programme or frame of reference. Quite a special role among these councils (Soviets) was played by the Petersburg Soviet, the best organized and the most authoritative one, in which prominent leaders of the revolutionary movement were active.

The revolutionary wave brought Parvus into the Petersburg Soviet. Parvus, the theorist, came to the conclusion that one could not reconcile oneself to a strikingly incongruous historical situation which would allow the bourgeoisie and the nobility to exploit for their own benefit the defeat of the Tsarist autocracy inflicted on it

*It may be worth recalling Witte's note on the incompatibility of absolutism and the Zemstvo movement, the note which Nicholas II rejected on the advice of another, more cautious, pillar of Tsarist bureaucracy I.L. Goremykin.

by proletarian forces. His theoretical speculations prevented him from realizing the historical fact that the whole state apparatus and its army were still in Tsarist hands, that they were still not wrenched from these hands, and would not be wrenched from them by the liberals in the camp of the bourgeoisie and nobility. He saw before his eyes only the power of the working class which manifested itself in the general strike; and this power seemed to him decisive and invincible. He was under the spell of that power and saw its true embodiment in the Petersburg Soviet of Workers' Deputies. The Russian working class should, maintained Parvus, by its own strength introduce and establish its own political dictatorship over Russia; such an example — a legendary victory and the new revolutionary method which assured that victory — could not but inspire the international labour movement in its striving for a revolution in the advanced European countries. This victorious socialist revolution would, maintained Parvus, spread from Russia across national frontiers and develop into a "permanent" revolution until the full victory of socialism on a world scale. Such was Parvus's theory devised in the days of the Russian revolution of 1905. Some of his comrades from the Petersburg Soviet were carried away by it, among them Trotsky, who became its main exponent and with whose name it was linked later on, when its true author's name was consigned to oblivion.

Lenin rejected this theory for which his mind was too rational and lucid and his manner of thinking too historical and too solidly based on the analysis of world politico-economic situation. Parvus, for all his talents, sharpness and boldness of ideas, was also a great fantasist and no mean adventurer (which showed itself so clearly in his subsequent career). Lenin saw what Parvus, blinded by his passionate temperament, could not see. Lenin saw that in the industrialized countries there existed at that time no economic or psychological premise for a socialist revolution: in short Europe was not in a revolutionary situation. But there was no economic, social or political premise for the victory of revolution in Russia either. The Russian working class could not defeat absolutism and the bourgeoisie all by itself, without an alliance with the peasantry and without the peasantry's support. The overwhelming majority of the Russian peasantry, regardless of the genuine development of the agririan movement, was not ready to take the revolutionary road under the leadership of the proletariat and as its ally. The peasantry was not ready, nor was the army which in its class content was largely a peasant army. In such historical circumstances the programme of "permanent revolution" was nothing more than an empty fantasy, an adventurist dream. And Lenin rejected it as completely unacceptable.

3

The course of events fully confirmed the correctness of Lenin's view. The cause of workers' revolution in Russia did not move forward. The uprising in Moscow, in December 1905, was drowned in blood. It remained isolated; it provoked only disparate and intermittent action, but received no united and synchronized support in the country as a whole. Even the proletariat of Petersburg, which had produced the standard bearer of the revolution — the Petersburg Soviet of Workers' Deputies — did not move to assist the Moscow uprising: it proved psychologically and ideologically not ready for action. The Moscow rising was a repetition, on a smaller scale, of the Paris Commune of 1871. In 1905, in Russia, it proved just as isolated and doomed as was the Paris Commune in France, in Europe, of 1871. Lenin knew that the rising was doomed, but he also understood that the duty of the revolutionary workers was nevertheless to support it, to take part in the action which was unavoidable because it was the only outlet for the energies of the Moscow proletariat, which would not have understood if that outlet were blocked by a section of the working class.

The defeat of the Moscow rising brought despondency to the ranks of the Russian workers and their ideologues. G.V. Plekhanov uttered his historic phrase: "One should not have taken up arms". How far away was this Plekhanov from the one who, in 1876, on the steps of the Kazan Cathedral in Petersburg led the historic demonstration which ushered in the epoch of open revolutionary struggle of the Russian working class.* Not only the Moscow rising, but the whole Russian revolution (the "proletarian" revolution especially), was defeated by the armed strength of Russian absolutism, furtively supported by Russian liberalism more or less openly in sympathy with it. The European proletariat did not budge! The workers' revolution did not reach beyond the Russian frontiers.

---

* The author refers to the demonstraton organized by *Zemlya i Volya,* on 6 December 1876, at which Plekhanov delivered an impassioned speech in defence of the imprisoned Narodniks. — *Trans.*

The "permanent" revolution did not manifest itself. Parvus's theory was refuted by the course of history. Lenin's opinion that the theory was an adventurist dream was fully confirmed. The Petersburg Soviet was dispersed; its leaders were arrested and sentenced by the Tsarist courts to exile in Siberia; the majority of them, however, managed to escape.

Alexander Parvus, the author of the theory, under the influence of this heavy blow, lost faith not only in "permanent" revolution but in any proletarian revolution. The bourgeois economic and social order began to look to him unshakable and within it he started to search for a place for himself. He became a considerable financier and entrepreneur in the old German empire and even extended his activities beyond its frontiers; he became a businessman on an international scale.

Trotsky did not follow in his footsteps. He remained in the ranks of the Russian Social Democrats and the Second International. But he talked no more about the theory of the permanent revolution. (He returned to it much later, during the party discussions after Lenin's death, and attempted, contrary to historical fact, to prove in his political biography that he had never discarded this theory.) In the period between the two revolutions, from 1905 to 1917, Trotsky was advocating another idea, quite different from that of the permanent revolution — the idea of socialist integration, that is of an organizational unification of all adherents to the socialist movement of all shades, from revolutionary Bolsheviks to Mensheviks, including the "liquidators".* Such a unification seemed to him necessary for a speedy overthrow of Russian autocracy and, after the February upheaval, for a further development of the revolution and the accomplishment of its historic tasks.

4

In 1905-06 Lenin rejected the theory of permanent revolution·as not applicable. Ten years later, in his theoretical thinking he began to consider the idea of uninterrupted revolution, in its conclusions very close to the theory he had previously rejected. Trotsky's polemical allegation that Lenin revised his views and accepted the theory of permanent revolution is not correct. As Trotsky put it: "I

* "Liquidators" advocated the abandonment of all underground activity and concentration on legal forms of struggle. — *Trans.*

did not come over to Lenin, but Lenin came over to me''. (Incidentally, his attempt to present Parvus's theory as his own was also wrong.) No, Lenin did not revise his previous evaluation of the "permanent revolution"; he conceived a new theory, akin to the rejected one, but based on quite different historical material, in a different historical situation, and with different economic, social, and political premises. The situation essential for the advance of socialist revolution was, according to him, created by the world war which broke out in 1914 and fundamentally changed the pre-war European order. The war was to end in a world proletarian revolution — there was no other way. Such was the basic theoretical conclusion at which Lenin arrived soon after the outbreak of hostilities. And, indeed, as Lenin had foreseen it, the war dragged on year after year; neither of the belligerent coalitions could achieve victory; the holocaust threatened to engulf other small and medium size bourgeois states. The armies were dug in and hardly advanced. Yes, "All was quiet on the Western front". Lenin's diagnosis looked more and more convincing. What still had to materialize was the second part of his theoretical formula: the prelude to the revolution, the first revolutionary flame in any of the belligerent countries. And such a flame suddenly burst out and brightly illumined the whole horizon.

The flame burst out in Russia in February 1917. Age-old autocracy, the pillar of world reaction throughout the whole of the nineteenth century, collapsed like a house of cards. It collapsed under the blows of workers' revolution in Petersburg which was, unlike the Moscow rising of 1905, supported by the troops of the Petersburg garrison. The soldiers of the Petersburg garrison were under war conditions quite numerous, and the garrison in its social composition represented fully the whole Russian peasant army mobilized for war. The Russian peasantry of 1905, rent by various rebellions and by unrest, had not been ready to support a workers' revolution in the capital; the young peasants recruited into the army had not been ready to break the discipline and openly to rise against the Tsar. Things were different in 1917. The war proved a great school for the Russian peasantry. Into the army were now recruited not only young men, but the whole active peasant population, youngsters as well as forty-year-old heads of families. They were all drawn into an organization which, in cities, especially in Petrograd, put them in direct contact with the working class, and prepared them psychologically to place themselves under the political leadership of the proletariat and to take over its ideology.

155

Hence the unparalleled victory of the February revolution, which spread like wildfire over the whole empire. Once victory was assured, there came into being not only the bourgeois Provisional Government, preoccupied with its legalization by the overthrown imperial administration, but also another purely revolutionary authority: The Soviet of Workers' — *Workers'*, as well as *Soldiers'* — Deputies. There were no Soldiers' Deputies in the Soviet of 1905 and this circumstance definitely determined the historic destiny of the Soviets of 1917, which sprang up after the revolution with the same breath-taking speed all over the country, not only in the centre, but also in the front-line zones. This immediately gave to the Soviets a wide national character, because the whole able-bodied male population of the countryside which was in the army, and the whole working population of the cities, were represented in the Soviets.

The discrepancy between the form of power which emerged in February 1917 as the power of the bourgeoisie, and the form of organization as constituted by the Soviet of Workers' and Soldiers' Deputies which represented the broad masses, became manifest. But this historic discrepancy was not immediately recognized either by the political leaders of the bourgeoisie and the intelligentsia (including the Cadets), or by the leaders and ideologues of socialist parties including those Bolsheviks who were in Russia right after the bourgeois upheaval. All of them were somehow thinking in "all-national" terms, which had seemed to demand the application of old classical parliamentary forms with elections according to a special electoral law, carefully and scrupulously worked out. The Mensheviks and the Social Revolutionaries were completely under the spell of the old formula of a "National Constituent Assembly", and did not even begin to realize what was the content of that new formation — the Soviet of Workers' and Soldiers' Deputies — thrown up by the revolution. ˙ It seemed to them something transitory to a degree, something which was bound to be wound up and replaced by "normal" organs of State power, constituted according to the canons of bourgeois law, and pursuing the aims of the democratization of the bourgeois social order and bourgeois regime of the country. They did not feel the historic atmosphere of the revolution, the revolutionary heartbeat of the country; they were not aware of the historic role of the Soviets, and they did not even ponder the problem. And at the time this was so with all the leaders of social democracy and the Social Revolutionaries of every political complexion, from G.V. Plekhanov on the far right (with his ideology of "Unity", that is national unity without class distinction) to the Zimmerwaldist "defencists" (Chernov, Dan, Tseretelli) including Martov's "internationalsits" who came to Russia with Lenin in the same "sealed train".* Even the Bolshevik leaders then in Russia, like Kamenev and Stalin, were not free from this ideological tie, which was binding together representatives of socialist thought of various tendencies in their incomprehension of the role and meaning of the new political organ. True, within that tangle they were on the left, but they were in it nevertheless. They were thinking in the same political terms as the other socialists, though they advocated different tactical methods and means of political struggle.

5

It would be wrong to maintain that until Lenin's return to Russia nothing foreshadowed the future historic role of the Soviets of Workers' and Soldiers' Deputies. In the turmoil of the first post-revolutionary days there appeared a document which prophetically foreshadowed the future importance of the Soviets. This was "Order No. 1". While the Provisional Committee of the Duma was trying to form a new government and to assure its juridical legitimacy as a successor of the old power and to obtain the Tsar's signature under the nomination of Prince Lvov as Prime Minister, a turbulent crowd of deputies, soldiers and sailors was gathering for the first session of the Petrograd Soviet and meeting in the hall the workers' deputies. These soldiers had just fought the police on the streets of Petrograd; the sailors had just thrown Admiral Nepenin and other hateful commanders into the sea. For these soldiers and sailors the revolution meant in the first instance freedom from the humiliating forms of discipline prevalent in the Tsarist army and navy. The newly won freedom had to be given an official confirmation, some solemn declaration about the end of the "ancien régime" in the armed forces. From whom could they expect such a declaration? The Provisional Government was only now beginning to take shape and nobody knew what in fact it would represent and how it would manifest itself. And here on the square, in front of the Tauride Palace, were gathering the representatives of the revolution — the workers and soldiers, the flesh and blood of the working masses, expressing their feelings

---

* The author is mistaken: Martov came a month later than Lenin. — *Trans.*

and their thoughts, drunk from the unexpected victory. They awaited or even demanded that this victory should be immediately made secure and that a "new deal" should be proclaimed for the army and the navy which joined in the workers' revolution. Such was the unanimous wish and demand of the Soviet Deputies. A proclamation to this effect, the "Order", could come only from the Petrograd Soviet, from the standard bearer of workers' and soldiers' revolution. The necessity to issue such an order precisely in the name of the Petrograd Soviet was recognized not only by the rank and file deputies, but also by the leaders of the Soviet directing it (if it was at all possible to "direct" it in any way in this turbulent situation) in the first days of its existence. Who then were the leaders of the Soviet? Who was responsible for drawing up and issuing this unprecedented historic document?

The first session of the Petrograd Soviet took place in the hall of the Duma in the Tauride Palace. Such was the overwhelming impression of the power of the soliders' and workers' revolution that the State Duma retreated before its authority and moved to the side wing of the Palace, yielding the central White Hall to the Petrograd Soviet. Here the gathering deputies were received by the Social Democratic and the "Trudovik" members of the Duma, who acted as hosts and to a certain extent as organizers of the Soviet. They were warmly greeted by the deputies, who regarded them as genuine leaders of the revolution and its prophets. In this atmosphere of general enthusiasm Nikolai Semenovich Chkheidze, the head of the Social Democratic fraction of the Duma, was chosen as President of the Soviet. Nobody asked whether Chkheidze was a Bolshevik or a Menshevik, nobody bothered about this as the question seemed without importance. Chkheidze mounted the rostrum and presided over the meetings. But did he direct the Soviet? For this he was not equipped. Tired and worn out by innumerable meetings, plenary sessions of the Soviet, meetings of the Executive Committee, of the Conciliatory Commission and Provisional Committee of the State Duma, by deliberations of the Provisional Committee itself and a multitude of political organizations, including those of the Menshevik Party, Chkheidze endeavoured to keep order in that turbulent sea of the Soviet and was carried on its waves not quite aware whither he was carried. Among his "comrades", that is his deputies, had to be counted also Kerensky and Skobelev, both members of the Duma.

Kerensky was fully absorbed in intrigues. By means of intrigues he managed to push himself into the Provisional Government, and to obtain the much desired portfolio of the Minister of Justice, which Miliukov graciously offered him instead of offering it to the Cadet Maklakov who had originally been designated for the post.* The business of the Soviet was of no interest to Kerensky: it was not there that he saw the road to power about which he dreamt. About Skobelev it is not worth talking. Politically he was an insignificant man who had no understanding of his own role or of the events he had been witnessing. No, these members of the Duma did not constitute the brain of the Executive of the Petrograd Soviet in the first days of its existence. On the Executive there were three prominent men who had found themselves in Petrograd during the February revolution, had considerable political experience, and were well known in revolutionary circles. They were Nikolai Nikolaevich Sukhanov, Yuri Mikhailovich Steklov, and Nikolai Dimitrovich Sokolov. Sukhanov possessed a considerable literary talent, and became known to the socialist intelligentsia mainly as a result of Lenin's political attacks on him. During the February revolution he tremendously impressed the representatives of the bourgeoisie and of the nobility in the Duma by his appearance and his refined intellectual manner. Shulgin said that meeting Sukhanov was like meeting "the secretary of the devil". But Sukhanov was not an orator; he did not impress the masses of soldiers and workers and did not evoke great confidence. He was fully engaged on his new literary enterprise: he had just become the editor of a great political journal *Novaya Zhizn*. Steklov was a no personality: first copies of the *Izvestiya* [*News*] *of the Petrograd Soviet* appeared under his editorship. But he also was essentially a *littérateur*, not very impressive as a speaker addressing large audiences. He was known among the intelligentsia, but not among soldiers and workers. Sokolov's position was quite different. He was well known to the Petrograd proletariat as the foremost counsel for defence in the political trials, as a lawyer with wide practice specializing in workers' affairs, and, last but not least, as the Bolshevik candidate of the city of Petrograd for the Duma. He impressed by his self-confidence, his inspiring presence, resounding voice and clear way of speaking. In the Soviet he immediately gained popularity and authority. He was looked upon and listened to with respect. When Chkheidze was prevented from presiding over a meeting of the Executive, he called upon Sokolov to replace him Sokolov conducted the debates with greater assurance and

* Cadets — Constitutional Democrats. — *Trans.*

formulated the decisions with greater precision than Chkheidze.

When a clamour spontaneously arose in the Petrograd garrison for an official affirmation and ratification of the "new order" introduced in the army and navy, all eyes turned towards Sokolov. It was he who had to draft the "Order" proclaiming the new rights of soldiers and sailors. Sokolov did not decline this task which was unequivocally assigned to him. He drafted this "Order", which he simply called Order No. 1. Not realizing either the future role of "Order No. 1" or its historic significance, Sokolov imagined vaguely that it would be followed by further Orders, a whole series of them. The draft of "Order No. 1" was first read at the plenary session of the Executive Committee of the Soviet and approved by it without reservations. After that it was read at the plenary session of the Soviet where it was received with enthusiasm and tumultuous applause. Published in the *Izvestiya of the Petrograd Soviet,* it was distributed all over Russia in tens of thousands of copies. It was read with delight by soldiers in the front line and in the rear. The mass of soldiers looked upon it as upon a new "fundamental law" proclaimed by the Petrograd Soviet of Workers' and Soldiers' Deputies. Nobody asked whether the Petrograd Soviet had the right to proclaim such a law, nor did anybody ask why the law was proclaimed by the Soviet and not by the Provisional Government, which had just announced its formation and the beginning of its activity.

What was the actual content of Order No. 1? The most important was the declaration of the right of the soldiers to organize and to send their representatives to the Soviets from all sectors of the armed forces. Soldiers' soviets had been formed anyhow quite spontaneously even before, at the first news of the revolution in Petrograd and of the appearance of the Soviets of Deputies. But Order No. 1 confirmed the legality of soldiers' organizations. The masses of soldiers were most impressed and most enthusiastic about the change in the manner of saluting the officers. This symbolized the downfall of the *ancien régime* and the new dignity of the rank and file. The officer corps received Order No. 1 with resentment. Other parts of the Order were less important. However, its meaning and its historical significance did not lie in its content, but in the very fact that a legally binding Order was issued in the name of the Petrograd Soviet which thereby acted as the supreme revolutionary power in the country, as the organ of revolutionary dictatorship. It amounted to a declaration of the dissolution of the Provisional bourgeois government formed by the

State Duma and approved by the abdicating monarch. This government was anxious to assure its status as the legitimate successor of the age-old forms of administration. It was mainly interested in the juridical procedure, though the order was drafted by a professional and practising lawyer. The Soviet was based not on legalities, but on the will and strength of the masses which joined the revolution and accepted the leadership of the working class. And these masses of soldiers — the armed peasant army — were the only real force in the country on which until then the power of Russian tsarism had rested. From the moment when the army and navy went over to the side of the workers' insurrection and supported the creation of the Soviets, it was precisely the Soviet which could become and had to become the only authority in the country.

Such was the reality of the historic situation. This reality found its expression in the promulgation of Order No. 1. This in no way diminished its significance as a declaration of the approaching proletarian revolution, which was invincible because it had the allegiance of soldiers and peasants. The Order was the precursor of an imminent establishment of the Soviet rule. The fact that N.D. Sokolov did not realize the full importance of his "literary exercise" did not deprive him of the title of the prophet of the October revolution, of the victory of Soviet power over the antiquated form of government.

6

"Order No. 1" was received with full approval and joy by soldiers all over the country; it was met with fury and indignation by the nobility and the bourgeoisie, and by the officer corps. What? A usurpation of the power of the "legal" Provisional Government? And who are the usurpers? Some illiterate workers! Some insolent soldiers! This was an attempt at a "subversion" of the army! This amounted to the betrayal of the fatherland in the face of an outside enemy! "This is a betrayal not only of the fatherland but also of the revolution" exclaimed the zealous "defencists" in the socialist parties. A wicked, mad campaign was mounted against the authors of the Order, against the Petrograd Soviet. In the meantime the enthusiasm of the first days of the revolution somewhat subsided. The excitement which gave birth to the idea of the Order was no longer there. And the "idea" itself? Was not the "idea" itself extremely unclear to the authors? They had no clear political perspective as to the future of the Soviets of Workers' and Soldiers' Deputies; they were the prisoners of the ideology of democratic legality which demanded the calling of the "national" Constituent Assembly elected according to a special electoral law. The bourgeoisie derived much hope precisely from the "national" character of the Assembly: it assumed that the elections would take place after the victorious conclusion of the war brought about by the Provisional Government in an atmosphere of chauvinistic fervour, and that it would be easy to do away with the Soviet of Workers and Soldiers, as well as with the socialist parties. The patriotic outcry about the subversion of the army confused not a few leaders of the Petrograd Soviet, and some of them went over to the other side. The first one was Kerensky. Louder than anybody else, he shouted about the "subversion of the army", about the need to strengthen in it order "to save the Fatherland and the Revolution". A search for those responsible for issuing Order No. 1 began. Before long all eyes fell on N.D. Sokolov who was decried as a "traitor" and a "public enemy". He could not find convincing arguments to vindicate himself, because in fact he remained strongly influenced by the idea of "revolutionary defencism" and had no clear conception where the series of incriminating orders that were supposed to follow Order No. 1 was to lead.

The appearance of new leaders on the political scene of Petrograd had a tremendous importance. Old militants of socialist parties returning from Siberia and from emigration were pushing into the background those who in the first days led the February revolution and stood at the head of the Petrograd Soviet. Sukhanov, Steklov, and Sokolov were replaced by F.I. Dan, I.G. Tseretelli, and A.P. Gotz. Prominent members of the Social Revolutionaries, V.M. Chernov and N.D. Avksentiev, stood aloof. Political activity inside the Soviets, where the Social Democrats, especially the Mensheviks, played the leading role, did not appeal to them. They tried to organize a "counter-game" in the form of a separate Soviet of "Peasant Deputies". What sort of peasant deputies could there have been when the Soliders' Deputies were representing the active part of the peasantry? And they also raved about the "national" Constituent Assembly in which they (like the Cadets) dreamt of playing the leading role. Dan and Tseretelli became now the leading political figures in the Executive Committee of the Petrograd Soviet. But Tseretelli, a well-known Menshevik, lacked the necessary qualities of leadership, in spite of his fascinating manner of speaking and the oratory on which his reputation was based. He was incapable of independent thinking and he lacked ideological conviction, no matter how talented a speaker he was on the tribune. It was Dan who supplied him (and also the whole so-called Organizational Committee of the "united" Russian Social Democratic Revolutionary Party, as the Mensheviks called themselves) with a much needed ideological base. Both, Tseretelli and Dan, considered themselves during the war as "Zimmerwaldists", and adhered to the minority in the Socialist International, which condemned its chauvinistic attitude. At the time of the February revolution they exchanged their "inter-nationalist" banner for that of "revolutionary defencism". When they made their appearance in Petrograd (they had returned from Siberia), this became the official ideology of the Petrograd Soviet, and they were its chief spokesmen. Dan was no doubt an intelligent and widely educated man, and he was objectively convinced of the absolute orthodoxy of his "revolutionary socialism". But one could not imagine a man less suited to, and less capable of, political activity in revolutionary conditions, at a time of *Sturm und Drang* affecting broad masses, a man who would be less of a "revolutionary". The author of a known and popular booklet written before the revolution, under the title *National Constituent Assembly,* Dan conceived that Assembly as chosen according to the last word in parliamentary procedure, on the basis of a comprehensive electoral law, solidly, conscientiously, and unhurriedly worked out with the participation of and in consultation with the luminaries of the legal profession. He envisaged that in the Constituent Assembly and the future normal parliament the workers' Social Democratic Party would play the role of a numerically insignificant minority opposition in accordance with the insignificant proportion of the working class in Russia's population. The great historical role which, as a result of the formation of the Soviets, the Social Democratic Party came to play seemed to him neither real nor desirable. He viewed the mere existence of the Soviets as a deviation from a normal historical development and thought that they should be abolished at the first opportunity, that is as soon there come into existence the organs of the democratic autonomous government and the Constituent Assembly, all juridically elected. He did not feel the pulse of the revolution (which the poet Alexander Blok discerned so clearly), he disliked all revolutionary "excesses", and had no understanding for the logic of the revolution. With such a non-revolutionary and anti-Soviet attitude how could Dan view Order No. 1? He considered it to be a grave mistake, and regarded its authors, at best, as politically blind. Dan, and with him the whole new leadership of the Petrograd Soviet, severely censured the proclamation of Order No. 1, disclaimed responsibility for it, and disavowed it by putting out "Order No. 2" which by its formulation was supposed to annul Order No. 1. In fact, however, further events proved that the politically blind were not the authors of Order No. 1, which had entered history as a harbinger of the further development of the revolution.

7

Such was the political situation when Lenin returned to Russia. His very arrival, after a journey in the "sealed train" across German territory with the permission of the German government, was by itself a blatant violation of all the sacred principles of patriotic and defencist ethics. (True, "the father of Russian Menshevism," Yu. O. Martov came with Lenin in the same carriage).* The bourgeois press reacted with screams and roars of vilification. But the Petrograd Soviet possessed enough tact and revolutionary solidarity not to be influenced by this outcry. Its official delegation, under the Chariman of the Soviet, N.S. Chkheidze, met Lenin at the Finland Station and welcomed him on his return home. But the Menshevik leaders were not in a mood to greet the appearance of Lenin with joy. Among themselves they commented: "Well, it will all get going now! We haven't anybody to oppose Lenin with his mad and devilish energy, with his theoretical fantasies. In fact, even Dan wouldn't do; Dan is a sybarite! And Lenin — Lenin is a demon of revolution". In private talks they even dreamt of drawing into political activity Alexander Alexandrovich Bogdanov, as the only political figure allegedly able adequately to face Lenin.'

And indeed Lenin did show demonic strength. He began his political activity in Russia straightaway, on the platform of the Finland Station, by making a speech from a military lorry. He came with a programme of international socialist revolution which was to put an end to the war and to build, on the ruins of capitalism, a new socialist order in Europe — at least in Europe to begin with. Socialist proletarian revolution began in Russia. This was not an accident of history; there were definite historical

* See translator's note above.

164

premises for it. Even if such a revolution had not begun in Russia, this would have had no real and decisive importance. Once begun, it would continue and develop "uninterruptedly", passing across national frontiers until it embraced all countries involved in the world war. This was why Russian revolutionary socialists should aim at transforming the democratic revolution into a socialist one. Their immediate objective should be the withdrawal of Russia from the war and an appeal for peace addressed to all the belligerent nations.

A unique and favourable social situation for fulfilling this historical task had arisen in Russia: the revolution was achieved under the leadership of the working class joined by soldiers and sailors, that is, in fact, by armed peasantry. The soldiers wanted peace which would allow them to return to their homes; they also hoped that the revolution would bring them, as peasants, the land of the landowners. They had to be given peace. They had to be given land. And they would follow the working class that would give them peace and land. They would follow the path of socialist construction. And on that path the Russian workers and peasants would meet the European proletariat which would overturn its own bourgeoisie and imperialist rulers and, together with the Russian proletariat, build a socialist order, a socialist world. Lenin, with lightning speed, became aware of the political situation which he found in Russia. He realized that the Soviets which had come into existence were the best, the optimal, form of organization of armed peasantry, that is in fact of the whole armed population led by the working class. It was as if history had consciously created this form for the fulfilment of great tasks with which it entrusted the Russian proletariat. It would be unforgivable recklessness not to make use of this historic form in the interest of the proletariat, in the interest of socialism. The inert formalism of Dan or Chernov and other Mensheviks and Social Revolutionaries, who idly clung to the slogan of a Constituent Assembly without understanding the meaning and possibilities of a new political form, was completely alien to Lenin's way of thinking. And so Lenin conceived and proclaimed the idea: "All Power to the Soviets!" — not to the Constituent Assembly under the cover of which all bourgeois parties, with the Constitutional Democrats at their head, hoped to advance their own social and political programme, but precisely All Power to the Soviets of Workers' and Soldiers' Deputies — to the armed peasantry, to the armed nation led by the working class. History itself had prepared and put forward this instrument to achieve the dictatorship of the proletariat.

"Dictatorship of the proletariat" had been the aim of all socialists since Karl Marx; it was inscribed on the banners of the Second International; it was expounded by theorists such as Karl Kautsky, G.V. Plekhanov, Paul Lafargue, R. Hilferding, and others. The dictatorship of the proletariat was the theme of *Iskra* edited by Lenin together with Martov, Potresov and Plekhanov. Where were these men now? Plekhanov, in the name of national "unity" with the bourgeoisie and for the continuation of the anti-German war, broke his organizational ties with the Social Democratic Party. Potresov did not break them, but in the large mass circulation journal *Dien* (*The Day*) which called itself "the organ of socialist thought" completely followed Plekhanov's line. Martov took a somewhat different stand: he criticized from the left the leaders of the Social Democratic Party — Dan, Tseretelli, and Lieber — and their "revolutionary defencist" attitude. But even he did not realize in the slightest degree the historic meaning of the new political instrument which had come into being in the course of a natural development of events. Lenin stood in complete opposition to all these leaders and theorists. His flexible dialectical mind was not bogged down in conventional tenets of bourgeois state laws based on the experience and practice of Western Europe in the nineteenth century. Lenin's mind remained free to search and discover new organizational forms of state power which manifested themselves in the creative dynamics of the revolutionary process. It was precisely in this sense that he put forward the call "All Power to the Soviets". He was pointing to the political means which would help in the struggle for peace and for the transition to socialist society.

Three main elements constituted the substance of Lenin's "April Theses" which resounded throughout the world and stirred millions of people: First, the revolution began in Russia; it was a socialist revolution; it was uninterrupted in the sense that it was bound to spread to all capitalist belligerent countries of Europe. Second, that the most urgent task of the Russian revolution consisted of the immediate withdrawal from the war and a direct appeal to all the belligerents with a proposal for a speedy peace. Third, the accomplishment of these tasks — the conclusion of peace and the building of socialism — was to be preceded by the assumption of power in the Russian state by the Soviets of Workers' and Soldiers' Deputies. "All power to the Soviets" — this was in fact the substance of the April Theses.

These theses stunned the whole Russian intelligentsia and nearly the whole population of the former Russian empire. Abroad, the reaction was not so powerful. The foreign governments at first did not take these theses seriously, receiving them as one more pronouncement of a socialist eccentric. The west European proletariat did not immediately grasp their meaning. In Russia the response was of three kinds: the bourgeoisie, the bourgeois intelligentsia and the officer corps received the April Theses as an offence against the state, as an attempt to subvert, in time of war, the bases of state and society, and to deliver the country — disarmed and unable to resist — to the enemy. Immediately rumours were spread that Lenin was a German spy sent to Russia with subversive aims. The majority in the Social Democratic (Menshevik) and Social Revolutionary Parties, following their leaders, went on repeating that the Theses belonged to one of those "theoretical fantasies" of Lenin which one could expect from him, and which were characteristic of him in the whole course of his political activity. Although this "fantasy" had nothing to do with reality, its attractiveness made it a danger for the uncritical masses. After acquainting themselves with the April Theses, the members of the Bolshevik Party were also taken aback; but their reaction was different. In front of them, on the dark horizon, there appeared a glow which like a rising sun illumined the political situation and the prospects for the future.

Until that time the political line of the Bolshevik Party differed only slightly from the line of other socialist parties. The Bolsheviks viewed with greater scepticism and more critically the Provisional Government and the Duma, considering them intrinsically alien and even harmful to the working class. The Bolsheviks thought it necessary to keep their distance from the Provisional Government and to preserve full freedom to criticize its moves. For them it was imperative to demand a determined rejection of the imperialist war aims and a withdrawal, as soon as possible, from the war. But the party did not pose the question of power and of the immediate wresting of power from the hands of the bourgeoisie, considering that it was necessary to prepare the election of the Constituent Assembly, according to the result of which the party was to determine its strategy and tactics. The Bolsheviks proposed to fight for reforms in the interest of the working class within the framework of the existing social system, as they did not see the possibility of revolution in the near future.

Until Lenin's arrival it was Lev Borisovich Kamenev, back from Siberian exile, who played the role of the main ideologue and leader

167

of the Bolshevik party centre. Due to his previous work as the secretary of the Social Democratic Bolshevik fraction in the State Duma he was, more than anybody else in the party, familiar with the great political problems and better equipped to take part in dealing with them. Stalin, who had also returned from Siberia, became the editor of *Pravda* and, basically, followed Kamenev's line, in fact conducted literary-political work under his direction.

Now everything had changed. The publication of the April Theses, and of Lenin's *exposé* at the party conference in Petrograd, opened the eyes of the rank and file Bolsheviks as well as their leaders. With a rare and even unprecedented unanimity, the conference accepted the radical change of the party programme and of its whole activity in accordance with Lenin's Theses.* This was warmly supported by prominent party members: by Zinoviev, who had returned together with Lenin in the "sealed train", by Stalin, by Bukharin who represented at the conference the Moscow party organization, by Sverdlov and others. But this unanimity was broken by objections put forward by Kamenev. He did not, in fact, object to the slogan "All Power to the Soviets"; he understood and shared Lenin's evaluation of the historic role of the Soviets, and was not tied to the traditional idea of the "national" Constituent Assembly. Nor did he object to the demand for the immediate withdrawal from the war and the conclusion of peace. But he was not convinced by Lenin's arguments about the proximity of the international socialist revolution, in which he did not believe. To his mind the revolution was not imminent in any of the industrialized countries of the West, neither in England, nor in Germany, nor in France, Italy, or Austria. He maintained that the end of the war might and would be brought about by the bourgeois governments of the belligerent countries on the basis of a political compromise among them, a compromise which would in no way affect the capitalist system prevailing in those countries. He also argued that the proletariat in the West was psychologically not ready to enter the path of socialist revolution, and that was why such a revolution was not possible in the near future. As Lenin was thinking and speaking only in terms of the international proletarian socialist revolution, and viewed the approaching Russian socialist

*Most sources agree that at that time Lenin was isolated in his party. At the Bolshevik Central Committee at the beginning of April Lenin's resolution was defeated by thirteen votes to three with one abstention; at the end of the month, at the national conference of the party Lenin's proposals were finally accepted by 71 votes to 39 with 8 abstentions. In the first half of April Lenin wrote a great number of articles, comments, and theses to win over his party to his views. — *Trans.*

revolution only in the framework of such international events, Kamenev, by rejecting these prospects, was also *ipso facto* discarding the possibility of the transformation of the Russian democratic revolution into a socialist one. In his opposition to Lenin's views Kamenev remained practically alone; only a few individual members of the party shared his reservations. The whole party was full of enthusiasm and looked admiringly upon Lenin as a prophet of a new world, who was opening men's eyes to the true prospects of historic development and showing mankind new vistas of socialist revolution.

Order No. 1 published on behalf of the Petrograd Soviet was approved and acclaimed by soldiers and workers. It constituted one step on the road to taking power by the Soviets. Of this the soldiers and the workers were not afraid; they did want to see power in the hands of their Soviets. But the leaders of the Petrograd Soviet were frightened by their own move, made under the influence and according to the wishes of the masses. They disavowed their own act and searched for an excuse for their alleged mistake, maintaining that they had been misunderstood, and tried to put the "blame" on the author of the Order — N.D. Sokolov. This disavowal was condemned by soldiers and workers alike. They were dismayed and wavered in their trust in the leaders. Now that on Lenin's proposal the Petrograd conference of the Bolsheviks openly and fearlessly adopted the slogan "All Power to the Soviets", restoring thereby the validity of Order No. 1, all the fervour and affection of soldiers and workers went to the Bolsheviks; and Lenin personally became the real hero, courageously defending the interests of the masses. It was inevitable that in their minds they should compare him with the pusillanimous leaders of the Petrograd Soviet, with the confused Sokolov, the hapless author of Order No. 1. Such a comparison did not work to the advantage of socialist non-Bolsheviks. From then on began the mass withdrawal of workers, soldiers, and sailors from the Menshevik and Social Revolutionary Parties towards the Bolsheviks.

9

At that time the leaders of the Provisional Government were concerned not only with the cancellation of Order No. 1 by the Petrograd Soviet itself — and in this they had the ready services of their "loyal" colleague A.F. Kerensky — they were also anxious to appease "our Western Allies", perturbed by the news coming from revolutionary Petrograd and revolutionary Russia. The leaders themselves, P.N. Miliukov and A.I. Guchkov, did not understand what went on in their own country. Guchkov had no doubt that now, when he, Guchkov, had made the weak and sly Tsar Nicholas II, with his predilection for sudden political turns and "faithlessness towards the allies", resign his throne, the army and navy would be brought to complete submission and the war would continue to its "victorious conclusion".

That Guchkov reasoned in this manner was understandable. He was a wilful personality, not an intellectual, with a tendency to adventurism, without much education and without great pretensions. But Pavel Nikolaevich Miliukov, professor of Russian history, specialist in the history of Russian culture, the very head of Russian liberalism, a man of great political experience acquired during his period of service in the Duma, organizer and leader of the so-called "progressive bloc" in the years of the war! It was astonishing that he understood nothing of the course of events and the prospects of the Russian revolution, or of the psychology of the nation, of the psychology of the Russian soldier. He was still dreaming about the "victorious" end of the war, he was harking after "The Straits" (Bosphorus and the Dardanelles), "The Cross of St. Sophia" (the occupation of Constantinople) — in a word the realization of "the Greek Project" of Catherine II. (At the time the soldiers used to call him Miliukov-Dardanelsky. But it should be remarked that Stalin also dreamt about the Straits, as well as about all the annexationist plans of Miliukov with the exception perhaps of "The Cross of St. Sophia".) And so Miliukov and Guchkov decided to allay the anxieties of the Allies and to give categorical assurances to Allied ambassadors and military attachés that the Provisional Government was resolved energetically to pursue the war to a victorious conclusion and not to some kind of peace on the basis of fanciful "no-annexation-and-no-indemnities" about which some soldiers' Deputies so irresponsibly prattled. The statements of the two Ministers, the most authoritative figures in the Provisional Government, were published by the bourgeois press of Petrograd.

The soldiers of the Petrograd garrison were enraged. They were passionately waiting for auguries of peace and listening tensely to all rumours about political moves leading to peace, and then suddenly: "... to a victorious conclusion!"? There was also great indignation among the Petrograd workers when they heard the old familiar words of the Tsarist Ministers spoken by Ministers of the new "revolutionary" government. This meant not the "defence of the revolution", but the old imperialist war aims which had already brought chaos and hunger to the population in the cities! The streets of Petrograd filled with crowds of soldiers and workers shouting: "Down with Miliukov and Guchkov! Miliukov out of the government!" and carrying posters with similar slogans. The demonstrations were impressive by their turbulence and spontaneity and by the great number of soldiers of the Petrograd garrison who took part. It all smacked of the February events. The bourgeoisie lost its balance, and so did the Committee of the Duma. Miliukov and Guchkov resigned. There was a governmental crisis.

What were the means to solve this crisis? The leadership of the Petrograd Soviet, which already in panic had disavowed Order No. 1, was, of course, quite incapable even of considering the taking of power by the Soviets. What then? A simple re-shuffle of the Cabinet? But this was not what the crowds in the streets were waiting for! This was not why the hazy spectre of the February revolution appeared! Then — coalition? The forming of a coalition government with representatives from the State Duma and the Petrograd Soviet? Until then the government was not a coalition. Kerensky got into it by a trick: he cheated one side and the other, the Committee of the Duma and the Petrograd Soviet. "Unfortunately, yes", maintained F.I. Dan, "unfortunately a coalition is unavoidable. For us it is highly undesirable and yet unavoidable. We have to take part in the government, but we must be careful and limit our participation to a minimum". Among the Social Revolutionaries there were several tendencies. Chernov and other leaders of the party regarded the formation of a coalition government positively. Chernov himself was prepared to enter it on condition that Social Democrat Mensheviks would take part in it as well. He considered it also necessary to bring into the government the party of nationalist-socialists who at that time stood very close to the Social Revolutionaries. A different position was occupied in these days by young soldiers, members of the Executive of the Petrograd Soviet, representing the Petrograd garrison, and by the co-opted delegates from the front. Nearly all of them belonged to the party of Social Democrat Mensheviks. They were young, they felt the temper of the soldiers' masses, they were not impressed but, on the contrary, repelled by the toothless policy of Dan and his

Organizational Committee of the Mensheviks. They were, however, not ready openly to express their agreement with the Bolshevik slogan "All Power to the Soviets", though, in fact, it was close to their way of thinking. Had they not in all sincerity supported Order No. 1 and with a heavy heart accepted its cancellation? They imagined that the coalition would in fact transfer power into the hands of the representatives of the Petrograd Soviet who would be entrusted with principal Ministerial posts. On behalf of these young soldiers the writer of these lines proposed, at the session of the Executive Committee of the Petrograd Soviet, to appoint Tseretelli as the Minister of Army and Navy and F.I. Dan as Minister of Labour. It was also planned to insist that the Minister of Foreign Affairs should come from among the represenatives of the Soviet. But there was no agreement among the "young" as to the candidate for this post. The best one seemed to be G.V. Plekhanov, but on condition that he would agree to pursue a peace policy, that is, that he would energetically demand from the Allies the repudiation of their aggressive aims and secure their agreement to proposals for a compromise peace. If Plekhanov were not to accept such conditions, his candidature for the post would not be acceptable, as he would only turn out to be no better than another Miliukov. If not Plekhanov, then perhaps Chernov? Or perhaps Martov? But nothing came of the project of proposing Plekhanov as a possible Foreign Minister. F.I. Dan with indignation interrupted my statement and qualified my proposals as absurd. "We cannot even speak about Tseretelli as Minister of War. It's complete nonsense!" But he was even more incensed by the plan that he himself should become the Minister of Labour. "Where did you get such an idiotic idea from?" he exclaimed. "Did it occur to you that I am a Jew? It cannot even be conceived that a Jew should become a Russian Minister. How is it that you do not understand this?"

At Dan's suggestion the session of the Executive Committee was suspended, and the debate was to be continued in the Central Committee of the Menshevik and Social Revolutionary Parties. At the meeting of the Organizational Committee of the Mensheviks, Dan came forward with a new clarification of the attitude of the party to the question of the coalition government. Once again he stressed that for the Social Democratic parties under a bourgeois regime, such as the Russian regime still remained after the February revolution, participation in the government was in principle undesirable and even inadmissible. The theoretical fantasies of

Lenin could not, of course, be taken seriously. In this context Dan recalled the experience of the West European socialist parties in the period before the war. If in a revolutionary situation the conditions required the Mensheviks to enter the government, then only the least prominent members of the party and the least representative ones should participate in it, and in this way minimize the responsibility of the party for the government's activity. One such candidate would be M.I. Skobelev who should get the post of the Minister of Labour. In the existing circumstances, said Dan, Skobelev would be a suitable personality. Tseretelli should not, in any case, take part in the government. But Chernov, whom the Social Revolutionary Party designated as the Minister for Agriculture, had put Tseretelli's participation in the government as a condition for his own acceptance of the post. In view of such an ultimatum, Tseretelli would also have to enter the government. In order to render such a decision less harmful, Tseretelli should be entrusted with the least important and the least influential position. And so it was decided to form a new Ministry, that of Post and Telegraphs. Let then Tseretelli become the Minister of Post and Telegraphs. In such a way the responsibility of the Menshevik Party for the overall policy of the government would be reduced to a minimum. This strategic conception, this "philosophy of history", was approved by the Organizational Committee of the Mensheviks, and on such conditions Skobelev and Tseretelli were delegated to enter the government. The question of the candidate for the post of the Minister of Army and Navy remained unresolved. The Central Committee of the Menshevik Party and that of the S.R.'s had no definite views on the matter. It was proposed that Kerensky should remain the Minister of Justice as a second representative of the Social Revolutionaries together with Chernov.

10

It was in this atmosphere of an unresolved governmental crisis that, in one of the halls of the Tauride Palace, a session of the Executive Committee of the Petrograd Soviet was taking place. While various topical questions were being debated, a young student, one of the secretaries, reported that in the ante-chamber of the hall a delegation of the General Staff demanded to be received by the Committee. After a brief consultation with those sitting next to him, the Chairman N.S. Chkheidze proposed that the delegation should be allowed in. Three Colonels of the General Staff entered the hall: G.A. Yakubovich, Tugan-Baranovsky and Count Tumanov. Yakubovich spoke on behalf of the delegation and declared that the "revolutionary General Staff' demanded that its views should be taken into consideration in the appointment of the Minister of Army and Navy. The view of the "revolutionary" General Staff was that A.F. Kerensky should be appointed to this post. Having said this, Yakubovich looked around the gathering obviously trying to gauge the effect of his sensational statement. The effect was indeed tremendous — none of the members of the Committee expected such a proposal and nobody knew what was behind it. No enthusiasm was shown and the assembly behaved with great reserve. The Committee will give attention to the proposal, said Chkheidze, and let the Colonel depart. A decision could not be taken immediately; first, the whole question had to be discussed in the Central Committee of the socialist parties and Kerensky himself also had to be consulted. A few hours later he appeared before the Military Department of the Executive Committee — this was his first visit there. Having greeted in a friendly manner all the soldier members of the Military Collegium, having shaken hands with each of them, he said something to this effect: "I have been informed that the Central Committee had discussed my appointment to the post of the Minister of the Army and Navy. If the Executive comes to the conclusion that this is necessary, I shall be prepared to take upon myself this heavy responsibility. I am the servant of the revolution. If I am appointed, I shall, of course, conduct all my work together with you, comrades, together with your Military Department. We shall discuss and decide everything together. It cannot be otherwise; we are comrades, aren't we?" Somebody remarked that it would be desirable that, after consultation with the Military Department, a soldier should be appointed as assistant to the Minister to deal with political matters and those of the democratic reorganization of the army. "Of course, of course", exclaimed Kerensky eagerly, "we shall together agree on the candidate for this job. This would be very important for the morale of the mass of the soldiers and would make a splendid impression!" The members of the Military Department parted with Kerensky on most friendly terms.

The Central Committees of the socialist parties approved Kerensky's candidature, and he was confirmed as Minister of Army and Navy. F.I. Dan said that this was a real "treasure trove", a real piece of good luck that they found at last a volunteer for this accursed post, and moreover one who was acceptable to the General Staff. This was all the more valuable and a quite unexpected solution. Nobody mentioned the deceitful manner in which Kerensky had pushed himself into the first Provisional Government, assuming the post of Minister of Justice. Nobody liked to put even a drop of tar into this god-sent honey. A few days passed by. Kerensky did not appear any more in the offices of the Military Department of the Petrograd Soviet. When a delegation from that Department went to look for him at his home and asked for an audience, young and elegant officers, adjutants of the new Minister, informed the delegates that Alexander Fedorovich was very busy, that he had no time to spare, that he was either attending a session of the government or was preparing to attend one; in other words, the Minister was taking part in show-meetings where he played the role of a political prima donna. The delegation did not manage to see him. Two or three days later an official communiqué announcing changes in the leading personnel of the ministry was published: Colonel G.A. Yakubovich* and Count Tumanov were nominated as vice-ministers, Colonel Tugan-Baranovsky of the General Staff became the Chef de Cabinet of the Minister, and Colonel Baranovsky the head of his political bureau. The first three were known as members of the delegation which proposed Kerensky's nomination and also as members of the Special Commission for the reorganization of the army active during Guchkov's premiership. But who was Colonel Baranovsky? Nobody knew him. His name appeared for the first time on the political scene. What brought him to the position of the head of the "political" bureau of the Minister of the Army and Navy? An inquiry revealed that Colonel of the General Staff Vladimir Lvovich Baranovsky was a brother of Olga Lvovna Kerensky, the wife of Alexander Fedorovich Kerensky. All became quite clear. Alexander Fedorovich was honestly paying his debts. The highest appointments were given to those who "pushed through" his candidature with the Petrograd Soviet, and to his own brother-in-law who was his link with the General Staff. It was he who became the head of the "political" bureau of the "revolutionary" Minister! The image of Kerensky as politician, as revolutionary, as socialist became quite clear.

* Alexander Gavrilovich Shlyapnikov in his memoirs *The Year 1917* confused two men bearing the same name and belonging to two different branches of the same family. Shlyapnikov was indignant that Yakubovich as a friend of the Minister

At the end of March 1917 the delegates to the first All-Russian Congress of the Workers' and Soldiers' Deputies began arriving in Petrograd. The Congress was to take place in the building of the Cadet Corps, the former Menshikov Palace, on Vassili Island. A group of internationalist Social Democrats (in the political parlance of the day they were then called Mezhrayontsy — the Interborough Organization) had put forward a plan to try to unite Social Democrats of all tendencies into one Russian Social Democratic Revolutionary Party, as it was named at that time. With this aim in mind the Mezhrayontsy called a meeting of the delegates to the Congress, Social Democrats of all factions and groups, for a discussion on the possibility of unification. The rapporteur at that meeting was Nikolai Alexandrovich Rozhkov, a professor of Russian history at the University of Moscow, a long-standing member of the Bolshevik Party, in 1905-6 member of the Bolshevik literary and academic section, who in 1917 became an adherent of the Mezhrayontsy. Representatives of the Bolshevik centres as well as Menshevik "revolutionary defencists" and Menshevik "Internationalists", that is, Martov's followers, were all invited to participate in the debate. Nearly all the delegates of all the four Social Democratic groups came to the meeting. In his speech Rozhkov aimed at persuading the audience that it was in the interest of the revolution, of its further development and successful conclusion, to set aside all existing differences about particular and personal questions in the name of the common goal and common principle and to bring about a united Social Democratic party. Rozhkov spoke wisely and brilliantly, with a great deal of sincerity and conviction, but he did not present any concrete programme on the basis of which a unification could take place. He did not, and could not, have such a programme. Neither Lenin nor Martov attended the meeting; obviously they considered it useless and futile. I.I. Skvortsov-Stepanov spoke in the name of the Bolsheviks and O.E. Ermansky on behalf of the Menshevik internationalists.

spoke and acted quite differently from the way in which he spoke and acted at the first Congress of the Soviets of Workers' and Soldiers' Deputies. But Shlyapnikov did not know that there were two men called Yakubovich; one was Grigorii Adrianovich, a Colonel of the General Staff, senior assistant to Kerensky soon promoted to the rank of Major General, and the other, the author of these memoirs, a soldier in the Tsarist army, the chairman of the Smolensk Soviet from its inception on 1 March 1917, who spoke at the first Congress on the subject of the democratic reorganization of the army — *M.P.Y.*

These were not, of course, personalities with enough authority in their own organizations to be able seriously to discuss practical decisions. They limited themselves to presenting the political positions of their respective parties, which had been known anyhow, without any indication as to their readiness for a merger. Their speeches had a propaganda character, aimed at influencing those delegates who were not quite sure of the correctness of their own stand. The Menshevik revolutionary defencists were represented by their ideologue and leader F.I. Dan, who came forward with a lengthy declaration. But he did not try to find a way for any agreement with other Social Democratic groups either. His speech was full of reproaches addressed to the Bolsheviks who were allegedly disrupting the unity in the ranks of revolutionary democracy, disorganizing it by the adventurist slogan of "All Power to the Soviets", and subverting the army in the face of the enemy by their irresponsible anti-war propaganda. Dan maintained that the government should seek "nation-wide" support and should not rely on the Soviets, which could not provide such support. Until the convocation of the Constituent Assembly it was therefore necessary to have a coalition government which would include the representatives of the bourgeois parties. Russia could not by herself withdraw from the war; fighting had to continue for the foreseeable future, and for this the fighting capacity of the army had to be maintained; soldiers should not be encouraged in their illusions. In Dan's speech there were hidden but clearly perceptible threats against the disorganizers of revolutionary democracy and subverters of the revolutionary army. After such a pronouncement the gulf between the "governmental" socialist parties and the Bolsheviks obviously widened. And in fact, the result achieved was quite opposite to that which had been intended by the organizers of the all-social-democratic meeting.

The Congress opened on 1 June. Most numerous were the representatives of the revolutionary Menshevik defencists and the Social Revolutionaries. Together they constituted an absolute majority. Their political positions were similar. The Mensheviks set the tone, and the S.R.s followed them. But by that time the April slogans of the Bolsheviks, "All Power to the Soviets" and "Immediate Peace", had already gained great popularity among the soldiers of the Petrograd garrison and the workers of the city. The leadership of the Bolshevik Party decided to take advantage of this atmosphere and to organize a mass demonstration in order to exert pressure on the delegates to the Congress and force them to take into account the mood of the proletariat, of the same workers and soldiers who had, after all, elected them and on behalf of whom they were to speak. When the leaders of the Congress, that is, the Mensheviks and the Social Revolutionaries, learned about the planned demonstration, they were beside themselves with indignation. "Ban the demonstration! Prohibit it in the name of the Congress! Was not the Congress the supreme authority of the Soviets of Workers' and Soldiers' Deputies and were not its decisions binding on all workers and soldiers of Petrograd?"

Such was the initial reaction of the leaders. But soon caution and cool counsels prevailed: for such a prohibition the masses had first to be prepared; they had to be made aware of the attitude of the majority of the Congress. And so the Mensheviks and the Social Revolutionary delegates went to visit military units and industrial plants. But their perorations there made not the slightest impression. Moreover, some meetings ended rather badly: the workers and even more often the soldiers were interrupting the speakers, chasing them from the tribunes and shouting "Go away! We do not want to listen!" When some of the delegates went in their cars into the working class districts of the town and distributed leaflets, the workers eagerly read them, but then booed the intruders and shouted them down. It became clear that the ban on the demonstration would not be effective. What was to be done? There was great nervousness among the delegates.

An interval in the work of the Congress was announced in order to enable different fractions to discuss the problem in separate sessions. G.V. Plekhanov, who among other veterans of the revolutionary movement took part in the Congress as an honorary guest, walked up and down the corridors; he did not have "his own fraction"; the "Unity" group of which he was the head had no followers among the delegates. The author of these lines, having met Plekhanov in an ante-chamber, exclaimed: "Georgi Valentinovich! Let us go to the session of the social democratic Menshevik group. We are, indeed, living through a unique historic moment on which depends perhaps the whole course of the revolution! In such a moment one should not attach importance to formalities, to the fact that you do not belong to our organization. We are your disciples! We have all grown up with your ideas! We should learn what you have to say! Let us go!" After a slight hesitation Plekhanov said: "Yes, I agree with you, the present moment is of a unique and historic importance and one should disregard formalities ... I would be prepared to go to the session of the Menshevik fraction. But ... they will not accept me." "How? They will not accept you?" I said. "Wait a minute. I shall talk to them and they will ask you to take part in the session!" I ran into the room where the meeting was about to begin and proposed that in view of the significance of the problem to be discussed and in view of Plekhanov's role in the history of the party and of the revolutionary movement, he should be invited: "We should hear what he has to say, what course of action he thinks we should take in the present circumstances." F.I. Dan interrupted me: "Well, really, what nonsense you are talking! How can we invite Plekhanov if he does not belong to our party, has kept at a distance from it and has been attacking us sharply? He himself would never agree to take part in our meeting." "But he does agree. He is just outside, waiting for your invitation." This was quite unexpected. For a second Dan was taken aback. He got red in the face. But he quickly composed himself and said: "Even so, we cannot allow him to attend our meeting; he is our political opponent whom we have to fight and shall fight." Other leaders supported Dan; the rest of the delegates remained silent. One could not guess what they thought, and nobody asked them. The proposal to invite Plekhanov was definitely turned down. I was very upset and went out.

"They did not agree, Georgi Valentinovich", I said. He smiled sadly, and said imperturbably: "I told you so." He said no more. He shook my hand and walked away. This was how the attempt to bring Plekhanov back, at a most crucial historic moment, into the ranks of the Social Democratic organization failed. After many meetings and lengthy negotiations between various groups and with the Bolshevik fraction, a compromise solution was reached. The demonstration was to take place but under the auspices of the Congress whose delegates were to meet the demonstrators on the Mars Field. There, next to the graves of the victims of the February uprising, a tribune was raised for the delegates to the Congress. The demonstrators filed past in formations according to their place of work or to the military unit to which they belonged. They were carrying their banners and placards with slogans. The impression was truly staggering: all placards and banners read "All Power to the Soviets!" or demanded immediate peace. These were all watch-words supplied by the Bolsheviks. Inscriptions expressing support for the Provisional Government were carried only by workers from some printing presses, employed by the state, and by the members of the clerical union. There could be not a shred of

179

doubt that the Petrograd proletariat wanted all power to be vested in the Soviets and was crying out for an immediate withdrawal from the war. Nor was there any doubt that these demands put forward in Petrograd today would be taken up in all other cities of Russia tomorrow. They would be supported by soldiers at the front and in the rear, just as they all supported the Petrograd workers and garrisons in the days of the February revolution.

12

It was astonishing with what stubborn incomprehension the Menshevik and the Social Revolutionary leaders viewed the demonstration. They drew no conclusions whatsoever from the event, and obdurately went on repeating the theses they had once formulated, as if they were for ever fixed and learned by heart. There was no flexibility, not the slightest ability to think dialectically, no political realism. And yet did they not pride themselves on their "realism" and decry the "adventurism and fantasies" of the Bolsheviks?

At the Congress socialist ministers from the coalition government delivered the main speeches, which were pale and pitiable. Strikingly poor was the speech of V.M. Chernov, the Minister of Agriculture, who was the recognized leader of the Social Revolutionaries. One could have expected from him some political ideas on the future. Nothing of the sort. A few jokes about some "small estates" which the Russian muzhik would receive from the hands of the Constituent Assembly, for which allegedly the whole Russian nation was waiting. The Russian muzhik did not wait for the Constituent Assembly, but for land and, even more impatiently, for peace. The Russian muzhik in soldier's uniform did not want to die either for "annexation and indemnities" or for peace without "annexations and indemnities". He wanted to leave the trenches immediately and to take part in the distribution of landlords' estates. But Chernov, and not only he, but also Avksentiev, the delegate of the peasants, and other Social Revolutionaries, were carried away by the prospect of a Constituent Assembly in which they hoped to play a leading role, by the prospect of electioneering and propaganda manoeuvres, and looked respectfully on the Preparatory Commission dealing with the technicalities of the election procedure. And the war? How to get out of it? To this Chernov obviously had given no thought; he

considered military matters as the "speciality" of Kerensky, once
Kerensky had taken upon himself the duties of the Minister of the
Army and Navy. As his own "speciality" Chernov considered the
preparation of the electoral campaign and the prattle about "small
estates" with which the little muzhik would be generously endowed
by the Assembly. Incidentally, this Preparatory Commission on the
establishment of the electoral law and parliamentary procedure
worked without haste. It was presided over by the Principal
Secretary of the Provisional Government, Vladimir Dimitrevich
Nabokov, one of the more important leaders of the Cadet Party,
for years overshadowed by P.N. Miliukov who had been trying to
push him aside, considering him as a rival. Nabokov was a very
clever and a well educated man, an expert in West European
administrative law. He was unquestionably an authoritative and
competent head of the Preparatory Commission. But he was in no
hurry. Why should he be? He was not only, and not so much, a
"technical expert" on administrative law as a great political figure
representing a particular political tendency. He had his views on the
situation of his time. Could the Cadet Party in present
circumstances count on any significant electoral success? No, not
by any means. Wouldn't it then be better to delay the preparation
of the electoral laws and wait for a change of the political climate?
Everything was in flux. It was quite likely that the Allies would,
after all, vanquish the German coalition, especially now that the
United States had entered the war. Then, if Russia remained be it
even nominally in the Western camp, she could count on her share
of the war booty and the benefits accruing from robbing the
vanquished. This would also change the situation within the
country. The Cadets and other bourgeois-liberal parties could then
count on much greater gains in the elections. The victorious Allies
would also help to re-establish "order" in Russia and to liquidate
all those "illegal" organizations like the Soviets of Workers' and
Soldiers' Deputies. Nabokov was certainly not in a hurry. Nor was
the Commission. Chernov, Dan and others admired the "meticu-
lousness" with which the Commission worked, and were proud
that the electoral laws of Russia would be the most perfect in the
world and in history. They did not understand that revolution
requires speed — anyhow, they were not made for speed.

Of all the speeches of socialist ministers the best impression was
made by the speech of the Minister of Supplies, Alexei Vassilevich
Peshekhonov. He was a known *littérateur*, for many years a
political commentator of the Populist paper *Russian Wealth*, and

belonged to the Narodnik-socialists. His *exposé* was very lucid and
to the point, without superfluous verbiage and empty phrases. In
the introduction Peshekhonov stated that he had never forgotten
that he was in the government on behalf of the Petrograd Soviet
which he represented. The Petrograd Soviet in sending their
representatives to the government had acted in accordance with the
whole system of the Soviets of Workers' and Soldiers' Deputies.
The first All-Russian Congress constituted the only legal representative and the only organ of the will of the Soviets. Peshekhonov,
therefore, considered it his duty to subject to the scrutiny of the
Congress all his previous activities and on this basis to receive a
further mandate. This "Soviet loyalty" on the part of an extreme
right wing socialist made a great impression; the quality of the
speech also contributed to the general sympathy he evoked.
Peshekhonov was rewarded by tumultuous applause such as was
not given to Chernov.

After Peshekhonov Trotsky took the floor. After his return to
Russia he had joined the Interborough Organization, the
Mezhrayontsy. At the Executive Committee of the Petrograd
Soviet, Trotsky came forward with a sharp criticism of the
Menshevik-S.R. majority and denounced its policy of compromise
with the bourgeoisie. Now, at the Congress, Trotsky did not
explicitly support the Bolshevik slogan "All Power to the Soviets",
but implicitly approved of it. He stressed the impossibility of a
consistently revolutionary policy in a coalition with the bourgeoisie
which was counter-revolutionary. Such a coalition, he said, would
be quite unnatural. It would in fact result in socialist Ministers
following their bourgeois colleagues and pursuing their imperialist
line, inimical to the workers. Such subservience was shameful and
inadmissible. The time had come to set up a real socialist
government and exclude from it the Cadets and other bourgeois
parties. What are you afraid of? he went on. Why do you hesitate
to take power into socialist hands? We have just heard, he said
further, the sensible and businesslike speech of Peshekhonov, who
acquitted himself well of his task and followed the directives of the
Soviets. "We need a government of twelve Peshekhonovs"
exclaimed Trotsky.*

I.G. Tseretelli, the Minister of Post and Telegraphs, was the
next speaker. He did not say a word about his Ministry. Only his
comrade Chernov spoke about it next day. Contrary to Dan's

*What Trotsky actually said was: "Put twelve Peshekhonovs in power and that
would already be an enormous step forward" — *Trans.*

conception, according to which Tseretelli was not to play any role in the government, things in fact turned out differently. It was precisely Tseretelli who came forward at the Congress with a general political *exposé* on behalf of all the socialist Ministers to explain their policy of concessions to the bourgeoisie, of compromises with the Social Revolutionaries and the Western Allies, and of the continuation of the war. The main ideological part of Tseretelli's speech was a polemic against Trotsky's statement of the previous day (though he did not mention Trotsky by name), and an attempt to demonstrate the impossibility of forming a uniformly socialist government which could not — which would not — possess enough power to solve the complex problems besetting the country. For this, he maintained, a coalition of all political parties, socialist and bourgeois, was necessary, a coalition of all the "living forces" (this was then the Menshevik terminology) for the fulfilment of those great tasks. When the Bolsheviks called for "All Power to the Soviets", they in truth wanted to put the burden on Social Democrats and the Social Revolutionaries and themselves to remain on one side; they did not intend to enter the government and share all the responsibilities. And we were not in a position to take power. "I maintain", went on Tseretelli, "that today in Russia the burden of power is too great for any one party, and that there is not a single party which would be prepared to take power with all the responsibilities." At that moment came Lenin's historic interjection: "'There is such a party!" Lenin was sitting at the front desk together with the Bolshevik fraction. (The Congress was taking place in the theatre hall of the Cadet Corps, where school desks had been brought in to accommodate the delegates.) The whole audience gasped, and there was complete silence. Tseretelli too was dumbfounded and confused. All eyes turned towards Lenin. He rose, and, head high, looked straight at the podium, directly at Tseretelli, waved his right arm and banged his hand on the top of the desk. He repeated loudly and clearly: "There is such a party!" (I sat very near Lenin, in the same row, just across a narrow passage, also at a front desk.) There was commotion in the hall. Tseretelli, not a little perplexed, said: "Perhaps in a few minutes we shall hear a statement, but I still maintain that until now there has not been in Russia a single political party which would agree to take power in its hands all by itself, nor in a coalition with other parties." After this he added a few rather unconnected and obscure sentences to finish his speech, and got down from the podium. But hardly anybody listened any more;

everybody waited to hear Lenin's statement. The whole audience was anxious and perturbed. The Chairman Chkheidze said: "Comrade Lenin has the floor."

Unhurriedly Lenin mounted the rostrum. Obviously, he was quite agitated. He did not stand still, but moved backwards and forwards. But he spoke calmly, with conviction, clearly and impressively. This, his historic speech, is now known all over the world and has been published in many millions of copies in all languages. Lenin expounded his new conception which he had, in fact, elaborated only a few days before, and with which, on the eve of the session, he had already acquainted the Central Committee of the Bolshevik Party, receiving its approval and consent. His lively and searching mind was always active; he was unable just to go on repeating the same formulae and precepts in ever-changing historical circumstances; he could not, like Dan and Tseretelli, helplessly and stubbornly move round in circles. It was at his initiative that the party had adopted the slogan "All Power to the Soviets" and taken it to the masses of workers and soldiers who, in their turn, inscribed it on their banners and posters, carried in the streets of Petrograd ten or twelve days before. It was precisely during these days that it became abundantly clear that the Mensheviks and the Social Revolutionaries, constituting the majority in the Soviets, refused to take power, to part company with the bourgeoisie with which they were in a disgraceful coalition. Just now from the same rostrum Tseretelli had confirmed this officially in the name of both parties. What should be done? Not to yield. If the Soviets, led by Mensheviks and the Social Revolutionaries, were unable to assume power, the revolutionary workers and soldiers would place that power in the hands of the only truly revolutionary party in Russia, revolutionary not in words but in deeds, the party of the Social Democrat Bolsheviks. Will this be a party dictatorship, and not the dictatorship of the Soviets of Workers' and Soldiers' Deputies? Not "Soviet dictatorship"? Yes, and so what follows? It will be the "dictatorship of the proletariat", accomplished by the only revolutionary proletarian party based on non-party proletarian and democratic organizations, among others, on the Soviets, if they accept Bolshevik Party leadership and range themselves under the Bolshevik banner. Such was Lenin's conception, approved by the Central Committee and for the first time announced nation-wide by Lenin at the first Congress of the Soviets. The announcement was not formulated in exactly this way, but such was its real meaning, its true character. And it became prophetic. In Russia, later transformed into the Soviet Union, there came into being a form of party-Soviet rule, predominantly party rule, which was gradually strengthened in the course of historical events.

13

At the session of the Congress at which Lenin spoke nearly all the leaders of the Menshevik and Social Revolutionary Parties and all the socialist Ministers were present. On that day, just before the beginning of the session, Kerensky had appeared for the first time at the Congress. He entered the hall accompanied by a few of his young lieutenants with glittering spurs, and hastily moved towards the podium. After Lenin stepped down, Kerensky insisted that Chkheidze should let him answer Lenin straightaway. Kerensky delivered a loud hysterical peroration without any significant content. He ran around the podium, shrieking and sighing, bending down towards Lenin, shaking his finger and, like a sleepwalker, screamed: "I see! I can see ... behind his back there rides a general! A general on a white horse!" assuring his audience that Lenin was objectively playing the role of a counter-revolutionary. Having finished his hysterical performance and stepping down from the tribune, Kerensky fell into a swoon, probably well premeditated. The young lieutenants were helpless and agitated, some delegates gathered around the fallen man. However, he soon came to, got up, pulled himself together and ran away elsewhere to "save Russia". During Kerensky's speech and his attacks on Lenin, Lenin himself, his hands in his pockets, kept on looking straight into his face and laughing. The clown deserved nothing better. Having heard the two men, Lenin and Kerensky, one could not help but compare them. Lenin, the thinker, experienced political activist and writer enjoying world fame, calm, reflective, resolute and daring. Kerensky, the political clown, bungler and buffoon, babbler, dreaming of becoming a great national figure. One, a giant of deeds and ideas; the other, a nonentity, inflated and absurd. And history has placed two such men face to face and made them appear in succession at the first All-Russian Congress of the Soviets of Workers' and Soldiers' Deputies. (Incidentally, Lenin and Kerensky were kinsmen coming from the same town, having gone to the same school. Their fathers knew each other well and worked in the same field. Kerensky senior was a director of a boys' "gymnasium", and Lenin's father was the head of state schools. Lenin's final school certificate was signed by Kerensky senior. Lenin was 10 years younger than Kerensky junior.)

It should be remarked that Kerensky's speech was not an *exposé* or a report; he confined himself only to polemical attack against Lenin. Well, what in fact could he tell the Congress, especially as he was then secretly preparing a military offensive to oblige "our Western Allies"? Russian diplomacy and Russian military leadership under Kerensky did indeed play at that time a sorry role on the international scene. After Miliukov's dismissal, M.I. Tereshchenko was appointed as Minister of Foreign Affairs, having previously been in the first coalition government the Minister of Finance. It is difficult to say what were Miliukov's motives in promoting this man to this particular post. Tereshchenko was a rich young man who had never been politically active and never had any definite political views. He had also hardly any views on his own "finances", which were taken care of by commercial and financial experts. He was an intelligent person, well read, with a wide circle of literary friends, and he was an admirer of the poet Alexander Blok. He was a pleasant, even a charming companion, but he was neither a politician nor an economist. Perhaps Miliukov was impressed by his great wealth? In any case he recommended him to his party comrade Nikolai Nikolaevich Kutler, who himself was a really able financier and politician, former Minister of Finance in the Witte government before 1905, who later represented Petrograd in the State Duma. Many years later, in the period of the NEP, Lenin enlisted Kutler's services in the direction of the State Bank. Miliukov as Foreign Minister pursued an imperialist policy and foreign diplomats respected him and regarded him highly; he knew how to behave with dignity. Tereshchenko was a "poor little sheep", hustled by foreign envoys. They disdained him for his lack of competence and he played a disgraceful role.

The foreign envoys demanded a Russian offensive. Military attachés also pressed Kerensky for an offensive. Kerensky wriggled. He hardly dared to believe that history had thrust upon him such an exalted military-historic role, and he tried desperately to fit it. The nonsensical decision to start an offensive was taken, though the army was psychologically incapable of an offensive. The soldiers at the front and in the rear were dreaming about the armistice, about the return home, the return to the villages where the landlords' estates were being distributed. Without their supervision the womenfolk might be cheated, the kulaks might grab the land — "they are likely to trick us while we sit here in the trenches!" How could the soldiers, in such a frame of mind, go to the attack, to a certain death? In the name of "Fatherland and revolution"? For them "fatherland and revolution" meant a return home and participation in the sharing of land. At best the army was capable of defensive action if the Germans were to attack. But there could be no talk about a Russian attack. This neither Kerensky nor Tereskchenko could understand. They had at all costs to demonstrate to the Allies that they were real "Ministers", no worse than the Tsarist ones, and that they deserved the approval and support of the western governments. An offensive was a senseless adventure, but it was to take place on the Galician front. And it ended in the only way it could end — in a catastrophe, in a dishonourable defeat. The foremost battalions which consisted of volunteers were wiped out without having received any reinforcements from the rear; and at the first counter-attack of the Germans, who had arrived to support the Austrians, the Russian troops retreated much further back than the position from which they had started the attack. Here was a defeat unprecedented in the Russian army, and when the news reached Petrograd it caused a sensation among the workers and even more among the soldiers of the garrison. The result was, of course, quite opposite to that expected by Kerensky and Tereshchenko, by the Provisional Government, which trusted the two Ministers, and by the leaders of the Mensheviks and the Social Revolutionaries. The delegates to the Congress, who had not been informed about the impending offensive, were plunged in gloom.

The Congress was, anyhow, coming to a close and it ended in the last days of June. At the last sessions a new All-Russian Executive Committee was elected by the method of proportional representation of candidates of each fraction present. Chkheidze was chosen by common agreement as the Chairman of the Committee. When the delegates unanimously confirmed this inter-fractional agreement and greeted Chkheidze with applause, he addressed the Congress saying: "You have raised me to a very high post", and he repeated, "a very high post indeed. Watch that I should not fall to the ground, fall to the ground". These words, simple, plain, and wise, pronounced with a strong Georgian accent, pleased the audience, which continued to applaud him loudly. But hardly anybody among those present guessed how prophetic his words would prove to be. Nobody could now save Chkheidze from that vertiginous fall which tragically ended in emigration, in Paris, when with a razor blade he cut his own throat.

The newly elected Executive in its turn elected a permanent bureau of fifty members and a Praesidium consisting of Dan and Lieber, representing the Mensheviks, A.P. Gotz and Khrunshinsky, representing the Social Revolutionaries, and L.B. Kamenev on behalf of the Bolsheviks. Not a single soldier and not a single worker participated in it. The reactionary press took advantage of this in order maliciously to howl down the Gotz-Lieber-Dan rule of the Soviets of Workers' and Soldiers' Deputies.

14

The First Congress of the Soviets did not bring any changes into a situation which had existed in Petrograd at the time when it opened. No fundamental decisions were taken. But at the Congress five basic "conceptions" became crystallized.

The first was that of Kerensky, if one can call his point of view a "conception". And it consisted of this: not to let pass the lucky circumstance of the revolution in order to make a meteoric career and reach for power in the state. Power! As much power as possible! No matter by what means! By deceit he had managed to push open the door of the Provisional Government and occupy the chair of Minister of Justice. He deceived the Committee of the Duma, deceived the Petrograd Soviet. And he succeeded. Then he corrupted the Colonels of the General Staff and they pushed him forward to the post of Minister of the Army and Navy. True, he repaid them honestly by giving them high posts in the Ministry. Then, in order to gain the favours of the western governments, he ordered, according to their wishes, an offensive at the front. Well, in fact, it was a failure; but Kerensky's zeal had been clearly demonstrated. Now it was time to strive for the post of the Prime Minister. Slyness and some assiduity were needed. And all this under the guise of "saving the fatherland and the revolution" from enemies on the right and on the left. The Constituent Assembly would be grateful to him for its convocation. This gratitude would be quite useful. What a heroic perspective!

The second was the conception of Dan and Tseretelli. The Russian revolution was a bourgeois-democratic revolution. The restoration of the monarchy had been the only danger threatening it. Now the aim should be to establish a political regime on West European pattern, either a republic or a constitutional monarchy.

After all, there were only two republican regimes in Europe, in France and in Switzerland (if one did not count the micro-states of San Marino and Andorra). All efforts should be directed towards setting up a parliamentary rule with Ministers responsible to the elected representatives of the people. The Social Democratic Party, as a workers' party, should remain in opposition, just as it had been in Europe before the outbreak of the war. The Social Democrats should take no responsibility for the policy of the government. Preserve freedom of criticism and your clean conscience! The party's participation in the Provisional Government should end as soon as possible. In the Constituent Assembly the Social Democrats would be an insignificant minority. And this was excellent. If the Social Revolutionaries were to strive for (and if they were to succeed in achieving) a majority in the Constituent Assembly — then what? It was their business. Let them disentangle themselves as best they could. After all, they were not a workers' party but rather a peasant party. Let them take the responsibility! As to the war, well, one should be careful and avoid a breach with the western democratic Allies. The Soviets of the Workers' and Soldiers' Deputies were an accidental though historic phenomenon, which did not really fit into the normal political scheme of things; they should be liquidated at the first opportunity, as soon as the Assembly was summoned and "normal" democratic organs of government came into being. Kerensky? Well, just an upstart! He undertook to do the dirty work? This, thank God, saves other socialists, and most important, saves us Social Democrats from dirtying our hands.

The third conception was that of Chernov. Whether this was a bourgeois revolution or not was unimportant, he argued. The main thing was that it was democratic. Our chief and fundamental task was to secure for the Social Revolutionaries a majority at the elections to the Constituent Assembly, that is to secure the votes of the peasantry. And when the Constituent Assembly had been summoned and given us a majority, then it would become clear what has to be done. According to our party programme, we shall give the land to the peasants. We shall also try to disentangle ourselves somehow from our war commitments. How? This will also become clear later. And, anyhow, why should we look so far ahead? All our forces should be concentrated on the electoral campaign, on the achievement of a majority in the Assembly. As to Kerensky ... Well, for the time being he is perhaps useful. Later on we shall somehow manage without him.

The fourth conception was that of Trotsky. After the defeat of the first Russian revolution of 1905 Trotsky became disillusioned with the theory of the permanent revolution, and in fact forgot about it. During the years between the two revolutions he embraced the idea of "socialist integration", of unification of all socialist forces around a common tactical programme without which, according to him, the socialist movement could not achieve any real success. Such an integration was especially necessary in Russia where rampant reaction had lifted its head. This was why in 1912 Trotsky proposed that Social Democrats of all tendencies and shades of opinion, including the "liquidators", should participate in the Prague conference of the Russian Social Democratic Revolutionary Party. Lenin was irritated by such a proposal. Angrily he turned it down and in the heat of a very sharp polemics compared Trotsky to the chief character of Saltykov-Shchedrin novel *Porfir Golovlev*, calling him after Shchedrin, "Little Judas Golovlev". Of course, Lenin used this epithet in the sense of the Russian classical author accusing Trotsky of unprincipled compromise with an enemy. Later on, after Lenin's death, and during the sharpening of the inner-party struggle, Trotsky's opponents seized on this epithet maintaining that Lenin had accused Trotsky of treachery. This was manifestly untrue. There was no question, and there could be none, of any kind of treachery. Lenin accused Trotsky of opportunism and unprincipled "togetherness", and barred him from the Prague conference. Five years had passed since then. After the outbreak of the world war Trotsky joined the Zimmerwaldist Internationalists, but did not play any particularly radical role among them. He was not a "defeatist", nor did he adopt Lenin's view that only socialist revolution would bring peace. Trotsky's position was not very much different from that of Zimmerwaldists like, say, Yu. O. Martov. There was no visible sign of Trotsky's return to the idea of permanent revolution. On his arrival in Russia, after the February revolution, Trotsky spoke sharply against the participation of socialists in the coalition with the bourgeois parties. He insisted on the withdrawal of the Cadets from the government. In fact, he was supporting the Bolshevik slogan of "All Power to the Soviets", but avoided using this formula and preferred to call for a "uniformly socialist administration" or a "government of twelve Peshekhonovs", as he expressed himself in his speech at the first Congress of the Soviets. This formulation testified not only to the inconsistency of his political stand, to his refusal simply to acknowledge the necessity of placing all power in the hands of the Soviets, and his reluctance to give his straightforward support to the Bolsheviks but also to a wish to return to his 1912 idea of all-socialist integration, the idea which had earned him Lenin's severe censure and the epithet "Little Judas Golovlev". Trotsky wanted to prove that in his dispute with Lenin in 1912 he had been right; he also wanted to convince himself of his own acumen and clearsightedness. But in this case his mind was not flexible enough, and he showed no ability to think dialectically. And indeed, was it worth while now, in the course of the great revolution, on the crest of the revolutionary wave, to cling to old pre-revolutionary formulae and adapt them to the changing political circumstances? Was it not better to renew them, to fill them with a new content more in keeping with the revolutionary situation? Trotsky, with all his boldness of thought and predilection for unexpected ideological turns, showed in this particular instance some rigidity of mind, some egotistical stubbornness in remaining attached to his own formulations.

It should be remarked that the political situation in the days of the first Congress, and of mass demonstrations under the slogan "All Power to the Soviets", gave a splendid opportunity for impressive and new concrete political statements in the spirit of workers' and soldiers' demands, an opportunity to voice these demands and to re-define them. In this political atmosphere a new idea was born: to proclaim the first Congress *to be* the Constituent Assembly. If all power was to go to the Soviets, then let it really be *all* power, without reservations. How could "all" power be invested in the Soviets if there was still to come some other Assembly which could also claim "all" power? Where in fact will "all" power reside? This dichotomy was also exploited by all counter-revolutionary parties, socialist and bourgeois, in their struggle against the Soviets: they stressed that the Soviets had no full powers, and that genuine full power would belong only to the Constituent Assembly. In order to put a radical end to such argumentation and propaganda it had to be shown incontrovertibly that there was no dual power, that the Soviets and the Assembly were identical, that the Congress of the Soviets equalled the Constituent Assembly. Trotsky liked historical analogies and often looked back into history. He should have been reminded that, following Mirabeau's suggestion, the Third Estate of the States General had boldly proclaimed itself to be the National Assembly. Mirabeau had shown in this case an extraordinary resourcefulness, courage, and boldness, and by his move had turned a new page in the history of civilization. The Congress of the Soviets had no fewer historic and social rights to declare itself the National Assembly than had the Third Estate in 1789. Mirabeau was the genius of the French Third Estate which had acted under his inspiration. Trotsky, in 1917, did not attempt to make a similar move on behalf of Russian workers and sailors. The putting forward of such a proposal would in itself have been a tremendously impressive historic gesture, remembered for centuries to come. Yet Trotsky all through his life had a predilection for theatrical gestures, and quite often made them whether they were needed or not. In this case there was an opportunity to strike a historic pose unique of its kind, but Trotsky missed it.

The fifth conception was that of Lenin. In contrast to Trotsky, Lenin did not like gestures and never made them. But he was a true revolutionary, and his thought was stirred by the currents of the revolution. On his return from Switzerland he persuaded the party to start a campaign, unprecedented in its scope, under the slogan "All Power to the Soviets". In conducting this campaign he did indeed show, according to his opponents, a "demonic energy". Why had Lenin not put forward the proposal to proclaim the first Congress of the Soviet to be the National Assembly? Had this not occurred to him? No, one cannot doubt that it would have occurred to him if it had accorded with his understanding of the historic situation and of the tasks of the working class. However, during the first few months of the revolution, till the first Congress, it was quite clear that the influence of the Mensheviks and the Social Revolutionaries had grown and that the leadership of the Soviets was concentrated in their hands. The Mensheviks, incidentally, did not envisage a socialist revolution; nor did they consider a revolutionary withdrawal from the war. Their party was aiming at a speedy establishment of an "orderly" bourgeois-parliamentary regime of the west European type; they did not wish for anything else. And what about the Social Revolutionaries? They were "revolutionary" *vis-à-vis* the Tsarist autocracy, and their "social-ism" was of the vague kind and without any class content. Their course at the time was not very determined, but hesitantly veering towards reconciliation with the bourgeois-capitalist order. Was it then possible to transfer "all" power into the hands of the Congress which was led by such parties? Would the power become consolidated if the Congress declared itself to be the National Assembly? Not at all. Lenin would have undoubtedly rejected such a possibility if it had presented itself. In every new historical situation Lenin was searching for a new solution. His thought never stood still, but flowed with the revolutionary current. And he found a solution: all power should be assumed by one party, because only one party proved to be really revolutionary in the revolutionary situation. This party would be flexible and act according to further circumstances: when necessary, it would base itself on the Soviets, if it could sway them in a revolutionary direction and wrest them from the hands of the Mensheviks and the Social Revolutionaries. It may be that the party would make of the Soviets the main instrument to carry out its own policy and the main instrument of governmental power. But this was not the chief problem. Power should belong to the party, no matter to whom one or other element of power would later be entrusted, whether to the Soviets or jointly to the Soviets and the trade unions, to the Cooperatives or to the Komsomol. The centre of power should always lie in the hands of the party and its apparatus. The party should take it upon itself to fulfil the great tasks which history had thrust upon the proletariat. To this end the proletarian government of Russia should in the first instance withdraw from the war and declare peace. By doing this it would not only satisfy the clamour for peace so ardently desired by the soldiers; it would also appeal to the world proletariat to rise against the war. The revolution in Russia was not an isolated phenomenon, but the first act of an upheaval on a world scale. As the revolution began in Russia, it was the duty of the Russian proletariat to take power and use it for spreading the revolution to other belligerent countries. The mere fact of the establishment in Russia of a proletarian regime which called upon the world proletariat to end the war and take power would prove to be the spark starting a revolutionary conflagration everywhere. The revolution would become uninterrupted until it embraced all the industrial nations of Europe that were involved in the war. And then the international proletariat would join forces and begin to build a new socialist order on the ruins of capitalism. Such was Lenin's conception.

Apart from the five "conceptions" there were, in truth, another two. One, the sixth, that of Martov, which he in no way tried to press on the Congress, was purely negative, and concerned the practical activities of the Menshevik Party and its participation in the coalition with the Cadets; in principle it accorded well with the Dan-Tseretelli view. Martov also defined the Russian revolution as bourgeois-democratic and considered the Soviets as an accidental growth which, in the process of historical development, would soon be removed. He also maintained that the Social Democratic workers' party could and should not take upon itself the responsibility for the further course and for the outcome of the revolution, but that it was destined to play the part of a parliamentary opposition similar to that played by socialists in west European countries before the war. Where Martov differed from Dan and Tseretelli and the Menshevik Central Committee was in his rejection of the necessity for the Mensheviks to participate in the provisional bourgeois government. He saw such participation as unprincipled opportunism, an unavoidable result of the abandonment of Zimmerwaldist "internationalism" and the adoption of "revolutionary defencism" which in truth was indistinguishable from "simple defencism" of the Plekhanov brand. Not for nothing had the revolutionary defencists in their Organizational Committee declared their party a "unified" party, that is a party embracing former Zimmerwaldist internationalists and defencists of the "first vintage", as Plekhanov put it, such as Potresov and company. Martov did not agree with such "unification", and formed, at the First Congress, his own faction of "Menshevik-internationalists". But his faction had no independent programme of political action. It was preoccupied with its own sterility, not participating in anything and not taking any responsibility.

Finally, the last, the seventh, conception was that of Plekhanov which at the first Congress found no response at all. None of the delegates expressed any sympathy with it though he had perhaps a few silent supporters in the faction of the Nationalist-socialists. Plekhanov himself in his speech at the Congress refrained from a direct exposition of his conception, which was in fact one of unconditional support for the same ideas he had expressed in the first days of the war, under the impact of the advance of the German army on Paris and the threat to the freedom of republican France. Plekhanov apparently ignored the enormous political changes which had occurred since those days, and especially since the February revolution. In his reasoning there was not a trace of dialectical thinking. In his opinion the first and for the time being the only task of the proletariat was and remained the defeat of Germany and its allies, the defence of the democratic freedom of Europe from the Prussian militarism of the Kaiser. For this there had to be an unconditional national "Unity" regardless of class differences.

194

It is difficult to imagine, difficult to understand, how G.V. Plekhanov, such a prominent thinker, could become the victim of such political blindness, how he could think in such an undialectical manner, could manifest such a lack of comprehension of great historic events.

15

The first Congress of the Workers' and Soldiers' Deputies ended its debates. The delegates dispersed and reported on the work of the Congress to their own Soviets. What had the delegates of the Petrograd Soviet to report to those who had elected them, to the workers of Petrograd factories and soldiers of the Petrograd garrison? Rumours about the impending reshuffle of the coalition government to be headed by A.F. Kerensky, responsible for the disastrous military offensive? How could they explain this offensive, which proved to be the only direct answer to their demand for peace expressed with such unanimity in the June demonstration? And was "All Power to the Soviets" to be replaced by the rule of Kerensky and his friends?

The workers and soldiers of Petrograd were astir with indignation. The idea of staging another demonstration entered their heads: to go to the Tauride Palace and to demand from the All-Russian Central Executive Committee, formed by the first Congress, an account of what had been done in response to workers' and soldiers' demands. The plan of this demonstration was not put forward by Lenin or by the leadership of the Bolshevik Party, but they did not object to it either. They did not view the demonstration as an attempt to seize power. Lenin understood full well that for this the circumstances were not yet ripe, that people were not yet ready, that neither the propagandist nor the organizational work had been completed. The demonstration was seen as one of the stages of such preparatory work. But it was not in this way that the Menshevik and the Social Revolutionary leaders or the Executive Committee understood the rumours of the coming demonstration. They were seized with panic. They imagined that this was indeed going to be the way in which Lenin's statement about the taking of power by one party was to be put into practice. The state of mind of these socialist leaders was very reminiscent of that of the Tsarist authorities on the eve of the events of 9 January 1905. The Tsarist Ministers and the officers of the court had imagined that the workers would invade the Winter Palace, commit acts of violence and annihilate the Tsar's family. They had persuaded the Tsar that armed defence of the Palace was necessary. The Cossacks had been called out into the streets of Petersburg. Now panic confused the minds of the Menshevik and Social Revolutionary leaders to such a degree that, for the defence of the All-Russian Central Executive Committee at the Tauride Palace, they called out the Cossacks, the same Cossacks who for decades had been the main weapon of repression of revolutionary street demonstrations in which the Mensheviks and S.R.s had themselves participated, the same Cossacks who were the symbol of Tsarist autocracy. Such a decision can be explained only as a result of calculations made under the impact of hysterical fear. Workers and soldiers went out into the streets. Some soldiers, though by no means all, took their rifles with them. What for? They had no clear aim. It was simply that the rifle was a "tool", an implement, that a soldier never parted with his rifle and that it was an essential part of his equipment. Crowds of workers and soldiers moved in the direction of the Tauride Palace. The Cossacks barred the way. Skirmishes ended with armed clashes. This was unavoidable; it was to be foreseen from the moment when the Mensheviks and S.R.s called out the Cossacks. Who began the shooting? This was really of no importance, as the military clash had to come. It is quite possible that the first shots were fired from the crowd by some individual soldier on his own initiative. The Cossacks responded with volleys, and the mass of the soldiers with random shooting. There were many victims on both sides. That the demonstration had no aggressive aims, and that the fears of the Menshevik and Social Revolutionary leaders were without foundation was obvious: when the crowd finally reached the Tauride Palace, after the shooting, and surrounded it in a disorganized manner, no violent incidents occurred.

In response to the popular demand Tseretelli and Chernov came out of the building, talked to the crowd and answered questions. The attitude of the demonstrators was not friendly by any means, but the two men were not molested and the crowd dispersed peacefully. But on balance the day ended with the victory of the Cossacks. Most of the demonstrators scattered under the rifle fire and a great many of them were unable to reach the Tauride Palace. This "victory" was celebrated not so much by the Mensheviks and the Social Revolutionaries as by the open adherents of the counter-revolution, the Cadets and the straightforward monarchists.

They were delighted by the fact that, at last, recourse had been had to the Cossack forces and also because the Mensheviks and the Social Revolutionaries "saw wisdom" and understood how one should talk to the rabble.

Expecting an attempt at subversion, the leadership of the Executive Committee had not only called out the Cossack cavalry regiments, but also demanded that "loyal" detachments of troops be sent from the front to Petrograd to quell the Bolshevik "putsch". "Loyal" soldiers were picked out and a few days later appeared in the streets. They had been subjected to the most reprehensible brain washing; they were told that in Petrograd the revolution was in danger, that the soldiers of the garrison there had become the victims of the agitation of German *agents provocateurs* and spies, that they were refusing to relieve their exhausted comrades at the front, that they were subverting the revolutionary order and acted against the revolutionary government and that, generally, Petrograd was full of spies and traitors. The front line troops were quite willing to go to Petrograd — it certainly was more pleasant to fight in the streets of the capital than to sit in trenches under the fire of German guns. They were no longer under the command of Tsarist generals; their comander-commissar was a member of the All-Russian Central Executive Committee, the Social Democrat Menshevik, Lieutenant Yuri Petrovich Mazurenko. Objectively, he was not a counter-revolutionary. He viewed his function as that of obeying an order of the party and the revolution, but he became quite carried away by his task of subduing the "Bolshevik putsch". He strutted through the halls of the Tauride Palace carrying before him in both hands an enormous sword in a silver sheath, on which he leaned in a dramatic posture when sitting down. He imagined himself to be some kind of Count Ivan Andreevich Khovansky, the conqueror of a national rising in Moscow at the end of the 17th century who boasted that "without me you would all be up to your knees in blood". And although objectively Mazurenko was not a counter-revolutionary, the role of the troops under his command became in fact doubly counter-revolutionary. The bourgeoisie raised its head: it openly proclaimed in the streets of the city the necessity of dealing roughly with the "spies", demanding in the first instance the arrest of Lenin as "the main spy", sent to Russia by the Kaiser's Germany in a "sealed train". Instead of energetically putting an end to such provocative agitation, the government of Kerensky (who had at last reached the Prime Minister's chair)

197

spurred it on, and finished by issuing an order for Lenin's arrest signed by the new Minister of Justice Pavel Nikolaevich Malyantovich, a Moscow lawyer who during the February revolution belonged to the so-called "legal Marxists" and called himself a Social Democrat. Lenin, with complete self-denial, was ready to give himself up in order to expose the whole nonsense of this counter-revolutionary agitation and thus render it powerless. Among his party comrades there were some who approved of this plan (Stalin, incidentally, belonged to them). But the majority of the Bolshevik Central Committee firmly opposed it and insisted that Lenin should go into hiding, and organized his escape to Finland. This was an extremely wise decision. There is practically no doubt that in the atmosphere then reigning in Petrograd Lenin would have never had the chance to appear in court; he would have been murdered in the street by counter-revolutionary bandits just as a year and a half later Karl Liebknecht and Rosa Luxemburg were murdered in the streets of Berlin. Among people spreading tales about the "German conspiracy" behind Lenin's moves and about his "spying" were even men like G.A. Alexinsky, a former member of the second State Duma, who had entered it as a Bolshevik and reached a high position due to his oratorical talent. When the Social Democratic fraction of the Second Duma (the "unified" one of Mensheviks and Bolsheviks, after the fifth Stockholm Congress of the Russian Social Democratic Revolutionary Party) with Tseretelli at its head, had been exiled to Siberia on a charge of preparing a rising and engaging in revolutionary propaganda in the ranks of the army, Alexinsky had managed to avoid arrest and to escape abroad. At the beginning of the war he took the extreme "defencist" attitude of Plekhanov. In the summer of 1917 he joined the group "Unity" and there distinguished himself by his aggressive Bolshevik-baiting. With rousing speeches he addressed audiences such as the Society of the Army and Navy and in fact called for the annihilation of Lenin as a "German agent".

Together with Lenin, Zinoviev, denounced in virulent propaganda as a spy, an enemy agent and "the right hand of the political criminal" Lenin, also disappeared from Petrograd. Much play was made with his journey with Lenin in the "sealed train" and with his long political activity abroad as Lenin's closest collaborator and head of the Bolshevik party school at Longjumeau, where, it was alleged, Russian "spies" and traitors were trained. There was no doubt that Zinoviev's life in Petrograd was also in danger. The two main "criminals" hid themselves. According to Kerensky, they had fled from justice. It was necessary to search for offenders at the top of the Bolshevik Party. After Lenin and Zinoviev, L.B. Kamenev was the most influential in the Bolshevik centre at the time. He had been elected by the first Congress to the Praesidium of the All-Russia Central Executive Committee and it would have seemed that this by itself should have given him political immunity. But the government decided to strike not only at the leadership of the Bolshevik Party but also at the prestige of the Executive Committee.

The government demanded that the Committee should lift Kamenev's immunity and that the Ministry of Justice should order his arrest as suspected of collaboration in the anti-state upheaval. That Kerensky had the insolence to address himself with such a demand to the Praesidium of the Executive Committee of the Soviet of Workers' and Soldiers' Deputies on behalf of whom he occupied the post of Prime Minister was not surprising — such were the *mores* of this political upstart and adventurer; but how the leadership of the All-Russia Central Executive Committee can have agreed to surrender, without any proof of guilt, a member of its Praesidium duly chosen by the first Congress of the Soviets merely out of a wish to pacify a vituperative agitation and in order to please the "socialist" Prime Minister, is just as difficult to understand as it is to understand the decision to call out the Cossacks for the "defence" of the Executive from a workers' demonstration. This was a case of mindless paralysis of the leaders of the Executive, who by such action were trampling underfoot the authority of the highest organ of the revolution, and the authority of its leading "socialist" parties, before the very eyes of the working class. Kamenev was arrested and thrown into prison. Kerensky's justice triumphed over the Soviets of Workers' and Soldiers' Deputies. The workers of the Petrograd factories, the soldiers of the Petrograd garrison, were aghast at this uncontrolled surge of reaction under the protection of Mazurenko's "army of occupation"; and they seemed devoid of will, as if plunged into torpor.

Reaction lifted its head even higher. There was expectation of further arrests and persecution of individual activists of the revolutionary movement. Yu. M. Steklov, one of the main leaders of the Petrograd Soviet in the first days after the February rising, was among others the victim of baiting by the reactionary press indulging in offensive sneers about his Jewish family name Nakhamkes. He was afraid to spend the night in his own flat, expecting the attack of a squad of soldiers, and with Chkheidze's permission slept in his office in the Tauride Palace.

It was precisely at this time that the differentiation between socialist parties occurred which was to become fixed and irreversible. It was at this time that they placed themselves at the opposite sides of the barricades and were no longer comrades in arms, even if at particular moments they had been divided in their counsels, but enemies engaged in a struggle, unable and unwilling to find any way to a new cooperation. It was precisely in these circumstances that Trotsky and a number of other members of the Internationalists of the Interborough Organization modified their political stand. Not so long ago Trotsky, at the first Congress of the Soviets, had called for a government of "twelve Peshekhonovs". How could one now think about such a government when the "twelve" were throwing each other into prison for the benefit of those against whom Trotsky had demanded unity? How could there be a "uniformly" socialist ministry constituted by the prisoners and their jailers? By Malyantovich and Kamenev? Under the impact of events Trotsky abandoned his old notion of socialist integration and, having undergone considerable mental stress, decided to join the Bolshevik Party and embrace the idea of the revolutionary dictatorship of the proletariat. The same decision was taken by his other comrades of the Interborough Organization, by A.V. Lunacharsky, M.S. Uritsky, V.M. Volodarsky. The Bolshevik Party gained gifted and devoted fighters who in the further course of events played a prominent historical role. Trotsky did not limit himself to this revision of his previous political attitudes. He now recalled the half forgotten theory of permanent revolution. He was struck by the closeness of this theory with that of Lenin's "uninterrupted revolution". It was tempting to think that it was Lenin who recognized the historic validity of the theory of permanent revolution which he had at first rejected. It was tempting to close one's eyes to the profound differences in the historical circumstances in which these two theories were conceived, to the great differences in the socio-economic and political analyses on which they were based. One wished to trace the chronology of the development of the idea and, perhaps, establish one's own priority. But so far all such thoughts were hidden in the depth of the unconscious. Some time later they would come into the open and find their expression in open statements and in literary writings. For the present Trotsky acknowledged only the tasks of the Russian revolution. He acknowledged that the

Russian revolution was destined to become the torch which would start the fire of the international proletarian world revolution. It was with such a vision before him, and eager to serve this idea, that Trotsky decided to enter the ranks of the Bolsheviks — to become a Bolshevik.

16

The solemn memorial service for the victims of the armed clash on the streets of Petrograd between the demonstrators and the Cossacks became a striking illustration of the political differentiation between the socialist parties which occurred in July 1917. This memorial service, in St. Isaac's Cathedral, had indeed a symbolic meaning for all the further stages in this socialist differentiation. The whole contingent of the representatives of the bourgeoisie and of the officialdom of the capital came to the Cathedral; the upper hierarchy of the Cadets with P.N. Miliukov at their head; the leaders of the former Tsarist Duma led by Rodzianko; the high executives from the world of commerce and industry, the highest state officials, the generals and admirals on active service and those already retired, the officers of the army and navy — all with their wives in ceremonial attire. Alongside came all the members of the Provisional Government, including all the "socialist" ministers led by the "socialist" Prime Minister A.F. Kerensky. There was an all round fraternization of this government with bourgeois Petrograd, and mutual vows of fidelity! But what was even more astonishing was that the official delegation from the All-Russian Central Executive Committee of the Soviets of the Workers' and Soldiers' Deputies with Chairman Chkheidze also participated in this solemn ceremony. How could such a delegation appear there? How could the leaders of the Menshevik and Social Revolutionary Parties recommend to Chkheidze and some other members of the Committee to take part on behalf of the Soviets in this counter-revolutionary fraternization? Well, when they had called out the Cossacks to "defend" the Executive Committee they had acted in panic, but they must have recovered from panic by the time they despatched Chkheidze to St. Isaac's Cathedral? What were the leaders of the Workers' Soviets thinking about when they threw themselves into the arms of the counter-revolutionary bourgeoisie that was dreaming and preparing itself for bloody "settlement of accounts" with the revolutionary working class? No, they did not think at all. They simply floated with the tide without being aware of the meaning of historic events. They were just not equal to that role which the great historic epoch thrust upon them. They led their own parties into an impasse and to an ignominous end.

A Lie is Conquered only by Truth

Lev Z. Kopelev

Translated by Ellen Wood

I

"A Letter to the Leaders of the Soviet Union ..." was written and sent in September, 1973, when the author was being furiously attacked in print, at meetings, and in specially published lectures. It seemed as if all the incomparably vast power of the state — the innumerable forces of official propaganda, the thousands of dignitaries and bureaucrats involved in the administration of culture, state security, internal affairs, in party, trade union and other administrations — was ranged against him and Academician A.D. Sakharov. Fighting against them were public prosecutors and academicians, tireless detectives and popular artists, humble technicians of criminal investigation and winners of the highest prizes in art and literature, anonymous workers — postal censors, masters of telephone tapping and authors of popular novels, songs, and films ...

In spite of everything, in defiance of daily, hourly threats, curses, shabby treatment, Alexander Solzhenitsyn wrote appeals to "the Leaders of the Soviet Union", trying to instruct them, to inspire them with the principles that he felt could save Russia.

The author's long-standing duel with the government is marked by an unquestionable nobility and loftiness of purpose. Precisely how that purpose has been realised, therefore, must be examined with especial seriousness.

Solzhenitsyn's literary and civic activities, his well-deserved international fame, have placed him on such a high pedestal that every word uttered from that height is carried throughout the world and finds a host of readers and listeners, evading all censors, defeating all radio-jammers. Therefore, when the author of *One Day in the Life of Ivan Denisovich* and *Cancer Ward* publishes theoretical tracts, prophecies and appeals, their significance and their capacity to influence the most varied people is extremely great.

"A Letter to the Leaders ..." contains several ideas that are essentially new to the author, as well as thoughts already expressed by him earlier in his letter to Patriarch Pimen, in his "Nobel lecture", in interviews and in the article "Peace and Violence" (August, 1973). While Solzhenitsyn lived in Russia, criticism of him might have given aid to his persecutors. But now, when he is safe, when his exile has in fact only confirmed his spiritual victory over lies and tyranny, the need to examine impartially the historical, sociological, and political observations expressed in his publications becomes the more obvious. Any concessions or discreet silences out of respect for him and his merits, any attempts to throw a halo of infallibility and inviolability to criticism around the author, are only insulting to his true dignity and lead to a betrayal of the truth and concern for the good of Russia, that is, a betrayal of precisely those moral and social ideals that inspire his work.

Following Pushkin's precept — to judge an artist by the laws he sets himself — let us examine "A Letter to the Leaders" in accordance with the principles of love of truth, patriotism, and Christian morality, that is, those principles that Solzhenitsyn affirms as the laws of his life and work — both in literary works and in spontaneous confessional declarations and appeals. We shall trace his words and thoughts step by step.

★   ★   ★   ★

In the first section, entitled "The West on its Knees", there appears an unusually high appraisal of the success of the USSR's foreign policy ("Truly the foreign policy of Tsarist Russia never had any successes to compare with these"). The failures of Tsarist diplomacy are attributed not only to its "cumbersome, bureaucratic diplomatic service", but also to "a certain streak of idealism", which, supposedly, impeded "a consistent line in defence of the national self-interest". In contrast, "Stalin, who had always easily outplayed Roosevelt, outplayed Churchill too and not only got all he wanted in Europe and Asia but also got back (probably to his own surprise) the hundreds of thousands of Soviet citizens in Austria and Italy who were determined not to return home but who were betrayed by the Western Allies through a combination of deceit and force''.

"... the Western world as a single clearly united force, no longer counterbalances the Soviet Union, indeed has almost ceased to exist. For no external reasons the victorious powers have grown weak and effete."

"... the catastrophic weakening of the Western world and the whole of Western civilization is by no means solely due to the success of an irresistible, persistent Soviet foreign policy. It is, rather, the result of an historical, psychological and moral crisis affecting the entire culture and world-outlook which were conceived at the time of the Renaissance and attained the acme of their expression with the 18th century Enlightenment."

These introductory judgments are unconditionally categorical. And yet, Stalin's diplomacy was not at all so omnipotently victorious, nor did it overfulfil his plans; on the contrary. Thus, for example, the capture of the Dardanelles and Trebizond was already considered in the years 1939-40; but the attempt to realise these old claims of Russian superstate power as well as the more recent attempts to seize Iranian Azerbaijan and Manchuria, to penetrate into Greece, swallow up West Berlin and South Korea, move into Yugoslavia, "assimilate" Sinkiang (Chinese Turkestan), "Finlandise" all the Scandinavian countries — all these made up a long list of gross miscalculations and defeats of Stalin's diplomacy.

The "Western world" never was "a single clearly united force"; bloc alliances of states emerged in times of war and crises (the Napoleonic, Crimean, and First World Wars) and quickly fell apart or realigned themselves. Perhaps the first real united "West" emerged precisely in the years 1947-1949 in NATO, becoming the nightmare both of the Stalinist and later the Khrushchevian superstate.

On the other hand, Tsarist diplomacy had a well-deserved reputation as one of the most skilled in Europe; not without reason did Bismarck call himself a pupil of the Petersburg school of diplomacy. The successes of Russian diplomats firmly consolidated the conquests in Central Asia and the Far East, the annexation of Transcaucasia, and the suppression of Poland in spite of all the pro-Polish sentiments of Western Europe. When defeat in the Crimea in 1854-55 and heavy losses in 1877 weakened the arguments of the Tsar's ambassadors, while fear of the growing expansion of the Russian empire united Austrian and German diplomats with their British and Turkish counterparts and they outmanoeuvred their Russian colleagues, various loyal journalists like Katkov hastened to attribute the Russian failures to a chivalrous idealism. But even then only very naïve and ignorant patriots believed it; because the foreign policy of the Tsar and his ministers — beginning with Alexander I, who made Talleyrand his agent, right up to Witte, who paid the lowest possible penalty for defeat in Manchuria and at Tsushima — that foreign policy, including even the truly ill-fated diplomacy of the last years of the Romanov empire, never suffered from the slightest idealism, and both in its successes and its failures was always pragmatically governed by the selfish interests of empire.

Thus, *all the basic propositions* of the introductory section are essentially contrary to reality; nevertheless, they are by no means original. In them one can recognise echoes of the "anti-Westernising spirit of the old Slavophils, the more recent "Eurasianists" and the "Young Russia" movement, and that rejection of all currents of European secularism and humanistic thought, liberated from religious dogmatism ("conceived at the time of the Renaissance") which was expressed with similar feeling by many Christian and Jewish spokesmen, that rejection of the Enlightenment and all other kinds of scientific and philosophical positivism. The eschatological fervour of this section reflects, too — albeit with a certain superficial admixture — traces of the ideas of the cultural pessimists: Schopenhauer and Nietzsche, Danilevsky and Spengler.

Praise of Stalin's foreign policy, extolled at the expense of the "idealistic" diplomacy of the past, serves simply as an introduction to contrast with a different and this time critical thesis.

> "We ourselves bred two ferocious enemies, one for the last war and the other for the next war — the German Wehrmacht, and Mao Tse-tung's China ... We bred Mao Tse-tung in place of a peaceable neighbour such as Chiang Kai-shek."

The first part of this statement has a basis in truth. The government of the USSR in 1925-33 provided cover for the secret officers' schools of the Reichswehr (Lipetsk, Volsk), and in 1939-41 the sage Stalin supplied the Reich's war industry with raw materials and, above all, oil (in August, 1939, the aircraft, tanks, and motor-transport of the Wehrmacht had barely enough fuel for three months, while in 1941 they had stocks for five years). Nevertheless, it was not only we — indeed least of all we — who "bred the Wehrmacht." And to explain Stalin's aid to the Wehrmacht and Hitler as stemming "from an exact adherence to the principles of Marxism-Leninism" is possible only if one knows absolutely nothing about that subject, or if one deliberately employs patently absurd untruths as polemical weapons of propaganda.

It is difficult to suppose that the author really believes those speeches of Stalin, Molotov, and their official "theoreticians," in which they listlessly repeated empty phrases about their faithfulness to the principles of Marxism-Leninism even when together with Hitler they brought about the fourth partition of Poland, when they solemnly proclaimed the war against France and England a "just war of national liberation," or when Stalin playfully called Beria "our Himmler" and, greeting the New Year of 1941, drank "to the health of the Führer; whom the German people love ..." But then it can only be supposed that the famous demand "to live not by lies" applies only to one particular kind of lie, and that in order to refute it one must be allowed to stray very far from the truth.

The thesis of the "nurturing of Mao Tse-tung" is not only far removed from the truth, but is in direct opposition to it. Mao Tse-tung "grew up" not thanks to, but in spite of, all Stalin's policies in China and all his Comintern and military-diplomatic policies. Beginning in 1926-7, when Stalin, still with Bukharin, demanded that the Chinese Communist Party submit to Chiang Kai-shek, and later when the few Chinese Stalinists accused Mao and his adherents of "adventurism," of "partisanist," "national-peasant," and other deviations, and right up to 1947-8 when the collapse of the Kuomintang army and government had become evident, Stalin only impeded the Maoists, distrusting them, suspecting them of Trotskyism and "national-deviationism". The "Northern Campaign" of Mao and Chu's armies was not completed in 1931-33 contrary to the instructions of the Comintern. Mao was elected chairman of the CPC in 1935 instead of the rejected candidate Wang Ming, through whom Stalin had tried to get the Chinese Communists to join "a united anti-Japanese front under the direction of Generalissimo Chiang Kai-shek". From 1931, when the Japanese seized Manchuria, right up to 1945, the Soviet Union supported the same "peaceable neighbour, Chiang Kai-shek" in every possible way, supplying him with arms and strategic equipment, sending him both military advisers and pilots, while aid to the "Border Region" was limited to greetings and the dispatch of a few doctors and a few "political" representatives who were mainly intelligence-observers attached to the CPC. (See, for example, the recent memoirs of Vladimirov, in which he blurts out what American and German witnesses reported earlier.) In 1945, when the Soviet army occupied Manchuria, they did not allow the army of the Chinese Communists to enter. And when in 1946 Stalin, on the demand of the Anglo-American authorities, ordered a hasty evacuation of Manchuria, Mao Tse-tung was informed of it only after several of Chiang Kai-shek's divisions had been moved considerably closer in American planes. Thus, Mao's army which had been positioned considerably closer to Manchuria, succeeded in capturing only a few depots of old Japanese arms, "magnanimously left by their Soviet brothers," (who nevertheless completely dismantled even the railways near the areas occupied by the "fraternal" Communist armies). The equipment of these armies in 1946-48 consisted primarily of spoils — Japanese and American — captured from the Kuomintang; they also obtained many guns and machine-guns of Soviet make as spoils from Chiang Kai-shek's generals who had capitulated. The successes of the Chinese Communists alarmed rather than pleased Stalin. It was in that very year that the split with Yugoslavia began; and as a potential rival in the Far East, the refractory and impenetrably secret Mao was undoubtedly stronger and more dangerous than Tito or his possible successors. Therefore, after the complete and long since irreversible victory of the Maoists, Stalin, under cover of propagandistic noises and complimentary fanfares, imposed oppressive concessionary treaties upon the new China, fortified himself on the Chinese Eastern Railway, in the naval bases of Port Arthur, in Sinkiang. With typical Stalinist cynicism he granted Mao a Soviet agent — a member of the CPC Politburo, Kao Kang (see the "Memoirs" of Khrushchev), hoping with this magnanimous gift to win the confidence of the Chinese. At the same time, intelligence agents were being assiduously recruited among the Chinese students who had been generously invited to Soviet civil and military colleges, and Soviet military advisers were planted in all large units and institutions of the Chinese army. The Korean War was provoked by Stalin primarily to involve China in a local war with the U.S.A., to weaken China and make her as dependent as possible.

The facts of this history of Sino-Soviet relations are sufficiently well-documented by circumstantial evidence from many European and American witnesses, but are wholly and unequivocally confirmed in Vladimirov's book *The Border Region of China* and in the "Memoirs" of Khrushchev. The efforts by Khrushchev's government somewhat to improve these relations — the relinquishment of the Chinese Eastern Railway, of the concession, and of military bases, the cession of Sinkiang, plans to increase economic aid, etc. — were already inadequate from the point of view of the Maoist rulers whose attitude was rapidly hardening. All these concessions did not eliminate but simply released and brought into the open the previously latent, hidden contradictions. To spite Khrushchev Chinese propagandists extolled Stalin — though only in demagogic mass propaganda, primarily that intended for "export"; in serious "secret" or "half-secret" or confidential discussions with important foreigners they made no distinctions at all between Stalin and all the succeeding "new Kremlin tsars," "Russian social-imperialists," and so on and so forth.

II

In the second section, "War with China," the assertions made in the first part grow into formidable prophecies:

"One's heart bleeds at the thought of our young men and our entire middle generation, the finest generation, marching and riding off to die in a war. To die in an *ideological* war! And mainly for a dead ideology!"

"The main reason for this impending war,.... the chief and insuperable one, is *ideological*. This should not surprise us: throughout history there have been no crueller wars and periods of civil strife than those provoked by ideological (including, alas, religious) dissensions".

"And what do you think will happen?.... That sixty millions of our fellow-countrymen will allow themselves to be killed because the sacred truth is written on page 533 of Lenin and not on page 335 as our adversary claims?"

And as a natural conclusion of these premises, these exhortations ring out:

"Give them their ideology! Let the Chinese Leaders glory in it for a while."

"The main source of the savage feuding between us will then melt away ... and a military clash will become a more remote possibility and perhaps *won't take place at all.*"

"Ideological dissension will melt away — and there will probably never be a Sino-Soviet war. And if there should be, then it will be in the remote future and a truly defensive, truly patriotic one."

Thus, the "primary," "chief," "insuperable" cause of the threat of war with China turns out to be the same perfidious IDEOLOGY (in the text of the "Letter" this word is often written in capital letters), which is, at the same time, "dead" and, as it were, non-existent.

Let us leave to the author's conscience his categorically naïve generalisations about ideological wars; any serious historian, be he a believer or an atheist, a geo-politician or a Social Darwinist, a religious existentialist or a Marxist, will cite him scores of facts demonstrating that while ideological formulae and symbols may have a very great subjective meaning for many individuals and often serve as ornamental propaganda devices for military purposes, they are never and nowhere the "chief" or "insuperable" causes of war. After many years of fierce battles between Holy Leaguers and Huguenots, it turned out that "Paris is worth a mass," while the dispute over the keys to Christian temples in Jerusalem was only the pretext for the Crimean war of 1854-55.

What, then, is the real cause of the increasingly strained relations between the Soviet and Chinese governments; what are the real reasons for this dangerous hostility? Have they really arisen only now out of ideological disagreements and differences of interpretation?

The Great-Russian government from the very beginning of its existence sought to expand to the west, the east, and the south. The necessity of repelling the incursions and the claims of belligerent neighbours impelled the Grand Dukes and Tsars themselves to attack, to conquer, sometimes by force and sometimes by cunning to "bring under their hand" the Livonian lands and Novgorod, the Tartar and Siberian kingdoms, the Nogai and other borderlands. The reforms of Peter the Great were inseparable from the aggressive foreign policy pursued by all his successors. Russian troops advancing into the lands west of the Dniester and the Amur region, Finland and Turkestan, Caucasia and Kamchatka, were sometimes preceded and always accompanied by brave explorers, zealous missionaries, enterprising merchants, inquisitive natural and ethnographic researchers, resourceful diplomats ... And sometimes with bullets, bayonets, and case-shot, sometimes with the jingle of roubles, sometimes with pretty wares or witty words, sometimes with one and the other or all three together, Russian power overcame the resistance of native princes, kings, emirs, beys ... It also repeatedly overcame Chinese commanders, mandarin-governors, and mandarin-diplomats. Having already begun in the 17th century with the conquest of the Kazakhs by Khabarov, which was consolidated by the skill of ambassadorial secretaries; having in the middle of the 19th century seized the deserted northeast frontiers of China, and toward the end of the century penetrated Manchuria with the Chinese Eastern Railway, the Russian government in the 20th century began to appropriate Outer Mongolia and Chinese Turkestan, starting under the last Romanovs and continuing under Lenin and Stalin.

Ideological symbols changed in the course of the century, but the essence of relations between governments was more or less unaltered.

In the 1850's, a mass revolution broke out in central China — the T'ai-p'ing Rebellion, which sought to shake off the rule of the Manchu dynasty and to repel the incursion of foreigners. The ideological symbol of the T'ai-p'ing rebels was "Christianity", but both British and Americans were ready to lead a Chinese army against their Chinese fellow-believers in defence of the rule of Peking pagans. The Chinese revolutionary nationalists, who were led in 1900 by the "Society of Harmonious Fists" (the Boxers) and in 1911 formed Sun Yat-sen's Kuomintang party, regarded Tsarist Russia as one of China's most dangerous enemies; in 1927 Chiang Kai-shek broke with the Communists because he saw them as an "agency of Moscow"; in 1929 Chang Hsüeh-liang tried to reconquer the Chinese Eastern Railway. In the 20's and 30's, the various rival parties in China were fighting in particular over whom to regard as the chief danger to their country: Japan, Russia, or the "foreign devils". The essential characteristic of the Maoist party and the Maoist armies was not so much their more than dubious adherence to Marxism (about which even Mao himself had very vague notions, and millions of his supporters none at all), as the strictly centralised, strong national structure, a nucleus for the crystallisation of a new empire. For this reason, both the Japanese and Stalin preferred to rely on those political forces in China that generated destructive centrifugal tendencies: the Japanese on the Manchurian separatists and the Wang Ching-Wei faction, and Stalin on Chiang Kai-shek and the "Christian Marshal" Feng Yu-hsiang.

The hostility between the governments of Stalin, Khrushchev, and Brezhnev, on the one hand, and the governments of Mao, Chou, etc., on the other, was, is, and will be least of all "ideological". This hostility represents a consistent evolution of long-standing, many-sided and, in particular, geo-political contradictions between a strong, intensively and extensively developing Eurasian power, and an Asian country that not long ago was still semi-colonial and which, as a result of the profoundly altered power relations after the Second World War, after the defeat of the Japanese empire, the disintegration of the British French, and Dutch colonial systems, and the emergence of new states — India, Pakistan, Indonesia, the Indo-Chinese republics — is growing into a great power, incalculably stronger, both absolutely and relatively, than China has ever been at any previous time in her 4000 year history.

The new Chinese state confronts the Soviet Union as her chief adversary not at all because the Maoists want to read Marx and Lenin differently, but because after the American withdrawal from Vietnam and while Japan remains disarmed, our troops and our rockets along the entire long land border, enveloping Manchuria in a pincer-grip, and our naval vessels, rapidly multiplying in the seas that lap against China's shores, represent a major and immediate threat to them. And the claims of the Maoist government against us have no ideological sources either. They are notably "imperial," territorial, national and geo-political claims; some of them are based, for example, on the fact that in "inner" Mongolia — that is, within the boundaries of China — there live three times as many Mongols as in "outer" Mongolia, in the Mongolian People's Republic, which Moscow prevented from "uniting" with the Mongol majority; on the fact that a large number of Kazakhs, Uzbeks, Uigurs and Kirghiz live in Sinkiang, and Soviet agents have for a long time set them against the "Hans", that is, their own Chinese "elder brothers". The notorious ideological disputes which in the "Letter" are given such excessive importance emerged only fifteen years ago as propagandistic consequences, not as causes, of a real inter-state contradiction. These disputes are being vastly inflated both in China and in certain foreign communist parties, creating a screen of noise and smoke that obscures the real causes of the tragically insoluble conflicts between governments — and that means precisely between governments and not between peoples. The ideological noises of the Maoist press, radio, the "cultural revolution." and so on, are a means of internal and external propaganda intended to acquire friends and sympathisers in other countries and to create an artificial "moral political national unity" in China. This is a Chinese version of the very ancient methods of exaggerating external threats employed by all war-like despotisms. Thus Hitler frightened the Germans with the threat of international Jewry and international communism, and in 1939 with the threat of "plutocracy"; and thus the Stalinists frightened us before 1939 with the threat of international fascism and Japanese militarism and from 1939-41 with the Anglo-French imperialists and the "white-Finnish aggressors". During the war the threats were so real that any propaganda was weaker than the reality — but in 1946 they again began to frighten us, this time with the sharks of Wall Street, international Zionism, West-German revanchism ... In recent years our semi-official, "whispering" (and even more effective) propaganda has been persistently manipulating the Chinese threat.

Following in the wake of Yevtushenko, Voynesensky and those who address "closed" meetings, the truth-loving writer, hero and prophet now joins in this propaganda (though with some different, more nationalist attitudes, like those of the Vyeche group), adding his contribution to that scale of the balance which is so zealously weighed down by the publicists of the *Novosti* news agency and by official lecturers and versifiers and political officers in the armed forces.

The deplorable peculiarity of the "Letter to the Leaders ..." lies in the fact that it could equally serve both the semi-official "military-patriotic" educational work of the Komsomol, the DOSAAF*, and, at the same time, Chinese propaganda. Here it is, he says, a frank declaration by Khrushchev's favourite, by Russia's most famous writer: he calls upon the new Kremlin Tsars to renounce all international ties and commitments, openly to scorn those programmes and ideals which they in fact betrayed long ago, and having cast off all ornamental masks, to establish an isolationist, nationalistic "authoritarian" state. At the same time, it should flatter Chinese national vanity that this Russian writer, renowned throughout the world, a Nobel laureate, etc., preaches the ancient native Chinese principles of the "Great Wall," that is, national isolation and conservative authoritarianism shut off from everything foreign ... Using the text of the "Letter", Maoist agitators could enrich their arsenal with new arguments for rousing

*Voluntary Society for Collaboration with the Army, Air Force, and Navy.

213

hostility against Russia and the Russian people in Asian and African countries and among the people of some of our own republics. The "Letter ..." is capable of causing such two-edged damage because it is built on a double untruth — on a false conception of the history of relations between Russia and China and on a false interpretation of their present situation.

Nevertheless, the author is perfectly justified in the anxiety that impels him to seek a way out of the growing tension, which is expressing itself not only in propagandistic noises but in the ominous massing of troops on both sides of the border. Menacing symbols turned into into bloody skirmishes on Damansky Island — when on a narrow strip of sterile land on which no human being has ever been born, several hundred young men were killed — Soviet and Chinese soldiers. They killed each other not for ideology, but for possession of that very island — for land and for power, not for ideas.

The ideas and world-views that predominate in the USSR and in China differ fundamentally from one another: only an infinitely gullible newspaper reader can seriously think that they are simply different versions of a single ideology. In fact, the world-views and perceptions of a substantial portion of the ruling and intermediate party leaders, government officials, and scientist-technicians in the Soviet Union are much closer to the views expressed in the "Letter ..." than to those expounded in the Programme of the CPSU or the textbooks of Marxism-Leninism. And the ideas and ideals of a substantial majority of Chinese public figures have never even come near these textbooks. However, independently of all ideological differences — which are to a considerable degree ideally abstract, though complicated by demagogic and false propaganda — the real contradictions in the struggle for power and land, if the present tension persists, may lead to that fatal coincidence of circumstances when "the guns begin to shoot on their own". His recognition, his sense of this terrible threat is the source of the noble anxiety that inspires Solzhenitsyn's thought. But his published works and the recipes for salvation proposed in the "Letter ..." evoke only a sad perplexity in the reader who is acquainted with history and current affairs. If the author of the "Letter ..." really believes what he writes, then how ignorant and naïvely narrow-minded he must be. But if he is simply making deliberate use of assertions that he knows to be false though effective, reckoning on mass hypnosis, how is this to be reconciled with his appeal "to live not by lies"?

The rejoinders of A.D. Sakharov and Roy Medvedev to the "Letter ..." are objectively more well-founded and subjectively better thought-out. The claims of Chinese nationalists should not be countered with opposing nationalist claims about the primacy and legality of our Far-Eastern possessions. Here the candidly self-critical and at the same time pragmatic policy which Lenin tried to adopt in similar cases would be more helpful than a return to the orthodoxy of Russia before Peter the Great. This would mean openly declaring, as was acknowledged in the early post-revolutionary years, that the territories acquired by Russia from China in the past 300 years were taken as a result of conquests by the Tsarist army, on the basis of unequal treaties; but that much time has passed since then, the rights of the living rank higher than the rights of the dead, and Vladivostok is indisputably "our city,"* and all these regions have become ours. If we acknowledged this and admitted that Stalin's policy of genocide, which in the Far East in 1936-7 resulted in a general expulsion — and even extermination — of the Chinese and Koreans who lived there, was criminal, we would take much of the wind out of the sails of Maoist propaganda. And reference to the actual principles of that very ideology which the "Letter ..." demonises and mythologises might ease the search for real compromises, based on demilitarised borders, on facilitating contacts between the Mongols of the Mongolian People's Republic and the Chinese People's Republic, on concrete long-term agreements concerning economic and scientific-technological cooperation, protection of the environment, a joint battle against the pollution of air and water, against hunger, disease, natural disasters .... Today such a programme is utopian, but in this utopia there is a living grain of truth, capable of growing in favourable conditions; while what is proposed in the "Letter ..." as a means of preventing or postponing an already impending war is not even a utopia, but a combination of abstract logical formulae, extracted from extremely distorted conceptions of reality and supplemented with incantatory commands.

III

The third section, "Civilisation in an Impasse," also arises out of a just concern. Many people in the most varied countries are alarmed by the poisoning of the biosphere, the exhaustion of natural

*A reference to Lenin's comment on its recapture in 1922 — *Trans.*

215

resources, and all the other multifarious destructive consequences of unrestrained and uncontrolled technological progress. It might have been only a matter for rejoicing that an outstanding Russian writer has joined those who are seeking ways and means to overcome the malignant forces that threaten all mankind. But the author of the "Letter ..." contends that the root of all these evils lies in the same causes to which he attributes the "catastrophic weakening of the Western world and all Western civilisation," namely in the "false ideas" "dinned into our heads by the dreamers of the Enlightenment." And he proposes to solve all these formidable and complex world-wide problems literally in the same way as the problem of a possible war between the USSR and China.

"I would not have mentioned this danger in this letter if the solution to both problems were not identical in many respects, if one and the same turnabout, a *single* decision would not deliver us from *both* dangers."

What single means of salvation is this that will save us from such different disorders? The renunciation of ideology. Because "... there is a road-block on the path to our salvation — the sole Progressive World-View."

And, as the first consequence of this first renunciation, there follows another renunciation of the fact that earlier in our history (in the time of Peter) we "... so unthinkingly, so blindly copied Western civilisation," because "... it was perfectly possible for ... Russia ... to find its own particular path."

The last proposition becomes somewhat more concrete in the next section, the fourth ("The Russian North-East"), in an appeal for the renunciation of all international ties; because, if the "Letter ..." is to be believed, such ties can only take the form either of "busying ourselves with world revolution," a preparation for "the cataclysm which is perhaps ripening, perhaps will even come to pass, in the Western countries"; or of the profligate enrichment of foreigners whom "we, ... like the meanest of backward countries, invite to exploit our mineral wealth, and to whom we suggest that they take our priceless treasure — Siberian natural gas."

In this last connection, he says:

"for half a century, since 1920, we have proudly (and rightly) refused to entrust the exploitation of our natural riches to foreigners."

This seems remarkable: the very same ideology did not interfere with a "proud and just" national economic policy. However, there is a single way out of all dangers:

to "*throw away the dead ideology* that threatens to destroy us militarily and economically, throw away all its fantastic alien global missions."

The paragraph, which began with praise of the half-century of "proud and just" economic policy, ends with a sorrowful complaint:

"We would have had plenty of other fine goods to barter if our industry had not also been built chiefly on ... ideology. Once again ideology stands in the way of our people."

It remains incomprehensible why before 1917 the managers of the Russian economy, who were very far from this malignant ideology, encouraged foreign concessions on such a grand scale throughout the country from the Lena to Baku, while from 1920 to 1970, during the allegedly autocratic rule of ideology, everything was, in contrast, "proud," etc. It is even less comprehensible how one builds industry "on ideology," or exactly what kind of "fine goods" we would have produced if industrial plans and orders had been established not by economists who had once studied dialectical materialism, but, let us say, by piously Orthodox planners ... I should guess that even a very rich literary imagination would find it difficult to answer these questions.

The preaching of national isolation, the return to an Old-Muscovite — not to say Chinese — "wise ignorance of foreigners" in our time sounds more than naïve. Such isolationism was possible for a while in a world that did not know aviation, radio, intercontinental missiles, atomic energy, cosmic research, and world wars. To rest one's hopes on the redemptive qualities of a "Great Wall" or an "iron curtain," which would shut off thriving farmsteads and monasteries in the Russian North-East from disasters that threaten the entire planet, means to doom Russia to the fate of a pious City of Kitezh, having completely lost any real conception of history and the contemporary world. It remains incomprehensible how such Manilov-like utopias can be reconciled with the perfectly sensible arguments that precede and follow them, concerning *every possible* kind of vital problem on the solution of which depends nothing more nor less than the existence of mankind.

IV

At the end of the fourth section, the author announces that he considers it "moral" "to recommend a policy of saving only ourselves when difficulties are universal" because "our people" have "suffered more in the 20th century than any other people in the world."

The idea of "superiority" in suffering, already proclaimed in the Nobel lecture, repeated again and again in interviews and articles, brings to mind those claims clearly expressed earlier at the beginning of the 30's, that our country was superior among countries of the world, that it was exceptional, historically elect ("we are the only country in the world in which socialism has triumphed ... The main criterion for distinguishing between good and evil on earth is the attitude toward our Homeland — the fatherland of all workers.") All kind of "firsts" were then claimed; "rootless cosmopolitans" and "grovellers before foreigners" were persecuted (how many of them filled the islands of the Gulag Archipelago from 1947 to 1953!); a wholesale xenophobia was propagated of a kind that did not occur even to the persecutors of the "Latinists" before Peter the Great. The change of a + to a - sign, the substitution of claims to primacy in progress by claims to superiority in suffering does not alter the essence of this zealous Old Testament belief that we are the elect. The "Muscocentrism" of the Stalinist who repeated that "the very least Soviet person" is higher than "the most highly-placed bourgeois," etc., directly and immediately prefigures the martyr-like pride of the author and those who share his views. For them, too, "the world begins with the Kremlin." This notion gives birth to an arrogant scorn for the sufferings and miseries of people in any other part of the world. "Would that we had your troubles ..."; what are they all, the Greeks, Indonesians, Chileans, "and all those others," compared to our torments and our victims! The publicists A. Solzhenitsyn and V. Maksimov devote many pages to this kind of attitude to the world; and though they both call themselves Christians, there is as much Christianity in their bookkeeping calculations — we have a million victims, you only thousands (even if we assume these calculations to be correct) — as there was patriotism and Marxism among those who accused the "rootless cosmopolitans".

★   ★   ★   ★

The section "Internal not External Development" expresses a justifiable anger and sorrow about our life. The bitter truth about the destruction of the countryside, about the thoughtless expenditures on arms, about the millions of people ruinously being driven to drink and about the pursuit of quick profits, about the ugly degeneration of our cities, about the decline of education, about the terrible irreversible damage done to our moral and intellectual development, impresses the reader with the author's high-minded anxiety, his sincere concern.

But when he tries to explain the reasons for most of these disasters and to propose ways of overcoming them, the author, with the fervour of Cato, speaks again of the same Carthage — "ideology".

"... Our ideological agriculture has already become the laughing-stock of the entire world."

"at every step and in every direction, it is *ideology* that prevents us from building a healthy Russia"

This section ends with an appeal to "first of all give up an ideology" and the next (6th) section is even entitled "IDEOLOGY."

This ideology, it seems, is

"not only decrepit and hopelessly antiquated now; even during its best decades it was totally mistaken in its predictions and was never a science. A primitive, superficial economic theory .. It was mistaken when it forecast ... It misssed the point ... It was mistaken through and through ... It miscalculated ..."

"Marxism is not only not accurate, not only not a science, has not only failed to predict a *single event* in terms of figures, quantities, time-scale or locations..., it absolutely astounds one by the economic and mechanistic crudity of its attempts ..."

"It was ... that same antiquated legacy of the Progressive Doctrine that endowed you with all the millstones that are dragging you down: first collectivization; then the national-ization of small trades and services ...; then the obstacles in the way of industrial development and technological reconstruction;

then religious persecution ...."

The growth of criminality is also attributed to the same cause, because "... for the believer his faith is supremely precious," while Marxism, which teaches atheism, "insists on" ... the encouragement of criminality,

> "just as it insists that you, the rulers of a super-power, deliver accounts of your activities to outlandish visitors from distant parts — leaders of uninfluential, insignificant Communist parties from the other end of the globe, preoccupied least of all with the fate of Russia."
>
> "Patriotism ... *means* rejection of Marxism. For Marxism orders us to leave the North-East unexploited and to leave our women with their crowbars and shovels, and instead finance and expedite world revolution."

In the following paragraphs this seemingly omnipotent ideology undergoes something of a transformation; it turns out to be already dead.

> "This ideology, which is driving us into a situation of acute conflict abroad, has long ceased to be helpful to us here at home .... In our country today *nothing constructive rests upon it*, it is a sham, cardboard, theatrical prop — take it away and nothing will collapse, nothing will even wobble. For a long time now everything has rested solely on material calculation ...."

(This is an unexpected tribute to the same ideology which is both a "millstone weighing us down," and a "sham cardboard prop.")

> "This ideology does nothing now but sap our strength and bind us. It clogs up the whole life of society — minds, tongues, radio and press — with lies, lies, lies."
>
> "Precisely because our state...continues to cling to this false doctrine ... it needs to put the dissenter behind bars. For a false *ideology* can find no other answer to argument and protest than weapons and prison bars. Cast off this cracked ideology! ... Let it pass from our country like a storm-cloud, like an epidemic ... Let us all pull off and shake off from all of us this filthy sweaty shirt of ideology which is now so stained with the blood of those 66 million that it prevents the living body of the nation from

breathing. This Ideology bears the entire responsibility for all the blood that has been shed ... Do you need me to persuade you to throw it off without more ado? Whoever wants to can pick it up in our place."

Such extensive quotations have been presented here so there can be no doubt about the accuracy of this account of the author's views. But it is confirmed even by the language and style of the letter, so exalted, so choked with the passionate obsession of his incantations and heedless of the involuntary humour of his tropes ("pull off from all of us ... this shirt"), all of which testifies to the sad unity of form and content.

The conviction that "ideology" is in fact guilty of the disasters of uncontrolled industrial-technological progress, the destruction of the earth's atmosphere, the growth of criminality, of women labouring beyond their strength, does not bear simple comparison with well-known facts. Surely the pollution of air, water, and soil, the harmful effects on the health of millions of people produced by contemporary industrialisation and even by the existence of large cities, breathing in the poisonous vapours of motors, deafened by noise and cacophony, clashings and clangings, stunned by speed and commotion, the rush of people and cars, dazzled by intolerably strong light, glittering and flashing, by glaringly bright colours — surely all this is considerably more characteristic of those countries in which a completely different ideology prevails. The newest plagues of the world afflict the life of the inhabitants of Tokyo and other large Japanese cities even more than the life of Parisians or Londoners, who might still be accused of faith in the "dreamers of the Enlightenment" who are also condemned in the "Letter". Even the most conservative jurists of West Germany do not believe in the contention that Marxism with the help of atheism encourages criminality, since they know that in the Marxist and atheistic GDR every type of criminality puts out much weaker shoots than in the soil of West Germany, which is governed by Christian parties. Even the states of the USA, where not only Marx but Darwin was forbidden not long ago, surpass all "Marxist" countries in the growth of criminality and drug addiction, in the number of perversions of the "sexual revolution," no less radically than in the number of automobiles and all kinds of goods, as well as in the number of churches and houses of prayer ...

We shall not enter into a debate about the historical fortunes of Marxism. The very concept itself has so many meanings today and is interpreted in such contradictory ways by both its adherents and its adversaries that such a debate would take up immeasurably more time and space. We shall confine ourselves to recalling the most elementary facts and simplest points that follow from them. Whatever may have been the errors or miscalculations in the economic, philosophical, and sociological writings of Marx and Engels, even the grossest of them could not have been either the cause or the source of that method — and then the theoretical methodology — of *party* discipline, which originally arose out of the political practice and the polemical work of Lenin, drawing above all on the experience of the Russian revolutionary movement of the 1870's and 80's, and later was developed into the harsh military-political doctrine of Stalin, and which today represents one of the principal foundations of the actual ruling ideology, or rather of that system of governmental propaganda, in which ideas and ideals, slogans and divergent political conceptions, can be exchanged and substituted with comparative ease without altering its essence. One can call oneself an internationalist and preach the most primitive chauvinism, the hatred of Germans or Americans; broadcast one's commitment to democracy, freedom, humanism — and with all the means of power, education, and propaganda teach a slavish disposition, meek submission to tyranny, a blind faith in the authorities, contempt for individuality, a self-denying service to the idols of party, government, and army, implant samurai virtues, make heroes out of spies and boors. To suppose that all this is related to the ideas and ideals of revolutionary socialism and, in particular, Marxism, is to believe unthinkingly in our crudest propaganda.

Stalinist ideology, which in fact predominates to this day in the consciousness of a majority of our prominent figures, in school and university programmes, in popular literature, films, newspapers (the 6th section of the "Letter ..." even speaks of "ideology in the form of newspapers"), bears the same relationship to Marxism as the ideology of the "Journal of the Moscow Patriarchate" or the semi-legal samizdat publication "Vyeche". Rudimentary formulae that have long ago lost all meaning, celebratory slogans and other ritual phrases, which are supposed to reflect something of the ideas of Marxism-Leninism, have the same relationship to reality as do our "constitutional freedoms".

To accuse Marx, Engels, or even Lenin of responsibility for "ideological agriculture," that is, for destructive collectivisa- tion, for the miscalculations and the incoherence of industrial development, and for the emergence of the threat of "technological ruin" is no more just than to condemn the Evangelists for the barbarities of the inquisition, to regard as Christian the ideology of the "Grand Inquisitor," or to consider Darwin or Haeckel responsible for the crimes of the Hitlerites, who, when they were elaborating racist laws and creating extermination camps, cited the doctrine of "natural selection".

Collectivisation in the USSR was not prescribed by any theoretical ideological programmes; it began suddenly — after Stalin's appearance at some mythical meeting of "Marxist students of agrarian questions" (which had never been mentioned before and has never been mentioned since, and of which there are no known participants). "Thorough"collectivisation based on the liquidation of the kulaks was carried out in 1929-30 in a crudely administrative manner and only received a "theoretical" foundation with a garnish of Marxist-Leninist phrases while it was proceeding, or even later. It was precisely then that the notorious four-part formula, "the doctrine of Marx-Engels-Lenin-Stalin," emerged. In Poland, where the ruling party also considers itself Marxist, after 30 years they have still not made up their minds to carry out collectivisation. And in the GDR, Hungary, and Czechoslovakia, all countries governed by "Marxists," the agricultural cooperatives are not even comparable to our kolkhozy: not in profitability or in the standard of living of the farmers, not in the system of legal and social relations. Indian agricultural cooperatives, Israeli kibbutzim, and the collective farms emerging in several Asian and African countries — often in religious communities — are being created by people professing the most varied ideologies, which are very far from Marxist.

The essential ideological premises of Stalinist collectivisation belong to the social and moral-psychological traditions of serfdom and the ancient "mir" community. These traditions were kept alive in the social utopias of the Slavophiles and Narodniki, the Tolstoyans and the earliest Soviet communards. There were attempts to overcome these traditions by Stolypin, A. Krivoshein, those "economists" from business farms to whom, in particular, quite a few pages are devoted in *August, 1914*, and those Soviet figures who put their stakes on the "cultured farmer," among them also Marxists: Bukharin, Rykov, Eichenwald, Stetsky, and others who in 1929 were vilified as "right deviationists," and in 1937-1938 were exterminated as "enemies of the people". The *mores*, the ideological, social, and administrative traditions of serf communities proved to be very tenacious, withstanding even the pressure of bourgeois-Stolypinist progress, revolutionary up-heavals, and NEP; and in the following decades — in that most terrible, most disastrous period in the long history of the Russian, Ukrainian, Byelorussian, Moldavian, Baltic, Central-Asian, and Transcaucasian peasantry — these very traditions became the basis of our "socialist" economy. Stalinist serfdom was more destructive to the Russian, Ukrainian, and Byelorussian peasants — probably because for them it was a crudely violent turning back, the destruction and devastation of the new property and social relations that had already developed, at the same time as nearby cities were growing very rapidly, sucking out, draining strength and people from the newly enslaved countryside. In the Central-Asian and Transcaucasion villages, auls,* and kishlaks,† the transition from the old community to the new was "smoother," the flight to the city less massive. Therefore, the peasantry has survived even to this day. For different reasons, the later collectivisation of the Baltic republics took place somewhat more happily than in Russia and the Ukraine. Even during the warmest period of Khrushchev's "thaw", in 1961, not one newspaper here, not one little pamphlet, made the slightest mention of the centenary of the abolition of serfdom. No one dared remind the passportless peasants of their ancestors' fate.

Similarly, Maoist "workers' communes" in China have above all inherited the traditions of the age-old community structure of the Chinese village, ruled by landlords and elders; these have now been replaced by party officials, who call themselves Marxist-Leninists with the same right as Stalin's executioners. And the differences between the Chinese communes and our kolkhozy are differences not in the interpretation of Marxism, but in the nature of national conditions and in the characteristics of the immediately preceding social developments. Thus, in their communes, which emerged out of still undecayed patriarchal communities and on land that had just been taken from the landlords, action really generated by the masses is more significant, and bureaucracy is combined with Red-Guard ochlocracy.

* Mountain village in the Caucasus.
† Village in Central Asia.

V

The "Letter ..." asserts that today's dominant ideology demands weapons and prison bars for dissidents. This is true, but precisely what kind of ideology is it that dominates, and precisely what kinds of dissidents are suppressed by weapons and put behind bars?

The heralds of Great-Russian superstate chauvinism operate unhindered in many publishing houses ("The Young Guard," "Soviet Russia," the regional publishing houses of Rostov, Krasnodar, Saratov, et al.), on the editorial staff of the daily newspaper "Soviet Russia," the magazines "Ogonyok," "Young Guard," "Moscow," "Neva," "Don," "Volga," and many other publications; they head the "Society for the Protection of Monuments," which has become in essence a legal association of new Black Hundreds; and they occupy posts in the most varied ideological institutions. Writers and scientists who openly call themselves admirers of the Romanov dynasty, supporters of the monarchistic nationalist views of K. Leontiev, Danilevsky, V. Rozanov, remain members of the CPSU, publish books, poems, and articles, hardly disguising their ideas, which are unconditionally hostile to any version of Marxism. A few years ago, a certain Skurlatov, member of the Moscow municipal committee of the Komsomol, distributed mimeographed "theses" in which he called for the introduction of laws to preserve racial purity and prohibiting interracial marriages, demanded an intensification of "heroic-military-patriotic education" with the aid of corporal punishment, barrack drill in school, the suppression of any kind of "debilitating intellectualism". After these theses had aroused loud — though only intramural — protests, their author was transferred to another job, again an ideological one, and, of course, remained a member of the CPSU; while his accusers were dismissed after a few months with extremely unflattering references.

At the same time, any attempts to concern oneself seriously with the problems of Marxism, and especially attempts to investigate history and the contemporary situation with the aid of the Marxist method of social-critical analysis of economic and social relations, provokes the harshest measures of repression. Members of the Krasnopevtsev group at the Moscow State University in 1957, members of the Leningrad "Union of Communards" (1965) and the "Marxist-Leninist" youth circles in Gorky, Vladimir, Ryazan, Kharkov and other cities (completely peaceful, naïvely dogmatic study groups which emerged in 1966-1969) were arrested and sentenced according to clause 70 to long terms of imprisonment. General P.G. Grigorenko, a convinced Marxist, languished for five years in a psychiatric hospital by decision of a court. Adherents of that ideology which the author of the "Letter ..." hates so much are persecuted by the KGB, public prosecutors, and the courts, no less harshly than are supporters of national determination for the Ukraine, Moldavia, Lithuania, Latvia, Estonia, Armenia, Uzbekistan — those republics that are supposed to be threatened by "bourgeois nationalism". To concern oneself seriously with Marxism is no less dangerous here than to disseminate Samizdat or to join the Zionists, the Baptists, the Jehovah's Witnesses, the "true Orthodox faith," the Buddhists, or to defend the Crimean Tartars who still remain in forced exile. On the other hand, the crudest abusers of "khokhols" (Ukrainians) "yids" etc. at worst hear fatherly reproaches and receive a symbolic cursory punishment.

Thus, if one can speak of the existence in our country of a single ruling ideology, it is about as close to Marxism as the sectarian doctrines of the Khlyst sect or the skoptsi are to the teachings of the apostles or to the world-views of S. Bulgakov or Florensky.

In the "Letter ..." it is repeatedly asserted that this ill-fated ideology imposes burdensome international obligations on Russia and even requires "the rulers of a super-power to deliver accounts ... to leaders of uninfluential, insignificant Communist parties." Such astonishing — or questionable — trust in the text of official news communiqués simply turns the facts inside out. The Comintern, established in 1919 by Lenin and his foreign supporters as a "general staff" in expectation of a world proletarian revolution in that year, within a few years had already become an instrument of Soviet internal policy, and in many cases even simply an instrument of military intelligence. (The most important agents of the GRU (Main Intelligence Directorate) — Trepper and Rado in the West and Sorge in the Far East — were originally agents of the Comintern.) From 1937 to 1953, many times more Communists from various countries were annihilated in Stalinist torture chambers and confined in Stalinist prisons and camps than in all the Fascist and other reactionary states of the world put together. In 1938 by a special decision of the Executive Committee of the Comintern, Communist parties that did not please Stalin were simply liquidated, in Poland, the Western Ukraine, and Western Byelorussia; two years later hundreds of German and Austrian Communists were handed over to the Gestapo and Stalin was prepared to join the anti-Comintern Berlin-Rome-Tokyo pact; and in 1943 the Comintern "dissolved itself" — to pacify the Western Allies. Those Communist parties that have firm ties with Moscow and receive economic aid are obliged to carry out almost all the orders of the Soviet hierarchy and not seldom to sacrifice not only the interests of their own people, but even blood and lives to the state interests of the USSR. This was the case in 1939 when the Communists of France, Britain, Finland, Belgium and Holland were obliged to become defeatists; not long ago the Communists of the Arab countries, Israel, Cuba, India were, indeed even now are, obliged to act similarly and to submit to ruthless leaders (Nasser, Fidel, Boumedienne, et al.) or to obstruct the national liberation movements of their own fellow-countrymen (for example, the Kurds in Iraq). The uprising in Hungary in 1956, the split with China and Albania in 1960-61, the invasion of Czechoslovakia in 1968 provoked various crises and conflicts in the Communist parties of various countries. Since then many Communists in Italy, France, England, Spain, and the Scandinavian countries have carved out a certain independence; in their newspapers there appear approving references to the work of A. Solzhenitsyn and Roy Medvedev, comments on the absence of free speech or on anti-semitism in the USSR, sympathetic articles about China, about Czech intellectuals persecuted by the Husak regime, and so on. But the "leaders of the USSR" have never been and never will be "accountable" to any foreign Communist parties, and expenditures on these parties are anything but disinterested assistance to the "world revolution," which no one thinks of any longer even in "Homes for Aged Veterans of October". These indeed great expenditures assure our government the kind of mass and often truly self-sacrificing foreign support of which tsarist general staffs could not even dream. Of course, before 1937-1939, and even until 1968, that support was both numerous and energetic; however, even that which for the time being still remains — especially in Asia, Africa, Latin America — vastly exceeds similar support for other great powers.

VI

In the seventh and final section, "But how can all this be managed?" a so-to-speak positive programme is presented. What exactly does the "Letter to the Leaders ..." propose to replace the present, different "ideological" system, so pregnant with threats of destruction? The first proposition sounds attractive:

> "Competition on an equal and honourable basis — not for power, but for truth! — between all ideological and moral currents, in particular between *all religions*: there will be nobody to persecute them if their tormentor, Marxism, is deprived of its state privileges."

The appeal for toleration, freedom of thought and speech is so good in itself that we may pass over the customary remark on the Marxist "Carthage"; let this fantastic scarecrow be, if only for the author's amusement. The more so as there follows immediately a very reasonable and just rejection "... of all revolutions and all armed convulsions".

However, the more concrete political prescriptions unfortunately contradict the opening abstract declarations of good intentions — and even contradict one another.

An appeal for an "authoritarian order" is introduced and supported by fastidiously scornful arguments about "democracy run riot" in the West, examples of which are: Presidential elections in the USA, the acquittal of the scholar-pacifist "who, during an exhausting war, steals and publishes War Ministry documents", and the activities of trade unions, which seek to

> "grab as much as they can for themselves whenever their country is going through a crisis".

All these very categorical but not very competent judgments are entirely in keeping with the opening section of the "Letter ..." ("The West on its Knees") and reiterate several earlier statements by the author (in the article "Peace and Violence"). *As political thought they are closest to the world-view of the Odessa citizens in "quilted waistcoats" described in the novel of Ilf and Petrov.* The notions about the "decadent West" which are the source of these ideas are obviously based on those remarks about "false bourgeois democracy" that have permeated both the old Bolshevik propaganda and all Soviet text-books, beginning with "A Short Course on the History of the CPSU," as well as current scholarly, literary, journalistic, and satirical works on foreign themes. Indeed, the thesis that Russia is "completely unaccustomed" to and "completely unprepared" for democracy is reminiscent of certain other kinds of political sophistry that at one time or another appeared in

Suvozin's "Novaya Vremya," "Grazhdanin," and later in "Vozrozhdenie". In fact, in the polemic against "decadent liberals" and "democratic babblers," the extreme "left" and the extreme "right" are often almost identical in the heat of their passion, in their ideas, and even in their style of polemical eloquence.

In place of hopeless democracy the "Letter ..." proposes an "authoritarian order"; and, anticipating possible dangers, the author assures us that he has in mind a kind of authoritarian order that

> "does not necessarily mean that laws are unnecessary or that they exist only on paper ... Nor does it mean that the legislative, executive and judicial authorities are not independent" and it "is founded on love of your fellow men".

Fine words; however, on the previous page it said:

> "For a thousand years Russia lived with an authoritarian order — and at the beginning of the 20th century both the physical and spiritual health of her people were still intact.... That authoritarian order possessed a strong moral foundation ... not the ideology of universal violence but the administration of justice and Christian Orthodoxy, the ancient, seven-centuries-old Orthodoxy ... before it was battered by Patriarch Nikon and bureaucratised by Peter the Great."

This paragraph, which began on a triumphal note, ends in a lament:

> "... From the end of the Moscow period and throughout the Petersburg period, once this moral principle was perverted and weakened, the authoritarian order gradually went into decline and eventually perished."

It appears that the healthiest system of all, which preserved even up to "the beginning of the 20th century both the physical and spiritual health of the people," was the one that existed before Nikon and before Peter.

A truly wonderful trick of historical thought! So, the massacres of Novgorod and Pskov — the extermination of tens of thousands of people, the oprichnina of Maliuta, the enslavement of peasants;

the Time of Troubles when boyars and priests swore allegiance to one pretender or another; such benefits of the early Romanovs as, for example, the monopoly of "intoxicating beverages" and the harsh punishment of women who dared to wean drunkards away from the "royal taverns" — all this does not prevent one from regarding this authoritarian system as "just." And before Nikon, did not Ivan the Terrible's massacres of the clergy "batter" the centuries-old Orthodoxy? Or were they balanced in favour of the Tsar's piety by the zealous references to him in the prayers of all the priests and laymen executed and martyred by him?

In fact, after Yaroslav's "Russkaya Pravda"* it was not until Alexei Mikhailovich and Peter that the administration of justice was even seriously thought about — that is, after the "battering" and the "bureaucratisation." According to the retrograde scheme of the "Letter ...", we must also include among the eras of ruinous decline the period of reform of the 1860's — that is, the period of truly great renewal and reform in Russia. During the half-century after the abolition of serfdom all the material and intellectual forces of our country developed rapidly and fruitfully; the economic, scientific, artistic, and literary treasures that were accumulated were such that they continued to bear fruit even after the terrible devastation of 1914-21 and after all the subsequent, incomparably cruel persecution of national culture in the 30's, and after a new ruinous war and new massacres.... The most powerful and inexhaustible sources of spiritual and material energy that have created Russian national culture were first liberated, or were even first born, with the reforms of Peter and especially intensively during the years of the great reforms in the 19th century.

The sketch of Russian history, outlined so inconsistently and with such internal contradictions in the "Letter ..." in order to demonstrate the necessity of an authoritarian system based on old-rite Orthodoxy, is no less far from the truth than all the other sketches that precede and accompany it. Even the wish for an authoritarian system that would permit freedom of speech, a variety of ideologies, independence of the judiciary, and so on, resembles nothing more than the dreams of the heroine of Gogol's "The Marriage" ("Zhenytba"), who wished she could combine the nose of one suitor with the figure of another and the disposition of a third ...

Apparently recognising how unconvincing are its references to ancient piety, the "Letter ..." suggests as a more recent example of

* Earliest Russian law code (11th century).

good authoritarianism "the soviets before July of 1918". But this is again a grotesque contradiction: precisely these were still democratic soviets in which representatives of different parties participated, and it was precisely they who tried to oppose authoritarian centralism.

The assertion of the possibility of an authoritarian system based on free soviets is an abstract logical construction of the type "fried ice-cream."

★　★　★　★

Thus, the basis of the critical parts of the "Letter to the Leaders ..." — the unmasking of "ideology" — proves to be a not too original trick of hypnotic propaganda: the exploitation of a demonology, much as the Nazis exploited the myth of "international Jewry," and the Stalinists and Maoists the myth of "international imperialism".

Untruthful and unjust critical premises inevitably lead to untruthful and unjust general conclusions. The appeals for the isolation of Russia from the world, for the creation of a most unusual authoritarian system are — undoubtedly against the author's will — closer than anything else to the ideals of Stalinist autarchy of the "1948-53 model" and to the programme of the Maoist "cultural revolution," which combines a cult of the absolute authority of Mao with demands for an unbounded freedom for the "line of the masses" — the compulsory replaceability and "openness to criticism" of all strata of government, party, and even the military apparatus.

The critical judgments of the "Letter ..." are far removed from reality both past and present. Let us hope that the author's wishes, admonitions, and prophecies will prove to be no less far removed from future reality; because his naïve political-economic fantasies, which A.D. Sakharov has rightly called "religious-patriarchal romanticism," for all their Avvakum-inspired old-rite idealism, reveal organic connections with those contemporary ideologies and socialist notions that have brought and will bring only new miseries to mankind.

A telling sign of this unnatural but nevertheless coherent convergence is the following respectful approbation of Stalin, completely unexpected from the author of *The Gulag Archipelago*:

"From the very first days of the war, Stalin refused to rely on the putrid, decaying prop of ideology. He wisely discarded it, all but ceased to mention it, and unfurled indeed the old Russian banner — sometimes, indeed, the standard of Orthodoxy — and we conquered!''

This approbation is the more deplorable because it is based again on a distortion (and is it only unconscious?) of historical facts. Stalin discarded Marxism not ''from the first days of the war,'' but a decade and a half before, when he proclaimed ''the building of socialism in one country'' as the real objective and the basic symbol of his party faith. And he was not the only one to rally round the ''old Russian banner.''

In 1919, by order of Trotsky, the uniform of the Red Army was modelled on the old dress of the Russian armies: the ''bogatyr'' helmet — it was actually called by this name in the regulations until it began to be called the ''budyonnovka'' — the galloon-tabs of the strelets on the chest and sleeves; Soviet propaganda against foreign intervention and against Wrangel — in particular, the poems of Demian Bedny — was based on nationalistic slogans no less than on ''class'' slogans; in 1920 Brusilov and Trotsky together waved the ''old Russian banner'' when the invasion of Pilsudski's army began, and in 1923 this banner was raised in rejecting Curzon's ultimatum, and in 1927 against Chamberlain, and in 1929 against the Chinese offensive against the Chinese Eastern Railway. In 1930 Stalin in his report to the XVIth Congress* began the fiercest campaign against the traditions of Russian national culture, abusing the Russian past with boorish ignorance (''Russia was always beaten ...''). That same year hundreds of churches were destroyed, among them the temple of Christ the Saviour and the Iberian chapel in Moscow, the treasures of the Hermitage were sold (tractors are more necessary than old pictures), and so on. And just as after the ''exaggerations'' of collectivisation that he himself had conceived he cynically charged his obedient executors with responsibility for the ''giddiness of success,'' so after the terrible famines of 1933, after Hitler's accession to power and the expansion of Japanese conquests in China, he understood the danger of the national nihilism he had set in train and in 1934 he suddenly reversed himself, fell upon Pokrovsky and Demian Bedny, ''unfurled the old banner'' and introduced the ''law on treason to the Homeland'' (earlier, the very notion was absent from his vocabulary). From that time onwards, he never furled the banner. It

*Actually in a speech of 4th February 1931 — *Trans.*

232

waved in history textbooks, beside which Solovev and Klyuchevsky looked like revolutionary Marxists, in the epic of Minin and Pozharsky and in mass literature. And after the war, when according to the strange assertions of the "Letter ..." "the Progressive Doctrine [was] taken out of its moth-balls," Stalin in fact raised the same "old banner" higher than ever. The glorification of Ivan the Terrible and the "progressive" oprichnina; the official canonisation of Yuri Dolgoruki, who in previous centuries had been regarded as a provincial princeling of dubious character; violent torrents of jingoistic literature, drama, cinematography and "popular-scientific" tracts grew until 1953 and, incidentally, have not been exhausted even today. All this was accompanied by such an unbounded orgy of xenophobia as only the most fanatical Old Believers could have dreamed of. The expulsion of "intractable" ethnic groups — Kalmyks, Germans of the Volga region, the Balkar, Chechen and Ingush peoples, Crimean Tartars, Greeks; the expulsion of Germans from East Prussia; the law punishing women with imprisonment for marriage with foreigners ... Both the Shamil who actually existed and the mythological hero of Kirghiz and Turkman folklore were subjected to posthumous condemnation — for having waged war with Russia! Shrill praises of real and imagined "firsts" of Russian science and technology alternated with frantic abuse of every possible foreign evil past and present, the spread of hostile, or at best arrogant, condescension to all foreigners and an open and "half-open" anti-Semitism. These allegedly patriotic feelings have permeated the consciousness or subconsciousness of many people, affecting prose, drama, and poetry; they have seeped even into the perceptions of the author of the "Letter ...", who has found it possible to approve of Stalin's sensible attitude toward the "old Russian banner — sometimes ... the standard of Orthodoxy."

It will not do simply to forget that this good sense of Stalin's appeared long before the war and grew unswervingly after the war and that it is completely inseparable from all the achievements of his superstate power, among them those recorded in the *Gulag Archipelago*. The shameless claims of the Stalinist to Marxism which the author of the "Letter ..." so naïvely believes — or pretends to believe — are as legitimate and well-founded as were the claims of Hitler or Mussolini to socialism, or Catholic and Protestant terrorists in Ireland to Christiantiy. All the external and internal policies, all the ideological, propagandistic, and educational activity of the old and new Stalinists vividly illustrate the historical laws propounded by N. Berdyaev:

"Revolution ought always to introduce a new life. But the nature of the objectivised world is such that in it the worst evils in the old always enter with the new. It is an illusion that revolution breaks with the old; it is only that the old makes its appearance with a new mask on. The old slavery changes its dress, the old inequality is transformed into a new inequality". (*Slavery and Freedom*, London, Geoffrey Bles, 1943)

Maximilian Voloshin poetically expressed the same sadly justified thought in many historical-philosophical verses and, in particular, in the poem entitled "The North-East" (!): "Hundreds of years of cruel, monstrous torture, and still the scroll is not fully unfolded and the hangman's register is not closed." These prophetic words were written in 1923! And in the same poem: "... the ravings of the secret police, the extreme terror ... in commissars is the folly of autocracy; in tsars the outbreak of revolution." A half-century ago the poet perceived clearly and acutely the tragic laws of his country's history. And he was not alone. Not long afterwards Anna Akhmatova wrote: "One cannot live in the Kremlin, that transformer of laws! Here the microbes of ancient fury still swarm: the wild fear of Boris and the malice of all the Ivans, and the arrogance of pretenders, instead of the people's laws." This is both a poetic and a historical truth about the traditions of the "authoritarian" superstate, passed on from Shemyak and Skuratov to Yagoda, Yezhov, Beria. The "imported" ideology to which the "Letter ..." ascribes such excessive importance is just one of the temporary decorative ornaments.

The actual ideology of the Stalinists, which still lives today, permeating our social existence and our daily "private" existence, our school books, newspapers, and literature, is an ideology of authoritarian bureaucratic party discipline, of superstate chauvinism, of unprincipled pragmatism in the interpretation of history, the contemporary world, and economic or ethical questions. Any such interpretations are determined by the immediate current needs of external or internal policy, so that any of today's "theoretical" pronouncements may be directly contradicted by tomorrow's.

Authoritarianism, chauvinism, and pragmatism — these are the integrally essential characteristics of the really dominant conservative ideology, while all the conventionally sacred (revolutionary, internationalist, democratic, socialist, humanistic, and so on) formulae or even lengthy outpourings are in essence simply decorative trinkets, purely external ritual relics, "vestiges", like the form of address "comrade" or the motto "workers of the world unite". In its true essence the Stalinist ideology is significantly farther both from the old Bolshevism and even more from all varieties of Marxism, old and new, than from certain contemporary conservative nationalist and religious ideologies — among them the "neo-Old-Belief" which permeates the "Letter to the Leaders ...". The angrily passionate revelation of the supposedly universal power of a naïvely caricatured "Marxism," the ideals of national isolation and exclusiveness, the apologia for an authoritarian system, the organic hostility to democracy and all kinds of humanism (Renaissance and Enlightenment), the very methodology of arbitrary manipulation of facts, anti-facts, and omissions — all this is heir to the basic elements of Stalinist ideology. These have, of course, been adopted unconsciously and are devoid of the rudimentary revolutionary and quasi-Marxist trappings, or have even been provided with contrary symbols: + instead of -, or the reverse. But in their essence the two ideologies are related.

VII

Nevertheless, everything in this "Letter ..." that seems to us inaccurate, unjust, and even dangerous in its possible consequences does not exhaust its content and its general significance.

The agonised alarm for the fate of Russia and Russian national culture is fully justified and timely. As many as possible of our fellow-countrymen should hear its appeal to rid themselves of the lies of official self-satisfaction, its arrogant boastfulness, and should seriously reflect on solutions to the crucial, vitally important problems of our spiritual and material existence.

The "Letter's" demand that we preserve, cherish, and vigilantly protect our country's natural environment and the monuments of national culture, that we reconstruct what has been destroyed and regenerate the abandoned sources of national creativity, is only to be welcomed — and this demand absolutely must be concretely expressed again and again by every available means in print and in social organisations.

The just reflections on the need decisively to transform the methods of planning and managing agriculture and industry, to discard methods based on the authority of incompetent, indifferent administrators and to be governed by the real vital needs of the people, as well as by the interests of future generations — all these are convincing.

One appreciates the clearly expressed rejection in the "Letter ..." of any form of violence, the conviction that today our social and governmental system can be reorganised and improved only "smoothly," that is, without violence.

Russia has experienced enough mindless and ruthless fratricidal bloodshed. The sensible words of the "Letter ..." oppose the verbiage of those extremists of old and new emigrations who — some out of a self-deceiving fanatical ignorance, some out of self-interested political calculation — howl about the necessity of a new Russian revolution.

A vivid pain permeates the lines about the hard fate of Russian women, about the miseries of mass drunkenness, about the decline of education.

All these unquestionable merits of the "Letter to the Leaders ...", although they do not atone for, do not balance, its defects — which are unfortunately not accidental, indeed only accentuate the very elements of "Bolshevism inside-out" which have appeared in previous journalistic works by the author and in *The Gulag Archipelago*, especially in the second volume — nevertheless, on their own, they can and must bear fruit.

Repentance: its Theory, History and Prescription for Today

Sergei Elagin

Translated by Vera Magyar

"Repentance, open the Gates for me"
(Supplication from the Lenten triode,
during the week of Mytar and Pharisee)
"And did they drag Pyatnashkin to the bureau?"
"They did."
"And what happened, did he repent?"
"He did ..."
(From a contemporary conversation)

I

In the volume of essays which Solzhenitsyn has edited*, the two essays which he has written himself ("As Breathing and Consciousness Return" and "Repentance and Self-Limitation in the Life of Nations") are the most important. They set the tone and determine the meaning of the rest. They contain the "general concepts" reflected in the others, in the form of prescriptions and arguments.

These concepts are the following:

1) "No socialist doctrine contains intrinsic moral demands as the essence of socialism; morality is merely promised as self-shedding, to fall from heaven like manna, after the socialization of

*From Under the Rubble, by Alexander Solzhenitsyn, Mikhail Agursky, A.B., Evgeny Barabanov, Vadim Borisov, F. Korsakov and Igor Shafarevich. With an introduction by Max Hayward. Collins, London, 1975.

237

property."

Solzhenitsyn himself wrote earlier, in *Cancer Ward*, about "moral socialism", "discussed as a conjecture", as he said, and "severely censored by the responsible speaker". So now we are to assume that the result of this discussion was enough for him to repudiate the validity of the term altogether.

2) "External, social freedom is very desirable for our undistorted development, but it is no more than a condition, a medium ... We can firmly assert our inner freedom even in externally unfree conditions ... In an unfree environment we do not lose the possibility of promoting moral goals ..."

It is very strange to hear such an argument from the author of *Gulag Archipelago* and, at any rate, it is impossible for the *reader* of that work to accept it. More precisely: should someone begin to expound such theories in my presence, my one and most irrefutable argument would be: "I see you did not read *Gulag*. Read this epoch-making book and you will never dare to say that 'we can firmly assert our inner freedom in externally unfreee conditions'."

3) The notion that "people's lives are tolerable" not only in democratic but also in "authoritarian states".

"Russia, too, lived through many centuries under various forms of authoritarian rule and yet preserved herself and maintained her health ... and for ten centuries millions of our peasant ancestors died telling that they did not live too intolerable lives."

Does it not follow, then, that serfdom was not too bad: *ten centuries*, it is no joke!

It is difficult to argue, since somehow one feels ashamed to ask Solzhenitsyn to re-read this country's history. Yet it will have to be done. And more than once. For there is, in life and in history, something indisputable, like a mathematical axiom that need not be proved. Must we start tearing down open doors by shouting that serfdom was evil, the greatest anti-human, anti-Christian evil, and that generations of Russian peasants lived "unbearable lives"?

The very fact of a declaration to the contrary is most likely the symptom of the morbid, vehement passion, that "succession of convulsive and instant self-denial and self-destruction, which is so fatal for us and which is so peculiar for the Russian character at various decisive moments of their lives", of which Dostoevsky, feeling it sharply, had warned us, and into which Solzhenitsyn has now fallen.

4) And the following statement can be explained only by straightforward ignorance of Russian history: "The autocrats of past religious centuries, though their power was apparently unlimited, had a sense of responsibility before God and their own consciences".

For pity's sake, Alexander Isaevich, did Ivan Kalita have "a sense of responsibility before God and his own conscience" when, wishing to conquer Tver, he brought on it the Tartars and drowned the Christian city in blood? Or Ivan III when, in 1502, condoning the rage of the well-known prior Iosif Volotsky, famous for his cruelty in persecuting any kind of free thinking, he consented to heretics being burnt in wooden cages? The historian may not care to remember that our Orthodox Church used to burn people alive, just like the western inquisitors — but it happened all the same.

And the ferocious internecine wars of Russian grand dukes struggling for power in the fifteenth century, when they sought out their enemies in churches, during prayers, when they blinded each other, imprisoned children, etc.!

The case of Ivan the Terrible merits special discussion, for most probably there was no more abominable despot than this tsar-hangman in a monk's habit ...

Solzhenitsyn, contending that the state structure is of secondary importance, since it is possible to be "internally free" in "externally unfree conditions", depicts "religious attitude", "religious bearing" as the most reliable criterion of truly humanistic behaviour. Further, the task of "liberating one's own soul" is an "accessible moral step for each individual man".

This liberation can be achieved through repentance by each individual man and nation, and after repentance should follow self-limitation.

Upon reading these essays by Solzhenitsyn I was reminded of the daughter of a mid-nineteenth century court architect, Elena Shtakenschneider, known by literary historians rather than by the general reading public. She was deprived of the capacity to lead a normal life by a vicious malady, but this, obviously, sharpened her intellect, her power of observation and her thirst for spiritual impressions, so abundant in the Russian society of 1850-1860, the period preceding the turning point.* Elena Shtakenschneider had left behind a diary, characterizing vividly the period and many of

*Following defeat in the Crimean war discontent and peasant revolts were widespread, and Alexander II had to initiate some reforms, the most important being, in 1861, the Edict of Emancipation — abolition of serfdom. — *Trans.*

its personalities. When she got to know P. Lavrov, later a famous publicist, she immediately singled him out from the rest of her acquaintances "who only fling questions at each other, but do not give any answers, because they cannot or do not want to. Lavrov with his classical, Plutarchian character, must be able to give the answers and must want to. I only hope he has no 'Achilles' tendon'! I hope I would not have to see his tendon!" — she siged with feminine helplessness. This supplication about Achilles' tendon came to my mind with particular clarity probably because one always tumbles upon it in the throes of a strong passion. And how bitter it is when one is forced to notice the 'tendon' after all!

These essays of Solzhenitsyn's seem to me, without any doubt, his 'tendons of Achilles', and at the same time they betray the weaknesses of the whole volume.

Every homily, every teaching needs disciples or apostles who work out in detail the thoughts the master hints at and who propagate widely his ideas. For every thinker, therefore, it is very important in what kind of an environment he advocates his teachings; it is vital whom he addresses himself to, who is capable of listening to him. Moreover, it is not a matter of indifference how the listener will understand and respond to these ideas, and above all how he will act upon them. Will the new teachings remain empty words for him, for whose sake he would not even dream of changing his life? Or will he respond with all his being, will he feel the ideas vitally necessary and wish to share them with those around him? And this does not depend on the listener, the disciple, the medium alone. It is determined to a much greater extent by the presence or absence of vital power in the teachings. Let us glance through, even if only in general outlines, the ethos of the basic religious essays in the volume. With this background perhaps Solzehnitsyn's recipes will become more comprehensible.

II

"I do not like it when people with a general education only, poke their noses into discussions regarding special fields. And we have plenty of it. Civilians love to discuss matters of a military concern, even field-marshals' business, while people trained in engineering make judgements on questions of philosophy and political economy." (Dostoevsky, *Diary of a Writer,* 1878)

"And he longs to believe but does not ask about faith" (F. Tyutchev)

The essays of a strictly religious trend, "Personality and National Consciousness" by V. Borisov, "The Schism between Church and the World" by E. Barabanov, "Russian Destinies" by F. Korsakov, "The Direction of Changes" by A.B., and also I. Shafarevich's "Does Russia Have a Future?", together with the former, in spite of some differences in emphasis, are all following the tone and trend set by Solzhenitsyn.

With the exception of the gifted and passionately religious sermon by F. Korsakov, who does not pretend to provide forecasts, directions and methods of salvation, all the others are marked by a deductive, hopelessly abstract way of thinking and by a rather mediocre knowledge of history. I. Shafarevich, for instance, in order to prove that the "ideal goal of socialism is the destruction of human existence" and that "among the fundamental forces, operating over the course of history is an urge to self-destruction, humanity's death-instinct", presents instances taken from popular booklets about Mesopotamia in the twenty-second and twenty-first century B.C., about the Inca empire, etc. (the essay "Socialism ..."). In the essay "Does Russia Have a Future?" Shafarevich echoes Solzhenitsyn, saying that "the road to freedom begins within ourselves, when we cease clambering up the ladder of career or affluence". Declaring further — contrary to historical facts — that "Christianity originated at the moment when the ancient world was at the peak of its flourishing" — while it is well known that Christianity appeared when antiquity was in the process of complete decomposition and it was a herald and sure sign of its end — he gives the optimistic forecast: "In our time, too, as in the first centuries of Christianity [!], there are small circles measuring their values by standards completely different from those of the world outside. Once this movement gets stronger, broader — we shall achieve a freedom we cannot even contemplate at present." Can a view be further removed from history than this? By the way, Solzhenitsyn spoke about this sort of inner freedom, contradicting himself, in the article "The Smatterers", where he made fun of "thinking fearlessly" in smoking-dens: "If making a gesture of contempt inside your pocket is inner freedom, what is inner slavery then?'' For in the liberal "groupuscules" of Moscow, where — according to Shafarevich — "there are different standards of value", making contemptuous gestures is becoming a most subtle form of conformism and adherents are becoming excellent virtuosos in the art. The members of these Moscow circles have learnt very well the rule of "rendering unto him what is God's after Caesar had extracted what was his" and there are no better skilled time-servers in our society than the Moscow "inner-freedom"-lovers engaged in wool-gathering in their kitchens.

This sort of idle gossip-club was ridiculed with hatred some time ago by Andrei Belyi who, in his reminiscences, had compared the attitudes of Blok, avoiding the tittle-tattle of such circles, "the fuss about completely aimless resolutions and protests of useless social groups eventually swept away by life's maelstrom, believing meanwhile that the vortex was created by them." As an example, on the other hand, of the "stilted public spirited personalities" more interested in their own vainglory than in the country's needs, Belyi invokes Merezhkovsky and his group: "their religious-philosophical conversations, with a background flaming with real catastrophe," seemed like " a lame caricature".

And this is how Blok himself describes his attitude to this sort of "group life":

"Idle talk has recommenced now, but all these embittered learned intellectuals, engaged in daily discussions about Christ, with spouses and sisters-in-law in pretty little blouses; philosophers and priests contemplating a multitude of problems, shining with self-satisfaction, they are all aware that behind the door there stand spiritual paupers.... And there is a cold wind in the street, the prostitutes are freezing, people are starving, others are being hanged, and the country is 'reactionary', it is hard, cold, loathsome to live in Russia. But even if all these chatterers would wear themselves to skin and bones with their hard work of research ... — it would make no difference whatsoever for Russia." (*Russia and the Intellectuals*)

Our Moscow circles did not get any further than those detested by Blok — only, perhaps, their phraseology became somewhat richer.

Of course, Shafarevich's Mesopotamia and Inca empire, Barabanov's Byzantine emperors provide the authors discussing Russia's destiny with a certain appearance of highfalutin abstract thinking — and abstraction has long been recognized as a superior form of thought. However, Hegel has already ridiculed this blunder in his fine satirical pamphlet "Who is an abstract thinker?" He gives an example of the most obvious abstract speech: "The marketwoman swearing and showering selected abstractions at a customer who found the eggs she sold were rotten ... She thinks in abstractions, that's all. She considers everything and everyone, from hat to stockings, from head to toe, together with daddy, mummy and the rest of the relations involved in the customer's crime of having found the eggs rotten."

"Truth is concrete" — this is such an old platitude that it is embarrassing to recall it. All the same, it is the first reproach one feels like addressing to the authors of the volume. The Vekhists'* tradition which the authors of *From Under the Rubble* wish to continue, was highly cultivated and rich in taking stock of the various spiritual quests in Russian society, in striving to give an answer to every question posed by life. Since then more than half a century had passed, cruel and testing years. New questions arose, new problems came to the surface. Nevertheless, the authors of *From Under the Rubble* seem to overlook all that their predecessors struggled with. They do not, or pretend not to notice the burning problems that need examining and solving. They cut the Gordian knots with their words. And as in classical tragedy, when the hero's life and destiny are tangled and tied up in a knot impossible to untie, there comes the *deus ex machina:* God descends from heaven and categorically and peremptorily resolves everything, as would befit an antique self-willed god who, as we know, had no pretensions to high justice. This is the kind of God who appears on earth in the pages of the volume. The religion the authors cause to descend from heaven, without proof or foundation, is something high and powerful that will redeem everything. There is no room for doubt ...

In the light of this divine simplicity the Vekhists seem like pitiful metaphysical philosophers coming from Khemnitser's famous fable. As we know, in the fable the philosopher falls into a pit and when they try to pull him out, with the aid of a rope, he blabbers confusedly: "What is a rope? A rope is simple cordage". But he is

---

* *Vekhi* (= Landmarks) published in 1909, was a collection of essays published by a group of writers, scholars and philosophers, disillusioned former Marxists and radicals, searching for different solutions. The second collection, published in 1918, just before the contributors emigrated, was entitled "Iz glubiny" (= *De profundis*) and M. Hayward points out that the title of this volume *Iz pod glyb* is an allusion to it.

unable to get hold of the end of it, having used up all his energy in the mental effort of defining the rope. The authors of *From Under the Rubble* bypass their spiritual fathers' doubts and anxieties, they put into gigantic brackets, in advance, all the tormenting problems as obvious metaphysical futilities — "a rope is simple cordage". It is no accident that the panacea they recommend is presented in its most abstract form — religion. *Not even Christian* religion, but generally *religion.*

Not bread that satiates hunger, not water that quenches thirst, but nourishment. Not a sky with clouds, but space. Not the child dear to you, but the human unit. Not love, but the biological function of the reproductive organ. Of course, in science it is possible and necessary to speak of nourishment, space, the problems of increasing birth-rates. On the other hand, one remembers from school the mathematical balance, the inseparable link between *necessity* and *sufficiency.* Abstraction is always necessary, but is it sufficient? Clearly not, when it is to do with the destiny of a man, a nation, a country.

Hegel asks in his satire: "Who thinks abstractly? — Uneducated, entirely unenlightened people. I remember, from my youth, a certain burgomaster who complained that writers undermined the foundations of Christianity and of law and order, one of them dared even to justify suicide. Terrible thought! From further explanations it transpired that the burgomaster had in mind *The Sorrows of Werther.* This is what I call abstract thinking!..."

Yet the distinctive characteristic of the religious articles in the volume is first of all their striking abstractness and consequent dryness. This is what the authors have to say about religion:

I. Shafarevich: "One must not forget about the sphere of cultural activity that is perhaps more important than anything else for the healthy existence of science — about *religion.* For hundreds of thousands of years* religion was the most powerful and noblest motive force of mankind, yet, in the space of a few decades, we have broken with it — not because we have found something nobler to replace it with ... And by now the third generation lives in a terrifying world, deprived of God. Here, I would say, is the key to

---

* The remains of *Sinanthropus* show that he lived four hundred thousand years ago. For modern man, one can scarcely speak of several hundred millennia! Moreover, religions did not appear at once: the rudiments of Hinduism originate from the second millennium B.C., Zoroastrianism from the turn of the second and first millennia B.C., and Hinduism proper from the first millennium B.C. All other religions appeared much later. — *S.E.*

the whole problem. *The life, death or resurrection of Russia depends* on the efforts exerted to solve it."

V. Borisov: "Mankind as the Church is the fulfilment of the future, towards which the constantly changing reality of the existing world must strive in order to become one with its Creator."

E. Barabanov is preoccupied with "the problems of Russia's Christianization ... Clearly, Russia's better future is inseparable from Christianity. And if Russia is destined to have a renaissance then it can be accomplished *only on a religious foundation*."

A.B. in the essay "The Direction of Change": "It is Christianity, precisely, the fermenting agent, the 'yeast of the world' that has caused and will cause history to rise like dough in a trough. We are firmly convinced that only Christianity possesses enough motive force to inspire and gradually transform our world. Therefore the *only* question is how profoundly we succeed in understanding this and convert it into fact in our lives in our times ... And until we have changed ourselves, even the best and most honest attempts to reconstruct anything 'from outside', by decree or by force, are doomed at best to come to naught ... There is no need to search for such external resolutions. We must achieve such internal (spiritual) condition that enables solutions to be dictated from within, by the immutable laws of compassion and love."

It is difficult to raise any objections to these excellent counsels. Russia did, however, have plenty of them in the past, too. Let us remember, for instance, L.N. Tolstoy's homily: "The truths, common to all religious people of our times, are so simple, so comprehensible and near to every man's heart that, it seems, it would be enough if *parents, leaders and teachers* ... impressed upon children and adults those simple and tangible truths common to all religious men ... The practical rule is that every man must treat his fellow man in a way he himself would like to be treated, thus human life as a whole would change by itself ... And instead of unreasonable struggle and discord, very soon and *without the aid of diplomats, international law, peace conferences, political economists and socialists of all types*, there would come to mankind a happy and peaceful life of complete accord directed by a single religion." (*What is Religion and Wherein Lies Its Essence?*)

Tolstoy's article dates from 1902. Imagine, what mankind could have avoided had they at once taken heed of Lev Nikolaevich's advice! There would have been no First World War, no Second World War, no revolution, etc. But his "mad world" lives according to its own laws which do not follow even the wisest

245

advice of the wisest old man. And to ignore objective reality in the second half of the twentieth century would constitute unforgivable levity.

Vladimir Solovev, discussing "temple religion", recognized its necessity: "it must exist, first of all, *because on earth the external comes always before the internal*". He distinguished "private religion" from "temple religion". The department of the "private" (or domestic) religion is "the internal individual life ... the personal life and private affairs of man".

This "private religion" — which, together with "temple religion", was ridiculed by L.N. Tolstoy — is recommended to us by the authors of *From Under the Rubble* as the means of Russia's salvation.

For V. Solovev, however, it clearly did not suffice, since it "leaves the whole universal human world, all social, civic and international affairs" to the mercy "of wicked, antichristian forces". To this a Christian philosopher could not reconcile himself and therefore he considered that the task of creating "universal Christianity" which "must be disseminated among the whole of mankind and applied to all human affairs" is the enormous task of the future.

The authors of *From Under the Rubble*, carried away by proclaiming that religion is the only means of relieving our country of all its troubles and curing all its diseases, have left completely out of consideration the rich heritage left to us by the Russian school of philosophy, and among them the thinkers of "Vekhi". The method itself, of declaration without presenting evidence, is not very effective in our times. For one can declare whatever one pleases: in medieval times phlebotomy was held to be a cure for every illness; Mechnikov recommended sour milk to everyone; Repin fed even his guests with hay, considering it the healthiest nourishment. When, however, the matter in hand is the life and destiny of a country, a nation, we have every right to demand substantiation from the doctors, instead of arbitrary statements. The authors of the religious articles in the volume, having taken over Solzhenitsyn's concept of the feasibility of spiritual freedom in "unfree conditions," disregard entirely the problem of "unfree conditions" as though it did not exist. Hence, they ignore the real conditions of people's lives — something Christianity had never permitted itself to do. Thus a paradoxical situation arises: while speaking of change, of a transformation of life, they scorn that very life, look down on it, recommend and consider the plausibility of concentrating merely on "one's inner self". This, as has been repeatedly proved, is a pure chimera.

The strength of Christianity is precisely in that it is concerned with man's existence on earth, finds out how to console him, what hopes to give him, how to reinforce his strength to face the struggle against the temptations of evil. Had Christianity scorned "external" life, men's existence, it could not have preserved itself throughout the two thousand years of its cruel, sanguinary history.

Socialist doctrines took over the concept of man's universal equality precisely from Christianity, and it was just this that provided them with such force and vital capacity. There are not many today who believe in the present "realized" socialism. After the raging violence of the Inquisition in the middle ages, after the stakes, there appeared in Christian Europe the demand for a "criterion for the truthfulness of faith" (V. Solovev). Protestantism appeared with its rationalism which impregnated the whole of the eighteenth century Enlightenment and "served as a leading idea for the first French Revolution." We are living in a similar situation now. Christianity was not destroyed either by the Inquisition or by Protestantism, Rationalism or Revolution. We do not know whether socialism will be as enduring. In any case, both these mighty forces — Christianity and socialism — are mighty exactly because they were never so naïve as to scorn the real contents of human life, and the social "medium" — to use Solzhenitsyn's expression. The history of religious thinking shows that an idea was always the more powerful the better it succeeded in creating a close and firm link between the religious and the social, between the social and the spiritual. And this the authors of *From Under the Rubble* cannot and will not do.

The other day I happened to have an unexpected conversation on the subject with a taxi driver. We were passing by a practising church, people were just leaving after service. The driver said to me: "Once I took an old woman to church, and she was enticing me to go in, telling me how beautiful it is in there, what a wonderful feeling it gives."

"And what happened? Did you go in?" I asked curiously.

"No, I didn't. What do they have? The kingdom of heaven and priests. But who believes, in our day and age, in the kingdom of heaven? As for the priests, they are just like our party organizer."

The driver began to laugh: "I remember how, when I was a child, our priest used to get drunk, and carry on outrageously. The same with the party organizer nowadays: as soon as they get the power they forget about the people. And wherever you look, it is the same everywhere. Not only in our depot ... All the same, somehow it seems more natural to believe in communism than in the kingdom of heaven", my interlocutor concluded unexpectedly.

Interesting conversation, is it not? One cannot help recalling Herbert Spencer who warns us very correctly in "Approaching Slavery": "The citizens' natural shortcomings unavoidably appear in the bad functioning of any social construction. There is no *political alchemy* that could help attain excellent behaviour from swinish instincts". But, then, not only political, *religious alchemy* does not help either! What struck me in the foregoing conversation was that for my interlocutor communism constitutes an equal competitor in the question of faith, an alternative, a possible choice of object for belief: Christianity or communism. It is interesting to juxtapose this to the statements of a man of very different background, views and fate, the Hungarian Cardinal Mindszenthy. "Communism is a special kind of religion, admittedly religion in the negative sense, but with its own dogmas and hierarchy." (*Face to Face with New Tribulations.*)

There is another substantiation of the same view. A hundred and twenty years ago, in 1851, after thirty years of penal servitude, one of the brightest and most unappeasable minds among the Decembrists wrote to his friend:

"Lately, I have become very interested in questions of socialism and communism. I have read a great deal on the subject — *for* and *against*, more against — but still remained convinced that at the basis of these new ideas, *unknown to the initiators themselves*, there *lies concealed a Christian idea*: love of the nearest — brotherly love ... Admittedly, many may talk about this, not always with the purest of intentions, possibly even for mercenary motives. This can be observed with Christian teachings, too, from the lips of — taking a Roman Catholic example — Jesuits, but others as well ... Nevertheless, I am convinced that socialist and communist doctrines will not remain without followers and will bring desirable fruit. This will come about when the doctrines become *imbued with Christian spirit* [my italics — S.E.] which is the only thing that can lead to betterment, perfection and bliss in this world as well as in the one beyond. If mankind has not yet achieved this, it is because they are not yet impregnated with the spirit of Christ. This spirit exists in individual persons, but not in society as a whole. Society remains heathen in its notions, customs, morals, in its way of life, even in its laws. God's kingdom exists in some souls but not in the world — yet it must become all-embracing ... Then the church and human society will be one.... The democratic republic is the most suitable form of Christian society." (*In Memory of the Decembrists*, Moscow-Leningrad, 1926. Letters of M.A. Fonvizin to P. Obolensky.)

There are a number of remarkable thoughts in this letter. A sincere, profound faith; pondering on how to transform Christianity from the property of individual persons to the property of society as a whole; and in this connection reflections about the democratic republic as the nearest to and most suitable form for Christianity. The conviction that in time "socialist doctrines will become impregnated with Christian spirit" seems also interesting. This last thought, at any rate, has not lost its relevance for our times. The "Statement on Socialism and Religion", issued by the Conference of Socialist Parties in 1953, declares: "In Europe the Christian Gospel constitutes one of the spiritual and ethical sources of socialist ideas." It is permissible to disagree with the statement, but then the contrary must be *proved*.

And finally, the last evidence: contemplations of the gifted Vekhist philosopher, N.A. Berdyaev, who, in his spiritual road-seeking underwent many a trial. In his book *The Sources and Sense of Russian Communism* he has set an example of objective, unprejudiced examination of the nature of Russian atheism which, according to him, is closely connected with socialism and "is a religious phenomenon". "At its root is the love of truth. This is an atheism made up of moral pathos, love of goodness and of justice." Berdyaev holds that Russians become atheists because they cannot "accept a Creator who produces a cruel world full of suffering. They want to form a better world themselves." The endeavour to create a better world is the spiritual objective of every revolutionary aspiration and at the same time a religious dream. Submit or transform — this is the question that lies at the root of human activity. To pass out of cruelty's way or to wipe out cruelty? This is not only a social-political, but also a theological question. Indeed, Solzhenitsyn, too, offers his own solution for the transformation of the world. The word of Repentance, according to him, is so omnipotent that it has the power to change everything. He is, however, sadly deluded. Let us recall the Gospel and Christ's preaching. He understood human nature and did not in the least believe that *His Word* is capable of transforming life, of getting people to live according to the law advocated by him. He expressed this awareness in the parable of the sower and the seeds:

"The sower soweth the word. And these are they by the way side where the word is sown; but when they have heard, Satan cometh immediately, and taketh away the word that was sown in their hearts. And these are they likewise which are sown on stony ground; who, when they have heard the word, immediately receive it with gladness; and have no root in themselves, and so endure but for a time: afterward, when affliction or persecution ariseth for the word's sake, immediately they are offended. And these are they which are sown among thorns; such as hear the word. And the cares of this world, and the deceitfulness of riches, and the lusts of other things entering in, choke the word, and it becometh unfruitful." (Mark IV, 14-19.)

Solzhenitsyn is much more self-confident. He is sure everyone who hears him will carry out his counsel, certain that his word is stronger than the devil, more powerful than "this century, corrupted by wealth and troubles".

The utopianism of such hopes has been understood long since by Christian thinkers, who even in purely theological works showed excellent examples of analyses of the *social* reality that Solzhenitsyn has decided to leave out of account.

This is what Evgenii Trubetskoy wrote about the objective existence of evil in the world and about the necessity of overcoming it, objectively as well. In his last book, *The Sense of Life*, written in 1918 and influenced by the 1917 revolution, he says:

"A human condition, where evil is restrained by at least exterior material barriers, is naturally much better from a Christian point of view, than a condition where evil is not contained at all ... And Christ himself imposed upon Christians the duty to pay taxes for the upkeep of Roman legions! The Gospel values the state not as a possible component of the Divine Kingdom, but as a step in the historical process that will eventually lead to it. He who wishes the human world to be transformed one day into paradise, even if only within earthly limits, must give his blessing to the force, *be it only external,* [my italics — S.E.] which prevents the world from becoming in the meantime hell... Not only the anti-state, anarchistic frame of mind in the literary sense of the term, but also a neutral, *indifferent* attitude to the state must be condemned. Once the positive role of the state is recognized, even if its value is only relative from a Christian point of view, every Christian is duty bound to fight for it. The stronger and more persistent the attempts to turn it into a kingdom of beasts plunging into the abyss, the more we Christians must strive to keep the state in our hands, transform it into an obedient weapon in the struggle against bestial existence in the world.''

Essentially, Trubetskoy advocates the same "universal Christianity" in which Valdimir Solovev and the Decembrist M.A. Fonvizin see the goal of the future: a Christianity which does not merely take care of the salvation of individual souls, but looks after the world and its needs. Thus, the necessity to think about the life of society and the state unavoidably arises. It becomes imperative to pose the problem: what is better for Christians and Christianity, a totalitarian state or a democracy? To the authors of the volume, nevertheless, any struggle for the improvement of the state and social organization seems unnecessary, fruitless and, in the last analysis, simply harmful.

Yet without establishing real democracy, so completely scorned by Solzhenitsyn and his fellow-contributors, true faith is not to be achieved; and it is so hard to comply with religious rites that an ordinary citizen can hardly overcome the difficulties (for instance, baptism of children). Barabanov is right when he says that the Russian Orthodox Church is undergoing a crisis, "in a special form. *External lack of liberty paralyses its life and is being internalized* [my italics — S.E.], it is taking root in the consciousness and becoming identified with Church hierarchy." But what happens in the church goes on also in all other ideological, social and public fields: in the educational system, in the health service, etc. There, too, "lack of freedom paralyses life and is being internalized". And one can simplify the equation even further: just try to go to one of the Moscow churches for Easter Liturgy. Your endeavour will cost a great deal of trouble and will not necessarily be crowned with success. Obviously, the state is also of the opinion that "inner freedom" is enough for Christians and that is why we have so few functioning churches. At Easter Night, the most frequented churches are surrounded by militia picket-lines and details of the *druzhina** in order to prevent a crowd forming

*Volunteer militia — *Trans.*

around the church. The members of the *druzhina* are usually students. An insignificant proportion of our students are inside the church with the believers, a part of them are picketing with the militia to "prevent disorder", while the great majority are at home, occupied with their "private lives".

Once upon a time the Slavophils tried to convince everyone that the Russians were a Godfearing nation. Yet the subsequent course of history did not prove this contention. It is too early to speak now about the "renaissance" of Christianity in Russia, and the religious intellectual circles in Moscow, in whom I. Shafarevich places his hopes, are evidently very small in number and their religious enthusiasm is much too superficial, not serious enough. It is more a question of paying a tribute to fashion and covers everything from collecting ikons, antique furniture, precious china and cut glass to practising yoga and engaging in "Vekhism".

There is only one thing missing: wholehearted adherence to any sort of world outlook, whether Eastern Orthodox or Buddhist or anarchist. They are all carried away by "God-constructing" which reminds one of the fantastic world of the Dutch painter Hieronymous Bosch, — in whose pictures the head of a horseman may be a thistle burr sitting on a bird's body with human legs, the horse itself may be an enormous jug, or a woman may be a dry tree with mermaid tails — rather than a brotherhood of people in search of God. For how else can one regard that concoction, made up of the most heterogeneous ingredients, drawn from orthodoxy, judaism, buddhism, "Vekhism", monarchist-nationalist ecstasy, catholicism, corrupted humanism, a misuse of Russian revolutionary tradition and the yoga system — which is served up all together in any of the Moscow circles under the name of the "modern quest"? Yesterday's atheists today become catholics, judaists, buddhists — and all more lightheartedly than one changes jobs. As V. Solovev said: "It is dreadful not to believe in God, but even more dreadful to half-believe"

The religious articles in *From Under the Rubble* bear the marks of this ideological impotence, confusion, of this "half-faith" in God which is really only a craving for faith. They are "dilettantes of religion" as Herzen says.

The authors of the volume want to burn their bridges, leaving on one side of the river everything material, social, political, and on the other all that is spiritual, religious. However, this is in contradiction to the whole culture, the essence of Christianity, as well as to the real existence of people.

252

Christ taught that "man does not live by bread alone", but he never preached this to hungry people. He gave food to the hungry, to great crowds of five thousand, not counting women and children, and on another occasion to four thousand people. Let us recall the beautiful story about this from the Gospel according to Mark:

"In those days the multitude being very great, and having nothing to eat, Jesus called his disciples unto him, and saith unto them, I have compassion on the multitude, because they have now been with me three days, and have nothing to eat: And if I send them away fasting to their own houses, they will faint by the way: for divers of them came from far. And his disciples answered him, from whence can a man satisfy these men with bread here in the wilderness? And he asked them, How many loaves have ye? And they said, Seven. And he commanded the people to sit on the ground: and he took the seven loaves, and gave thanks, and brake, and gave to his disciples to set before them; and they did set them before the people. And they had a few small fishes: and he blessed, and commanded to set them also before them. So they did eat and were filled ..." (Mark VIII, 1-8.)

Here lay the strength of Christ's teaching: feed the hungry, but remind them of the higher interests of the human soul. After two thousand years of Christianity's existence it would be madness to renounce this dialectical relationship, Christ's humanism.

III

"The word of the Lord came unto me again, saying, What mean ye, that ye use this proverb concerning the land of Israel, saying, The fathers have eaten sour grapes, and the children's teeth are set on edge? ... But if a man be just ... he shall not die for the iniquity of his father, he shall surely live. The soul that sinneth, it shall die. The son shall not bear the iniquity of the father, neither shall the father bear the iniquity of the son." (Ezekiel XVIII.)

"We have so bedevilled the world, brought it so near to self-destruction, that the moment has arrived when it is high time to repent: not for the sake of a life beyond the grave (this is thought comic nowadays) but for the sake of survival here on earth ... If we add to this the inflamed atmosphere of international and inter-racial tensions, then we can say, without stretching the point, that we are very unlikely to survive without *REPENTANCE* ... Not the bitter strife between parties, between nations, not the dragging of every tension along a fight to delusive victory — but only *repentance*, the search for our own mistakes and sins" — writes Solzhenitsyn. He sees in repentance the way out of the hopeless situation not only for each individual human being, but also for the world, for all nations who wish to live in friendship and harmony. In our days, perhaps more than ever, he who has faith is happy. Though, in Herzen's words "religious positivism has but feeble effect at the present stage of spiritual development." Writing in his diary about the death of his friend Vadim Passek, he gives an account of how frightening it was when Passek's wife stood by his grave, the coffin already buried, listlessly, without a tear. The archimandrite went up to her and said: "That's enough. This is not our way. Come with me to the church and pray to God." This produced a strong impression on Herzen: "Here is the strength of religion. In such moments one is ready to do anything to find a way to reconciliation. Religion cures everything."

Only faith in the immortality of the soul can reconcile man to death. The Christian tenet, the dogmas of Christianity possess a strength which preserved the Christian idea itself, as well as the church, through all the rationalistic revisions and in spite of all the victories of enlightenment.

Dostoevsky held that without believing in the immortality of the soul man cannot remain man but slides unavoidably into baseness. He saw the way out, the solution of the problem of problems, in the creation of a church-state, in "religion for all" and not merely for high intellects.

Tolstoy, the reckless "revisionist" of Christianity — to use a fashionable term — who had the audacity to rewrite the Gospel, showering abuse on the Orthodox rituals, recommended to mankind all sorts of abstention: celibacy and vegetarianism, non-resistance to evil.

Solzhenitsyn takes over much of this. Repentance, which he recommends to Russia, is in fact only one of the seven Christian sacraments, together with baptism, confirmation, the eucharist, holy unction, matrimony and ordination.

Why repentance in particular? When I had read Solzhenitsyn's appeal "Do not participate in the fraud" I was immediately struck by it: yes, this is what is needed, only thus is redemption possible. But does *this* change life? No, for *everyone's* strength is different and it cannot be demanded of *everyone* to enter the field as a warrior. And if he is no warrior? My colleague said to me shortly afterwards, getting ready to go to a meeting: "I am off to participate in the fraud. What can I do? After all, in a year's time I shall be retiring ... I cannot remain without a piece of bread for my old age ..."

And can repentance change life?

The first question that comes to mind is: if we are to repent, who to and of what? And at once a whole chain of other questions follows: what is repentance? What did it serve in history? What did it mean in Christian life? And is Solzhenitsyn right in saying that "Ivan the Terrible's terror never became so widespread and systematic as Stalin's, to a great extent because the tsar came to his senses and repented"?

The *Pocket Dictionary for Atheists* (Moscow, 1973) informs us that repentance "is when the believer confesses or repents his sins before the priest, then the latter absolves him in God's name."

In the Gospel, on behalf of Christ, it is firmly established that "Joy shall be in heaven over one sinner that repenteth, more than over ninety and nine just persons, which need no repentance."

Nowadays the practice in churches is mainly "collective confession".

Solzhenitsyn says that "we were invested generously with the gift of repentance, once it used to flow through and through the nature of a large proportion of Russians. *Not by accident has the Day of Forgiveness occupied such a prominent place in our calendar of festivals*".

But then, since olden times, the Day of Forgiveness in Russia was the end of carnival, the most pagan period in the "calendar of feast days", which the church could not master, even though carnival week is the last week before Lent, preceding Easter. Merry-making, outdoor carousal, parties, feasts with the traditional Russian pancakes, the procession with a straw dummy in a woman's dress burnt to the accompaniment of cheerful singing — this is now Shrovetide used to be celebrated in Russia. On the last day, Sunday, when the dummy was being burnt, everyone had to ask each other's forgiveness. They even went down on their knees, this was part of the ritual and of the heightened atmosphere, the festive mood, after the long winter and before the seven weeks of Lent. It was more of a feature of conventional behaviour, an act of "mummers" than real sincere repentance. The *Day of Forgiveness* was the last day of authorized revelry, of getting satiated on pancakes, the day when everyone was free *himself* to forgive his fellow men for offences, a day of almost complete freedom, or, as one could now say, of "letting oneself go"! No one looked upon this ritual of asking forgiveness of his relatives and neighbours as a sincere religious repentance. How could they, over pancakes! More likely it was done so that on the last day of carnival *everyone* should be in good spirits.

The fasting that started after the *Day of Forgiveness*, on Purification Monday, was another matter. Here the church demanded repentance, and one had to kneel before the ikons and not in front of the neighbours. Tsar Aleksei Mikhailovich who, according to Solzhenitsyn, was aware of his "responsibility before God and his own conscience", gave orders to apply the utmost severity to those who did not repent, did not confess their sins as befits a Christian during Lent: "And if there are any who did not come to *repent* in the first week of the great Lent, they will be tortured. And such disobedient, shameless creatures we, the Great Sovereign, shall thrust into disgrace without the least pity."

Why such severity, such concern on the party of "Caesar" for the execution of a Christian ritual, when he had no business whatsover to take care of how people "render unto God what is God's"?

Repentance is the only Christian sacrament which affords constant and regular access to the soul of every Christian, to his everyday secular life, with all his thoughts and hopes.

Not for nothing did the Holy Synod, during the reign of Peter the Great, issue a decree obliging priests to inform the authorities "if in the course of confession before his spiritual father someone told about any — not even committed but contemplated only — theft, and, more importantly, about treason or mutiny against the Sovereign or the state, about malicious thoughts against the honour or health of the Sovereign or His Highness's family".

This decree, very likely, is still in force. "In the spirit of pre-Petrine Russia [says Solzhenitsyn] there were waves of mass-scale *repentance* — *more precisely religious repentance*, starting separately in individual hearts and merging into torrents." This is true. It is well known, for instance, that in the year 1492 after Christ was born and seven thousand years after Creation, the end of the world was expected in Russia. During the night of March 25 — the day of annunciation — it was expected that the archangels

Michael and Gabriel would blow the trumpet and announce the end of the world. Therefore people gave away their property, bought their coffins and that terrible night went to sleep in them instead of their beds. However, the fateful night passed, the 7000th year everyone so feared had ended, and life recommenced: together with repentance and sin, half and half. There was a similar occasion in Europe in A.D. 1000. This is how Hegel writes about it:

"Universal fear spread all over Europe. The dread was provoked by the expectation of an approaching terrible judgement, and by the belief in the imminent end of the world. The feeling of terror induced people to commit senseless acts. Some donated all their property to the church and spent their time in repentance; the majority abandoned themselves to dissoluteness and squandered away all they had."

But can one see in similar moods of mass fear a respectable phenomenon, "the superior, true road of nation-wide repentance" as Solzhenitsyn asserts? Obviously not, for what is induced by fear — and this sort of mass frenzy can be caused more than anything, by fear — "crosses the borderline of tragedy" when "struggle is not possible". (Herzen)

In order that repentance should not be the desperate act of those about to die, of suicides, but a creative force, capable of influencing future life, clear recognition of sin and the wish to overcome it are needed. Of what sin and to whom must Russia repent? What crime? That for more than half a century she has been leading a desperate life, becoming more exhausted than anyone in the course of a race? Ivan Lestvichnik said of the way of repentance:

"Repentance is ... promising God to live differently ... condemning voluntarily the evil in oneself, unperturbed self-scrutiny, it is the door to hope and to the renunciation of despair. The repentant is a non-disreputable convict. Repentance is reconciliation with the Lord by way of good deeds — deeds that are contrary to sin — the cleansing of conscience, voluntary forbearance of every grief. The penitent is the discoverer of punishment for himself."

Thus, repentance must, of necessity, contain the readiness to "do good deeds that are contrary to sin" — i.e. still the same age old question (so hateful to Abram Tertz) "what is to be done?" It is the "promise of leading a new life", i.e. not only recognition of one's sins, but also recognising the road that lies ahead. Consequently, repentance alone brings no salvation. One cannot run away from the inevitable — but what comes after? How to build up a new life?

Otherwise — and Ivan Lestvichnik warns about this, too — one can fall into the sin of conceit: "False contrition breeds conceit, but true contrition provides consolation."

Repentance, as a sure way to keep all matters under close control and at the same time lead mankind in the desired direction — this secret was well-known to the Catholic Inquisition.

The fourteenth-century French inquisitor, Bernard Guy, wrote: "The task of the Inquisition is to destroy heresy; heresy cannot be liquidated unless heretics are exterminated; heretics cannot be exterminated without the destruction of those who conceal, defend them, sympathize with them." Hence the other slogan of Inquisition: "Destroy them all — the Lord will recognize his own".

At the same time, all the efforts of the tribunals and inquisitors aimed not so much at discovering the heretic, as at compelling him to appear voluntarily before the tribunal, repent, and, as a sign of sincere repentance, give away all "those who concealed, defended him and sympathized with him".

Repentant sinners and heretics persisting in their errors — these were the two categories appearing before the Inquisition. The repentants were dressed in the special robes of the "penitent sinners". They could count on clemency from the Inquisition: they were not to be burnt alive, but to be strangled or beheaded first.

Galileo, who "abjured, cursed and detested" his errors, was locked up in prison after his repentance. "For your penitence, to deliver you from your sins, we order you to read seven psalms of repentance once a week for three years." (From the sentence of the Inquisition.)

But there were also those persistent enough to withstand any effort directed at forcing them to confess their sins, to repent of their errors. On 25 October 1599 the following entry was registered in the minutes of inquisitional trials: "Giordano Bruno, son of the late Giovanni of Nola, friar of the Order of Teaching Brothers, Master of Divinity, declared that *he does not need and does not wish to renounce,* has *nothing to renounce*, can see no grounds for *renunciation* and does *not know what he should renounce*."

During investigations in the Petrashevsky case, when Dostoevsky was arrested, he was questioned by Yakov Rostovtsev, a member of the investigating commission who had also brought the Decembrists to trial. On behalf of the tsar he promised to "pardon" Dostoevsky, provided he repented and was "willing to give an account of the whole affair". "I cannot believe that the man who wrote *Poor People* could be in concert with these vicious people." Dostoevsky did not accept the offer and was sentenced to penal servitude.

Martyrdom-persistency or repentance-apostasy: this is the frequent dilemma posed by a proposal to repent.

Repentance, in essence, means indeed renouncing all that one has done before, what one thought, how one acted. It means "promising God to live differently".

How, then, can one propose repentance *to all*? To the sinner and the righteous? For how can the righteous man renounce his previous sinless life? Those "born angels who weightlessly glide on the surface of this life (the swamp), never sinking into it even when their feet come into contact with it" about whom Solzhenitsyn writes. They "are the just, we have all of us met them".

It was not by accident that the Inquisition came to my mind, for to compel everyone to repent by force is the same as "dragging and squelching through the stinking bog of a society based on violence and fraud". It is, indeed, violence and fraud, only in the guise of Christianity.

For the innocent there is nothing to repent of, while the guilty do not repent. And nothing — no "millions pouring out their repentance", especially if they do not do it publicly, "but among friends and acquaintances" as Solzhenitsyn recommends — will cure our social life in the same way as will *public trials* of the surviving perpetrators of Stalin's camps. "What way is there if not the way of delivering ourselves of the burdens of our past, and this *only* through penitence, for we are all guilty, all blemished?" says Solzhenitsyn. But not everyone is guilty, not all blemished. The Judaean high priests demanded that Christ be executed. The Judaean Governor Pontius Pilate "washed his hands". Judas betrayed him to the executioners. The Roman soldiers nailed Christ's body to the cross, many shouted from the crowd "Crucify him!" "A great number of people and women ... mourned and lamented over him." Are they all "equally guilty, equally blemished"?

There was a woman in the crowd when Jesus was being led to execution, who held out her cloth to wipe the sweat from his forehead, and Christ's face became imprinted on the cloth (see the ikon "The Saviour on the cloth"). There was Joseph of Arimathaea who asked for Pilate's permission to bury Christ's body; there were the disciples, the women who came to the grave. Society always has its Pontius Pilate, who allows all passions to come to the surface, "washing his hands" before power, while he himself is part of it. But even Pontius Pilate's guilt differs from that of the soldiers, who spat on Christ, "and took the reed, and smote him on the head. They gave him vinegar to drink mixed with gall ... and they crucified him, and parted his garments, casting lots ..."

Is it possible that our hearts can permit that the "great number of people and women" who escorted Christ to the execution and mourned and lamented over him, are as guilty as the Roman soldiers who taunted Jesus, as Judas, as the high preists? Their guilt, their "partaking in the fraud" consisted of not throwing themselves, unarmed, against the Roman legionaries' swords and spears. Does one insist that they should repent? That they should shout about their "share" in the murder of Christ?

Solzhenitsyn feels sorry that "nowadays we, Russians, are not floating towards heaven, shining in glory, but are sitting, perplexed, on smouldering spiritual ruins". We shall not shed tears for heaven — leave it to the angels. Otherwise we may end up like the magi Simon, who got to the gates of heaven with the aid of sorcery, only to be turned away by St. Peter. For any smouldering ruin can be rebuilt and the terrain used for crops — if there is strength enough and if there is "external freedom" to apply the energy.

And finally, the last "historical reminiscence", about Ivan the Terrible's "coming to his senses and repenting".

As is well known, in Stalin's times one was not allowed to say a bad word against Tsar Ivan, since Stalin saw in him his own remote spiritual father and precursor.

We shall not call on the Russian historians, from N.M. Karamzin to S.B. Veselovsky, for evidence on Ivan the Terrible's bloodthirstiness, on his pathological personal cruelty, on the desperate and ravaged state he dragged the country into, submitting it to bloody terror; he — in the words of the annalist — "devastated his land ... he would have gone out of his mind and destroyed all the land had the Lord not put an end to his life".

We shall not quote statistics about the respective number of victims in Stalin's and Ivan IV's times in proportion to the population. We shall only try to recall and contemplate the features of the Tsar who "came to his senses and repented", and whom the slavophil A.S. Khomyakov called "ferocious and wild madman, slavedriver of Christians, crowned enemy of his native land" (in his play "Ermak").

In 1570 the Tsar raided Novgorod and Pskov. This is how the annalist reports on the event:

"He sacked the Cathedral of St. Sophia and took the miracle-working ikons and all the treasures, all valuable things; robbed the archbishop's palace, and all the monasteries and he tortured all the people and many orthodox believers with terrible tortures. And other people — they talk about sixty thousand men, women and children — were driven into the great Volga river, they say the river became dammed. And in other towns of Novgorod he also took people away and robbed monasteries and churches."

Let us not forget that all this was done by "an autocrat of past religious ages", one who "in spite of his apparently unlimited power had a sense of responsibility before God and his own conscience" — as Solzhenitsyn tells us, carried away by abstract enthusiasm, without taking a look at actual Russian history.

The Tsar particularly distinguished himself at Pskov. At that time the prior of the Pecher Monastery was its founder Kornilii, a renowned architect of monastery fortifications and well-known for his scholarship. When Kornilii came out of the monastery gates to meet the Tsar with the cross, Ivan drew his sword and severed his head with one blow. However, he "repented at once and, lifting the corpse, carried it in his own arms into the monastery". The road soaked in Kornilii's blood, along which the Tsar walked with his body in his arms, to the Church of Assumption, is called the "Bloody Road" in memory of the event. As evidence of Tsar Ivan Vasilevich's repentance he presented sacrifices to the Pecher Monastery of Pskov after Kornilii's death.

According to legend, Kornilii himself walked, following the Tsar's footsteps, holding his own severed head in his hands, and died only when Ivan the Terrible had repented and started to pray.

In the same year the unfrocked metropolitan Phillip Kolychev was murdered in the prison where he was held, by one Malyuta Shuratov. Kolychev had dared to "argue" with the Tsar. At the Uspensky Cathedral of Moscow, when Ivan the Terrible came to liturgy with his mob of oprichniks — "devils", as they called them in Russia — in black cassocks and black helmets, with their knives and daggers bulging out under their cassocks, the metropolitan not only refused to bless the Tsar, but made a courageous and daring speech about innocently flowing Christian blood. To Ivan's threats Kolychev replied: "I am pursuing the truth and no suffering can compel me to be silent". There followed punishment for all his relatives and death for the metropolitan himself. Is this "coming to one's senses and repenting"?

To top it all, Ivan the Terrible was an unusual sort of religious fanatic. In sixteenth century Russia the cult of ancestors was very strong and the firstborn had to take care of the cult. Therefore the Tsar, whenever someone fell out of favour, did his best to exterminate the whole hated family, all kinsfolk, even distant relatives with their wives and children. Thus there was no-one to remember the souls of the victims. "In order that he should not have time for the last confession and to make the necessary preparations for death, the victim was murdered unexpectedly. So that his body should not benefit from Christian burial, he was dissected and thrown into the river under the ice, or flung to the dogs, birds of prey or wild beasts. To deprive him of the last hope for redemption of his soul, he was robbed of the chance to be remembered", writes S.B. Veselovsky discussing how Ivan the Terrible tried to condemn his enemies at once to the torments of hell, by not allowing them to have a Christian funeral. This was "more terrible than physical pain or death itself, as it affected the fate of the soul for eternity".

One would think that Solzhenitsyn judges Ivan the Terrible's "coming to his senses and repenting" on the basis of I. Repin's melodramatic painting. Like all paintings with an historical theme, this has little to do with history. This is how, in fact, Ivan became his son's murderer:

He struck his pregnant daughter-in-law, the Crown Prince's wife, with a metal rod and when her husband came to her aid Ivan hit his son on the forehead, dealing a fatal blow. The Crown Prince's wife, after the attack, gave birth to a dead child and soon died herself as a result of the wounds.

Ivan the Terrible sent to the Monastery of Trinity-Sergiev five thousand roubles — an enormous sum of money by contemporary standards — as an offering to the memory of his murdered son's soul. Here it is — the price of Ivan the Terrible's "coming to his senses".

True, there is an unfinished testament Ivan the Terrible wrote twelve years before his death, where he repents of his sins in the most self-abasing terms, declaring himself guilty of covetousness, murder, gluttony, drunkenness, lechery and even perversion. Of course, one ought not to take this stereotyped pseudo-Christian humility at its face value.

This repentance did not prevent Ivan the Terrible from continuing, to the last day of his life, to commit crimes against the people and against his own state. His actions were not guided at all by "a sense of responsibility before God and his own conscience", but by taking all the liberties of an unlimited autocracy, feeling "free to pardon or put to death any of his subjects at will" — as he said in a letter to Kurbsky.

Evidently, the brilliant sixteenth century Russian free-thinker Fedor Ivanovich Karpov was right when he said that the ideal state should be guided by a principled rule of law: "Public affairs in towns and principalities are getting into a disastrous state due to long suffering. For when people must endure lack of justice and legality, this brings the cause of the good of the people and of public affairs to ruin. It leads to a void, to the kingdom of morals of violence."

Solzhenitsyn considers "any other solution" except repentance as a "temporary social delusion". And in repentance "even sins of the distant past must not be overlooked", one must accept in advance that there is not one neighbour against whom one has not sinned. As on the day of forgiveness, one begs everyone's pardon.

At first sight, this idea seems very effective and satisfactory. Indeed, one wishes to be loved and forgiven by all neighbours and relatives. But very soon — on thinking it over — one realizes that it is a mirage, an abstract vision, taking the square root of the Christian ideal. How can nations forgive each other — through diplomatic notes, or by convening conferences for the purpose? Or at a gathering of collective repentance, about which the *Pocket Dictionary for Atheists* speaks? And how to account for the sins of the distant past?

Solzhenitsyn says: "If those whom we offended have previously offended us, our guilt-feelings are less hysterical: mutual offences always throw a mitigating shadow. The Tartar yoke Russia was held in, mutes our possible sense of guilt toward remnants of the Golden Horde." Well, I never! Here we are, back to square one, as the saying goes. What was the use of talking about repentance at all, if we cannot forgive in any case, if after hundreds of years we still harp on old offences? So the Tartars Stalin deported from the

Crimea were "remnants of the Golden Horde"? Thus it turns out that he dealt political justice and we are not to feel guilty toward them for Stalin's cruel deed? Such reasoning is anti-Christian, or rather, anti-human.

According to this reasoning, then, there is no one to ask forgiveness from, since someone, sometime was sure to have offended us. Fine day of forgiveness it would be, if, on the pretext of peacemaking repentance, all nations started to present their neighbours with centuries-old accounts of who conquered whom and why ... It would be difficult to collect the bones after similar days of forgiveness. Such a turn of mind, by the way, is not unexpected with Solzhenitsyn. He has not distinguished himself at all by Christian humility or magnanimity, but is rather given to accusations and the most rigid categorical judgements. "Our sense of guilt before the Estonians and Lithuanians is always more painful, more shameful than the guilt feeling we have toward the Latvians or Hungarians whose rifles rattled often enough in the cellars of the Cheka and in the backyards of Russian villages." No, with such rancour in the heart, it is senseless to talk about Christian repentance and, in the final analysis, even about simple friendly co-existence.

Solzhenitsyn's second recipe, self-limitation, is no more encouraging. He maintains that his compatriots in Russia are fully capable of depriving their children of "oranges and butter", and that they must show "their love of the fatherland according to the proverb 'bread and water make a fine meal'".

Russians, as far as memory goes, never had their fill, and even now, in many industrial towns, too, there is a shortage of meat and other basic foodstuffs.

Russians, alas, are quite used to the "fine meal of bread and water". But to declare that this is how it ought to be, and this is how it should go on, is simply immoral, to put it mildly. Anyone is free to retire to a monastery, to go to the stake or get himself arrested, but to force everyone to follow suit — is it not a form of spiritual violence?

"After the western ideal of unlimited freedom, after the marxist concept of freedom as the yoke of recognized necessity, here is the truly Christian definition: *freedom is self-limitation*" — writes Solzhenitsyn. This seemingly spectacular definition is, in essence, an empty, abstract sophism which means not freedom, but natural slavery.

How much more correct and profound is the Russian poet V.A.

Zhukovsky's definition of freedom, in his letter to the future Alexander II, then Crown Prince, dated 1833:

> *"Man can be just and correct at any given moment, this is human freedom. There is no doubt about what is just at the moment* ... Who can answer for the future? Even the next moment does not belong to us: it is the province of Providence. Only by remaining within the boundaries of humanity, by *recognizing clearly what is just*, can our actions be wholesome, i.e. moral. On the contrary: by entering the territory of Providence and trying to produce in the space of a minute by force what Providence will accomplish in time, we destroy others and ourselves. What, then? Must we condemn ourselves to inactivity and inertly submit to the power of time? ... No ... Follow time step by step, listening to its voice, and do what it demands. To stay behind is as harmful as to run ahead of time. Don't try to move mountains, but do not just stand there helplessly when they start to fall down. In the first case you yourself would cause the destruction, in the latter you could not prevent it, and in either case you would perish. But by working relentlessly, tirelessly together with time, *separating* from the *living* that which is already put to death by life, *nourishing* what is *budding* with *life* and protecting what is *ripe and full of life*, you ... either create the *necessary new*, or destroy the fruitless or harmful *old*. In short, live and let live, and do not — by any means — stray into the province of God's truth." (Zhukovsky, *Collected Works*, ed. by A.S. Arkhangelsky, vol.XII, 1902, p.29).

How all-embracing and human, how tolerant and noble his idea is, in spite of the remoteness of his situation and concepts for us! While precisely these Christian qualities are missing in Solzhenitsyn. His didacticism is rigorous and stringent, his boundless self-confidence is harsh and unkind.

It so happens that there is no more unpopular idea in Russia at present — after the Tolstoyan rice cutlets and the bolshevik "we must suffer in the name of the future", must go without today for the sake of a "bright tomorrow" — than self-sacrifice. One can preach self-sacrifice to a country or a person who is well-fed, leads an easy and satisfying life. But to set the standard of "bread and water" to those only just rising from bitter, hungry deprivation and not yet quite risen out of it, is unforgivable, anti-human callousness. It means the idea is more valuable than people. And of that concept we have had more than enough!

In today's Russia there is no word less respectable than *repentance*. To this day the repentance by victims of the 1930's trials, crimes they have never committed, remains an unsolved puzzle. To this day it is customary to "call to task" errant writers, urge them to public penitence — at meetings or in the press.

And the first "Russian question" is always in readiness: "And what happened? He didn't repent, did he?" — one asks with terror, hope and pain when the latest victim's turn comes.

They hate repentance in Russia nowadays. Repentance and denunciation — these are the two control levers of any totalitarian system. With their aid tenacious people are driven into submission and the rest forced into silence.

Herzen wrote more than a hundred years ago:

"The trouble is that the way our country is governed ... the censor kills the word before it is formed. And should it break through now and then, there comes the secret instruction, post-haste by messenger troika — and that's the last you ever see of the author. Just imagine, if Jesus Christ himself started to preach a sermon somewhere on Admiralty Square or in the Summer Gardens — there would not be any need for Judas. The first police officer would take him to the 3rd department, and from there he would be transferred to the army, or — even worse — to the Solovetsky Monastery." (Letter to Tsar Alexander II.)

These words of Herzen's we can repeat today as well.

Russia is in no need of either repentance — she suffers enough from it in its basest and vilest forms — or self-sacrifice — we have had enough pharisaical exhortations about the necessity for self-sacrifice. What Russia needs is true democracy. Only that can assure national progress: spiritual, moral, religious and political development.

The Christianity of L.N. Tolstoy and of the Contributors to "From Under the Rubble"

German Andreev

Translated by Vera Magyar

"Tolstoy awakened religious sentiments in a society that was indifferent to religion or hostile to Christianity."

(N.A. Berdyaev, *The Russian Idea*)

"The enemy of Christianity, and of any kind of religion, is not the communist social system — more suitable to Christianity than capitalism — but communism's pseudo-religion which they want to substitute for Christianity. The communist pseudo-religion, in its turn, came into existence because Christianity had failed to fulfil its task and had become distorted. The official church took up a conservative attitude to state and social life and submitted to the old regime with servility." (Ibid.)

"No matter how often a man, whose relations with the world are determined by working for the good of his family, his kinsfolk or his nation, repeats that he is a Christian, his morality will always remain a family or national morality, but not Christian morality."

(L.N. Tolstoy, *Religion and Morality*)

"Take therefore no thought for the morrow: for the morrow shall take thought for the things of itself. Sufficient unto the day is the evil thereof."

(Matthew, VI, 34).

'I cannot stand it when even most high-principled people depart from the ideal of the Virgin Mary and end up with Sodomian ideals. What is more terrible, even with Sodomian ideals in their hearts, they do not discard the ideal of the Madonna, but continue to talk on behalf of their hearts, sincerely, sincerely as they did in their younger, sinless days."

(F.M. Dostoevsky, *Brothers Karamazov*)

"The gist of my idea is that since the depraved are in unison and constitute strength, decent people must do the same."

(L.N. Tolstoy, *War and Peace*)

"... it would be desirable to hear a voice in the press discussing events of the day from a higher, Christian, conciliatory point of view instead of a partisan one."

(From L.N. Tolstoy's letter to Godyansky, 1.1.1906.)

I

You can frequently observe an amazing resemblance in attitudes to social problems in people who, to all appearances, occupy opposing positions in principle. When you try to define what exactly seems so alike in the writings of these people who disagree with each other on every question, you discover that it is their common method, the method of partisanship.

The method of partisanship is characterized by some striking features.

The partisan publicist "supercharges" the quantity of facts selected to support his case, while ignoring those facts that would frustrate his concept. He has a tendency to generalize ideas and statements, without paying much attention to the accuracy of such generalizations. He is interested in his opponents' errors only, and refuses to take notice of their achievements. If history does not fit into his constructions, he says: "So much the worse for history". He is inclined to discredit his adversary's personality. In the partisan publicist's works the world appears impoverished, for he tries to squeeze all the diversity and colour of real life into his absolute system. He does not lend an ear to Goethe's Mephisto, who made the wise observation: "Theory, my friend, is grey, but the tree of life is eternally green." He judges people by their declarations, not by their deeds.

As is well known, the word "partiya" (party) comes from the English word "Part".

A partisan disposition to truth drives people into opposition to

268

one another instead of uniting them. The Christian, aiming at universal cohesion, and the partisan thinker are incompatible. The distinguishing feature of the partisan manner of thinking is that it considers strife, class struggle, international, inter-state armed conflict, and conflict generally between people, to be inevitable and therefore justified. The partisan thinker assumes that conflict is ineluctable, while peace and love between men are temporary and accidental.

For the Christian, on the other hand, love and unity between men is truth, conflict is negation.

During quieter times partisan dispute leading to the triumph of certain theorists and to the defeat and disgrace of others, preserves its academic character and is relatively innocuous for those not concerned with the problems under discussion. When, however, there are threatening clouds on the horizon for a nation or for mankind and evil threatens, partisan feuding between Christians becomes dangerous. It may be a matter of life or death for many people, but the incensed disputants do not take heed; they consider that the main point is to assert truth as they see it; it makes no difference to them by what means, or at what price, they will achieve their aim. In fact, incorrect methodology — and in the field of social thought there is no more harmful method than partisanship — cannot lead to truth, and what is more important, it cannot recruit supporters for the truth either.

Should we have, one day, an intelligent machine, capable of extracting the method of argument in works of sociology, regardless of their contents and wording, and should we give it the task of analysing *From Under the Rubble*, the machine would come to the conclusion that the contributors are, to all appearance, the same people who in the Russia of the mid-twentieth century published, in huge editions, textbooks entitled *Scientific Communism, The History of the Party* and similar propaganda material. The same confidence of possessing ultimate knowledge, the same urge to browbeat instead of providing proof, to ram their dogmas down the throats of the uninitiated, the same contempt for all those who think differently can be found in both. They have the common tendency to mystify, to manipulate historical reality, to fall back on stereotypes (class, nation, Orthodoxy, East, West, etc.). Both mistrust individual freedom of choice.

And so Russia, by fits and starts, proceeds towards the kingdom of the Grand Inquisitor. One can detect the contours of the society foreseen by George Orwell in *1984*. Those few among the inhabitants of Russia who do not care about "the growth of national well-being", and at the same time sense, with horror, the decline of moral well-being, those few who, miraculously, still have a glimmering awareness of inner freedom, pounce eagerly upon everything forbidden in the field of ideas, especially if the forbidden is sanctified by the name of the truly great Russian writer, Solzhenitsyn.

Just as the wayfarer in a desert, who for want of clear water has had to drink with abhorrence the dirty liquid from stagnant wells, throws himself at a fresh spring, so the inhabitant of Russia reaches out for pages filled with words of freedom. He turns the pages written by Solzhenitsyn and those near to him with trembling hands, looking forward to unprecedented delight in truth.

What weight of responsibility these publicists must feel, having achieved the right, long forgotten in Russia, to speak to their readers without interference by the censor or the bureaucrats of the Central Committee!

It is well-known that freedom from external constraint is no guarantee against slavery to internal prejudice. Freedom is a gift: like fire, it can illuminate truth, but it can also incinerate it.

And is there one truth or are there as many truths as parties?

II

One should think that there are only two truths: God's truth and the devil's truth. Dostoevsky saw the struggle between God and devil in man's soul: Tolstoy replaced the term "devil" by "beast" (though in some of his works he also called it "devil"). Solzhenitsyn in *Gulag Archipelago*, a work where religious integrity reaches its summit, says: "the line dividing good and evil crosses through every man's heart". On one side God, on the other — the devil.

But, then, God is interpreted in many different ways, even a Christian God. Where is the true God?

Upon examining the history of man's search for God, one arrives inevitably at the conclusion that however differently people understand God, there is something in common in every one of these notions. What they have in *common* is the true God, because truth is in unity. And the differences in ideas about God stem from prejudice, from human "darkness", and from the strong influence of pagan beliefs.

The great, eternal and timeless importance of Tolstoy — the fifth

Evangelist, to my mind, and a true interpreter of Christ — is that he cleared the concept of God of human superstition, and more importantly, of partisan controversy about the divine essence. Tolstoy found that common interpretation of God which is truth, in all those who believe in him: Christians and Buddhists, Muslims and Judaists, Lao-Tse and Kant, Socrates and Schopenhauer, Harrison and Bondarev, Orthodox believers and Catholics.

"I believe in God, whom I conceive not as a part but the principle of all things."

Who Do We Belong To?

"My life awareness, the awareness of freedom, is God." *Ibid.*

"When there is a choice (man's life is no life without the recognition of this), man seeks the best, the most compatible with reason and its laws (the laws of God). And whatever is not compatible with the laws of wisdom, that is what I call beastly."

Ibid.

"No-one ever saw God. If we love each other, then God is within us."
"God is the Beginning of all beginnings and man senses Him in himself as love."
"God is love."

The idea that man is physically finite in time and limited in space, while his spiritual self is infinite, runs through all Tolstoy's religious writings. The awareness of our links with those who lived before us and those who will live after us, as well as with those far away from us, awakens God within our souls. Man's love for his own limited self, for his flesh, comes from the devil. Man's love of the infinite comes from God. Reason prompts man to recognise the petty and insatiable nature of the flesh and the greatness of the free soul and the feasibility of its demands. "Man, try as he may, cannot please his body, because what the body claims is not always attainable, and when it is, it is through strife against others." *Love Each Other.*

There have always been two beliefs on earth. According to one: man exists for the sake of his immortality, but his physical being cannot be infinite, for flesh is mortal. According to the other: man lives once only, his soul is born together with his body and dies together with it. Both these concepts of life are beliefs, since there is no empirical evidence for either the immortality or the mortality of the soul. It is impossible to prove that one must live for the sake of one's body, and it is equally impossible to substantiate that one must live for the sake of one's soul. One can demonstrate only the different personal and universal consequences of life according to the laws of the Soul and of life according to the claims of the flesh.

People can be distinguished as religious or atheistic not by their abstract ideas on the essence of existence, but by the way they live. The atheist lives for the sake of wealth, of power over other people, he longs to dominate others, his actions are directed by the craving to gratify his flesh. He who believes in the true God, on the other hand, lives for the diffusion of Love, truth and freedom. "The concept of God, like that of the soul, is indubitable for me and for all believers, only as the opposite pole to everything material." (*Criticism of Dogmatic Theology*) When Man has to decide between two alternatives: carnal well-being or the good of the soul, through his choice he commits himself to God or the devil. It is for this reason that he who asserts that he does not believe in God, but when faced with an alternative, sacrifices the welfare of the flesh, in the name of the good of soul — he is religious. He who worships God in the temple, but takes more than he earns and outside the temple strives for the well-being of his flesh — is an atheist. For we are told: "Not everyone that saith unto me, Lord, Lord, shall enter into the Kingdom of Heaven; but he that doeth the will of my Father which is in Heaven." (Matthew VII, 21.)

He who believes in God will never serve any sort of human association — party, class, nation — and will take even greater care not to serve a state, an organization created specially to violate people, to limit their freedom.

Obviously, man cannot be entirely independent of all human associations. Every believer participates, to some extent, in some kind of human union. But the believer serves an organization, particularly in the case of the state, only up to the point where God forbids us to step further. We can quote, as exemplary for a believer, the patriarch Tikhon's answer at the Moscow trial of 1922 when the chairman of the court asked him: "Do you consider existing state laws binding for yourself for not?" Tikhon worded his attitude to the state with great care: "Yes, I do, as long as they do not contradict the rules of devoutness". Tolstoy, in his *Short Summary of the Gospels* (I came to consider him as the fifth Evangelist when studying this work) disclosed the essence of

Christian attitude to the state, using Chapter XXII of the Gospel according to Matthew as his point of departure: "Render therefore unto Caesar the things that are Caesar's; and to God the things that are God's." (18-21)

A Christian cannot conceive how anyone could achieve a goal like the creation of a just society, by working for the state. "There is one way only to achieve this goal" said Tolstoy, "and it is the simplest and most natural one. It means leaving aside state and government, not bothering about them, and thinking only about one's own life and leading it according to the rules of clear conscience." (*About the Existing System*)

In every man there is a longing for God and at the same time resignation to the devil. Man, with the sinful part of his nature, belongs to the state, nation, class, family, and submitting himself to all these units, he pays tribute to the devil, to a greater or lesser extent. But a religious man is aware of the fact that any kind of human association means temptation, since the moment he serves one or another part of mankind, he ceases to serve God, and works only for the group of people he sees himself in. While Christ said: "And a man's foes shall be they of his own household. He that loveth father or mother more than me is not worthy of me: and he that loveth son or daughter more than me is not worthy of me." (Matthew X, 36). The term "household" must be understood in a broader sense, reaching beyond those who constitute your home. It covers all the associations you belong to. Tolstoy did not teach people not to love the Fatherland, people, relatives. He only spoke about the alternatives you may be faced with: association of people or God. You, as an atheist, give God up for them; you, as a Christian, give them up for God.

One of Dostoevsky's heroes says: "I believe in Russia, I believe in Orthodoxy ... And in God? In God? I ... I shall believe in God." Hence, Dostoevsky also acknowledges the incompatibility between faith in God and in some human unit. But while for Dostoevsky this dilemma seemed tragically insoluble so that sometimes he taught that we should serve not God, but the state and the Orthodox Church; for Tolstoy, who solved every problem on the basis of reason instead of dark unconscious instincts as did Dostoevsky, the answer was clear and simple. God comes first of all, then family, people, and as for the state, it is the last in the line.

Tolstoy taught people to believe only in their knowledge, and with certainty one can know only oneself. Therefore the believer does not aim at changing his external conditions, since those are

273

not dependent on him, but on the general outcome of the struggle between God and devil in the world. In order to further God's triumph, man can aspire only to his own moral betterment. In addition, he is entitled to remind others of the teachings of Christ, to help strengthen their faith, show them the good that comes to the world from holding to Christ's teachings. But the Christian does not participate in political activity, since the purpose of such activity is changing man's external life and the means to this end involve strife between people. Political struggle imbues man with characteristics such as unconditional belief that he knows how to transform life — something that other people do not know — and this is the sin of pride; hatred for those who think differently — which is breaking the doctrine of love; and greed for power. Tolstoy always insisted on the idea that only man can improve himself. And, indeed, this is the only way of transforming the world. This way a mistake in the course of accomplishing the transformation cannot cost more than one life, that of the transformer himself. And once every man had reconstructed the Kingdom of God within himself, it will bring along the triumph of His Kingdom on earth, of which Christians and communists dream (I have in mind those idealist communists who wish to replace the communist socio-economic system by the ideal of human freedom.) Tolstoy's are the only religious-social teachings free of the eternal contradiction between ends and means: to serve God and Love is end and means at one and the same time.

Tolstoy, though he often used the expression 'personal redemption', confirmed, in fact, the salvation of mankind through every man serving God.

The entire course of mankind's history proves that as soon as social reformers appear on the scene, you can expect blood, however fine (and sincere) the words they utter about peace, happiness, and brotherhood may be. Berdyaev was right in remarking: "There was never a single project conceived in the womb of the historical process that would have been successful". (*The Meaning of Life*) For in order to transform social conditions the reformer must take into account a vast number of interacting and mutually binding circumstances and it is not for man to know them all; only for God. And every reformer, though starting from the "ideal of the Madonna", ends up at the "Sodomian ideal", and establishes a system which is as unjust, and sometimes even more so, as the one he has just demolished. Having committed violence for the sake of the happiness of millions — and violence not against himself, but against those near him — the "great" reconstructor inevitably gets caught up in the law of "blood calling for blood". Forgetting his original aim, he exerts all his energy to prove that the first blood was not shed in vain, but in aid of "liquidating" or curbing the freedom of those who — as he saw it — obstructed the way to the great goal.

Tolstoy denied the value of "great men": no-one knows in whom God is more present than in the rest. The Old Believers bowed from the waist to everyone, knowing that there is a part of God in all beings.

Tolstoy taught us to love, not the abstract human being, but the man standing next to you now (his story "Where there is love there is God" is relevant), and not to plan people's future lives. This is taken from Christ's sermon on the Mount: "Take no thought for the morrow: for the morrow shall take thought for the things of itself. Sufficient unto the day is the evil thereof" (Matthew VI, 34). In the story "Three Questions" Tolstoy said: "And remember, the most important time is now. It is most important, because it is only now that we have power over ourselves ..."

For Tolstoy Christ was one of the greatest teachers of mankind. He only regretted that Christ himself did not write anything, thus his teachings are known only through the writings of people who were inferior to him in wisdom, infected by the prejudices of their own times, and often incapable of rising above pagan ideas. Tolstoy performed an enormous feat when he extracted from the Gospels all that is eternally valid, the great wisdom and supreme religious doctrine that can and ought to be comprehended and adopted by people of our own times. At the same time he cast out all that was mean, that would only alienate reasonable people from faith.

He said: "Religion is not simply a once and for all established belief in supernatural events that had apparently taken place once upon a time, and belief in the necessity of certain prayers and rituals! It isn't either — as scientists would have it — a remnant of superstitions stemming from ignorance in ancient times, which would have no meaning and relevance in our time, for our lives. Religion is *people's attitude to eternal life and to God, defined by reason and based on correspondence with modern knowledge*; it is the motive force guiding mankind towards its predestined goal." (*What is Religion ...?* My italics — G.A.)

Tolstoy extracted from the Gospels, as well as from other books that reflect modern man's superior wisdom, the most important elements, the quintessence of what links these writings to each other.

Tolstoy noted that all Christ's commandments were in the negative mood: you shall not commit adultery, you shall not swear, do not resist evil by evil. The basic postulate of Tolstoy's religious ideal, i.e. that man is finite in flesh and infinite in Soul, determined the nature of his teachings on moral improvement. Moral improvement means overcoming the desires of the flesh (and not the annihilation of flesh as the ascetics Hartmann and Schopenhauer preach), by liberating oneself from one's sins.

Tolstoy names six most terrible sins: lust (turning necessity into pleasure), sloth, covetousness, love of power, lechery and drunkenness. He says: "If there were no sins, there could be no poverty, no surfeit, no depravity, no pilfering, no robbery, no murder, no execution, no war." (*Christian Teaching*) Indeed, it must be obvious to everyone who sincerely wishes to create the Kingdom of God on earth that if people

1 did not try to transform the means of existence — food, clothing, shelter, — into the purpose of life and thus endlessly enlarge shelter — into the purpose of life and thus endlessly enlarge with expensive ornaments (the sin of lust);
2 did not expropriate the work of others (the sin of sloth);
3 did not accumulate whatever they do not need today (sin of covetousness);
4 did not seek power over other people (sin of love of power);
5 did not change sexual partners (lechery);
6 did not numb their consciousness by various means of intoxication, like vodka, drugs, exciting spectacles, i.e. parades, meetings, religious ceremonies (sin of drunkenness),

then there could hardly be grounds for war or violence.

Materialists contend that morality is a product of social conditions. This doctrine itself is immoral, it was created to justify human sin: "Society is divided into classes, in any case, such is the law of social-historical development, hence some must rule and some must submit" — says the power-loving atheist to himself and he acquires power by means of violence. But should the prevailing opinion in society hold that class struggle — or any other struggle — is sinful, and that love of power is a deplorable vice, he who craves power would at least acknowledge that his aspiration is shameful, unnatural and that no "dialectics of social development" justify his personal sin. Christ taught: "Let your communication be, Yea, yea; Nay, nay: for whatsoever is more than these cometh of evil" (Matthew V, 37). And yet all over the world monuments are erected to conquerors and revolutionaries, and children are told that though on the one hand it did not all happen without bloodshed, on the other hand these are great heroes and benefactors of the people ...

But if I believe in reason only, accepting deliberately Christ's teachings, why should I need to dim my conscience with vodka, with intoxicating spectacles like a patriotic demonstration, why should I listen to all kinds of demagogic speeches and thus give up my free reason to anyone but God? And if we do not all submit to this process of paralysing our minds, how can they compel us to participate in savagery of all sorts, like war, persecution of people objectionable to the authorities, etc.? When the sin of drunkenness disappears, there will be none of these horrors.

And the same applies to all other sins.

All healthy thinking people are dissatisfied with the world they live in. Without nonconformism there would be no progress of any kind, hence no moral development either. The only distinguishing feature is that truly religious people, Christians in particular, pursue the transformation and improvement of the soul, their own soul, while atheists transform the world at their own discretion, wreck that which they did not create and construct that which is not for them to build. He who changes the world, sows discord, he who transforms the soul according to Christ's teachings, promotes unity. The Christian becomes a source of light for those around him, and the more light, good and justice is emitted by each man's soul, the brighter the world becomes.

The Christian does not recognise human organisations like parties, nations, churches, for all these associations stand between man and God. The Christian does not serve God through men, but serves men through God.

It is not true that Tolstoy taught us to love our nearest as strongly as ourselves. He was aware that it would be unnatural. He who loves God in himself, and hence lives according to Christ's commandments, will do no harm to others, will not sow evil in the world. The Christian cannot be responsible for his feelings, since they are dictated by his flesh; but for his actions he can and must assume responsibility, for these are guided by his religious conscience.

Tolstoy differentiated between reason and common sense. The latter is a slave of the flesh, it always finds explanations for deeds committed according to the demands of our physical being. Man's awareness of reason is the only one given to man by God to help him find truth: "... the only tool man possesses for acquiring knowledge is his reason ... therefore any preaching that maintains something contrary to reason, is deception." (*Christian Teaching*)

III

While athiests believe in the flesh only (though of course, as a rule, in spite of their being servants to the flesh, they take cover behind the mask of idealist phraseology), Christians have another temptation: the church with its dogmas, hierarchy, with its pretensions to a mediatory role, and — most importantly — with its allegations that one can gain admittance to the world beyond with the aid of pagan devices and tricks: bowing before ikons, Eucharist, anointing, baptism, extreme unction etc.

In people's minds nowadays, at least in Russia, Christianity and Church are inseparable. This is why it is so difficult to convince modern man of the truth of Christianity. A contemporary man says, with the ironic scepticism so characteristic of the twentieth century: "But isn't Christianity all about the creation of the universe from chaos? About immaculate conception? About the resurrection of the dead? About turning your left cheek to anyone who strikes your right cheek? About loving your enemies?" Remaining on the grounds of dogmatic theology there is no chance to attract to Christianity any significant number of Russians in search of the truth. Therefore it is imperative to give them a prompt answer in Tolstoy's words: "The Christian religion and the Christian Church are not one and the same and we have no right whatsoever to suppose that what is characteristic Christian religion is also characteristic of the Christian Church." (*About Tolerance*).

In our day and age, religious ideas can be disseminated only through appealing to reason, only by renouncing church partisanship and the dogmatism that follows from it. That the spreading of religious ideas is vitally important, that the redemption of mankind lies only in a religious attitude to life, needs no proof. It is enough to look back on the bloodstained history of the twentieth century, brought about by athiests.

★   ★   ★   ★

Basically, Russia has known only two historical roads: that of the state church and that of the state party. We have not so far experienced the third one: the road of Christian redemption in Tolstoy's sense of the words.

I suppose, had Tolstoy been alive now, he would not notice any qualitative changes in the beliefs of post-revolutionary Russians. (Let us remember that Tolstoy did not evaluate people's faith according to brochures, newspaper articles, prayers or scientific booklets written by them, but by their way of life, by their attitude to God.) He would see a difference in institutions standing between man and God; (before — ideological justifications of violence came from the state/church, now — they come from the state/party). He would observe that violence has increased quantitatively and become more frightening. But, I repeat, he would not notice either a particular decline or, still less, a rise in the level of religious awareness. If before the revolution evil reigned and good was suppressed, the same applies after the revolution. As before 1917, Russia abounds in Christians and atheists and the correlation between moral and social values remains unchanged: the higher a man rises on the social ladder, the more his bond with God loosens. Before the revolution there was an institution — the church — to manipulate people's conscience with the aid of myths, now there is a similar institution — the party.

The Russian Orthodox Church in view of its entire historical practice, has no grounds on which to claim the right to lead the Russian people toward Christianity, which was destroyed as early as the fourth century, and not without the help of the church hierarchy.

Tolstoy maintained, not without foundation, that unadulterated Christianity existed only up till the Council of Nicaea (325) and the first Council of Constantinople (381), where people who arbitrarily declared themselves as the only representatives of God on earth, invented a creed consisting of twelve articles and demanded unconditional and blind faith in these articles from orthodox believers. (Naturally, one of these articles, the ninth, calls for belief in the one and only Holy and Apostolic Church.) Consequently, from that day on, the church demanded of the orthodox, loyalty to itself in the first place and to God only after that. As recently as 1956, the "Journal of the Moscow Patriarchate" admitted that "from the very beginnings of its history the Church does not tolerate ... and excommunicates all those who deviate from its dogmatic doctrines, though it manifests a certain lenience towards

279

those who break some moral codes." (J.M.P. 1956. No. 8, p.47.) Tolstoy, on the other hand, never recognised faith without deeds: "... faith ought not to be separated from deeds ... deeds are the essential consequence of faith." (*Criticism of Dogmatic Theology*)

It goes without saying that Tolstoy's Christianity is incompatible with Orthodoxy. Tolstoy separated church from Christ to the same extent to which the Synod separated itself from the church. Both the Synod and Tolstoy acted logically. Tolstoy could not accept the church as a true Christian institution, since he did not recognise, on the whole, any intermediary in the matter of communication between man and God. He could not see the church as a true Christian institution, moreover, because its doctrine and its entire historical practice did not correspond to Christian morality, while its dogmas and rituals could not stand up to criticism at all.

It must be said that the church, by the character of its actions and the nature of its doctrines has in fact separated itself from Christ.

I shall permit myself a short excursion into the history of the Orthodox Church in order to support this idea.

Already the very first action of the Church, immediately after Russia's conversion to Christianity, strikes one with its utter disregard for Christ's commandments. In the "Russkaya Pravda", the first code of laws in Russia after the adoption of Christianity, they included — following a proposal by the episcopate itself — articles prescribing the most cruel punishment for brigandage. (And we know who the brigands were: peasants robbed of their livelihood by the princes, and ruined townspeople.) Up to the moment of the episcopate's intervention, brigands used to be punished by "fines to be paid in money", then by "complete destruction", i.e. confiscating all their belongings and selling them, together with their families, as slaves abroad. Hence, already in the tenth and eleventh centuries, the church participated in breaking the Christian law "do not resist evil with evil", and was even the initiator of reprisals against unfortunate people.

We know, from the laws of Yaroslav, Prince of Kiev, that church representatives formed a part of the ducal courts of justice and that the penalty extracted from an offender was shared between the prince and the metropolitan. Thus the church, from the very beginnings of its existence in Russia, disregarded another commandment of Christ, "judge not that you be not judged", as well as that of "render to Caesar what is Caesar's and unto God what is God's".

Tolstoy's Christianity and "From Under the Rubble"

The historian V.O. Klyuchevsky points out that in Yaroslav's days there were prison cells attached to churches and that prisoners were beaten. By an order of Metropolitan Ivan (1080-1089), sorcerers (i.e. those who did not accept orthodox dogmas and authority) were to be submitted to exorcism and then "violently punished but not beaten to death".

All through its subsequent history the church was competing with secular powers in breaking Christ's commandments and was highly successful in the enterprise. At the same time it was always slavishly serving authorities. Not the bolsheviks, but the tsars after Peter the Great in 1721 placed lay authority at the head of the church, abolishing the Patriarchate and replacing it by a permanent council called the Holy Synod. And what happened? Did the church go underground? Not at all! It grew accustomed, quite easily, to subjection to the sovereign, since church princes always had no less wealth and power than the secular princes, and they preferred mammon to God. And Christ said: you cannot serve God and mammon.

Russian tsars closed monasteries without any special protest from the church. As we all know, Catherine the Great was no communist, yet she succeeded in closing down almost five hundred monasteries out of eight hundred and eighty-one that had existed before her reign. The church swallowed this, too. Nowadays some Orthodox believers, in particular one of the contributors to *From Under the Rubble*, blame the Soviet authorities (and quite rightly) for not allowing the church any say in secular matters. But, then, neither did Catherine: "Your essential duty is to govern the churches, take care of performing the sacraments, preach God's word, defend the faith, to pray and to fast," i.e. it seems that she would take what is Caesar's and what is God's should be rendered unto the clergy. Catherine, the "Tartar in a skirt" as Pushkin called her, had the same attitude to the church (like all other rulers, by the way) as that adopted by today's rulers in their treatment of philosophers: work out your theories, seek religious (philosophical) justification of our right to rule by force, praise us to the skies, anathematize our enemies and we shall help you to find a comfortable corner. But if you do not fulfil these tasks — you have only yourselves to blame! You will be confined to a monastery (as in the case of Nikon, who had dared to say that the "tsar may be a lesser authority than the archbishop"); to a lunatic asylum (as with Grigorenko or Zhores Medvedev). And the church did the homework set by the authorities. As early as 1549, out of sixty-nine people canonized by the church, seventeen were princes, fourteen metropolitians and bishops and twenty-three founders of monasteries. At the same time the church excommunicated enemies of the state, like Stenka Razin, Yemelyan Pugachev and even Tolstoy. So it turned out that daylight robbers and oppressors — the princes — were saints, while those advocating non-violent resistance to evil were pronounced villains. And no wonder. The church is an organization, made up of people torn by the same passions as ordinary human beings. Priests are no better and no worse than other people. Yet it would be wrong to label them atheists. There were true saints among the Russian clergy, like Sergius of Radonezh or the patriarch Tikhon. There were scoundrels, too, like Petr Myslovsky, who under the guise of confession elicited the names of their confederates from arrested Decembrists and received the Order of St. Anna for his services. (Just as the Soviet power gave orders of merit to priests who were far from being saints, for collaborating with the authorities.) But, then, communists are not all "bluecaps" either. There were saints among them as well (General Grigorenko, for instance, is a communist). Does the holiness of certain individuals, though, entitle us to historical rehabilitation of the party whose doctrine and practice are based on violence? A Christian must be consistent and admit that the church also served violence, just as any party in power of striving for power.

Let us recall the scene of prayers at Razumovsky's private chapel in *War and Peace*. "We offer ourselves and our lives to our Lord Christ" — Natasha, listening to these words, feels happy that at last she can grasp the supreme truth: "My lord, I put myself in your hands" — she murmurs to herself. And suddenly, the deacon takes a new text and reads it "in that serene, bombastic and gentle tone ... which works so irresistibly on the Russian heart." Only this new text is a complete contradiction of the one he had just read, which was really in line with the commandment to love God, all our friends and enemies. This time he is bidding his listeners fight the enemy who had invaded Russian soil. And Natasha, with her sense of truth, "could not bring herself to pray for treading the enemy under our feet, when only a *few minutes earlier* she was wishing to have more enemies in order to love them and pray for their souls." (My italics — G.A.) The deacon had no spiritual qualms about changing the principal message of the prayer when it suited the interests of the state, but in the religious conscience of the girl, not spoilt by the church, there arose a confusion.

The whole history of the Orthodox Church is the history of

robbery and deception, committed jointly by church and secular powers. It is the history of substituting the doctrines of the church hierarchy for Christ's teachings. The living Christian doctrine that was comprehensible to everyone was transformed into a code of dogmas acceptable only if reason was renounced altogether.

To claim truthfulness for church dogmas can lead to a situation where no thinking man takes religion in general seriously. Tolstoy gave his warning of this danger: "Having freed himself of the deception of hypnosis," he wrote, referring to a man who had earlier believed in church doctrines "such a man, filled with hatred for the lie he has just rid himself of, becomes a natural prey to advanced ideas according to which all religions are obstacles blocking mankind's road to progress." (*What is Religion ...?*)

On these grounds Tolstoy looked upon the church as a dangerous enemy of religion.

Nevertheless, I do not think Tolstoy would have been quite so militantly disposed against the church, had the clergy taught people, apart from the rituals, the essence of Christianity as well. But he witnessed the contrary: "... it is no use saying that Russian Orthodox preachers see the essence of the doctrine somewhere else, and that these (the rites) they regard only as old formalities not worth demolishing. It is not true. Throughout Russia, the whole of the Russian clergy — and with special intensity, of late — advocate only this belief in rites. Nothing else exists." (*The Kingdom of God is Within Us.*)

As an opponent of any kind of restriction, Tolstoy did not deny the right of the "dark ones" to participate in religious rituals. He only reminded believers that deeds are more important. "Do believe in Sunday, in paradise and hell, in the popes, in the church, in sacraments, in expiation", he wrote, "say your prayers as your creed demands, fast, sing psalms. All this should not prevent you from acting as Christ has shown us we should, for the sake of our salvation: do not be angry with your neighbour, do not commit adultery, do not swear, do not resist evil by evil, do not kill." (*What I Believe*)

Tolstoy did not so much blame the church for perpetuating these pagan rites, as charge it with betraying the essence of Christianity which resulted, first of all, in the birth of such a frightful combination of words as "Christian soldier".

The church deviated from Christ's commandments in all aspects: 1) it induced people to believe not just in the one and only God, but also in the Holy Mother, in angels, in a host of saints (it will be recalled that some of these saints were "nominated" by the church); 2) instead of "Thou shalt not make thyself a graven image" — worship the icons; 3) in the place of "do not swear" — they bless the troops; 4) instead of "honour your father and your mother" — honour also your sovereign and your superiors; 5) in place of "thou shalt not kill" — kill, at the command of your superiors, obeying state laws.

Consequently, neither its history, nor its symbols of faith, nor its rituals entitle the church to the role of representative — especially not the sole representative — of God on earth.

The Orthodox Church is a religious party that has discredited itself by its very partisanship.

Modern man witnesses how courageously reason probes into the secrets of matter, and it is impossible (but also unnecessary) to convince him that reason cannot find out the secrets of the soul. There is no sense in attempting to refer people of the atomic-electronic age back to mystical methods of puzzling out the laws of spiritual life. It was Tolstoy's deep conviction that man's religious consciousness, his awareness of links with eternity, grows and improves following the same line as the process of scientific cognition. Just as scientific knowledge has no need to return to already surpassed and discarded stages, so religious knowledge must develop, discounting errors committed by previous generations on their way towards God.

Tolstoy wrote: "... faith, religion, i.e. the interpretation of the meaning of life, throughout bygone ages, seemed possible only in the form of secretive, mystical, miraculous revelations and of relevant rituals. Now, on the other hand, mankind in its highest principles, especially with Christianity, has arrived at a point where mystical interpretations of the meaning of life, with their miraculous revelations and rituals imposed allegedly to please God, become unnecessary. A simple and reasonable explanation of Life's meaning, which is free of mysticism, becomes sufficient and even more convincing than hitherto; an explanation, which ensures the fulfilment of vital moral demands. (*Union*)

Russia has never yet tried the road of Christianity. Up to 1917 she followed the road characterized by the troika of "autocracy—orthodoxy—nationalism". After the revolution, Russia departed on an even more terrible road which can be defined as that of "oligarchy—pseudo-marxist ideology—moral-political unity of the people". Our thinkers have seen the viciousness of this second road. But are they wise to appeal to Russians, asking them to trust once again in already discredited ways of life and religious consciousness, which would be basically a continuation of the pre-revolutionary road?

This is the question arising in the wake of *From Under the Rubble*; with the very title the authors announce their intention to bring back from non-existence something that had long since disappeared into oblivion.

What is it they extricate from under the rubble? How should this volume be judged from the viewpoint of a maturing Christian awareness as understood by Tolstoy?

The history of Russia, as of any other country, must not be handed over to those who wish to forget it. The authors of the volume repeatedly reproach Soviet ideologists for their efforts to wipe out historical memory in people's minds. They appeal to us to remember the eternal values without which, as they suppose, Russia cannot proceed towards happiness.

Yes. A lot has been done in the past sixty years in order to make people forget their country's past including its recent past.

To justify the violence of today's rulers, ideologists do their best to blacken the regime that was overthrown.

For nearly sixty years historians and philosophers who serve the present regime, have argued that everything before 1917 was basically bad. Only what furthered the revolutionary cause was ever good, namely, revolts, activities of three generations of revolutionaries, Russian artists' criticism of the system and attempts to demolish it. Whatever could have held Russia back from revolution is either consigned to oblivion or attacked; in particular the entire Russian idealist philosophy, and most of all its religious theme. It can be stated, without any danger of erring, that the overwhelming majority of the Russians called "smatterers" by Solzhenitsyn, have no notion of such great philosophers (to mention only the latter part of the nineteenth and the beginning of the twentieth century) as V. Solov'yev, Tolstoy, Berdyaev, N.O. Lossky, or P. Florensky. To their mind Russian philosophy is limited to Belinsky, Chernyshevsky, Pisarev, Plekhanov and Lenin. Soviet ideologists, by taking out of its context one or another phenomenon of Russian life and Russian thought, turn the complex and to a certain extent harmonious history of Russian thought and truth-seeking into some kind of a freak. This is particularly so when they adapt concepts, sometimes even of theorists they disavow, to the expediency of their pragmatic tasks, consequently depriving them of their true identities.

I wish to emphasize that reinstating the truth about Russian thought is not a mere academic mission, but a crucial task. Russia today is a country whose spiritual life influences the fate of people all over the world. [It would exceed the task of this article to explain the reasons that lead to increasing ties between Russia and the rest of the world. — G.A.] God's triumph in Russia would mean that the danger of destruction of the soul and liberty on earth would be eliminated for a long time to come; the devil's victory would mean the whole world wallowing in the mud of animal existence, deprived of spiritual values and abounding in feuds, hatred and slavery.

Hence, the attempt by the authors of *From Under the Rubble* to reclaim certain past values can only be received with approval. For much of what goes on in Russia at present was forecast by the great prophets, first of all by Dostoevsky. Moreover, they recommended a number of ways for avoiding the evil they foresaw.

On the whole, in spite of the differences between individuals who constitute the history of Russian thought, it is not difficult to detect two harsh tendencies in the blue-print for Russia's transformation, a revolutionary and a conservative one.

The former is expressed most frankly, without any attempt at refined wording, in a letter by V.G. Belinsky: "I am beginning to love mankind in a martial fashion: in order to make the smallest part of it happy, I would — it seems — be ready to annihilate the rest with fire and sword." And elsewhere: "People are so stupid that they must be led to happiness by force. And what is the blood of thousands compared with the humiliation and suffering of millions?"

Champions of happiness for millions, from the narodniks to the bolsheviks, displayed a great deal of heroism and self-sacrifice. Much "blood of thousands" was shed by them or was their fault. Many of the rich and the oppressors were deprived of their wealth, their power, and their lives. And finally the fighters for the happiness of millions came to power. What followed, however, was not at all like their plans, but rather like Dostoevsky's forecast: "They mean to establish justice, but by rejecting Christ, they end up soaking the earth in blood; for blood calls for blood, and he who draws his sword will perish by the sword. And even if Christ's vow did not exist, they would still destroy each other, right to the last two men on earth."

Where revolutionary projects for Russia's transformation lead to, is convincingly demonstrated in the volume. The authors, as a rule, do not abandon the Christian standpoint when they treat events in present-day Russia, the fruits that the work of the champions of universal happiness have borne for the people. At the same time, it must be admitted that in this context the book does not represent anything new, compared with Solzhenitsyn's *Archipelago* or *First Circle*, which together amount to an entire encyclopaedia of Soviet life, evaluated from the moral altitude of Christian teachings.

Evidently, the compilers of the volume had a different aim. It is quite clear by now who is to blame, or rather, what is to blame (violence). The question worrying the authors is: what is to be done, who to learn from, which of the traditions of Russian thought must be resurrected and what is to be left buried under the rubble.

It is sad to discover that the authors would have no objection to anathematizing Tolstoy once again and putting in his place the very institution which at the time dealt with him summarily — the Orthodox Church.

This does not mean that the book represents a complete break with the essence of Christianity, as far as theological doctrines are concerned. No. Its strongest and most attractive point is precisely that the ideas contained in it are akin to Christianity's ethical foundations.

The analysis of Christian motifs echoing from certain pages of the volume is not within the scope of this essay, since they are above dispute among Christians. The inspired appraisal, from an ethical point of view, of the actions of not only individual persons, but also states and generally social systems that permeate the book, reminds one of Tolstoy's works. "There is no greatness where there is no simplicity, goodness and truth" — the criterion in evaluating people in social organizations applied by Tolstoy is also employed in *From Under the Rubble*. Socialist doctrines, in particular, receive judgement on an ethical basis: "In no socialist doctrine are moral demands seen as the essence of socialism — there is merely a promise that morality will fall like manna from heaven after the socialization of property" (from Solzhenitsyn's article). And indeed, it is absolutely clear — borne out by our whole historical experience — that the moral standards of society depend, first of all, not on the form of property, but on the extent to which its members are religious. In our times the bestial structures of capitalist Chile and of socialst China are almost equally immoral.

The suggestion of self-limitation is forever enhancing life, and so is the idea that man's physical being is perishable, while his spiritual principle is eternal — an idea that was always near to Tolstoy's heart. "The turn towards internal development, the triumph of inwardness over outwardness, if it ever happens" writes Solzhenitsyn — "... will be comparable to the transition from the Middle Ages to the Renaissance." Similarly, the recognition that man is sinful and the call for repentance can only be accepted by Christians.

The volume, as befits Christian publicism, is directed against all kinds of positivism, against definite forms of subordination of the human existence to any political or biological function whatsoever:

"Darwin, Marx, Nietzsche and Freud ... resolved the inconsistency each in his own way, leaving not one stone upon another in the edifice of blind faith in man's dignity. They knocked the *human personality* off its phantom humanist pedestal, tore off and ridiculed its mantle of sanctity and inviolacy, and showed it its true station in life — as the cobblestone paving the road for 'superman', or the drop of water destined with millions of others to irrigate the historical soil for the happiness of future generations, or the lump of flesh dragging itself painfully and uncomprehendingly to union with its fellows". (From Borisov's article).

Kant, whose doctrine of the categorical imperative is so near to Tolstoyan Christianity, was alarmed to observe, almost two hundred years ago, the theorists' disparaging attitudes to the divine essence of the inimitable human ego that was spreading all over Europe. (*The Foundations of Metaphysical Ethics*).

In the same article Borisov recognises the peculiar character of each man's road to God: "... every personality ... approaches this union [with the Universal — G.A.] in its own way, striving to achieve fulfilment *within* itself; only thus is the true whole fulfilled."

The volume is permeated with the absolutely correct idea that only through religious consciousness is it possible to proceed towards happiness: "And if Russia is destined to have Renaissance, it can be accomplished only on a religious foundation." This very conviction aided the authors in revealing just where the real greatness of Russian literature lies. Soviet literary historians, following in Lenin's footsteps, maintain that Russian literature has a revolutionary tendency. The authors of the book accomplished a great feat in showing the primarily religious significance of Russian literature: "... Russian literature — through Gogol, Dostoevsky, Tolstoy, Chekhov and Solzhenitsyn — is witness to the profound malady of our secular culture, the tragic absurdity of a godless existence" (from Barabanov's article). The history of religious searches by Russian writers is not yet written, and the author of these pages, determined to fill the gap, was happy to come across these lines in the article by a man who is close to the great writer.

The authors' deep aversion to revolution as well as counter-revolution and their call for a moral revolution: this is a basis on which it would be possible to unite Christians around the collection *From Under the Rubble.*

However, the authors recommend yet another basis for association: they invite Russia to take again the road she already passed along: that of orthodoxy, nationalism and authoritarianism (euphemism for despotism); a road that cannot (and ought not to) attract a single thinking man and is as distant from Christianity as revolutionary Marxism.

In their treatment of the past, the authors demonstrate the very partisan methodology I talked about at the beginning of this article, and, as a consequence, they inevitably deviate from Christianity in a score of their tenets. [Christianity as such, which would be interpreted in the same manner by everyone, does not exist. In this article Christianity is understood in its Tolstoyan interpretation. — G.A.]

Upon reading the volume, one is constantly reminded that all its authors passed through the Soviet brand of educational and instructional process. Having discarded the foundations of Marxist ideology, they did not prove capable of shaking off entirely the bolshevik manners of discussion. Doctrinairism, arrogance, [here is an example of a rebuff against those with a different cast of mind: "What a state of disrepair twentieth century Russian history is in, how distorted, twisted and full of obscurities it must be, if people who know nothing about it can pose as its self-styled conceited judges." This refers to those who interpret Russian history differently from the authors. — G.A.], implacability to everyone with a different cast of mind or acting differently from the authors, manipulation of historical facts to accommodate their partisan dogma — it all comes through with more or less prominence in these articles.

Carried away by their partisan zeal, the authors pay no heed to how far they have moved from Christianity, how they have substituted Orthodoxy for Christianity, nationality for divine personality, state system for freedom.

Apart from the illuminating and persuasive homily "Live without lies", none of the social proposals in the book have much in common with Christianity. Instead of advising Russian people to find their bearings away from the frightful road, they direct them towards the old path, already sufficiently tested, which hardly anyone deems attractive.

I shall dwell upon the authors' attitude to Russia's past, to the problem of nation and church, in order to prove that this is a repetition of the old ideology of "autocracy, orthodoxy and nationalism", and not even brought up-to-date at that.

V

"I love my fatherland but with a strange love —
My reason will not override it!
Neither her glory bought with blood,
Nor her peace instinct with proud confidence,
Nor cherished legends of dark antiquity
Stir comforting reveries in me."
                    (Lermontov, "Fatherland", translated by D.P. Radin.)

The authors state that the chief culprits of the Russian tragedy were "godless humanists" (what a strange expression, it sounds like "hot ice-cream"). The "godless humanists" — revolutionaries and even non-revolutionary intellectuals — frustrated Russia's peaceful, harmonious development, deprived Russia of her true countenance.

Turgenev uses the expression "general interchange of opposite places". Well, the authors reconstruct Russian history, using just this method of reversing places. Today the peasantry is soulless — before the revolution they were pillars of the divine cause. Today the peasant's toil is joyless — before the revolution it brought pleasure. Russia's national characteristics are now extinct — before the revolution she had a clearly etched national profile. Today's rulers are the embodiment of all vices — before the revolution they incarnated the guarantee for Russia's peaceful development. Modern, Marxist ideology kills the soul — pre-revolutionary orthodox ideology nurtured it.

"Russia, too, lived through many centuries under various forms of authoritarian rule and yet preserved herself and maintained her health and did not experience any self-abasement, as in the twentieth century, and ... millions of our peasant ancestors died telling that they did not live too intolerable lives" — reads one of the articles. This idyllic state was befouled by "godless humanists" who have led Russia to the present predicament of soulless slavery.

In this statement the partisan method, which contrasts with Tolstoy's Christianity, is particularly evident. Only with an eye to a partisan purpose, aspiring to confirm the righteousness of the group of people who interpret events thus and in no other manner, can one go to such lengths in disregarding historical facts. Leo Tolstoy always knew how to remain at a Christian, non-partisan level of contemplation. Here is, for instance, what he wrote at the time of the first Russian revolution, addressing himself to the people: "... now that the tsarist government call you to fight against your brothers, and the revolutionaries tell you to do the same, there is only one line of conduct for you, Christian workers, a single way compatible with your own interests as well as with the will of God and your very conscience: *do not side with either the old or the new government and do not participate in the anti-christian actions of either.*" (Address to the Russian People, 1906.)

Further, the compilers of the volume, by denying the Christian teaching on personal salvation, inevitably go as far as juggling with all sorts of generalized social concepts, like nation, Russia, people, when in fact at no time did a united Russia, with common history, with a single morality, with equal level of well-being and homogeneous features, exist. There were (and are) always people, personalities who each proceeded along his own path towards God (or evil), who were joyful or suffered, loved or hated, hoped or despaired in his own manner.

Tolstoy, even when he describes such an important historical event as the 1812 patriotic war in *War and Peace*, reminds the reader: "Meanwhile life, the real life of people, with their day-to-day cares about health, sickness, work, leisure, their interests in ideas, science, poetry, music, love, friendship, hatred, passion, went on as ever, independently of the political vicinity of, or enmity against Napoleon and regardless of any possible reconstruction."

This ability to see not only the general but also, and first of all, the particular, is what is lacking in the volume, hence the conclusion that before the revolution there existed a united Russia (a very good one, with some short-comings), and that now there is a united Russia (a very bad one, for the last of the orthodox believers).

There is no such thing as a homogeneous history of a united Russia. If there was anything that endured and endures through the whole of Russian history, it is the force of two types of power — state and church — against ignorant, tormented people, fleeced by all possible methods, and against the intellectuals who try to awaken human dignity in people.

Let us respond to the authors' appeal and switch on our historical memory.

First of all, the peasants who "lived not too intolerable lives" and their relationship to the masters of Russian lands.

We shall begin with the period when the Orthodox Church appeared in Russia.

In 1169 the Novgorodians defeated Suzdal and they sold their prisoners as slaves for "two nogatas" (three times less than the price of a goat).

The price of a Russian man was fixed by the "Russkaya Pravda" — compiled upon consultation with the higher clergy: the price was 5 grivennik (the fine to be paid for killing a "smerd").

This is how the character of Orthodox Russia began to shape itself.

With the passage of centuries orthodoxy strengthened its positions more and more and people's lives became harder and harder. By the fifteenth century a peasant's guilt was decided upon — not by law, not even by precedent or custom — simply at the landlord-prince's will (as later, at the end of the 1920's and beginning of the 1930's — at the will of the state). The peasants began their mass exodus from the land, a phenomenon reflected, as a matter of fact, in folk art, in the theme of seeking to find out about truth and falsehood, (which was employed by Nekrasov in "Who can be Happy and Free in Russia" and by Tvardovsky in "The Land of Muraviya"). And as early as the 1470's peasants lived in serfdom. Consequently one can see no sign of any sort of united Russia with a homogeneous aspect. The features of princes and boyars somehow did not resemble those of the smerds. (I assume there is no need to talk about differences in clothing and housing.) Centuries went by and yet Russia's uniform image still did not emerge. I shall take the liberty of quoting two literary portraits from "Who Can Be Happy and Free in Russia", that of a muzhik and that of a landlord. [I am aware that the authors of the volume treat revolutionary poets with a certain suspicion, therefore I would remind them that Dostoevsky held Nekrasov in high esteem — G.A.]

Here is the portrait of the muzhiki:

Poor, dishevelled Kalinushka
Has nothing to dandify himself,
Only his back is decorated with weals,
But that cannot be seen under his shirt.
From under his bast sandals and his collar his torn skin can be
    seen
His belly is swollen from chaff.
      Twisted and turned
      Whipped and tortured
      Kalina is hardly alive.

And here is the portrait of another Russian, the landlord:

The landlord was ruddy,
Snub, well-built,
Around sixty years of age;
His moustaches white and long,
His ways like those of a young man.
His jacket was laced like the hussars'
He had wide trousers.

Up to 1861, almost without any opposition on the part of the Orthodox Church or even with its connivance, peasants were being robbed, beaten, exchanged for dogs, driven into families like animals into herds, decked out in military uniforms and compelled to kill other people.

From the sixteenth century on, the state became yet another burden on the peasant's shoulders. Ivan IV's oprichniks trampled over fields and burned the grain. "The country became desolate", wrote Heinrich Staden, and added: "the peasant would like to bury himself alive to escape from injustice". And a foreigner, visiting Russia in the seventies (Daniel Prince) wrote that the peasants' conditions were the worst, "they are forced to pay a considerable sum each week to the prince as well as to their own landlords; thus, if they have cattle, fruit or any other product, they are obliged to sell it to neighbouring landlords, denying themselves everything and living, together with their wives and children, on black bread.

They live very badly." So those who fleeced the muzhik in 1920-40 had their historical prototypes. The Cossacks did not appear by chance in the sixteenth century, but because the muzhiks fled from the so-called "not so intolerable life".

During the reign of Peter the Great Russian people began to sell each other to the factories. And again, muzhiks were running away from the land. The bolsheviks were not the first, as the authors of the volume would have it, to knock out of the peasant his love of toiling on the land: already the 1710 census revealed only 635,412 peasant households, 20% less than at the 1678 census.

Under Elisabeth (when, as is correctly stated in *Archipelago*, there was no capital punishment in Russia) the "document of guarantee", i.e. passport system was invented which meant that without this document the peasant could not absent himself from the estate. As we know, this practice was also adopted by the Soviet authorities in the thirties and forties, but it was not invented by them. For a "lamentation" (complaint) against the landlord the latter condemned the plaintiff to penal servitude. Now we are approaching the nineteenth century. That is when peasants were used as stakes in card games, were exchanged for dogs (see Griboedov: "They were exchanged for three greyhounds"). Can this, too, be called absence of abasement of the Russian nation? In the journal of an estate manager (end of the eighteenth century) we can read: "From now on Thekla Yakovlevna must not be addressed by her name and patronymic, but everyone has to call her 'Cowardly liar'; and should anyone call her by name and patronymic, that person shall be flogged mercilessly, given five thousand lashes with the birch." Some respect for a nice Slav girl! And a hundred years later Nekrasov wrote about three nooses awaiting a peasant girl: "whichever she gets caught by, it does not make much difference to her lot".

"Three hideous portions to woman Fate gave.
The one: to a slave to be mated,
The second: the mother to be of a slave,
The third: to a slave subjugated.
And each of these burdens has heavily lain
On women of Russia's Domain." (Transl. by J.M. Soskice)

Solzhenitsyn, in his appeal to the leaders, accuses the authorities, passionately and very convincingly, of degrading women. But they did not invent this attitude either!

Moreover if we read the notebooks of Bolotov, the nineteenth-century diarist, we find him writing:

"Worried in case the good-for-nothing may die during flogging, I tried out a new method on him. I ordered him to be trussed up and thrown into the overheated bath-house. He was then fed forcibly with salt fish and guarded strictly to make sure that no-one should give him drink, under any circumstances. Thirst has tortured him till he was ready to confess."

We cannot forget what went on in *Gulag Archipelago*, but there is no need to forget that teachers of "bluecaps" are not trained at bolshevik schools alone. It is quite another matter that pupils have surpassed their teachers, according to all evidence. There no-one will dispute with Aleksandr Isaevich.

I am not going to talk about Russian people's conditions in the nineteenth century. Russian literature provides an ample view of it. Not a single, not even the most insignificant writer painted such a joyful landscape as the authors of *From Under the Rubble* somehow perceive it.

It is interesting, though, how reality breaks through now and again, and frustrates the book's basic tendency "... we managed to preserve serfdom for a century or more after it had become unthinkable, keeping the greater part of our own people in a condition that has robbed them of all traces of human dignity." Such sentences are utterly incompatible with the fundamental idea upheld by the majority of the articles, the idea of the allegedly united Russian nation. If the nation is a personality (we shall discuss this unchristian contention later), then who was it who held Russians in slavery? They themselves?

Slavery for the people has always existed in Russia, evidently in different forms. It was not invented by the bolsheviks. It is another matter that the road they recommended did not lead to justice, and even less to moral progress.

Furthermore, the value of the individual has considerably decreased, the degree of people's safety has fallen since 1917.

But Christians do not engage in gauging which power commits greater violence against people. "All governments are equal in the proportion of good and evil in their actions" — noted Tolstoy in his diary. Obviously, this is not entirely correct. It is not a matter of indifference for a man what sort of state he lives in: oligarchic, totalitarian, or democratic. The less oppressive the state, the less suffering Christians have to endure in serving God. But a Christian never whitewashes one state for the sake of revealing the criminal nature of another.

It must be stated categorically that robbery, violence, the curbing of liberty are not the results of Stalin's brainwaves. Solzhenitsyn has enough intellectual courage to deduce Stalin from Lenin (by the way, V. Grossmann did the same in his novel *Everything flows* ...), but somehow his courage stops short of admitting that Stalin means also the furthering of Ivan the Terrible's, Peter's, Catherine's, the Nikolais' ... and Nero's and Herod's causes.

All human history is a history of opposition between God and Caesar and behind the latter there is the devil. Hence a Christian writer — and we would like to see Solzhenitsyn as one — has no business to appear as defence advocate of certain rulers and as prosecutor of others, however terrible those others may be.

Solzhenitsyn's attitude though, is the logical consequence of his substituting the concept of nation for that of individual and the concept of state for the concept of nation.

Even infringement upon the freedom of the individuals persecution of dissenting intellectuals, prohibition of free movement, are not phenomena unique to the sixties of the twentieth century. The first "samizdat" dates back two to three hundred years. They "picked up" Latin icons and books as long ago as in Ivan Andreevich Khvorostinsky's times in 1616, and they exiled Radishchev, literally, for "samizdat".

Not the Soviet regime but Ivan the Terrible was the first to prohibit travelling abroad freely, even for people loyal to the authorities. This is what Kurbsky wrote to him: "... you have closed the frontiers of the Kingdom of Russia, in other words turned the once free environment of men into hell's stronghold. And if someone still dares to leave the country, to follow the prophets' orders, for it is written that Jesus preached all over Syria, you call him a traitor and if he is caught at the frontier, you punish him with terrible deaths." It could have been written today.

Kurbsky fled from "hell's stronghold", and Voim Afanasevich Ordyn-Nashchokin was, in contemporary terms, a "non-returner".

Thus, emigration is no novelty either. Once again, the authors of the volume, guided by their almost pathological craving for generalizations, and for the "general exchange of opposite places", do their very best to prove what cannot be proved, namely that exiles do not link their fate with that of the fatherland. They pose a rhetorical question: "... can we speak of any significant contribution on their part to the treasury of Russian culture?'' (Shafarevich's article).

True, the people who left Russia were very different from each other. There was G.K. Kotoshikin, a gifted man but without firm moral standards, who really did become a traitor. At the other end of the scale there were also the noble V.S. Pechorin (in the middle of the nineteenth century), the great Russian thinker A.I. Herzen, and after 1917, I.A. Bunin, S. Rakhmaninov, N.K. Metner, and one could continue the list. Can we call the contributions to national culture by such emigrants as V. Hugo, Heine, Herzen, Bunin, Thomas Mann, insignificant?

As we can see, the authors are again prejudiced, partisan, intolerant in their attitude to the individual.

Exile is not the emigrant's fault; as a rule, those in power are guilty. Emigré attitudes towards Russia are far from unequivocal, and not every emigrant gives less to Russian culture than those who remain with the frontiers. I shall take the liberty of quoting the words of a contemporary Russian artist whom the KGB has tried to persuade to stay and, when he refused, accused of being a traitor to Russian culture. He replied: ''Russia always remains at the heart of an artist. Wherever he goes he will serve Russia. But whom and what do you serve, here, in Russia?'' Needless to say, by quoting this example I do not intend to give judgement as to whether Russian culture derives more or less benefit from those staying. A Christian expresses his relations not to an association of people (in this case the sum total of emigrants), but to the individual personality.

Man is responsible before God for his own actions, there is no room for intermediaries. He who tries to place some kind of agglomeration of people or organisation between man and God, deviates from the course of Christianity and enters the marshy terrain of partisanship.

This is why it seems that the authors of the volume digress, to a considerable distance, from Christianity when they create, or rather reconstruct, unearth from under the rubble, the theory of nation-personality, thus repudiating the Christian doctrine of personal salvation.

VI

Perhaps the first Russian thinker to formulate the proposition of unity of the nation as personality, was V.G. Belinsky. He wrote:

"Nationality to mankind is what personality is in relations to the concept of man. In other words, nationality is the essence of mankind's personality. In respect of this question I would sooner support the Slavophils, than remain on the side of humanist cosmopolitians." (*Russian Literature of 1846*)

It seems like a quotation from *From Under the Rubble*. Yet it was written by Belinsky at a time when he was making a stand for revolution and socialism, with his customary ardour. Hence, the combination of Slavophil and revolutionary in a single person appears in the Russian social movement long before Stalin. In his article Borisov quotes Dostoevsky: "The nation is nothing more than the national personality". But Dostoevsky had taken the idea from Belinsky, whom he passionately loved and hated at the same time.

Belinsky committed a small offence against truth when he ascribed the concept to Slavophils alone. The idea was as much an official, government one as Slavophil. Nationalism, as part of the fulcrum power leans upon, figures in Uvarov's famous troika of "autocracy, orthodoxy, nationality".

As far as the Slavophils and those akin to them like Chaadaev are concerned, it must be said that although their attitude to the concept of national unity was free from fanaticism, their own ideas on the matter were inconsistent, contradictory and in this sense the authors of this volume have gone a long way beyond them.

This is how Chaadaev writes: "Nations are moral beings to the same extent as individuals. Centuries educate nations as years do individual people." ("First Philosophical Letter")

There seems to be a complete accord between Chaadaev and the authors of *From Under the Rubble* in believing that there exist common moral features in people belonging to the same nation. And suddenly, inthat very "First Philosophical Letter" Chaadaev says: "In our heads there is decidedly nothing uniform, everything is individual, and everything is precarious and incomplete." This phrase cancels out, once and for all, the one quoted earlier. Admittedly, Chaadaev notices this lack of national unity in Russians only (a hundred years, by the way, before the authors of this volume, who accuse Marxists and "godless intellectuals" of having destroyed this unity after 1917). Furthermore, if we look at yet another passage from Chaadaev's letter, where he appeals, after all, to personal responsibility, — "... now everyone must know the place allotted to him in the common mission of Christians, that is to say, what means he can find in himself and around himself for promoting the objective set before the whole of mankind" - then we can say definitely that Chaadaev, in the last analysis, preferred the idea of personal salvation to that of a nation's responsibility before God.

Even among Slavophils there are some who have their doubts about the unity of the nation as a personality. A.S. Khomyakov declares without enthusiasm: "In Russian history the rights of the individual were not only neglected, but sacrificed outright to the general structure." K.S. Aksakov remarked (before 1917) that "people and government now follow different courses, different principles. It is not just a matter of people's opinions never being asked. It means that no honest man dares to express his opinion."

The Slavophil standpoint did not coincide with the official one. The former, notwithstanding their orthodoxy, were able to come to a profound understanding of the essence of Christianity. They did not recognise power, and what is more, they separated God's authority from that of Caesar's. On the other hand, there could be no more biased supporters of "moral-political unity" than rulers. It is easier to rule a united people, and it is also more convenient to shift the responsibility — in case of misfortune — onto the whole nation. The call for general repentance by all Russians for everything committed by the authorities, must be music to the rulers' ears.

The view that a worn-out Russian peasant woman and, say, a village teacher are guilty of the Russian troops' brigandage in foreign lands; or that a milkmaid in the Netherlands or a British shepherd are guilty of colonial robbery, is a logical consequence of substituting the concept of state for the concept of nation and a result of denying the idea of personal salvation. At the beginning of the article "Repentance and Self-Limitation ..." Solzhenitsyn calls the state "an association of thousands and millions of people". A man so alert, who can see so vividly and describe with such painful sincerity the obtuse machinery of human power in *Archipelago*, regrets the Kuomintang representative's expulsion fron the U.N., because *thus* "ten million Chinese on Taiwan were thrown out of the human family ..." But they did not expel ten million Chinese, only a doubtful representative of one of the doubtful mundane governments. And when the U.N. did not admit the representative of the Chinese People's Republic, was it better? And is the U.N. a human family? Is it not a "family" of governments? What has a Christian got to do with godless politicians? Expose them? Yes! But to wish that one ruler replaced another? Neither the Slavophils nor, it goes without saying, Tolstoy have ever contemplated the question to which pretender's mercy people should be abandoned. When, during the Russo-Japanese war, Tolstoy was asked whose side he was on, the Russian or the Japanese, he replied as befits a Christian: "I am for neither Russia nor Japan; I am for the workers of both countries who are being deceived by their *governments and forced* to take part in a war that is harmful to their well-being and in conflict with their conscience and religion." The idea of accusing the people of being guilty in conducting war did not even cross Tolstoy's mind. Yet Tolstoy wrote much about repentance — repentance by each individual for his own sins. In *War and Peace* Platon Karataev talks about a merchant who had ended up in penal servitude for someone else's offence. The merchant, aided by his faith in God and having recognised his sinfulness, withstands suffering. When the real culprit is found, the merchant, grown old in servitude, says to him: "God will forgive you. We are all sinners before God. I am suffering for my own sins."

Solzhenitsyn's call to repent springs from the pure source of Christianity, and also from a natural aversion to Soviet propaganda which indicates to the Soviet people a selection of those guilty for their troubles — imperialists, zionists, etc. — in order to divert suspicion from the real criminals, or simply to cover up for failures and mismanagement. But ought one — while acquitting the falsely accused "offenders" invented by the authorities — to transfer the responsibility for the crimes onto the shoulders of the whole nation?

The denial of the idea of personal salvation leads Solzhenitsyn to prompting Abel to repent for Cain's sin.

And from here it is not far to nationalism, which has really nothing to do with Christianity. It is terrifying that Solzhenitsyn, in his article, completely forgets the commandment about enemies: "The memory of the Tartar yoke in Russia must always dull our possible sense of guilt towards the remnants of the Golden Horde." Are we to take it that we do not forgive the Tartars? That the deportation of the Crimean Tartars is less sinful than that of the Latvians or Estonians?*

Using the concept of nation (and country and state, synonymous terms for the authors) instead of that of the individual Solzhenitsyn

---

*Wishing to forestall the readers' obvious indignation, Solzhenitsyn writes: "I repudiate the inevitable noisy protests ..." "Repudiate" — what sort of an argument is that?

condemns and acquits entire nations: "Only God can know, it is not for us to judge, which country committed the most evil." That only God is our judge, it is true. It would be no bad thing if the compilers of the volume reminded themselves constantly of this truth. But evil deeds are committed by the rulers, not by the country; and we can decide ourselves, with God's help, which rulers committed the most evil deeds. The government which frustrated to a greater extent and more frequently Christ's commandments, is the guiltier. I believe that, say, Khrushchev brought less evil upon us and did more good, than Stalin, though Khrushchev, as all rulers, sinned more terribly against God's laws than any private person. Probing further into history, it can be decided also without much difficulty that Nero, Ivan the Terrible and Robespierre, very likely, were greater sinners than Marcus Aurelius, Alexander II or Lincoln, for instance.

Indeed, every man shares the guilt, to a certain extent, in the authorities' crimes. But he is guilty not before his nation, his neighbours, only before God. And, what is more, we cannot send for trial, to the same court, the marshal who gave orders to crush the freedom of Czechoslovakia and, say, a Russian peasant woman, mother of a large family, whom no one has asked what she thought of Czechoslovakia's road to socialism and who would not even have the leisure to ponder over the question. All the same, Solzhenitsyn· calls on all Russians, simply because they are Russians, to assume responsibility for all political actions carried out in Russia or in the name of Russia.

The Christian writer's task is to advocate non-participation, to hearten those whose spirits are failing, not to invite people to repent for the unchristian deeds of the authorities. When Solzhenitsyn launches the ardent appeal "live without lies", when Shafarevich motivates and supports this appeal, they are Christians. When they assemble people in various associations: nations, states, country — they are politicians.

And Solzhenitsyn's discourses about the quantities of deadly arms necessary to defend a nation (country, state) have really nothing Christian about them. "Yes, of course," writes Solzhenitsyn, who is generally given to sketching projects for state reconstruction, "defence forces must be retained, but only for genuinely *defence* purposes, only in proportion to the threat" [should Tolstoyans and other Christians refuse to take up the arms of "defence", in the state projected by Solzhenitsyn, would their fate be the well-trodden path to prison or expulsion? — G.A.]. But, then, the Soviet leaders, too, as well as all other rulers, keep tanks and missiles only for defence purposes, and generally, to preserve peace.

Tolstoy, on the other hand, who did not tolerate arms on any pretext, wrote: "Violence cannot be regulated and employed within defined limits only. Once violence is permitted, it always extends beyond the line we had intended to draw." (Letter to an American, 1902).

Leo Tolstoy was not alone in denying the concept of nation and man's duties to the so-called national mission. Religious thinkers like, for example, Berdyaev and Karsavin placed the rights of the individual above those of the nation, and especially above the rights of the state. Yet is is strange that Borisov, not content with such real allies as Dostoevsky, for some reason quotes Karsavin as an advocate of the theory of national personality.

N.A. Berdyaev, long before Heidegger and Jaspers, worked out his own philosophy of personalism and existentialism, based on Christian concepts, derived, to a great extent, from Tolstoy's Christianity. Moreover, Saint Augustine, who suggested the concept of the "subject", was also looked upon by Berdyaev as one of the sources of his own philosophy. To Berdyaev's mind "society, nation, state are not personalities; man as personality is more valuable than the former. Therefore it is the right and duty of man to defend his spiritual freedom against the state and society. In the life of the state, nation, society we can often observe a tenebrous, demonic force striving to subjugate human personality and turn it into a mere instrument for furthering society's own purposes." (*The Individual and Society*) According to Berdyaev, the process of objectification and the conditioning rules distort human conscience. He was right in reaffirming that "pure, true conscience can be present only in the individual personality and through it; everything must be submitted to the jurisdiction of this 'existential' conscience, unadulterated by objectification". (Ibid.)

Berdyaev can by no means be called a cosmopolitan. There is hardly anyone who did more for the research into particularities of the "Russian idea". Only, he left the individual alone with God, as a Christian should, and did not allow interference by any association of people. [I should point out that V. Grossman's profound understanding of the essence of Russian history is manifestly underestimated. G.A.]

L. Karsavin, too, treated the theory of national personality with extreme caution. He explicitly favoured the Christian idea as opposed to the national. He wrote: "an inevitable consequence of national egoism is the fragmentation of 'alienation' that permeates all aspects of life and *denies Christ's religious-social ideal.*" (*Dostoevsky and Catholicism*, my italics — G.A.)

The contemporary religious philosopher, Levitin-Krasnov, is similarly unequivocal: "... personality exists for the Christian, nation does not."

Hence, as our authors' serious allies, there remain only the atheist Belinsky, Dostoevsky tumbling between faith in God and faith in Russia, and also — unfortunately — the creators of "official nationalism" S.S. Uvarov and N. Kh. Benkendorf, as well as the present-day apologists for the "moral-political unity of the Soviet people".

Not trusting reason, drawn to mysticism, the contributors to the volume define even the concept of nation, so dear to their hearts, in an unscientific, illogical, purely mystical fashion. Solzhenitsyn writes: "the profoundest similarity between individual and nation is their mystical nature in that neither was created by human hands." Borisov seconds him: "Whatever new qualities a man may receive in the ups and downs of his life, in the innermost depth of his conscience, in his '*ante-memory*' (my italics — G.A.), he always preserves a vague notion of his origins, of his 'prototype'." But this is pure racism! Even if not aggressive (perhaps for the time being?), still mystical racism. Why is the term "ante-memory" any better than the "call of blood"?

If God — infinity and love — lives in man's soul, He, because He is infinity, binds together all God's creatures on earth. Tolstoy wrote: "Man's false corporations cannot be smashed by other corporations, only by the individual person's loyalty to God." (*What I Believe*)

Perhaps to confirm national unity could be harmless, were it not that it *always leads* to justification of international enmity. The contributors to *From Under the Rubble* have not escaped this danger either. They declare often enough, (Borisov, for instance) that all nations are equal before God, nevertheless, proceeding along this noble line, they frequently stumble. Thus, Solzhenitsyn predicates no more and no less than the existence of inborn national sympathies and antipathies. In reality, national sympathies and antipathies are *cultivated* with the aid of social pedagogy. This is known to atheists as well as to Christians. The philosopher I.S. Kon, in his article published some time ago in "Novyi Mir", exposed splendidly, without mystical haze, the sources of ethnic prejudices. And Lev Nikolaevich Tolstoy who, one would think, knew people as well as the authors do, maintained that he has never observed any national feelings in the *unspoilt* Russian peasant.

The existence of national feelings cannot be denied altogether, I suppose. The nation as a determined unit does exist. But there is obviously no such thing as national "ante-memory" or "prototype".

Every man is born in a certain land, among a certain tribe. From an early age he acquires, first unconsciously and later more and more consciously, his nation's language. Language remains the main, and perhaps only, thing that ties a man to his nation. Language is the only empirically perceptible common feature in people belonging to a given nation; language in the broader sense of the word, that is, embracing the language of musical sounds, of colours and lines as used by national painters, the language of words in which people think and in which the poet creates images in his works. Apart from language, there is *nothing* universal in people assembled in a nation. All other features of a nation are either sociologists' inventions, used to stretch the point, or absurdities (like common state territory), or myths (as for instance unity of national consciousness). History has played its frequent tricks on those who defined the particular features of a nation peremptorily. How are we to understand, for instance, the definition of the Russian nation given by an eminent specialist of national problems, K.S. Aksakov. "The Russian nation is not a state-nation ... It does not contain any political characteristics, consequently, not a single grain of revolution." How "accurate" this definition seems in the twentieth century, when the Russian people have participated in three revolutions in the space of seventeen years and found themselves locked up in a state the like of which history has rarely known before!

Chaadaev held that Russians do not constitute a "uniquely necessary portion of mankind". As though Lomonosov and Pushkin — about whom Chaadaev knew — had not been Russians, and as if one could imagine the history of mankind without Dostoevsky and Tolstoy — whom Chaadaev did not know!

It is curious, to what an extent the views of those formulating ideas about Russians, "coincide". Khomyakov said that Russians were born Christians, having been Christians almost before Christianity had reached Russia; Belinsky suggested to Gogol: "Look round very carefully and you will see that Russians are by nature a profoundly atheistic people". This is where myth-mongering leads! Evidently, there were people of very different convictions among Russians: revolutionaries and conservatives, advocates of a strong state and opponents of the same, profound believers and atheists — and all this had little to do with their nationality.

Nationalistic myth-mongering predominates in *From Under the Rubble*. It manifests itself most distinctly in Korsakov's article, who identifies the concept of Russia with that of Truth, and in Shafarevich's introduction to his collection of articles. They affirm that national life has some purpose!

All this has nothing to do with Christianity and it does not correspond to truth either, if, of course, one believes in truth and not in some sort of obscure "original sense" or ambiguous verity, "set down for eternity" — in Korsakov's words (only it is not clear where and by whom it is set down).

Tolstoy always fought against conceiving religion as myth-mongering. The rejection of Tolstoy's religion inevitably leads to the creation of myths, to mystification. This, in its turn, results in more and more people repudiating faith altogether, since, after Hitler's and Stalin's socialism, people will never accept spiritualist theories of the nation, in whatever noble shape they be served up.

As I have mentioned earlier, Tolstoy did not preach against loving one's country, although Swami Vivekananda's idea would very likely have been near to his heart: "Work as though you were strangers in this country who came here only in passing. Work, but do not attach yourself to anything. Every yoke is terrible." (*Karma-Yoga*) Man's love of his nation is a sentiment and it can rise in his heart like any other sentiment. Moreover, like every feeling, it can induce people to accomplish good as well as bad actions. There is only one feeling which cannot move man to bad deeds: love of God. It is precisely for this reason that nowhere in the Sacred Books is there any slogan inviting people to amalgamate in any kind of corporation like class, party. For the Christian, love of his nation, like love of a woman, of his children, is a temptation that can distract him from serving God. Let us remember that Christ said: "He who loves father or mother more than me is not worthy of me." This is not an appeal pleading: do not love your father, mother, son, daughter. It means that your love of God comes before any other love. There is nothing good or bad in being faithful to your father, mother, nation. There is only one important question: are you, at the same time, faithful to God?

Man's whole life is a journey towards (or away from) God. Truth is in approaching God. He who entices people to abandon serving God and demands that they serve something else, nation, for instance, is a propagandist of anything you may wish to call it, but not of Christian religion.

Love of his nation is a mere episode in man's life on his way towards God. In the field of art we find a brilliant representation of this process when Prince Andrei seeks the right path in *War and Peace*. Prince Andrei's road leads from serving himself (Napoleonism), through serving his nearest and dearest (life in the Bold Mountains), the state (serving on Speransky's commission) and the Fatherland (during the 1812 war) to serving God. This is an ascent from godless individualism to the discovery of God. Each stage of Prince Andrei's development brings him nearer to God. Clearly, the service rendered to his Fatherland is on a higher level than that rendered to his own ambitions, consequently it brings him nearer to God. Serving the Fatherland exclusively, however, is not Christ's religion, it is only a more attractive religion than that of serving oneself.

The authors of this collection, with their method of universalizing each moment of development, each condition of man in the world, condemn people who do not recognize national unity, without pausing to find out *in the name of what* do they deny this unity. Some say: "Russia is a bitch", and here the authors' wrath is understandable. Meanwhile others say: "Russia is dear to me, but God is even dearer".

Jesus said: "... believe me, the hour cometh when ye shall neither on this mountain nor yet at Jerusalem worship the Father ... But the hour cometh, and now is, when the true worshippers shall worship the Father in spirit and truth: for the Father seeketh such to worship him." (John, IV, 21-23). Love of God *contains* also love of one's father and mother, wife and son, Fatherland, but it is superior to all those other loves.

Each time a man launches an appeal for the Fatherland, if he is a Christian, he must pose himself the question: does this action of mine, for the good of the Fatherland, not contradict that which is demanded of me by God? And he does not look upon the Fatherland, under any circumstances, as his truth, his God.

However, by serving God, we do also serve the Fatherland, after all is said. The Christian serves his soul without taking into account how this will reflect upon any sort of human association. Man does not serve other men directly, but through God. This is the most important gem of Tolstoy's ideas. If I live according to God, you live according to God, he lives according to God, the Divine Kingdom will descend to earth, consequently to your Fatherland, too. Moreover, we can learn how to serve God from the Gospels, but how to serve the Fatherland — all ideologists teach us differently. Tolstoy wrote in a letter: "The goal Christianity sets before man is not the welfare of one or another association of people, achieved by fulfilling the will and laws of this association, but the supreme welfare of all men, of the whole world, which can be attained by fulfilling the will and obeying the laws of God". (1895)

VII

In the second chapter of this article I have shown that Tolstoy considered the church as a non-Christian institution, and have tried to support Tolstoy's views through a short excursion into the history of the Orthodox Church.

For the authors of *From Under the Rubble* the Orthodox Church, together with the Russian state and nation, are important pillars on which their faiths rest.

I find it unbelievable that the authors should be unaware of the dark side of church history. More than that: I am convinced that they know this history better than I do. My contention is based on the fact that certain data of this history come to the surface every now and then in the volume. Should one gather all the negative statements by the authors, regarding the church, and add to them the facts from Solzhenitsyn's letter to Patriarch Pimen,* one would arrive, without fail, at the conclusion that their sight is not impaired, they see the blind alley the church has led and still leads Christians into. Barabanov is particularly frank. He admits unequivocally that the church has long since betrayed the Divine Kingdom to Caesar's Kingdom: "... preserving our academic

---

*Prompted by Patriarch Pimen's Christmas message, Solzhenitsyn, in 1972, addressed an open letter to the Patriarch, asking why the call for religious education of children is addressed to emigrants only and not to those within the frontiers. He also reproaches the church for demanding passports from those baptizing their children and registering them, for thus secular authorities can easily check on identities, consequently this single act consumes all people's courage and religious enthusiasm and leaves no energy for the religious upbringing of their children. — *Trans.*

impartiality, despite the seductiveness of past eras with their majestic attempts at theocratic kingdoms and church-state 'symphonies', surely we shall be obliged to acknowledge that in Byzantium and in Russia ideas about the Kingdom of God and the kingdom of Caesar too often merged and became interchangeable.''

And how sharp, and indubitably justified are the accusations Solzhenitsyn throws at the church: "The church, grown utterly decrepit and demoralized by the time of the revolution, was perhaps one of the chief culprits in Russia's downfall ..."

Indeed, the road to salvation recommended by the church from the moment of its rise in Russia, was so repellent that Russians flinched from it and departed on the unchristian road of the revolution.

This is quite clear, it would seem.

Still, the authors' partisan methodology prompts them to frantic endeavours to save the church; not to save people from the church, but save the church at all costs.

In their attitude to the church they are nearest to those they themselves condemn, namely, their Marxist foes. "Our party has committed many errors (even crimes) but ... long live the party!" — say those Marxist-Leninists who are aware of the historical truth. Similarly, our authors reveal the fundamentally destructive role the church plays in the history of Christianity, and at the same time they are passionately partisan fanatics in appealing for the reconstruction of the church, together with its symbols of faith, its hierarchy, its servility to the state. They treasure the external, the ritual features of the church, and in order to preserve them, they are ready to forgive its antichristian actions. They go as far as ignoring the striking similarity between the activities of the church and those of the communist party leaders; a similarity that is most conspicuous in the way they treat those who think in a different way. The entire history of the church — up to the most recent years — is the history of castigating anyone with a different creed, excommunicating those who believe in a different manner, or whose ideals do not coincide with those of the church hierarchy. Tolstoy was excommunicated, now the church rejects Eshilman and Yakunin, while Ermogen Kaluzhsky is confined to a monastery. The patriarch did not stoop to reply to the twelve "vyatich" [these facts are included in Solzhenitsyn's letter to Patriarch Pimen]. In the same way they have expelled from the party such convinced Marxists as Grigorenko and Roy Medvedev and in the same fashion the Central Committee failed to reply to letters by communists who would have wished to purify the party of its sins.

Roy Medvedev, Grigorenko, other Leninist communists, are even more courageous, more consistent in criticising their church, that is the party. And they are not possessed by narrow-minded mystical faith in the bankrupt party, like the authors of *From Under the Rubble.*

"Russian Orthodoxy is the one and only true religion" — writes F. Korsakov, and with this single sentence separates from God millions of Buddhists, Moslems, Judaists, as well as non-orthodox Christians. And why, indeed, is only Orthodoxy ("the official party line") true? How can it be proved? It can't be. "... it is the very impossibility of finding a logical explanation for this reality that constitutes the church's mysterious secret and explains the Russian's inability to tear either himself out of the Church or the Church out of himself." Now even the Russians are not all recognized as Russians; for Korsakov presumably allows that nowadays not all Russians, to say the least, feel it "impossible to tear themselves" away from the church.

"If the Orthodox Church is the only true church, and if this truth cannot be proved, but only mystically perceived, then I prefer atheism with its logic, perhaps not always convincing, but at any rate, logic," — would be the reaction of many Russians, after reading *From Under the Rubble.* This is how Christianity loses hundreds more people who are seeking God.

Have the authors not considered whom (and why) Lenin considered the more dangerous for atheism, the orthodox clergy or Tolstoy? I wish to draw attention to the passage from Lenin's article "Leo Tolstoy as the Mirror of the Russian Revolution", where he accuses the great Christian of teaching "one of the vilest things on earth, namely, religion", of endeavouring "to replace officially nominated priests by moral conviction", i.e. the cultivation "of the most subtle and therefore most loathsome priesthood". Lenin sensed very distinctly that the orthodox priest "plays into the hands" of atheism, as they used to say in party literature. Tolstoy is dangerous. Lenin devotes seven articles to combating Tolstoy's teachings, for he undertands that it is Tolstoy who can attract Russians away from the revolution, not the orthodox hierarchy. All the church fathers do is thrust Russians into the arms of revolutionaries. (Berdyaev also saw this, by the way, and so does Solzhenitsyn.)

And now, once again, Tolstoy is excommunicated from the

faith. The act was performed by Korsakov. He cannot regard Tolstoy as a Christian, because he submitted to critical analysis and then refuted Incarnation, Resurrection, original sin, Atonement and the sacraments.

It was most probably with people like Korsakov in mind that Berdyaev wrote: "Orthodox extremists hate and discard Tolstoy, because he was excommunicated by the Church Synod. The big question is whether or not the Synod can be regarded as an organ of Christ's church. Is it rather an organ of Caesar? To reject Leo Tolstoy means to reject the Russian genius and, in the last analysis, Russia's mission in the world." (*The Russian Idea*) [Berdyaev's philosophy does not coincide in every respect with that of Tolstoy, nevertheless, N.A. Berdyaev was no partisan. As a religious theorist he recognized the immense role Tolstoy played in the dissemination of religious awareness in Russia. — G.A.]

The anti-Tolstoyan trend of the volume is a result also of the fact that the authors are not always discriminating enough in unearthing certain phenomena of the past from under the rubble. They compel us to re-read the most disgraceful pages from the history of Orthodox Church.

I shall take the liberty of quoting from the decision of the Holy Synod, No. 557, dated February 20-22, 1901. "Count Tolstoy ... preaches the abolition of all the dogma of the Orthodox Church and of the very essence of Christian faith with fanatical frenzy; he denies the living and personal God glorified in the Holy Trinity, Creator and Providence of the universe; he refutes Our Lord Jesus Christ, God made Man, Redeemer and Saviour of the world, who suffered for us and for our salvation, and who has been raised from the dead; he refutes the Immaculate Conception of the human manifestation of Christ the Lord, and the virginity, before and after the Nativity, of Mary, Mother of God, most pure and eternally virgin; he does not believe in the life hereafter or in judgement after death; he refutes all the Mysteries of the Church and their beneficial effect; and, flaunting the most sacred articles of faith of the Orthodox community, he has not feared to mock the greatest of all mysteries, the Holy Eucharist ..."

This is all true, except, to my mind, marking him as a fanatic. The fanatics were those who wrote this letter, not Tolstoy. But there is something else really significant here. The editors of decision No. 557 have listed all Tolstoy's sins against the dogmas of the Orthodox Church, but they did not present a *single* fact to prove (it cannot be substantiated) where Tolstoy undermines, as they allege, "the very essence of Christian faith." With this they confirm that for them the dogmas represent law and prophecy.

Such is the attitude to religion that the authors of the volume, attacking Tolstoy, wish to dig out from under the rubble.

It is interesting to examine how the style of the volume changes according to the nature of the phenomenon treated. When the authors turn to contemporary conditions in Russia, when they expose Marxists, their language is accurate, their phrases are clear, there are no metaphors and allegories. As soon as they begin to speak about religion, the style becomes enigmatically metaphoric, the layer of realism peels off and mystical romanticism gets the upper hand. Here is, for instance, F. Korsakov, quoting Florensky: "As the end of history approaches, the domes of the Holy Church begin to reflect a new, only vaguely perceptible rosy light of the Undying Day." Clearly, this is a metaphor. But F. Korsakov does not allow us to interpret the image as such. He explains it: "What Father Pavel says here is obviously [!] not intended as a metaphor or image [!!]; his words are the testimony of a Russian genius engraving in his work reality observed by him ..." Neither Tolstoy, nor religious philosophers like N.A. Berdyaev, N.O. Lossky, S. Bulgakov expressed themselves in such language. The essential is, however, not the style, but the interpretation of religion. While for Tolstoy religion is an important matter for every man and hence it should not be clothed in enigmatic, mystical forms, its language ought not to be that of sooth-sayers, for the contributors to the volume Christianity is a collection of mysteries, it is the other world inaccessible to the ordinary man's reason.

The most absurd ritual, Eucharist, quite justly called by Tolstoy in his reply to the Synod "base, crude magic", is once again given the utmost importance for Christianity, and this is worded in the most obscure manner.

"The Eucharist", writes Barabanov, "is the peak of tension, the culmination of the most important in man's existence. God and man meet in the most intimate, unsunderable way. And in this incomparable joy of man's union with the absolute Reality, the God-man Jesus Christ, everything is filled with unutterable light and exultation." One can understand it when a man, who had lost his ability to think as a result of religious ecstasy induced by self-excitation and by dimming conscience under the influence of peculiar temple conditions and still persisting pagan beliefs, has such sensations. But a thinking Christian who takes up the pen (or the typewriter?) and works in a calm condition, with lines like these provokes — to put it mildly — perplexity.

Without the aid of metaphoric language today, in the age of reason's triumph, it is impossible to repudiate Tolstoy's judgement on the Eucharist (and generally on all church rites and symbols of faith), in *Resurrection* and in his other religious writings. This is what he writes about the Eucharist, referring to the scene from *Resurrection*: "Quite true, I wrote down simply and realistically, without faltering, what a priest does in preparation for the so-called sacraments. But that this so-called sacrament would be something sacred and that merely writing down how it is performed is blasphemy, is utterly untrue. Blasphemy is not in calling a partition a partition instead of iconostasis,* or a goblet a goblet instead of a chalice, etc. The most abominable, unceasing, outrageous blasphemy is when, using every possible means of deception and hypnosis, they persuade children and simple-minded adults that cutting a piece of bread in a special way, pronouncing at the same time certain words, and placing it in wine means the bread contains God; that he, in whose name the piece of bread is taken out, will be healthy if he is a living man, or if he is deceased, he will be happier in the other world; and that the person, who swallows the slice, receives God himself. But this is terrible!" (Reply to the Synod, 1901) (And I would add: reply to the authors of *From Under the Rubble* published in 1974.)

Tolstoy demonstrated that the Christian religion does not amount to a score of pagan rituals, pleading prayers, or the preposterous belief in the trinity and at the same time one and only God, or in the Immaculate Conception. It is an awareness, clear and comprehensible awareness of man's responsibility before that spiritual, infinite principle, the source of love, which is God. Such interpretation will enlist those millions and millions of twentieth century people who wish to live for the sake of bringing light to earth, and not for the limited "I" of the flesh.

★   ★   ★   ★

From the days when the first Christian communities came into existence, right up to our own time, there was never a homogeneous doctrine of Christ that would unite all those who testified to his

---

*Eastern Eucharist is celebrated at the altar which is partially concealed from the congregation by a screen, decorated with icons, behind which the heavenly mysteries are enacted.

name. In a world where atheism was persecuted and unconditionally refuted (if only in words), the lack of Christian unity did not constitute a threat of doom for religion in general.

In our times, when people regard atheism as a quite natural frame of mind, disputes about Christianity are ruinous: they convince the godless that religious doctrines are as unsubstantiated as party-ideological ones.

The world, and Russia therefore, can be saved only if *all* believers unite in the struggle against atheism. We must take precise stock of and cast aside all that divides believers. We must carefully consider and foster all that unites them. It is obvious to all Christians that heresy was the outcome of commentaries to the Holy Writ, of differing attitudes to the Holy legend, various interpretations given to rituals, and of contradictory views on church organization. Hence, for the salvation of Christianity — and of the world — all believers, even if they do not renounce their own views on the Church, on relationships between the individual and the nation, on rituals, must forgo the pride and certitude that only their interpretation of faith is true.

Unity must be founded on the basis of what all believers agree upon.

Tolstoy's teaching seems to me the basis upon which such unity is feasible, since partisan orthodoxy and sectarian intolerance are absolutely alien to Tolstoy's religion.

Comparing Tolstoy and Dostoevsky, N.A. Berdyaev, who was no unconditional supporter of Tolstoy's religion, nevertheless declared: "He [Tolstoy] awakened religious sentiments in a society that was indifferent to religion and hostile to Christianity. He stirred up the search for the meaning of life. Dostoevsky influenced a relatively small circle of intellectuals with complicated souls. Tolstoy, as religious and moral teacher, influenced a much vaster circle, embracing popular strata as well." (*The Russian Idea*).

Tolstoy's teaching is to be extracted from under the rubble. The authors of the volume have every right to deplore the destruction of temples. They have every reason to suffer, witnessing the lack of sacred books in Russia. But Tolstoy's religious works are also virtually banned: in thirty-seven years of Soviet rule they were published in full only once, less often than the Bible. The Holy Scripture is published in Russian by the patriarchate, and for this they deserve our thanks. But Tolstoy, who was expelled from the church by the Synod, and from philosophy by Lenin, is buried under heavier rubble than the Holy Scripture. And one ought not to dump yet another stone on the heap, as the authors of *From Under the Rubble* have done.

What is most important for Tolstoy in Christianity is not to utter the word "Lord! Lord!" but to accomplish deeds that please God.

There is no deed more vital for Russia today than the moral revolution urged by Solzhenitsyn. In this revolution everyone is ready to participate, without sparing himself: orthodox believers, and non-orthodox Christians; humanist intellectuals who consider themselves atheists; advocates of democratic socialism and opponents of the socialist organization of production; champions who live in Russia and those, perhaps weaker ones, who have emigrated; too narrow nationalists as well as too broad cosmopolitans.

All these groups and "groupuscules", while differing in their objects of worship, are united in their awareness of the doom threatening Russia and the world. And they are all one in serving God, refusing to serve mammon; all prepared to suffer for the truth, for God-love, God-Freedom, God-Spirit, illuminated for us by Leo Tolstoy.

So let us listen to him:

"The gist of my idea is that since the depraved [i.e. atheists] are in unison and constitute strength, decent people [i.e. religious — G.A.] must do the same."

(L.N. Tolstoy, *War and Peace*)

314